THE UNEXPECTED LEGACY OF DIVORCE

A 25 YEAR LANDMARK STUDY

BOOKS BY JUDITH WALLERSTEIN, PH.D.

Surviving the Breakup
How Children and Parents Cope With Divorce
with Joan Berlin Kelly, Ph.D.

Second Chances
Men, Women, and Children a Decade after Divorce
with Sandra Blakeslee

The Good Marriage
How and Why Love Lasts
with Sandra Blakeslee

The UNEXPECTED LEGACY of DIVORCE

A 25 YEAR LANDMARK STUDY

Judith Wallerstein, Julia Lewis, and Sandra Blakeslee

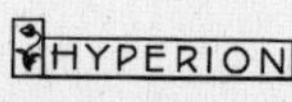

New York

Library of Congress Cataloging-in-Publication Data

Wallerstein, Judith S.

The unexpected legacy of divorce : a 25 year landmark study / by Judith Wallerstein, Julia M. Lewis and Sandra Blakeslee.—1st ed.

p. cm.

Includes bibliographical references.

ISBN 0-7868-6394-3

1. Children of divorced parents—United States—Longitudinal studies. 2. Divorce—United States—Longitudinal studies. I. Lewis, Julia. II. Blakeslee, Sandra. III. Title.

HQ834.W356 2000

306.89'0973—dc21 00-035071

PAPERBACK ISBN: 0-7868-8616-1

Book Design by Cassandra J. Pappas

FIRST PAPERBACK EDITION

10 9 8 7 6 5 4 3 2 1

This book is dedicated with gratitude, admiration, and affection to the women and men in this book who are the vanguard of an entire generation of young Americans raised in divorced families. We thank you for sharing your lives with all of us over twenty-five years and for helping millions of other children and young adults to understand that they are not alone.

Contents

Acknowledgments

WE WOULD LIKE TO ACKNOWLEDGE a profound debt to the Zellerbach Family Fund, which funded the original "children of divorce study" in the early seventies and has continued to support this work for twenty-five years. In a culture where foundations prefer quick results and time-limited programs, the Zellerbach Family Fund has had the wisdom and courage to recognize the matchless contribution of long-term follow-up studies of children. Throughout most of those years, the foundation's executive director, Edward Nathan, provided the professional leadership and vision that made what we have achieved possible. We are also profoundly grateful to the San Francisco Foundation, which, under the direction of former executive director Martin Paley, established in 1980 the Judith Wallerstein Center for the Family in Transition—a nonprofit, free-standing agency that brings together a range of educational and counseling services along with research and advocacy projects aimed at helping divorced and remarried families. The Center, which has served over six thousand children and their parents, is a tribute to Mr. Paley's enlightened leadership and remains the only such facility in the world.

We have been enormously helped throughout the writing of the book by eminent demographers and sociologists who have been generous with their knowledge.

We are especially grateful to Norval Glenn, Ashbel Smith, Professor of Sociology at the University of Texas at Austin; to Larry Bumpass, professor of sociology, Center for Demography and Ecology, University of Wisconsin, Madison; and to Nicholas Wolfinger, assistant professor of sociology at the University of Utah.

Colleagues and friends in different disciplines have read the manuscript and given us the benefit of their expertise and recommendations. We are especially grateful to Jan Blakeslee, whose comments were wonderfully supportive and instructive in the final stages of the book; Janet Johnston, executive director of the Judith Wallerstein Center and associate professor of sociology in the administration of justice department at San Jose State University; and to Mary Ann Mason, professor of social welfare at the University of California at Berkeley. All gave excellent advice on different sections of the book. We have benefited from consultations with Mary Halbert, J.D., who practices family law in Marin County and enlightened us about negotiating custody and visitation plans. We thank Amy Freidman for helping us locate members of our comparison group and Marci Hansen, professor of special education at San Francisco State University, for sharing her informed perspective on divorce and stress in families with vulnerable children.

We received expert consultation about the impact on children of witnessing domestic violence and advice about court-related programs for families and children from Professor Jeffrey I. Edleson, director of the Minnesota Center Against Violence and Abuse (MINCAVA) at the University of Minnesota School of Social Work in St. Paul, and Susan Hanks, Ph.D., coordinator for special services in the Office of Family Court Services of the Judicial Council of California.

For consistency of style, this book was written as if the senior author had interviewed all the subjects. In real life this daunting task was shared with others over a five-year period. We want to thank Christina Rodriguez, our project coordinator, for her gentle, tactful persistence and organizational skills. Our heartfelt appreciation goes to many students in the psychology graduate programs at San Francisco State University for their dedication and time: Christina Rodriguez, Karen Flynn, Mary McGrath, Carmelina Borg, Kate Donchi, Kristen Reinsberg, Hector Menendez, Rachel Lentz, and Sophia Nahavandi.

We want to say a special thank-you to our literary agent, Carol Mann, who was wonderfully supportive throughout and always there when needed. Also, we owe a debt of gratitude to Irene Williams for her remarkable talents as publicist and good friend. And finally we want to acknowledge the many people at Hyperion who made this project possible. Special thanks to Bob Miller, Martha Levin, and Jennifer Landers for bringing this book to light and especially to our editor, Peternelle van Arsdale, for her sustained efforts in helping us tell our story.

Finally, we want to acknowledge our spouses and families. Judy wants to thank Bob Wallerstein for his helpful and wise consultation on research methodology throughout the life of the study and for his love, support, and confidence in her work over so many years. Julie gives thanks to Eric, Michael, and Marina Multhaup for their great generosity in sharing her with this endeavor. Sandy is grateful to her partner, Carl Moore, for his ever constant love and support.

Prologue

PUBLISHED ONE YEAR ago, our book hit a raw nerve in America. It broke through an almost conspiratorial silence about the true nature of our divorce culture and how much growing up in America has changed in recent decades.

The major contribution of this book has been to recognize, for the first time, that when children of divorce become adults, they are badly frightened that their relationships will fail, just like the most important relationship in their parents' lives failed. They mature with a keen sense that their growing-up experiences did not prepare them for love, commitment, trust, marriage, or even for the nitty-gritty of handling and resolving conflicts. In the book they say, "I never saw a man and a woman on the same beam." Their decisions about whether or not to marry are shadowed by the experience of growing up in a home where their parents could not hold it together. They are no less eager than their peers who grew up in intact families for passionate love, sexual intimacy, and commitment. But they are haunted by powerful ghosts from their childhoods that tell them that they, like their parents, will not succeed.

On the positive side, many young adults who weathered their parents' divorce are extremely successful in their chosen careers, having learned how to be independent, resourceful, and flexible. Having invented their own moral path, they are decent, caring adults who managed to build good marriages in spite of their fears. Many are excellent parents. In the book they say, "I never want to let happen to my children what happened to me." Others turned their lives around by dint of their own courage, insight, and compassion.

The response to our book was phenomenal. Oprah Winfrey invited me to be on her show twice. Realizing she had tapped into concerns that deeply affect millions of young adults in her audience, she invited them to speak out. And they did. With tears and anger, they said:

"This book is talking about me. This is what happened to me. This is what I am feeling today."

"I'm still angry that my parents never explained the divorce to me."

"When my dad remarried I lost him to his new family. Two sets of children were too much for him. I'm happily married and I worry all the time that I will lose my husband. It's like I'm always waiting for that second shoe to drop."

After the book came out, thousands of people from all over the country and Canada called in to radio talk shows to describe their feelings.

Children of divorce wrote and e-mailed to tell me that they no longer felt alone. Many were vastly relieved. The stories of other young adults in the book enabled them for the first time to make sense out of their own lives:

"You are right on the mark. I kept seeing myself over and over in the book. I've given copies to my sister, my stepchildren, and friends of my stepchildren. I know so many people who should read it."

"A child of divorce since age seven, I am still recovering from the effects it had on my life. Your book has confirmed the notions I've held for 23 years and helped to consolidate my feelings."

"When I picked up your book, I finally found someone who spoke for my experience. Your book described what I have lived through in an honest way that no one else was willing to discuss. I am amazed to hear that you know so intimately the grief of children who have lived through divorce."

Another said, "As I am a child of divorce, your book was very meaningful to me. My parents divorced when I was five and I grew up fully immersed in the divorce culture. Finally I feel freed of the burden of pretending that the divorce did not matter. Your book helped me understand how much my parents' failed marriage set the stage for the emotional entanglements that would come later."

I did not talk much in the book about religious beliefs in the context of divorce. But several people reported that their faith in God was shaken for several years by their experience as children. Most of these were adults who had been abandoned by a parent when they were very young. It appears that their disappointment stood in the way of relying on their religion for support. On the other hand, some described how religion had helped them, especially in providing the rules and structure that they found lacking in their lives. Others found the community of the church or synagogue a source of comfort.

A few letters talked about an enduring anger at aging parents. One woman said, "My parents are getting old. My father is getting frail and my mother needs special attention from time to time. But I still feel so much anger because of their neglect of my feelings over more than 25 years. I am hardly capable of giving the attention that I would normally give. And when I do take care of them, it is without any pleasure at all, only a sense of duty."

One change that may come from these sentiments is that adult children of divorce are starting to speak out. Realizing that their contemporaries share many of the same feelings, they're no longer ashamed to admit how much their childhood grievances and disappointments have endured. As they search for ways to help one another and put their fears to rest, we may see the rise of groups that focus on the experience of having grown up in divorced families.

Another change is that many people are seriously considering the benefits of staying together for the sake of their children. They're examining what they have as a family and are taking a more realistic look at what divorce entails. Combining a full-time job, courtship, and parenting requires the speed and agility of an Olympics champion but without the training that the champion brings to the race.

We are also seeing a rise in interest in premarital education and marriage enrichment programs. Several states have enacted marriage license incentives that encourage people to take a four-hour class in marriage education for a reduced fee and immediate granting of the license. To cut down on impetuous weddings, Florida put in a three-day waiting period. Illinois has legislation to make people wait sixty days. Other states are considering legislation to improve preparation for marriage. There is greater community interest in marital counseling programs and conflict resolution courses that are aimed at teaching people to stay in the marriage and resolve the friction rather than turn to divorce. It is still far too early to know whether these or other education plans will be effective, but they reflect the rise in community concern about children and the search for new ways to improve marriage.

When I have presented my findings to judges and attorneys at national conferences, many admitted that they were stunned to learn that highly educated, affluent parents were not sending their children to college, especially when a second set of children was born into a remarriage and children from the first marriage were pushed aside. They were also surprised to hear that many adolescents are furious at the court system for ordering strict visitation agreements with no options for adding flexibility or change down the road.

The extraordinary reception to our book has encouraged me to hope that change is on the way. This younger generation has no illusions that divorce is easy or quickly over for children or parents. They, like we, are in favor of divorce where the marriage is cruel, exploitative, or dangerous or even when one or both partners are miserably unhappy in the relationship. But they are also acutely aware of how difficult it is to raise children alone or as coparents in separate homes. They know how hard it is for the youngsters who grow up in divorced homes to create the relationships that they long for when they come of age.

Greta, who is 23 years old, is an example of the hope I see for the future. She wrote to ask my advice regarding her problems with men:

"Your book taught me a lot about myself that I never put together before. My parents divorced after 23 years of marriage. My major fear is that if my parents were together that long, and the marriage was fine, how can I possibly see 23 years down the road for myself? So I get scared and don't want to marry at all, even though I desire marriage more than anything. I also am afraid that any man I love will be gone the next day. *Every* relationship I have ever been in ended because I was so clingy. I was afraid that the guy would not like me tomorrow. As a result my clinginess made them do just that. They left. I try to control it but it's really hard because I get so scared. I want to find a great marriage and say to my parents, 'Hey, look. I did it and you couldn't.' Thanks again, Greta Saunders."

Greta is a member of a plucky generation in which men and women have evolved their own values that were not part of their upbringing. They are tackling the life tasks of adulthood with courage despite their many fears. They're eager to help themselves and each other to succeed where their parents failed. And, as we report in our book, many of them eventually triumph.

JUDITH S. WALLERSTEIN
SANDRA BLAKESLEE
September 2000

Preface

In the fall of 1994 I received a phone call that was to entirely revise my understanding of divorce and how it has changed the nature of American society. On the other end of the line was Karen James, one of the children in a longitudinal study on divorce that I began in 1971 and last wrote about in the late 1980s. I remembered her well. Karen was a charming, lively child who was ten years old when her parents separated. I had interviewed her then, and again when she was fifteen, twenty, and twenty-five years old. The last time we met she was miserable, living with a man she didn't love. I recalled how concerned I was about her despair.

But the voice on the phone sounded strong and vibrant. "This is Karen James," she announced. "I'm calling from North Carolina. How are you?" After we exchanged routine pleasantries, she said, "I'm going to be in the Bay Area next week. Do you have time to see me?"

"Of course," I answered. "I've thought about you many times."

"I'm in a whole other place than our last meeting," said Karen. "It's all new. I'm coming to town to get married next Saturday but I can come up to Marin on Thursday afternoon. Would that work?"

I told Karen that I was honored that she could fit me in during such a busy week, and we set a time to get together. I was absolutely delighted by her call. Karen is one of the many children who, after divorce, moved into the vacuum created by parents who are overwhelmed by the changes in their lives and unable to carry on as they had before. Divorce often leads to a partial or complete collapse in an adult's ability to parent for months and sometimes years after the breakup. Caught up in rebuilding their own lives, mothers and fathers are preoccupied with a thousand and one concerns, which can blind them to the needs of their children. In many such familes, one child—often the oldest girl—takes on responsibilities far beyond anything she has done before. These young caregivers quietly assume the nurturing and moral guidance of their younger siblings and also serve as confidant, adviser, caregiver, and even parent for their own parents during the years that follow.

Karen followed this script to the letter. From a merry, outgoing ten-year-old, she soon became a somber young woman. I remember her telling me when she was only eleven, "I'm really worried about my brother and sister. I have to set them a good example so they'll be good. That means I have to be good. They fight all the time since my parents broke up. I try to stop that and teach them to talk instead of hitting. I'm also worried about my mom. Since Dad left she cries every day when she comes home from work. I try to comfort her and also to warn her about her new boyfriend. I think that he'll hurt her feelings even more." Karen shook her head sadly. She was overburdened by her new responsibilities but felt that she had no choice but to forfeit her needs to the needs of her family. High school, she explained at our meeting several years later, was a blur because her home situation had hardly changed.

At out last meeting, when she was twenty-five, I was very concerned about Karen's inability to break free from a young man she was living with but did not love. She tried to explain: "You remember that when I was dating guys in college, I became very frightened that anyone I really liked would abandon me or be unfaithful, and that I would end up suffering like my mom or my dad? Well, choosing Nick was safe because he has no education and no plans, which means that he'll always have fewer choices than me. I knew that if we lived together and maybe got married someday I wouldn't ever have to worry about him walking out." With tears in her eyes, she added, "Nick is very kind and caring. I'm not used to that."

Although I understood that Karen felt starved for kindness, it baffled me why a bright, attractive woman like her would feel she had so few options other than a loveless relationship. She cried bitterly as she described the loneliness of her life with Nick and the strain of his passive dependence on her. "I knew it was a mistake one day after we moved in together," she said. "But I can't leave him. There's no way I could hurt him that way." And that is how I left her, standing at a crossroads, struggling with a decision whether to leave or stay.

Thus I awaited her arrival the following Thursday, two days before her wedding, with equal measures of hope and concern—hope that she had turned her life around and worry that she hadn't. What had she done between age twenty-five and thirty-four? Had she broken free of her fears? Of her sorrow? Was she still taking care of her family while feeling guilty for never doing enough? Was the man she was marrying a good choice? Was she no longer afraid of loving and being loved?

As Karen came through my front door, she looked radiant. I was suddenly aware that in all the years we've known each other, I had rarely seen her happy. She was dressed very simply in black wool slacks, white pullover, and herringbone suit jacket, and as always, she was beautiful. The last few years had made her somehow softer, more relaxed in her shoulders and arms. Her stunning blue eyes had a new twinkle that flashed as we greeted each other warmly.

I told her how lovely she looked and congratulated her on her forthcoming marriage. "Who's the lucky man?"

"We're both lucky," she said, settling on the sofa. "Gavin and I did everything differently compared to how I lived my life before." And she launched into her story. Within months of our last meeting, she had moved out of the apartment she shared with Nick and said good-bye. As she had anticipated, he was devastated, begged her to come back, wailed, and made her feel guiltier than ever.

"How were you able to leave?" I asked, aware of her long-standing difficulty in turning away anyone who needed her care.

She was silent and then answered slowly, her face pale. "I felt like I was dying. It has to be the hardest thing I've ever done and it took all my courage." She described how she would come home after work and find her partner lying on the couch, waiting for her to take charge. It was just like taking care of her mom. At that point, she realized she had to get out. Her escape took her to the East Coast, graduate school, and ultimately into a dream job—directing a regional public health program for handicapped children in five southern states.

It was there that Karen met her fiancé, Gavin. As she told me about him, I smiled and said, "I remember when you thought you didn't have choices. It looks like you've made quite a few recently."

"You mean, how did I decide to marry Gavin?" She blushed ever so slightly. "It's a long story. We met at a party not long after I moved to Chapel Hill and he called to say that he would love to get together. He's an assistant professor of economics at Duke and even though I knew absolutely nothing about his field, we hit it off instantly. I wanted to see him again right away but I waited a discreet week and then I called him back. Well, we were together every day from then on and about six months later I moved in with him. He says that the day I moved in was, in his eyes, the day we married, but I didn't see it that way. I wasn't ready quite yet. I was scared."

"So you were hesitating. Was it about Gavin or about marriage?"

"About marriage. About being happy. You see, it's not all behind me. Part of me is always waiting for disaster to strike. I keep reminding myself that I'm doing this to myself, but the truth is that I live in dread that something bad will happen to me. Some terrible loss will change my life, and it only gets worse as things get better for me. Maybe that's the permanent result of my parents' divorce. Gavin says I'm always waiting for the other shoe to drop. I've learned to contain it. I no longer wake up in terror when I go to sleep happy, but this feeling does not ever go away."

"So how did you make up your mind to marry him?" I asked.

"Well, it's strange, but a near catastrophe made me change my mind. Gavin was in Nashville, giving a talk, and on the drive home was caught in a freak ice storm. He got pulled off the road in the middle of nowhere by the highway patrol and couldn't get to a phone for eight hours. I was home, waiting for him, hearing about all sorts of fatal accidents on the roads. I was beside myself. Anything could have happened to him."

"You must have been scared out of your mind."

"Oh, yes," said Karen. "It was ghastly. I just knew it was the disaster that I always expected and that it would blow my life away. But something really important happened to me at the same time. I realized that whether we married or not, life is always chancy. If I marry him, I might lose him. If I don't marry him, I might lose him. So I could lose him either way. And that's when I realized that I want to hold on to Gavin for the rest of my life and for whatever happens. I said yes, let's get married."

Smiling at her calculation, I said, "So you decided to take a chance, to reach out for what you really want?"

"That's right, although it's still hard for me to know what I want. But I've learned what I don't want. I don't want another edition of my relationship with Nick or with my mom or dad."

"And what do you want?"

"I want a lover and a husband. I'm no longer frantic to find just anybody. I'm no longer afraid to be alone. I can stand on my own two feet."

Her last words were unforgettable. She seemed to be talking more to herself and only partly to me. "My co-workers say that I have an old soul. I've always felt that I would die young, that so much unhappiness was compressed into the early part of my life that it made sense. But maybe the second half of my life is the part that I will enjoy more. I never had a childhood. I always took care of everything." A smile broke across her face. "You know, I like the kind of woman I'm becoming. I love the man I'm marrying. I like my kindness and my sensitivity. I love my work. I'm on a good path. I can finally be who I am."

Our meeting had lasted three hours and both of us were spent emotionally. It was a sad, moving, gallant story, and Karen had told it vividly. Both of us cried as she spoke and both of us ended up smiling and thankful that she had ended on a note that was at least partly upbeat and hopeful. She was on her way to her wedding day. I'd been granted a great privilege to share her life. I wished, as I so often do, that I were a novelist so that I could capture the richness of her feelings and the amazing sweep of changes she had made in her life.

As we embraced, I thanked Karen for her generosity and candor. I told her how impressed I was with her, how proud I was of all she'd done, and how much I hoped the years ahead would make up for her past sorrows. She invited me to stay in touch and offered to send me snapshots of their new home.

The door was almost closed behind Karen when she turned back and pushed it open. Smiling, she said, "Maybe your next book should be about what happens to all of us when we grow up." Little did I realize how prophetic her words would turn out to be.

• • •

After Karen left, I sat for a long time thinking about the unexpected twists and turns in her life. Did her parents have any idea of what they had started twenty-five years ago when they filed for divorce? If they had known the long-term consequences for their children, would they have done things differently? Would they have divorced? Like most people back then, they probably thought divorce was a minor upheaval in the lives of children. They undoubtedly expected that family life would soon resume its normal course and that parents and children alike would benefit from an end to marital conflict. Surely they did not foresee lasting effects that would extend into the fourth decade of Karen's life.

I thought back on the lovely, wistful child who had tenderly taken care of her distraught mother, younger siblings, and father when he became a "basket case"—and how she had forfeited her own teenage years. I could see her face contorted with grief when in her early twenties she told me how she anguished over whether to leave the young man she had committed to simply because he had been kind to her. Preoccupied with fears of loss, betrayal, and abandonment, she was still locked into the self-sacrificial caregiver role of her childhood and had reinstalled it in her adult relationships with men.

But Karen had turned her life around. I was stunned by how much she'd changed since our last meeting. Karen was absolutely on target when she announced, "It's all new." She had come to see me at age thirty-four in pride and triumph, having broken free of her long-playing role as family rescuer. Karen's story was tantalizing, for it raised questions that I simply could not brush aside. I had assumed that when the children in the study entered adulthood ten or fifteen years after the breakup, I would be able to accurately report the long-term effects of divorce on their lives. In a best-selling book titled *Second Chances: Men, Women, and Children a Decade after Divorce*, I described what these children were thinking, saying, and doing in their late teens and early twenties as they went in search of intimate relationships, started their careers, and began to assess the personal impact of divorce on their lives. I found that many children of divorce were caught in an intense inner conflict—afraid of repeating their parents' mistakes while searching for lasting love. Many were either avoiding commitment or jumping impulsively into relationships with troubled people they hardly knew. I left them feeling worried about their futures but hopeful that they would find a way to overcome their fears.

The changes I saw in Karen pointed to an enormous untold story about her generation. If Karen was able to turn her life around, what happened to the others? Did her story reveal a general pattern that I had not seen because I stopped too soon? I realized there must be others like her, and I had to wonder when, if ever, the story of divorce is reasonably complete.

And then it hit me. We have not fully appreciated how divorce continues to shape the lives of young people after they reach *full adulthood.* For example, we know from surveys that grown children of divorce have a higher divorce rate, but that does not tell us anything about their intimate feelings, the major turning points in their lives, how they made the choices they did, and how they think about love and marriage and being parents themselves. The only way to get to the heart of what they think and worry about is to follow them over their entire life course, from early childhood to middle adulthood. Why was it so hard for Karen? Why did it take her so long to take a chance on love? Demographers now tell us that a quarter of adults under the age of forty-four are children of divorce. We are talking about millions of people who are struggling with the residue of an experience that their parents would rather forget.

One thing was crystal clear. I *had* stopped too soon in my inquiry of children from divorced families. Karen's visit had opened a set of questions and challenges that I found irresistible. Within a few weeks of her visit I decided to undertake a sequel to *Second Chances* with the hope of finding out how others were faring at the twenty-five-year mark. This is the longest close-up study of divorce ever conducted. The youngest "children" are in their late twenties and the oldest in their early forties. This book explores what has happened to them in adulthood. How are they getting along? How many of them are happily married? Do they have children? Have many divorced or rejected marriage? Do they still consider their parents' divorce to be the main, defining event of their young lives? Are they angry at their parents? Do they now approve of the decision? Are they compassionate? Are they cynical? Are they worried, and if so, about what? What values do they espouse in love, sex, marriage, and divorce? How disappointed or contented are they with their lives? By getting into the heads and hearts of this generation, I hope to shed light on deep changes in American attitudes that are shaping the future in unexpected ways.

I also wanted to learn, this time around, about the lives of the adults who grew up next door but whose parents did not divorce. What did they learn from their parents? Are children from very unhappy intact families any different from children raised in very unhappy divorced families? Are children raised in happy intact families "immunized" against divorce or are they no less vulnerable to failure than their age-mates? How does our divorce culture affect their attitudes toward marriage, commitment, and divorce? What happens when they marry children of divorced families? Does this become an issue in the marriage? Do they worry that their own marriages are more fragile because marriage is more fragile? I realized I would need a comparison group to answer such questions.

To carry out this new round of research on the lives of young adults whose parents divorced twenty-five years ago, I invited two colleagues to join me. Both have worked with me on earlier projects. Julia Lewis, professor of psychology at San Francisco State University, was associate director of research at the Judith Wallerstein Center for the Family in Transition when it was founded in 1980, and director of research for the ten-year follow-up study. She is co-principal investigator of the twenty-five-year follow-up study. Sandra Blakeslee is an award-winning science writer for *The New York Times*, who collaborated with me on two earlier books. Her task was to help write our stories and findings in a clear accessible style. She also contributed her personal experience and broad compassionate understanding of many parts of our society. Both have been my valued partners.

Consider, then, that this book is a report from our children in their own words—knowledge that everyone, including parents, grandparents, and policymakers, has been waiting and wanting to hear. After twenty-five years the jury is no longer out. Divorce has entered the lives of an entire generation and changed the way they and we think about marriage and commitment. Children of divorce who were rendered mute by the legal system have returned to give us their verdict, and we are obliged to listen.

JUDITH WALLERSTEIN,
Belvedere, California, 2000

Introduction

IN JULY 1999, *Sesame Street* aired an episode in which Kermit the Frog, dressed as a reporter, interviewed a little bird asking her where she lived. The happy little bird chirped that she lives part of the time in one tree where she frolics in her mother's nest and the rest of her time in a separate tree where she frolics with her dad. The little bird concluded merrily, "they both love me," and ran off to play. This, of course, restates the beguiling myth of divorce. Watching this, we are meant to understand that divorce is a minor upheaval and normal occurrence in the lives of children and adults. Not to worry, it says to the child. Your parents will continue their loving play with you as always. Your life will be exactly like it was before, only it will now take place in two locales. The story may provide bland comfort to some worried children. But I suspect most know better. The story of the little bird in no way matches their experience of growing up in a divorced family, be it in one home, two homes, or any combination of living arrangements over the years.

The story is nevertheless important because it has deep roots in our contemporary culture. It describes several abiding myths that have guided our community opinions and policies for three decades. Up until thirty years ago marriage was a lifetime commitment with only a few narrow legal exits such as proving adultery in the courts or outwaiting years of abandonment. American cultural and legal attitudes bound marriages together, no matter how miserable couples might be. Countless individuals were locked in loveless marriages they desperately wanted to end, but for the most part they had no way out. Then, in an upheaval akin to a cataclysmic earthquake, family law in California changed overnight. A series of statewide task forces recommended that men and women seeking divorce should no longer be required to prove that their spouse was unfaithful, unfit, cruel, or incompatible. It was time, they said, to end the hypocrisy embodied in laws that severely restricted divorce. People should be able to end an unhappy marriage without proving fault or pointing blame.

The prevailing climate of opinion was that divorce would allow adults to make better choices and happier marriages by letting them undo earlier mistakes. They would arrive at an honest, mutual decision to divorce, because if one person wanted out, surely it could not be much of a marriage.

These attitudes were held by men and women of many political persuasions, by lawyers, judges, and mental health professionals alike. The final task force that formulated the new no-fault divorce laws was led by law professor Herma Kay, who was well known as an advocate for women's rights. In 1969, Governor Ronald Reagan signed the new law and people were jubilant. It was a time of hope and faith that greater choice would set men and women free and benefit their children. Within a few years, no-fault divorce laws spread like wildfire to all fifty states. People all across the country were in favor of change.

But what about the children? In our rush to improve the lives of adults, we assumed that their lives would improve as well. We made radical changes in the family without realizing how it would change the experience of growing up. We embarked on a gigantic social experiment without any idea about how the next generation would be affected. If the truth be told, and if we are able to face it, the history of divorce in our society is replete with unwarranted assumptions that adults have made about children simply because such assumptions are congenial to adult needs and wishes. The myths that continue to guide our divorce policies and politics today stem directly from these attitudes.

Cherished Myths

TWO FAULTY BELIEFS provide the foundation for our current attitudes toward divorce. The first holds that if the parents are happier the children will be happier, too. Even if the children are distressed by the divorce, the crisis will be transient because children are resilient and resourceful and will soon recover. Children are not considered separately from their parents; their needs and even their thoughts are subsumed under the adult agenda. This "trickle down" myth is built on the enduring fact that most adults cannot fathom the child's world view and how children think. The problem is, they think they do. Indeed, many adults who are trapped in very unhappy marriages would be surprised to learn that their children are relatively content. They don't care if Mom and Dad sleep in different beds as long as the family is together.

Fortunately this myth has come under strong attack in recent years with reports from parents, teachers, and researchers like me who found that the children were suffering. The euphoria of the early 1970s soon gave way to a rising tide of concern about the impoverishment of women and children, the high distress among the many parents who did not agree with their spouse that their marriage was on the rocks, and the fact that children did not bounce back quickly. Children in postdivorce families do not, on the whole, look happier, healthier, or more well adjusted even if one or both parents are happier. National studies[1] show that children from divorced and remarried families are more aggressive toward their parents and teachers. They experience more depression, have more learning difficulties, and suffer from more problems with peers than children from intact families. Children from divorced and remarried families are two to three times more likely to be referred for psychological help at school than their peers from intact families. More of them end up in mental health clinics and hospital settings. There is earlier sexual activity, more children born out of wedlock, less marriage, and more divorce. Numerous studies[2] show that adult children of divorce have more psychological problems than those raised in intact marriages.

Although many people no longer believe the myth that children always benefit from a divorce that makes parents happier, it continues to exert subtle, unconscious influences on how we think about divorce and our reactions to it. It has encouraged parents to expect that their children will approve their decision. Actually, as you will see in the chapters that follow, this is hardly ever true for children who have not yet reached their teens. It has made it harder for parents to see or believe that their children suffer with fears and sadness after the breakup. And it has made it harder for parents to prepare their children properly for the forthcoming divorce and provide them with the comfort they need. The fact that many men and women get caught up in the search for new lovers or taxing new jobs after divorce—both of which make parents less available to their children—only serves to compound their desire to hold on to this myth.

A second myth is based on the premise that divorce is a temporary crisis that exerts its most harmful effects on parents and children at the time of the breakup. People who believe this leap to the happy conclusion that the key to the child's adjustment is the settlement of conflict without rancor. Thus the spotlight of our attention in terms of resources and interventions has been on the breakup. If the two parents don't fight, at least in front of the children, and if they rationally and fairly settle the financial, legal, and parenting issues that divide them, why then the crisis will resolve itself in short order. The two lucky adults will have broken free of their troubled marriage and, along with their children, can move forward to build happier lives. The children will resume their usual round of play and school activities. They will make the transition easily to having parents in two locales and dividing their days and nights between separate homes in different neighborhoods. Their lives will proceed as before, only much improved as compared to their experience in the predivorce family. This is all supposed to happen regardless of any betrayal, abuse, or abandonment that caused the divorce that left at least one person reeling in pain and one or both parents hardly capable of thinking clearly about their children. The belief that the crisis is temporary underlies the notion that if acceptable legal arrangements for custody, visiting, and child support are made at the time of the divorce and parents are provided with a few lectures, the child will soon be fine. It is a view we have fervently embraced and continue to hold.

But it's misguided. Our willingness to believe this notion has prevented us from giving children and adults the understanding they need to cope with the divorce experience *over the long haul.* It has kept us from making long-term plans for our children and from acknowledging the fact that their needs change as they grow older. It has prevented us from listening to their serious complaints and easing their suffering. Thankfully, this second myth is also beginning to unravel because of a new voice that is just now emerging on the national scene. That voice belongs to the children of divorce now grown to adulthood. In this book, you will hear them challenge these myths firsthand. Now that they are grown up, have marriages, divorces, and children of their own, they speak with an authority we dare not ignore.

Adult children of divorce are telling us loud and clear that their parents' anger at the time of the breakup is *not* what matters most. Unless there was violence or abuse or unremitting high conflict, they have dim memories of what transpired during this supposedly critical period. Indeed, as youngsters then and as adults now, all would be profoundly astonished to learn that any judge, attorney, mediator—indeed, anyone at all—had genuinely considered their best interests or wishes at the breakup or at any time since. It's the many years living in a postdivorce or remarried family that count, according to this first generation to come of age and tell us their experience. It's feeling sad, lonely, and angry during childhood. It's traveling on airplanes alone when you're seven to visit your parent. It's having no choice about how you spend your time and feeling like a second-class citizen compared with your friends in intact families who have some say about how they spend their weekends and their vacations. It's wondering whether you will have any financial help for college from your college-educated father, given that he has no legal obligation to pay. It's worrying about your mom and dad for years—will her new boyfriend stick around, will his new wife welcome you into her home? It's reaching adulthood with acute anxiety. Will you ever find a faithful woman to love you? Will you find a man you can trust? Or will your relationships fail just like your parents' did? And most tellingly, it's asking if you can protect your own child from having these same experiences in growing up.

Not one of the men or women from divorced families whose lives I report on in this book wanted their children to repeat their childhood experiences. Not one ever said, "I want my children to live in two nests—or even two villas." They envied friends who grew up in intact families. Their entire life stories belie the myths we've embraced.

The Longitudinal Study

THE ADULTS ON whom this work is based are among the vanguard of an ever increasing army of adults raised in divorced families. Since 1970, at least a million children a year have seen their parents divorce—building a generation of Americans that has now come of age.[3] It bears repeating that they represent a quarter of the adults in this country who have reached their forty-fourth birthdays.[4] Demographers also report that 40 percent of all married adults in the 1990s have already been divorced.[5] The lives of these children of divorce now grown to adulthood and the important lessons I have learned from them are the main topics of this book. It is the only study in the world that follows into full adulthood the life course of individuals whose parents separated when they were young children. From the beginning, my interest has been in the inner world of these people as they matured. I've tried to see the world through their eyes and to explore the quality of their relationships over many years with parents, stepparents, lovers, husbands, and finally their own children. As the study proceeded I became especially intrigued with the turning points along their life journey and with the ways they were finally able to overcome unexpected legacies from their parents' divorce.

The core group of 131 children and their families were recruited in 1971 when my colleague Joan Berlin Kelly and I began asking open-ended questions of families going through divorce. The children came from middle-class families and were carefully prescreened so that everyone chosen was doing reasonably well at school and was developmentally on target during the predivorce years. Naturally I wanted to be sure that any problems we saw did not predate the divorce. Neither they nor their parents were ever my patients. I have been following their lives in intimate detail, seeing them and both of their parents for many hours of interviews, at least every five years since 1971. My findings at the eighteen-month, five-, ten-, and fifteen-year marks were reported in two earlier books.[6] At this, the twenty-five-year follow-up, I was able to locate close to 80 percent of the "children" in face-to-face interviews that each lasted several hours. They are now twenty-eight to forty-three years old.

This book also contains knowledge that I have gained from working with more than six thousand children and their parents who came to the Judith Wallerstein Center for the Family in Transition—a nonprofit agency that since 1980 has provided mediation, counseling, and education for Marin County families going through divorce.[7] Throughout the 1980s and 1990s, the staff and I have done pioneering research on a wide range of current issues, including joint custody, high-conflict families, overnight visiting for infants, and court-ordered visiting, and that research has influenced public policy and the courts and informed the work of pediatricians, teachers, and clergy. The center, which is nationally and internationally renowned, also provides training for legal and mental health professionals who work with families in separation, divorce, and remarriage.

Finally, this book draws on extended interviews with a comparison group of adults from intact families who were the same age and were raised in the same neighborhoods and schools as those in the long-term study of divorced families. My goal in comparing the two groups was to enable the growing up experience and adulthood of each group to stand out in bold relief. I soon found that intact families come in all shapes and sizes, ranging from harmonious to wretched. I was particularly interested in comparing the lives of those raised in troubled families that remained together with those in the divorced group. These comparisons shed light on the life of the child in a troubled family that did not divorce and provide a good basis for addressing the frequently asked question: for the sake of the children, is it better to divorce or to stay in an unhappy marriage?

What I Have Learned

When I began studying the effects of divorce on children and parents in the early 1970s, I, like everyone else, expected them to rally. But as time progressed, I grew increasingly worried that divorce is a long-term crisis that was affecting the psychological profile of an entire generation. I caught glimpses of this long-term effect in my research that followed the children into late adolescence and early adulthood, but it's not until now—when the children are fully grown—that I can finally see the whole picture. Divorce is a life-transforming experience. After divorce, childhood is different. Adolescence is different. Adulthood—with the decision to marry or not and have children or not—is different. Whether the final outcome is good or bad, the whole trajectory of an individual's life is profoundly altered by the divorce experience.

We have been blinded to this fact by the sheer numbers of people affected and by the speed at which our society has been transformed. Many people today think divorce is a perfectly normal experience. It's so common, children hardly notice it. No stigma. No big deal. After all, if half the child's schoolmates come from divorced families, how could divorce be so traumatic? And isn't it true, they say, that children raised in bad intact families are no better off? Everyone who grows up in America today is affected directly or indirectly by divorce, so everyone has the same worries. In other words, they argue that divorce places no special burdens on individuals (remember, it's a normal experience). Indeed, if researchers were to compare groups of eighteen-year-olds from divorced and intact homes and then groups of twenty-two-year-olds and so forth they would probably find that most children of divorce and children from intact homes often hold similar views. It's true that most young people are worried about similar things.

But I have found what I think are deeper truths to this superficial impression. First, each child experiences divorce single file. Just because others are suffering does not reduce their suffering. Would it lessen a widow's sorrow to have five other widows on the same street? Would that make her feel less pain? Numbers provide no consolation for children or adults in many of life's traumas. People who believe that numbers mute the individual child's suffering have simply not talked to the children. Each child in a classroom half full of children of divorce cries out, "Why me?" Moreover, by following the life of one child of divorce, and then another and another, from early childhood through adolescence and into the challenges of adulthood, I can say without a doubt that they have worries apart from their peers raised in intact homes. These worries are reshaping our society in ways we never dreamt about. That is the subject of this book and a challenge to all of us in coming years.

THE PAGES THAT follow contain many themes that are entirely new to our understanding of the long-term effects of divorce. For example, Karen was the first grown child of divorce who described that she lived with the fear that disaster was always waiting to strike without warning, especially when she was happy. As I soon found out, these fears were common among young adults who grew up in divorced families. If happiness increases one's odds of experiencing loss, think how dangerous it must be to simply feel happy.

Contrary to what we have long thought, the major impact of divorce does not occur during childhood or adolescence. Rather, it rises in adulthood as serious romantic relationships move center stage. When it comes time to choose a life mate and build a new family, the effects of divorce crescendo. A central finding to my research is that children identify not only with their mother and father as separate individuals but with the relationship between them. They carry the template of this relationship into adulthood and use it to seek the image of their new family. The absence of a good image negatively influences their search for love, intimacy, and commitment. Anxiety leads many into making bad choices in relationships, giving up hastily when problems arise, or avoiding relationships altogether.

As we will see, the divorced family is not a truncated version of the two-parent family. It is a different kind of family in which children feel less protected and less certain about their future than children in reasonably good intact families. Mothers and fathers who share their beds with different people are not the same as mothers and fathers living under the same roof. The divorced family has an entirely new cast of characters and relationships featuring stepparents and stepsiblings, second marriages and second divorces, and often a series of live-in lovers. The child who grows up in a postdivorce family often experiences not one loss—that of the intact family—but a series of losses as people come and go. This new kind of family puts very different demands on each parent, each child, and each of the many new adults who enter the family orbit.

Moreover, divorce brings radical changes to parent–child relationships that run counter to our current understanding. Parenting cut loose from its moorings in the marital contract is often less stable, more volatile, and less protective of children. When that contract dissolves, the perceptions, feelings, and needs of parents and children for one another are transformed. It's not that parents love their children less or worry less about them. It's that they are fully engaged in rebuilding their own lives—economically, socially, and sexually. Parents and children's needs are often out of sync for many years after the breakup. Worried children watch their parents like little hawks, looking for signs of stress that will affect their availability as parents.

As the stories you are about to hear reveal, children are not passive vessels but rather active participants who help shape their own destiny and that of their family. They make gallant efforts to fit into the new requirements of the postdivorce family although they hope for many years that their parents will reconcile. Because they are in their formative years, the new roles that they assume in the family are built into their character. Some move into the postdivorce vacuum and become principal caregivers of their families. Others learn to hide their true feelings. Some get into trouble hoping that they can bring their parents back together to rescue them. The roles they adopt to adjust to the new circumstances in the divorced family are likely to endure into adulthood and are frequently reinstalled in their adult relationships.

And finally, we see that many children of divorce are stronger for their struggles. They think of themselves as survivors who have learned to rely on their own judgment and to take responsibility for themselves and others at a young age. They have had to invent their own morality and values. They understand the importance of economic independence and hard work. They do not take relationships lightly. Most maintain a reverence for good family life.

The Life Stories

THIS BOOK IS organized around the life stories of five adults raised in divorced families and several others who were raised in intact families. Each of these individuals is prototypical, carefully and thoughtfully chosen to represent the experiences of large numbers of people from similar backgrounds. Their stories are interlaced with writing that draws on current research and studies carried out at the Center for the Family in Transition, reflecting our most recent dilemmas in family law and policy. Other essays present my own formulations about growing to adulthood in a divorced or intact family, how the experiences are alike or different, and how adult expectations are forged in the crucible of family life.

In choosing to portray the whole lives of a representative few rather than brief vignettes or group data from many, I hope to capture an in-depth view of how divorce shaped and reshaped the lives of the children as they grew into adulthood. Many large-scale studies are based on census data about divorcing families and provide useful demographic information about the high incidence of divorce among the adult children of divorce, high school dropout rates, difficulties in adult relationships, and the like. But those studies all rely on structured telephone interviews or questionnaires that elicit superficial information or even mechanical responses about the inner feelings and thoughts of people. Only face-to-face interviews over many hours within the context of a trusting relationship, where the interviewer is free to follow unanticipated topics that arise in natural conversation, lead us to the human experience behind the statistics. This kind of intensive interviewing is necessarily confined to a limited number of people because it is so time consuming. But this well-known research tool is the only way to gain access into the hearts and minds of the people themselves, to understand who they are and how they view themselves and others, how they got to where they are today.

This book is organized into five parts, each of which centers on the life story of an adult who was raised in a divorced family. Each section recapitulates the life course of that individual from the time his or her parents separated to life today, twenty-five years later. Throughout these main stories I have interwoven counterpart stories or shorter vignettes drawn from the lives of adults who were raised in intact families.

Part One is about Karen, a child who takes on adult responsibilities at the breakup and continues in this caretaker role throughout her growing-up years. This experience shapes all of Karen's adult relationships and her view of motherhood in unexpected ways. I compare her development to the life story of Gary, a young man who was raised by two parents who resolved to stay married despite their unhappiness with each other. Gary's story addresses the question of when and whether people who are unhappy can or should stay together for the sake of their children.

Part Two is about Larry, a boy who was raised amid scenes of domestic violence. When his mother left the marriage, seven-year-old Larry was enraged and sought to restore the marriage with the collusive help of his father. I compare Larry's life to the experiences had by Carol, a young woman whose parents engaged in lifelong violence with zero intention of ever separating. Larry and Carol shed light on the perceptions of children and adolescents raised in violent families and how these attitudes affect their adult lives.

Part Three is about Paula, a young child who suffered intense loneliness after divorce when her mother had to go to school and work full-time. In adulthood, Paula is herself a single parent who is starting over after a wild adolescence and an impulsive early marriage. Her story enables me to explore the long-term effect of court-ordered visiting, joint custody, and other court policies that shape children's lives and attitudes toward their parents. No person in our comparison group suffered an experience equivalent to Paula's sudden loss of a loving protective environment, and so they are not included in this section.

Part Four is about Billy, a child who was born with a congenital heart condition and who had special needs that prevented him from adapting to his parents' new lives. Divorce is particularly challenging for such vulnerable children who are not able to handle change very well. In this section, I also explore the issue of who pays for college when obligatory child support stops at age eighteen.

Part Five is about Lisa, who was raised in a family where every effort was made to keep the peace. She grew up in comfortable surroundings with the support of two loving parents and an affectionate stepmother. Nevertheless, when Lisa entered adulthood she encountered serious problems in trusting men. She struggled with feelings that stemmed from the long ago divorce. Compared to Betty, who was raised in a very happy intact family, Lisa is not sure that she can find a life partner, raise children, and trust in the institution of marriage.

In telling these stories, I realized that adults raised in divorced families carry within them a unique kind of history. They are the product of two distinct families and the transition between them. Their lives begin within an intact family that one day vanishes. This is replaced by a series of upheavals that leave them confused and frightened. The next chapters of their lives occur within the postdivorce family, which can take many forms. The family can expand to include a new cast of characters—other adults or children who are temporarily or permanently a part of their lives—or it can contract into a diminished version of the predivorce household. And it can be everything in between. These disparate parts of their histories continue to occupy their minds as they mature. At each new developmental stage, they assess anew what they have lost or gained from the divorce. Often the balance sheet changes as circumstances and relationships change. At each stage they reach new conclusions about themselves, their parents, and their stepparents, and they arrive at a perspective that they then carry into their adult relationships.

The life stories of those raised in intact families reveal that children of divorce live in a separate but parallel universe. We found similarities and differences between the two groups all along the life course. I did not expect to find these contrasts so clearly defined between youngsters brought up on the same block and attending the same schools.

All the people in this study have been given new names and other disguises to protect their privacy. Sometimes we used composites based on the stories of several young people to strengthen the disguise. But apart from these changes, their words and the major events of their lives are unedited. I've discovered over many years of interviewing children and adults that people rise to lyrical heights when they feel that someone is finally listening.

One final note. I am not against divorce. How could I be? I've probably seen more examples of wretched, demeaning, and abusive marriage than most of my colleagues. I'm keenly aware of the suffering of many adults and their long-lasting efforts to improve their lives after divorce. I'm also aware that for many parents the decision to divorce is the most difficult decision in their lives; they cry many a night before taking such a drastic step. And I am, of course, aware of the many voices on the radio, on television, and in certain political and religious circles that say divorce is sinful. That it is always detrimental to children and that people who divorce are selfish, only concerned with their own needs. But I don't know of any research, mine included, that says divorce is universally detrimental to children. People who espouse this view speak earnestly from their own lofty values, but I suspect they have not spent time with families facing intractable problems that can lead to divorce.

In truth, people seek divorce for reasons beyond the wish to escape a wretched or frightening marriage. A driving force in the thousands of divorces that I have seen close-up is the wish to surmount the quiet loneliness and disappointment of a loveless marriage. People understandably reach out for another chance at happiness and companionship. Indeed, these troubled feelings merit our deep respect and understanding. But the parent's agenda may conflict with the wishes of the children who need a stable home while growing up. Put succinctly, unlike other social ills such as poverty or community violence, where the interests of parents and children converge, divorce can benefit adults while being detrimental to the needs of children. Our moral vision and our family laws have been built on the assumption that members of a family, big and small, have the same interests. But divorce challenges this assumption straight on. We have been reluctant to face this dilemma in its full complexity. I will take up this issue of when and whether to divorce or stay together for the children's sake in coming pages. I believe guidelines can be drawn from the life stories you are about to read. I also address whether new policies and practices by the courts and parents could better meet both the wishes of parents and the needs of children. Can we do things better is the core question of this work.

Who This Book Is For

THIS BOOK IS written for those of you who grew up in divorced families and want to know why you *feel* and *act* the way you do. Each of you believes that your suffering was unique. You've struggled with inner conflicts and fears whose source you don't comprehend. You've lived for years with fear of loss and the worry that if you're happy, it's only a prelude to disaster. You fear change because deep down you believe it can only be for the worse. You've been worried about one or both of your parents all your life, and leaving them has been a nightmare. Like most adult children of divorce, you've never confessed to anyone how terrified you are of conflict because the only way you know to handle it is to explode or run away. You've lain awake night after night struggling with anxiety about love and commitment. You know far too much about loneliness and too little about lasting friendship. But you were too uncomfortable to mention these feelings because you had no idea that you were part of a large and growing army of millions of young adults who were raised in divorced homes and who share your bewilderment and concerns. The feelings that confuse and trouble you have deep roots in your history. By seeing how your life has been different from that of people raised in good intact families, you will begin to understand these roots for the first time. Your fears may not vanish, but they can surely be muted. That's my first purpose.

This book is also written for those of you who are married to a child of divorce. Why is it that in dealing with your spouse you so often feel as if you're walking on eggs? Why do you have to be so careful about even trivial disagreements, and why is it so hard to change your plans? In deciding to have children, you may have run into an emotional blockade, and when it comes to getting along with your spouse's family, the complications never cease. Your spouse has deep anxieties that seem strangely out of sync in such an otherwise highly functioning person. But if you can understand your spouse and accommodate to special needs, he or she will be profoundly grateful. Children of divorce have not had many people in their lives who understand how scared they sometimes get in situations that others take for granted.

And, of course, this book is written for those parents who are standing at the crossroads. Should you decide to divorce, what will happen to your children and how can you help them? Should you decide to stay together, what will be the price for you and your children who grow up in an unhappy marriage? I have drawn on many decades of research on divorce to offer advice to parents at the time of the breakup and during the years that follow. I have spelled out how to tell children of your decision to divorce. This is very important in setting the stage for the postdivorce family. Your child will never forget what you say (or fail to say) and the emotional ambience of the family meeting. I also explain in detail how to choose a custody arrangement that will benefit you and your child, and how to modify this arrangement as the child grows and her needs and interests change. Among the many issues I discuss is how to help your child when there has been violence in the home; many children witness it as the marriage comes to a stormy end and people who would not normally strike one another do so with abandon. I have been concerned for many years about the child's sense that as a child of divorce she has fewer rights and less influence on her life compared to her friends in intact families; I suggest many ways that parents can help the child feel she is loved and respected. Finally, I have some special advice about remarriage and building relationships between a child and a stepparent. All of these issues are central to the child's well-being in the divorced family and are areas of concern for which the parent has very little preparation or guidance.

Finally, I have another important audience in mind. This book is also written for concerned judges, attorneys, mediators, and mental health professionals who work with the courts and families. All of you are caught in dilemmas created by a legal system that gives priority to the rights of parents but is mandated to protect children. I invite you to hear the voices of these young adults who have grown up under the policies of our legal system. Few of you have ever had the opportunity to find out what happens to such children after agreements—in which they have no voice—are signed, sealed, and delivered. This is your chance to hear from these children. They speak from the heart.

I begin with the rest of Karen's story.

THE UNEXPECTED LEGACY OF DIVORCE

A 25 YEAR LANDMARK STUDY

PART ONE

Parallel Universes: Karen and Gary

ONE

When a Child Becomes the Caregiver

Karen James's visit drove me to continue probing the long-term effects of divorce on children. The minute she left, I went to my study and drew out her family's record to refresh my memory. I have copious files on each family member in our study, including verbatim transcripts of past interviews, letters from teachers, notes describing dollhouse play, children's drawings, comments from parents about their own lives and their beliefs about their children, comments from children showing an astonishing difference in perceptions, and my own margin notes about what each family represents. The first item that caught my eye was a drawing Karen had done when we met. (Children's drawings often tell you what they are feeling and reveal far more than spoken words.) Karen had depicted each member of her family in meticulous detail—her mother, father, eight-year-old brother Kevin, and six-year-old sister Sharon. Dressed in bright colors, they were standing very close together, each smiling broadly. Even the cat was smiling. "My Family" was printed across the top in large block letters. I was intrigued by Karen's capacity to maintain an image of serenity in her drawing because by now I was privy to the shrieking disorganization in her family life. Karen's wish for peace and family togetherness was poignantly clear. As I was to learn, this was the central desire of her life.

The James divorce totally bewildered the children. Though on a rocky course for several years, the marriage was functioning (in the children's eyes) and family life seemed pretty stable. The father made a good living as a dermatologist who worked long hours in a private practice with four other physicians. The mother was furious at her husband, complaining that he was never available, spent zero time with the children, was cold and aloof as a husband and incompetent as a lover. He paid almost no attention to what he called her "yammering." She was a strikingly beautiful woman who worked part-time in an upscale floral shop making elegant, expensive flower arrangements. The job engaged her artistic streak and enabled her to be at home in the afternoons when the children got home from school. She was a strict, demanding mother. He was an emotionally distant father—when he was around. The parents yelled at one another, barking grievances that made no sense to the children, but there was never any talk of divorce. As the three siblings told me, Sturm und Drang were part of normal family life.

The real storm began with the sudden traumatic death of Mrs. James's mother, who was killed in a highway accident. Mrs. James collapsed with grief. She had depended on her mother for advice, affection, and help in maintaining the social façade of a happy marriage. The death precipitated an agitated depression in Mrs. James, who became increasingly angry at the world and critical of everyone around her. She turned to her husband for solace, love, compassion, and sexual intimacy. He became the chief target of her rage because he did not provide the help she needed. Quarrels that were part of the marriage began to magnify and cascade as the anger took on a life of its own. Soon their life was nothing but a series of arguments, each louder than the next. Dr. James was badly frightened by the intensity of his wife's needs and withdrew further. Reeling from both losses, she attacked him more and more wildly. Stung by her loud accusations of his failings, he countered with accusations of infidelity, long-standing frigidity, and incompetent mothering. As best I could make out, the final trigger was Dr. James's departure for a two-day dermatology convention. Consumed by her anger, she impulsively sought legal counsel and filed for divorce.

As I looked over the record and searched my memory, I was surer than ever that the James's quarrels had more passion than content. They were not fighting over infidelity—which was apparently old hat—so much as wanting to hurt each other. Each heatedly denied the other's accusations. Yet, like so many divorcing couples, they fought savagely, as the children looked on helplessly or ran away and hid. As happens in many families, there was no disagreement around child custody or visiting. Mrs. James would have done anything to irritate her husband, including making him take the kids—as long as that is what he did not want.

Anger Doesn't End with Divorce

THE MARRIAGE WAS dissolved amid rising chaos within the family. The parents' fury at each other did not subside over the years that followed, although it was never fought out in the courts. This is a familiar situation for those of us who work with divorcing couples. Contrary to what most people think (including attorneys and judges), the vast majority of divorcing parents do not drag their conflicts into the courtroom. The 10 to 15 percent of couples who do fight in court consume the lion's share of our attention but they do not represent the norm.[1] Most parents negotiate a divorce settlement, decide on custody arrangements, and go their separate ways. Unfortunately, many of them stay intensely angry with one another. In our study, a third of the couples were fighting at the same high pitch ten years after their divorce was final. Their enduring anger stemmed from continued feelings of hurt and humiliation fueled by new complaints (child support is too burdensome or too little) and jealousy over new, often younger partners. The notion that divorce ends the intense love/hate relationship of the marriage is another myth of our times. Like many divorced people, Karen's mother frequently called her ex-husband and got into shouting matches. As a result, the children were exposed to the hurt and anger that led to the breakup throughout their growing up years. Millions of children today experience the same unrelenting drama of longing and anger that refuses to die.

It is, of course, hard to know how often divorce is precipitated by factors outside the marriage. I have seen a good number of such instances. Indeed, it is one of the common causes—or more precisely, final triggers—of divorce, yet few people seem to recognize its importance. Whenever people are shaken by a serious loss in their lives—be it the termination of a job, death of a parent, serious illness in a child, or any grievous event that can evoke powerful and primitive passions—the bereaved person will turn to their spouse for comfort. If the partner responds with understanding and tenderness, the marriage can be forever enriched. But the tragedy can also split people apart when the bereaved person is deeply disappointed in the partner's response and feels rejected in his or her hour of greatest need. Grief turns to rage as the two people end up irrationally blaming the other—one for not having empathy, the other for making insatiable demands. The initial loss is soon compounded, anger and accusations take over, and the marriage cascades downward. Mrs. James followed this script to the letter.

It's especially tragic when divorce occurs as the sequel to a serious life crisis. The suffering person loses whatever support there was in the marriage and confronts the transition from marriage to singlehood in a depleted state. The children are badly frightened and apprehensive about what lies ahead. It's as if the entire family at its weakest point is expected to deal with an earthquake and its aftershocks.

What happened to this family is instructive. Many people, including lawyers, judges, and mediators, don't understand how often in divorce seemingly rational complaints cloak powerful, irrational feelings. Or they assume that the complaints always reflect anger at the spouse and not some other deep sadness. However familiar Mrs. James's marital troubles sounded to her attorney, her anger did not arise from the marriage per se but from a secondary loss that fueled her rage. Ideally, her grief over her mother's sudden death and her inability to mourn should have been addressed before she moved ahead to make thoughtful decisions about her divorce and her children.

This is the kind of rage that can last for decades after divorce and it is the kind of anger that leaves lasting residue on a child's personality. As an adult, Karen is terrified of conflict because it's so dangerous. But we're getting ahead of our story.

Becoming a Caregiver Child

Six months after the divorce, Dr. James married a much younger woman whom the children liked very much. She was lively, funny, and did not try to intrude into their lives as a rule-making stepmother but rather befriended them and treated them warmly. Unfortunately, Dr. James carried some baggage into his second marriage and it, too, was stormy, featuring many unexplained weekend departures by the second wife. Three years later, she kissed the children good-bye and left to marry another man. "I was a basket case," Dr. James told me during one of our follow-up interviews. The children were stunned, bereft of explanation for the second loss in their family life.

Nor did Mrs. James find much happiness in the years after her divorce. She had several love affairs followed by a second marriage. The new husband, who ran a landscape business, could not tolerate the children and soon grew bored with his pretty wife. The marriage lasted less than five years, throwing the mother into continued turmoil.

For Karen, the legacy of divorce was that she moved into the role of substitute parent for her younger siblings and of confidante and adviser to her troubled mother and father. It was an entirely new role for this child who, like many others before the divorce, had been leading a fairly protected life. Yet Karen undertook the classic role of caregiver or "parentified" child with aplomb and grace. In fact, she was a model parent. "My brother is scared of a lot of things," she once warned me.

"What is he scared of?"

"Of the dark. Of going upstairs. Of being alone. I try to take care of him. I go into his room every night, so he won't cry." Many young girls voluntarily move to fill the vacuum created by parents who collapse emotionally, and sometimes physically, after divorce. The caregiver child's job, as she defines it, is to keep the parent going by acting in whatever capacity is needed—mentor, adviser, nurse, confidante. The range is wide depending on the parent's need and the child's perception. One ten-year-old in this group got up regularly with her insomniac mother at midnight to watch television and drink beer. She frequently stayed home from school to make sure that her mother would not become depressed and suicidal or take the car out when she was drinking. A father told me how his twelve-year-old daughter had packed his clothing, helped him to find an apartment, and arranged to do his shopping. She called him nightly to make sure that he had gotten home safely, and to beg him to stop smoking. Although most caregivers are girls, we've seen several dramatic instances of boys who undertook similar roles. One fourteen-year-old boy, whose mother abandoned the family, stopped going to school and undertook all of his mother's responsibilities, including shopping, cooking, cleaning, and caring for his father who was in a state of collapse.

Such children soon sacrifice their friends, school activities, and, most important, their sense of being children—childhood itself. In return, they gain a sense of pride and the feeling that they have saved a parent's life. When there are siblings at home, the caretaker child moves forthrightly into the parental role and takes charge of running the house, making dinners, seeing that homework is done, putting little ones to bed, cleaning bathrooms late at night. Karen was well suited for this caretaking job and quickly learned to keep her own feelings under tight control. To her great credit, Karen had enormous compassion for both of her parents and was especially comforting to her mother, who in turn acknowledged how much she depended on her ten-year-old.

With no hint of embarrassment, Mrs. James told me, "Karen takes care of me. She understands me without words." Like most parents who come to rely heavily on their children, she had little or no awareness of the child's heavy sacrifice of her own playtime and friendships. She wasn't aware of the fact that Karen was missing school and not paying attention to classroom work. Instead, she spoke as if Karen were an adult or even a much older person. "When she sees me sitting alone in the evening, she knows that I feel sad and she puts her arms around me. She is also very wise. She told me to get rid of my boyfriend. 'He will only hurt you,' she said. I've learned to listen to her."

And who, I wondered, does Karen turn to for soothing words? Who does she have to comfort her in the years following divorce? Or does she gradually learn to block her own feelings and needs because they are too painful?

Karen told me how she liked to sit alone in her grandmother's garden where it was quiet and she felt safe. I regretted that she didn't have many friends but was pleased to hear she had at least this one oasis. I remember Karen years later telling me, "My grandmother saved my life."

There's no way for a sensitive child to see her mother cry or her father fall into depression without worrying that she's the cause of it—and so she takes full responsibility for her mother's tears and father's moods. I watched Karen with a feeling of great helplessness, realizing there was nothing I could do to alleviate her pain or slake her thirst for protection. I remember once asking her, "What will you be when you grow up, Karen?"

She blushed. "I want to work with children who are blind or retarded or who can't speak." I thought of Karen's mother who sat alone and cried, of her brother who was afraid of the dark, of all the sorrowful people in this family, including herself, whom this amazing child wanted to rescue and I almost cried.

When a child forfeits her childhood and adolescence to take on responsibilities for a parent, her capacity to enjoy her life as a young person, develop close friendships, and cultivate shared interests is sacrificed. Beyond this loss, there is a major psychological hazard if the upside-down dependence goes on too long. The child may become trapped into feeling that she alone must rescue the troubled parent. When she attends to her own needs and wishes, she feels guilty and undeserving. This happens if the parent's unhappiness continues for years and the parent comes to rely on the child for comfort or when the child herself assumes the role and won't give it up. Whatever its origins, the child feels obliged to care for the parent in whatever capacity is needed—as caregiver, companion, mentor, or the person who keeps depression at bay. Karen said, "My mom has no one. Only me."

As strange as this sounds, many of these youngsters believe that it's their duty to keep their parent alive. Without them, the parent would die. This is an awesome responsibility, especially for a child who has no one to confide in. It is far beyond the kind of help a devoted child gives to a parent in a temporary crisis, divorce or otherwise. It is an overburdening that seriously inhibits the child's freedom to separate normally and to lead a healthy adolescence. Bound to the troubled parent by unbreakable strands of love, compassion, guilt, and self-sacrifice, the child is not free to leave home emotionally or to follow her heart in love or marriage. In fact, the parents and siblings may not feel able to function without her. They may cling to her and block her exit. As I was to learn later, many of these child caregivers reinstalled the rescue relationship that they had with their parents into their adult relationships with the opposite sex. This is a serious long-term consequence of divorce for those who become caught up in the caregiver role.

The Diminished Parent

By the time Karen was fifteen, her home situation had changed very little. She made no waves in high school and got just passing grades. Her teachers described her as being quiet, reserved, and ladylike. They made no inquiries about her frequent absences, perhaps assuming too easily that someone at home was ill and she was needed. Clearly she was not working to her potential. How could she?

Again I asked Karen about her plans for the future and she replied in what had become her customary grave, thoughtful manner. "I'd like to get married and maybe have kids. But you never know, you might get a divorce. I don't ever want that."

To understand how divorce affects children over the long haul, we need to explore the fact that the divorced family is not just a cut-off version of the two-parent family. The postdivorce family is a new family form that makes very different demands on each parent, each child, and each of the many new adults who enter the family orbit. For millions of American children the experience of growing up—of simply *being* a child—has changed. For millions of adults, the experience of being a parent has been radically transformed.

The first thing we need to acknowledge is the close link between the marital bond and the parent-child relationship. Every parent and child knows this is true. When the marriage is working and the couple is content, the parent-child relationship is nourished and rewarded by the parents' love and appreciation for each other and supported by their cooperation. But when the tie is severed, the break sends messages throughout the system that quickly reach the children. The first message is that parenting is diminished. The adults are now each on their own and occupied with building separate lives. How will I manage and where am I going and how can I put my life together?

How does this diminished parenting show up? Ask any child of divorce. In every domain of the child's life, parents are less available and less organized, provide fewer dinners together or even clean clothing, and do not always carry out regular household routines or help with homework or offer soothing bedtime rituals. But the big picture is more troublesome than the details. When the marriage breaks, children take on a new meaning for their parents. They may become a much heavier burden. Or they are an unfortunate residue from a dream that failed. Or they may give hope and meaning to a parent's life.

After divorce a surprising number of otherwise well-functioning adults reach out to children for help with their grown-up problems. In Karen's case, this kind of behavior became the norm, leading her into the role of caretaker child. But in many families, the reversal of parent and child roles is more or less temporary, albeit shocking. One father told me that he revealed all his business and personal plans in Castro-like lectures to his seven-year-old son who "understands everything." In our playroom, this child's play consisted of running a Mack truck over a little car. Parents who are otherwise mature and responsible in their social and professional commitments will choose to be vulnerable in front of their children. Suddenly they place tremendous stock in the child's opinion—even when the child knows absolutely nothing about the issue at hand. Thus the adult will ask for advice about a lover, how and where to live, whether or not to remarry, and whom to choose. Others share their disappointments in love with very young children. I was startled when Sammy, who was four, comforted his grieving mother whose lover had just left by saying, "He shouldn't quit in the middle. That's not right."

The parents' motives are not hard to understand. Even women who choose to leave their marriages and have successful careers will feel alone and beleaguered as they face new responsibilities and have to make decisions alone, without advice from a partner. Men are also depressed and lonely at this time. They need help setting up a home for themselves and to be reassured that their children want to see them. Men and women alike feel isolated and alienated from former friends who may be reluctant to take sides—and thus stay away from both. Other friends are concerned about the cracks in their own marriages and will keep a safe distance. Family members often disapprove of the divorce and do not hesitate to say so. Feeling hurt and defeated, each parent naturally turns to the children as their most loyal confidants. Both rely heavily on their offspring for sympathy and companionship. These youngsters literally help keep the parents going. They are remarkably intuitive about adult depression and protect their parents from pressures outside and inside the home. Twenty-five years after divorce, many men and women still say to me, "I would not have made it except for this child."

Given how emotionally dependent on their children many parents become, it's not surprising to see bitter custody or visitation fights over who has priority in the child's life. Many parents come to believe that without that child, they have no one. Their only remaining important life relationship and loyal support lies with that child. Thus the legal battle often has its roots in adult despair and not, as many people think, in the parents' simple desire to spend more time with the child. Men and women tell me that when the child is with the other parent they become seriously depressed and wander restlessly from room to room unable to bear their loneliness. Sometimes this behavior occurs only during the months following the breakup. But it can also endure, providing the basis for endless litigation over custody and visiting. Such battles may distract parents from their personal misery but they hardly resolve it.

As these relationships develop, parents and children often become more like peers than separate generations, which in turn can make the children more independent and responsible. They are justifiably proud of their achievement. Many of our efforts to understand the impact of divorce on children have assumed incorrectly that the child is a passive vessel who is shaped by the changes ushered in by a divorce. *But the child is an active agent.* (This is a theme I will develop in depth in a later chapter.) No one asked Karen to step forward. She did it on her own. Her role in the postdivorce family was entirely different from her role in the predivorce family. In some homes, everyone benefits from the child's new role. Adults gain needed help. Children gain maturity and self-confidence. They also show a moral sensibility and compassion for others far beyond their years, which they can draw upon later in their adult relationships and often in their career choices. Karen's decision to study public health and to develop programs for crippled children was by her own account rooted in the early responsibility she took as a child. For the fortunate parent who is able to rely on the child to get through the extended divorce crisis, the child's availability may tip the balance between chronic dysfunction and recovery.

Of course, caregiving by a child can occur in intact families when a parent is ill or troubled. I recall one little girl, Martha, the oldest of three siblings, who took over running the household for a year when her mother was recovering from a serious car accident. Martha and her father shared in parenting the younger children and in taking care of Martha's mother. The difference was that although the mother was in a wheelchair for many months, she maintained close touch with what was going on in the home. Both parents maintained adult responsibility for all their children at home. Martha matured as a result of her experience and was rewarded by both parents with appreciation and praise. In many immigrant families one of the older children often is responsible for helping the adults to understand the new language and strange culture. Here, too, the child performs vital functions that enable the family to keep going, but the adults maintain their responsibility at the head of the family.

In contrast, in a postdivorce family, the child often takes responsibility for the one or both parents who are temporarily or lastingly overwhelmed by the crisis. This situation can be compounded by the adult's subsequent disappointments in relationships. A formerly competent mother or father is unable to carry on as before. Recovery from a divorce is a lot harder than we have realized and it lasts a lot longer. As a result, the burden falls on the child who steps forward to take charge—out of compassion and often out of unrealistic guilt. This is one way that divorce profoundly changes not only the child's experience but, as Karen illustrates, the whole personality of the child as she grows up and becomes an adult. Caregiving that involves sacrificing one's own wishes for the needs of others is poor preparation for happy choices in adult relationships, as we'll see in coming chapters.

TWO

Sunlit Memories

The more I thought about Karen, the more I wondered what I would find in talking to young adults who were raised in unhappy intact marriages—whose parents were similar to Karen's parents before their divorce. Would these children move into the breach as caregivers or would they somehow be protected by their parents' decision to stay together? Would they be able to keep their distance from their parents' unhappiness or, like so many children of divorce, be drawn into the vortex of ongoing conflict?

Thus I was eager to meet the young people we recruited to serve as our comparison group for the adult children of divorce. When we began, I honestly didn't know what we'd find. If we could lure them into participating, how candid would they be? As busy adults with families and jobs, would they be willing to talk with my colleagues and me for several hours at a time? Would we end up, as many researchers do, talking only to women, who tend to be more comfortable discussing relationships?

At the outset, I was sure of only one thing: we needed men and women who would match our divorce sample. That is, they would have to be the same age, have similar backgrounds, and have grown up in the same neighborhoods as did the children in the divorce study. We found many people by asking those in the divorce study to put us in touch with their childhood friends who had grown up in intact families. These were adults who literally grew up alongside their friends who were part of our twenty-five-year study. They went to the same schools, played the same sports in high school, attended the same parties, and talked the same slang. Their parents were in the same socioeconomic group and had similar educational backgrounds. Eventually we settled on a group of forty-three people. I decided to keep the group small to begin with because frankly I had no idea what kinds of territory we'd get into. I was not so much interested in outcomes as I was in their total life experience as children and as young adults. As these young men and women shared their memories and details about their lives today, I found rich veins of material to explore and, most important, to compare with the memories and lives of the children of divorce whom I have come to know so well.

I asked many questions about their growing up experiences from childhood through today. What does each person remember about his or her years in grade school, high school, and college? What was their family like? When did they first fall in love? When and how did they decide whom to marry? As adults, how do they feel about marriage and parenthood? How do they get along with their own parents? What are their attitudes about divorce and marriage, betrayal and trust? In looking for answers to these questions, I wanted to get a deeper understanding of the statistical differences sociologists are finding between children of divorce and people raised in intact families. Most large studies of divorce are conducted using questionnaires or other survey techniques administered by people who never see those they are questioning. Researchers gather data from large numbers of families and then segregate children into two big categories—from a divorced family or from an intact family. Such "controlled" studies indeed show that children of divorce and those raised in second marriages are a whole lot more troubled than children from intact marriages are. Researchers have found significant differences in learning problems, school drop-out rates, early sexual behavior, incidence of divorce, physical illness, anger toward parents, and a host of other very important social measures.[1]

But these large-scale studies, while worrisome, usually don't answer the questions that parents want answered. And one reason for this is that subgroups (within the larger legally defined samples of divorced versus not divorced families) are not examined separately. If we really want to tease out the long-term effects of divorce on children in contrast to the effects of being raised in a culture where divorce is rampant, we need to look at similar kinds of families in both groupings. For example, some intact families are characterized by enduring love and friendship with a primary commitment to parenting. Some divorced families are characterized by a lasting sense of attachment with a similar commitment to parenting, despite the breakup. These would be roughly comparable. However, some intact families are enmeshed in mutually destructive behavior, driven by alcoholic rages, in which the children are not protected. Similarly, some divorced families suffer the same kind of chaos where the children are not protected either before or after the divorce. Again, these subgroups are worth comparing. The middle group, where parents are very unhappy in the marriage but want to protect their children, is the largest of all, and indeed, this is where the question is hardest to answer. Many parents in our divorce group had marriages that were of "middling" quality but they decided on balance to go their separate ways. And most of the young adults who were raised in intact families in our study described their parents' marriages the same way—not very happy but they stayed together anyway.

Until this study, no one to my knowledge has ever directly compared the experience of growing up in divorced or remarried families with what it's like to grow up in intact families—yet this is exactly what we, as a society, need to know. Parents want to know how the lives of their children will be different if they decide to stay married or to get a divorce.

That said, these young adults did indeed describe three kinds of intact families. At one end of the spectrum are the highly dysfunctional, bordering-on-cruel families revealed by Carol's story in Chapter 7. These are homes where the children do not feel safe, where the adults are often out of control, but where the parents stay together for reasons I'll explain later.

At the other end of the spectrum are those families that seem to someone like me, who is so used to family troubles, too good to be true. The parents not only get along, they genuinely love each other and continue to show one another respect and affection. The children feel that they are central to their parents' interest and that the family is a priority to both adults. It's very important to understand that these happy families suffer the same kinds of setbacks—automobile accidents, job loss, death in the family, bouts with cancer—that other families encounter in everyday life. They are not immune to tragedy or blessed by incalculable good luck. It's just that they negotiate these issues in ways that preserve the rock solid marriage. In several instances, as people talked lovingly about their parents and their parents' marriages, I felt like I had wandered into another country where the inhabitants look familiar but the language and customs are new. I have grown so used to talking to children of divorce that I hadn't given much thought to what it would mean to grow up in a very happy family in our divorce-ridden culture *from the child's point of view.* How would their life experiences and perceptions of the world differ from the young people down the street being raised in divorced families?

Finally, there is the largest group comprising all the families in between. These are homes in which there can be many serious problems—loneliness, infidelity, chronic illness, depression, sexual deprivation, and countless other woes—but the marriage stays intact. These are homes in which there are also gratifications, especially in shared concern and love of the children. There often is a history of love and friendship that still binds the couple together despite their growing distress and anger at each other. In other words, these are families that stay together in the face of adversities that drive many other couples into divorce court. As I learned more about these families, I began to recognize striking similarities to the families that divorced back in 1971 when my study began and to the thousands of divorcing families that we saw at the Center for the Family in Transition in the 1980s and 1990s. Families like these can go *either way* depending on a host of factors. At the core of their interactions and ambience, they are alike. These are the parents who are most likely to ask, should we divorce or would it be better for the children if we stayed together? What happens to their children is a key issue. How they decide creates striking differences in the entire life experience of their children, as Gary's story reveals.

Gary, the Fort Builder

"I've found some time!"

Although we had not met in person, Gary Bates and I had been playing phone tag for nearly three weeks, trying to set up an interview. As the owner of a successful hardware store, dedicated jogger, and father of three young children, time was his scarcest commodity. Gary's wife, Sara, was just leaving for a birthday party with the two older children, aged ten and seven. The baby was fast asleep inside the house.

"I'm really curious to know what you find out," she said, leaning out of her car window. "My sister just got divorced and sold her house. I haven't told her this but I think she's made a terrible mistake. Her kids are really young. I think she could have stayed in her marriage and toughed it out at least a little longer."

As Gary and I walked into the house, he confided, "Sara and Janine were raised in a very traditional family where divorce is unheard of. And so when Janine got a divorce, her folks were crushed. They just can't understand why she did it."

After we had settled down with "mid-morning depth charges"—Gary's name for his homemade double lattes—I asked him to describe his own family. What was it like growing up in a middle-class neighborhood in Marin County in the 1970s and 1980s?

Gary scrunched his face comically. "Do you want the outdoor version or the indoor version?"

"Both, of course."

"Well, the outdoor version is what I think of when I remember my childhood. We lived in a big, old Victorian house just a couple of blocks away from downtown. My folks still live there. All my friends lived close by, and by the time I was seven or eight I could ride my bike to their houses and we'd go all over to town together. I just remember being outside as much as I could. There was a huge old live oak tree in our backyard and we'd spend hours in it, pretending to be explorers or astronauts. My best friend Eric had a tree house in his yard and we used to build magnificent forts and whoop it up with war games that drove our moms crazy. That of course was the point. Another friend's house was right on a creek. When we got older we took great hikes up the canyon. We just were outside and going as much as we could. I remember how tough it was to come in for dinner, not to mention to have to stay in and do homework!" He laughed, obviously enjoying sharing his memories.

As I listened to Gary describe what it was like to play in his backyard, it struck me that children from divorced families do not talk this way. In all the hours I have talked with Karen through all the years, she never spontaneously turned to the subject of play. It turns out that children raised in very unhappy intact families also don't recall playing with friends, but we'll get to that in Chapter 7. As Gary remembered the forts that he and his friends built, how they screamed at each other like banshees, how they could have given Geronimo lessons, I realized that these were happy, sunlit memories. These were, as one novelist wrote, "those early amorphous years when memory has only begun, when life is full of beginnings and no ends and everything was forever."[2] Gary and his friends were playing the games that children have invented since the beginning of time. Of course the rough-and-tumble life of the school and playground has its heavy disappointments and its share of physical and emotional injuries. Children can be cruel. Those excluded from the inner circles suffer a lot. But as an adult, Gary remembered with amusement how he fell learning to ride a bike and his first soccer match when he ran down the field the wrong way and everyone made fun of him.

When children of divorce did remember playing with friends as an important experience of childhood, the memories were from before the divorce. No doubt many of them rode bicycles, climbed trees, and fooled around in backyards, but they *did not mention it.* Carefree play was not what came to mind when I talked with them at the time or when they reflected back on their younger years, in elementary school. Instead of caring about who finds who in a game of hide-and-seek or who is at bat in the local softball game, children of divorce have other, more pressing concerns. Is Mom all right? Is Dad going to pick me up tonight? Can I bring my new friend over to the house to play if no one is home?

The blunting of childhood memories about play is not restricted to children of divorce. Children all over the world experience war, famine, forced labor, and all kinds of traumas. Nevertheless the differences in play among well-to-do children from protective intact families and children of divorce who lived next door was an unexpected finding that came early in the study. These differences are important because play is a critical aspect of a child's social and moral development. It forms the basis of learning where you fit into the world of equals, how to share and when not to share, when to put up your dukes and when to run. These are all things that grown-ups can't teach. You have to learn them yourself. Unstructured play—where children build forts or tree houses to keep out the adults—is especially important. It enables a child to take a step toward independence and into the world of peers. It's the basis for honing leadership skills, for learning not to cry, not to run home to Mommy, but to trust yourself. It's climbing a tree by yourself and learning how to test the branch before you put your foot on it. Imaginative play is the basis for creativity and fantasy life.

Recent research has called attention to the central importance of peer relationships in the development of children and adolescents.[3] There's no question in my mind as to the significance of these friendships. How harmful is it in the long run to miss out on play? Many very creative people have had twisted childhoods and so we know that building forts is not a prerequisite for a successful adulthood. But it's clear that divorce shuts out some of the special happiness and early friendships that childhood can offer. For children of divorce, growing up is a lonelier road. One result may be a decrement in social skills. One father who grew up in an intact family and now coaches a Little League team said, "I can always spot the boys from divorced families. They get into more fights and they're sore losers. Not all of them, but enough so that they're a headache for all the coaches." Another result could be the kind of feeling I saw in Karen when she said, "My fiancé tells me that I'm too serious because I never learned how to play. He wants to teach me how. He's right. I never had a chance to do things for me. It's still hard for me to think about what I want for myself." She understood perfectly that play is something that one does for pleasure, for oneself. This is what she feels she gave up when she learned early on to think of others before herself.

It gradually dawned on me that children of divorce and those in happy intact families live in separate albeit parallel universes. I would not have seen this without their descriptions of play, and the lack of it, in their backyards after school. This finding has important implications for our social policy. When visiting and custody plans are made, the child's friendships and play activities are rarely considered by parents. The courts never acknowledge them. In the common scenario, parents are the major protagonists. Their schedules, wishes, and rights occupy center stage. In the hundreds of court evaluations and decisions that I have read and in thousands of conversations with parents, I've rarely heard a word about the importance of maintaining the child's friendships and play activities. The only exceptions are where a young adolescent is a gifted athlete or shows special promise in another field. In the view of officialdom, the only thing of value in a child's life is her time with each parent. It should be sobering to parents and others who allocate the child's time to take the memories of this generation into account. Peer play looms much larger in their fond memories than afternoons spent with either Dad or Mom.

Gary continued to reminisce nostalgically about his childhood. "Another memory I have was the crunch of the tires on my dad's car when he returned from work at seven o'clock every evening. It's funny but I can still hear that in my head. Supper was a family thing at our home. We had a special ritual. We used to go round the table and everyone said what they did that day. I still remember being included when I was three years old. I felt ten feet high!"

A lot of adults from intact families remembered supper as an important family event. Like today, many of the mothers who worked outside the home tried to arrange their schedules so they'd be home after school when the children were young. They made a point of having sit-down meals in the evening. Most of the fathers worked long hours, including some weekends. But in most homes supper waited until the entire family was assembled, if not nightly then several times a week. Sunday dinner was special in many homes. With a few exceptions, these were pleasant memories with games, rituals, and conversation that included the children and the grown-ups.

I was again interested that Karen and her peers from divorced families never spontaneously mentioned family suppers or other regular occasions happening *after* the breakup. Undoubtedly they shared evening meals when the family was together, and I suspect that they had many pleasant sit-down dinners with either parent at home after the divorce. But as children they did not mention these events and as adults they did not recall such dinners in their memories of growing up. Even the children in the remarried families did not talk about their family dinners together except early on in the remarriage when the children wondered where the new stepparent would sit and whether he would occupy Dad's or Mom's vacant place. Somehow these occasions lacked the symbolic power of belonging to a family, as they did for children in intact homes.

A Sense of History

WITH THE VISION of a mom and dad at either end of a dinner table, I said to Gary, "Tell me about your folks."

Gary leaned back and stretched out his long legs. Suddenly he jumped up, went over to the piano, and brought back a framed photograph. "This will help to explain it," he said, handing it to me. "It's my favorite picture of my parents." Taken when Gary's parents were in their twenties, the father was leaning casually against a tree, his head thrown back, laughing. He was tall and fair, with tightly curled blond hair, and he wore sideburns, which were then very fashionable. Gary's mother was much shorter than her husband and had very dark, exotic, Barbra Streisand–like looks. She was standing in profile, both hands around one of her husband's arms, looking intently up at him.

"That's kind of how they are," Gary continued, as both of us gazed at the photo. "They're so different but I think that's what brought them together, being really different. Later on, though, it caused a lot of friction." He set the picture on the coffee table in front of us.

"I'd like to hear about them."

Gary then launched into a detailed description of his parents' courtship—who said what, when, and where, almost as if he'd been a fly on the wall. As he talked, I mentally added him to the growing list of other children from intact families who recounted similar courtship stories. They described how their parents decided to have children, a fact (or myth) that was important because it cemented their sense of being wanted from the outset. In hearing these stories, I realized again how much these young adults saw themselves within the context of their family's history—and how children of divorce did not share this feeling. If the latter knew the story of their parents' courtship, they didn't mention it spontaneously. It probably would have been painful for them to think about. In some interviews, children of divorce asked me to repeat what they'd said at earlier meetings as if to turn the pages of an imaginary family photo album, enabling them to reconnect with the past. The loss of continuity with family history is a consequence of divorce that we have overlooked.

Gary had a lot more to say about his parents' marriage. This was a subject that was clearly "up front" and important to him, even though he hadn't lived with them for over fifteen years. "I think they were really happy in the early years," he said. "My dad inherited the business from his dad and always spent long hours at the store. Mom raised us and did the bookkeeping. It was hard to get away for vacations but they managed some camping trips. They'd close the store for two weeks in the summer and we'd tour the national parks. Mom was always real happy to get back to a shower and her kitchen. But early on it seemed like they enjoyed each other and there wasn't much tension."

Like remembering their play, most of the people raised in well-functioning intact families also remembered family holidays, vacations, and other social occasions that brought the family together. They described the abundance of good food, noise, loving interest from grandparents, and mischievous fighting with cousins. They also recalled tensions and some open antagonism among different family members. But these were secondary to the warm glow of the get-togethers. Family vacations were especially memorable. Camping trips were the best-loved vacations among these children who later recalled their escapades and misadventures. The children knew when one of the adults, like Gary's mother, did not share their enthusiasm. One young man guffawed when he recalled how his mom decided to do gourmet cooking over a campfire. Some of their fondest memories were about several families getting together to go camping, hiking, fishing, or boating. These were important communal experiences and the children were proud to do their share of the chores and planning. One young woman remembered how pleased she was that her parents invited her best friend whose parents were divorcing.

As I searched my memory I was hard put to recall children of divorce talking happily, after the divorce, about any holidays or family vacations. Thanksgiving and Christmas posed annual dilemmas. Along with the goodies came the question—whose turn is it to spend which holiday where? For many, these occasions were a mixed bag. Some recalled visiting grandparents alone without their parents, which gave many children a sense of belonging to an extended family, something youngsters in intact families took for granted. Most loved their grandparents very much. These were happy times in their grandparents' home that were long remembered. Some children liked spending separate vacations with their dad and his new family while others hated summer vacations because they were forced to go visit one parent under court order. Family celebrations like graduations, bar mitzvahs, weddings, and birthdays could be very happy. But they could also be marred by continuing tensions between parents, new lovers, and ex-partners. Will one of the adults ruin the occasion by acting out? The children would hold their breath until the event was safely over. The glow of a family get-together, where the older generations can relax and enjoy the food and laugh at the children's antics and the children can bask in the family's admiration, was not part of their storehouse of childhood memories in the same way that it was for those in most intact families.

Invisible Structure of Parenting

As Gary described how he spent his time as a child, it gradually dawned on me that in a well-functioning intact family mothers and fathers are in the background as their children grow up. Their role is to create a safe and supportive place for the children, whose job during elementary and junior high school is to go to school, play, make friends, and simply grow up. From the child's perspective, children occupy center stage. The parents' job as producers is to stay in the wings and make sure that the show goes on. They should of course encourage, applaud, feed, and clothe the players. If the children stumble, parents should come out of the wings, help them up, dust them off, and immediately get offstage again.

In families like Gary's, parents keep a close eye on what their children are doing "onstage" at every moment. If the play gets too rough or there is trouble in the classroom, they are front and center, ready to act. At home, they keep up the buzz of a "parenting dialogue," a conversation that begins with the child's birth and never ends: How is Gary doing? Does his teacher understand his aptitude for math? Should I talk with her? What should we do about his fighting in the schoolyard? What's the best way to handle the teacher's complaints? and so on. The litany is endless. Out of these ongoing dialogues, held after the children are asleep, or when they are thought to be out of earshot, parents evolve a domestic policy for the home and a foreign policy for outside the home. Later, at the dinner table, both adults present a united front to the children.

This invisible structure of parenting that supports the growing child and runs interference for her is weakened or lost in the breakup. Karen and her siblings felt that they had been suddenly abandoned, almost orphaned. Their mother was present but so distracted that they could hardly get her attention. And their father was morose and cranky. In divorce, even parents who get along well after the breakup rarely share a strategy for raising their children, although they may come together around an emergency or scheduling. Like quality time, parallel parenting—a term coined by mediators to mean that two parents who raise a child separately are comparable to two parents who raise a child together—is a great slogan, but it can't replicate the cooperative parenting that children and parents need. In a good intact family, a constant parental dialogue revolves around the day's events and interactions within the family. Daily conversations and the pillow talk that follows literally shape the child's environment to fit her needs as she grows up and changes. Such parental dialogue, if it existed, is abruptly shut off by divorce. As a result, the role of the parents as the child's champion is weakened. This is a serious loss in our crowded, fast-moving society, especially for the child who has special needs or who may be a late or an early bloomer. Of course single parents can take on this role to the extent that their busy schedule permits, but as they often tell me, they feel weighed down by the responsibility for making all the decisions themselves and by the pressures of time. Remarried parents can and do reinstate the invisible parenting structure, but that may not happen for several years. Even then, it takes on a different cast, as we'll see later in the book.

THREE

Growing Up Is Harder

One of the many myths of our divorce culture is that divorce automatically rescues children from an unhappy marriage. Indeed, many parents cling to this belief as a way of making themselves feel less guilty. No one wants to hurt his or her child, and thinking that divorce is a solution to everyone's pain genuinely helps. Moreover, it's true that divorce delivers a child from a violent or cruel marriage (which we will soon see in Chapter 7). However, when one looks at the thousands of children that my colleagues and I have interviewed at our center since 1980, most of whom were from moderately unhappy marriages that ended in divorce, one message is clear: the children do not say they are happier. Rather, they say flatly, "The day my parents divorced is the day my childhood ended."

What do they mean? Typically parent and child relationships change radically after divorce—temporarily or, as in Karen's family, permanently. Ten years after the breakup only one-half of the mothers and one-quarter of the fathers in our study were able to provide the kind of nurturant care that had distinguished their parenting before the divorce. To go back to what Gary said about his parents being "offstage" while he grew up, after a divorce one or both parents often move onto center stage and refuse to budge. The child becomes the backstage prop manager making sure the show goes on.

What most parents don't realize is that their children can be reasonably content despite the failing marriage. Kids are not necessarily overwhelmed with distress because Mommy and Daddy are arguing. In fact, children and adults can cope pretty well in protecting one another during the stress of a failing marriage or unhappy intact marriage. Mothers and fathers often make every effort to shield their marital troubles from their children. It's only after one or both have decided to divorce that they fight in full view. Children who sense tension at home turn their attention outside, spending more time with friends and participating in school activities. (Gary, whose parents' marriage was often unhappy, did exactly the same thing.) Children learn at an early age to turn a deaf ear to their parents' quarrels. The notion that all or even most parents who divorce are locked into screaming conflict that their children witness is plainly wrong. In many unhappy marriages, one or both people suffer for many years in total silence—feeling lonely, sexually deprived, and profoundly disappointed. Most of the children of divorce say that they had no idea their parents' marriage was teetering on the brink. Although some had secretly thought about divorce or discussed it with their siblings, they had no inkling that their parents were planning to break up. Nor did they understand the reality of what divorce would entail for them.

For children, divorce is a watershed that permanently alters their lives. The world is newly perceived as a far less reliable, more dangerous place because the closest relationships in their lives can no longer be expected to hold firm. More than anything else, this new anxiety represents the end of childhood.

Karen confirmed this change in several of our follow-up interviews. Ten years after her parents' divorce, I learned that she was attending the University of California at Santa Cruz so that she could run home on weekends and be available for crises. And there were plenty of those, mostly involving both her younger brother and sister. When she was twenty, she told me angrily, "Since their divorce I've been responsible for both my parents. My dad became a pathetically needy man who always wants a woman to take care of him. I'm the backup when his girlfriends leave him. My mom is still a mess, always involved with the wrong kind of men. I've had to take care of them as well as my brother and sister."

Many Losses

When most people hear the word "divorce," they think it means one failed marriage. The child of divorce is thought to experience one huge loss of the intact family after which stability and a second, happier marriage comes along. But this is not what happens to most children of divorce. They experience not one, not two, but many more losses as their parents go in search of new lovers or partners. Each of these "transitions" (as demographers call them) throws the child's life into turmoil and brings back painful reminders of the first loss. National studies show that the more transitions there are, the more the child is harmed because the impact of repeated loss is cumulative.[1] The prevalence of this instability in the lives of these children hasn't been properly weighed or even recognized by most people. While we do have legal records of second, third, and fourth remarriages and divorces, we have no reliable count of how many live-in or long-term lovers a child of divorce will typically encounter. Children observe each of their parents' courtships with a mixture of excitement and anxiety. For adolescents, the erotic stimulation of seeing their parents with changing partners can be difficult to contain. Several young teenage girls in the study began their own sexual activity when they observed a parent's involvement in a passionate affair. Children and adolescents watch their parents' lovers, with everything from love to resentment, hoping for some clue about the future. They participate actively as helper, critic, and audience and are not afraid to intervene. One mother returning home from a date found her school-age children asleep in her bed. Since they'd told her earlier that they didn't like her boyfriend, she took the hint. Many new lovers are attentive to the children, regularly bringing little gifts. But even the most charming lovers can disappear overnight. Second marriages with children are much more likely to end in divorce than first marriages. Thus the child's typical experience is not one marriage followed by one divorce, but several or sometimes many relationships for both their mother and father followed by loss or by eventual stability.[2]

Karen's experience is typical of many that I have seen. Her father's second wife, who was nice to the children, left without warning three years into the marriage. After she was gone, her father had four more girlfriends who caused him a great deal of suffering when they also left.

Karen's mother had three unhappy love affairs prior to her remarriage, which ended after five years. Obviously Karen and her siblings experienced more than "one divorce." Their childhoods were filled with a history of new attachments followed by losses and consequent distress for both parents. Karen's brother, at age thirty, told me: "What is marriage? Only a piece of paper and a piece of metal. If you love someone, it breaks your heart."

In this study, only 7 of the original 131 children experienced stable second marriages in which they had good relationships with a stepparent and stepsiblings on both sides of the divorced family. Two-thirds of the children grew up in families where they experienced multiple divorces and remarriages of one or both of their parents. Such figures don't capture the many cohabitations and brief love affairs that never become legal relationships. Given this experience, can we be surprised that so many children of divorce conclude that love is fleeting?

Ghosts of Childhood

When I turned to the notes of my interview with Karen fifteen years after her parents' divorce, the image of a young woman crying inconsolably entered my mind. Karen was sitting on the sofa in my old office, with her chin in her hands and elbows on her knees, telling me about her live-in relationship with her boyfriend Nick.

"I've made a terrible mistake," she said, twisting a damp tissue into the shape of a rope. "I can't believe I've gotten myself into this. I never should have done it. It's like my worst nightmare come to life. It's what I grew up dreading most and look what happened." Karen gripped her fingers tightly until her knuckles shone like moons.

"What's wrong?" I asked, as gently as I could.

"Everything," she moaned. "He drinks beer. He has no ambition, no life goals, no education, no regular job. He's going nowhere. When I come home after work, he's just sitting there in front of the TV and that's where he's been all day." Then Karen's voice dropped. "But he loves me," she said in anguish. "He would be devastated if I ever left him." Even in her great distress and anger she was intensely cognizant of her boyfriend's suffering. I thought to myself, this epitomizes Karen—she's always aware of other people's hurts and suffering.

"But then why did you move in with him?"

"I'm not sure. I knew I didn't love him. But I was scared of marriage. I was scared of divorce, and I'm terrified of being alone. Look, you can hope for love but you can't expect it! When Nick asked me to live with him, I was afraid that I'd get older and that I wouldn't have another chance. I kept thinking that I'd end up lonely like my dad. And Mom."

I looked at this beautiful young woman and shook my head in disbelief. Could she really think that shacking up with a man she didn't love was all she could hope for? Karen must have read my mind because she quickly said, "I know. People have been telling me how pretty I am since I was a child. But I don't believe it. And I don't care. Looks were always important to my mother. She wears tons of makeup and dresses like a model. I thought she was silly and still do. I don't want to look like her or live my life that way."

"How did you meet Nick?"

She sighed as she answered, "Well, we hardly knew each other in high school. We were never lovers or even friends. I think that he had a crush on me from afar. Then in my junior year I broke my ankle and during the six weeks that I was hobbling around, he was very kind to me, carrying my stuff and visiting me. He was the only one who took any care of me. He also comes from a divorced family with lots of troubles. When he dropped out of school, I felt very sorry for him."

"Then how did he come back into your life?"

"I was having a real bad time. My brother was getting into serious trouble with the law and my dad wouldn't do anything to help. I pleaded with him but he was totally indifferent. I was frantic and beginning to realize that all my efforts to hold my family together were wasted. So when Nick asked me to move in with him, I said yes. Anything to get away, even though I knew from the outset he had no plans for the future, no training, no formal education. After the first day, I said to myself, 'Oh, my God, what did I do?' But at least I know he won't betray me. At least I'm safe from that."

"Karen, this fear of betrayal is pretty central to you. You keep mentioning it."

"It's been central to my life," she agreed. "Both my parents played around. I saw it all around me. They felt that if you are not getting what you want, you just look elsewhere." (I've never heard anyone put the alternative morality of our divorce culture so succinctly.)

Karen took her hands away from her face and silently ripped the tissue in half. "There's another reason I moved in with him," she whispered. "It will probably distress you." Karen spoke hesitantly, clasped her hands in her lap, and elaborated slowly, as if every word were painful and she had to extract them one by one. "I figured that this is one man who will never leave me." Silence. "Because he has no ambitions, he will always have fewer choices than me. So if I stay with him and even marry him someday, I won't ever have to worry about his walking out."

Karen was right about my being distressed. Her statement was chilling. How utterly tragic that this lovely woman would begin her adult journey so burdened down with fears. What kind of life could she build on such fragile foundations?

Like a good caregiver child, Karen reinstalled her troubled relationships with her mother and father into her early relationships with men. As rescuers, most young women like Karen are used to giving priority to the needs of others. Indeed, they are usually not aware of their own needs or desires. Karen confessed that she had never in her life thought about what would make her happy. "That would be like asking for the moon," she said. "I was always too worried about my family to ask for me." As a result, these young women are often trapped into rescuing a troubled man. How can they reject a pitiful man who clings to them? The guilt would be unbearable. Others find troubled men more exciting. One young woman who had frequent contact with both parents during her growing up years explained: "I think I subconsciously pick men who are not going to work out. Men who are nice and considerate bore me. My latest is irresponsible. I don't trust him. I'm sure he cheats. But he's the one I want."

WHAT PROMPTS SO many children of divorce to rush into a cohabitation or early marriage with as much forethought as buying a new pair of shoes?[3] Answers lie in the ghosts that rise to haunt them as they enter adulthood. Men and women from divorced families live in fear that they will repeat their parents' history, hardly daring to hope that they can do better. These fears, which were present but less commanding during adolescence, become overpowering in young adulthood, more so if one or both of their parents failed to achieve a lasting relationship after a first or second divorce. Dating and courtship raise their hopes of being loved sky-high—but also their fears of being hurt and rejected. Being alone raises memories of lonely years in the postdivorce family and feels like the abandonment they dread. They're trapped between the wish for love and the fear of loss.

This amalgam of fear and loneliness can lead to multiple affairs, hasty marriages, early divorce, and—if no take-home lessons are gleaned from it all—a second and third round of the same. Or they can stay trapped in bad relationships for many years. Here's how it works: at the threshold of young adulthood, relationships move center stage. But for many that stage is barren of good memories for how an adult man and woman can live together in a loving relationship. This is the central impediment blocking the developmental journey for children of divorce. The psychological scaffolding that they need to construct a happy marriage has been badly damaged by the two people they depended on while growing up.

Let's look closely at the process of growing up. Children learn all kinds of lessons at their parents' knees, from the time they are born to the time they leave home. There is no landscape more fascinating to the baby than the mother's face. There is no more exciting image to the child than the frame that includes Mom and Dad kissing, fighting, conferring, frowning, crying, yelling, or hugging in the adjoining room. These thousand and one images are internalized and they form the template for the child's view of how men and women treat each other, how parents and children communicate, how brothers and sisters get along. From day one, children watch their parents and absorb the minutiae of human interaction. They observe their parents as private persons (when the adult thinks no one is paying attention) and as public persons onstage outside the home. They listen carefully to what the parents say (although they often pretend not to hear) and they ponder what the parents fail to say. No scientist ever looked through a microscope more intently than the average child who observes her family day in and night out. And they make judgments from early on. Children as young as four years old tell me, "I want to be a daddy like my dad" or "I won't be a mommy like my mommy." They have powerful feelings of love, hate, envy, admiration, pity, respect, and disdain. This is the theater of our lives—our first and most important school for learning about ourselves and all others. From this we extrapolate the interactions of human society. The images of each family are imprinted on each child's heart and mind, becoming the inner theater that shapes expectations, hopes, and fears.

But over and beyond the child's view of mother and father as individuals is the child's view of the relationship between them—the nature of the relationship *as a couple.* Our scholarly literature is full of mother–child and, more recently, father–child experiments, but as every child could tell the professors, the child sees her parents as a twosome. She is intensely and passionately aware of their interaction. What could be more important or more enthralling? These complex images of parental interaction are central to the family theater and are of lasting importance to children of divorce and to children from intact families.

All the young people in the intact families described the relationship between their parents as if they had followed them around day and night. They described their parents' laughter, their teasing, how they knew how to push each other's buttons and how they comforted one another. They even speculated in detail about their parents' sex life. They told me whether Dad kissed Mom when he returned home or whether he pinched her bottom or whether the parents were reserved. Others wondered what their parents had in common or why they stayed married. Along with these observations, they made moral judgments and they reached conclusions that had direct implications for their future lives.

How is the inner template of the child of divorce different from that of the young adult in the intact family—especially if the child of divorce, in accord with the current advice of mediators and court personnel, has access to both parents and the parents refrain from fighting during the postdivorce years?

As every child of divorce told me, no matter how often they see their parents, the image of them together as a loving couple is forever lost. A father in one home and a mother in another home does not represent a marriage, however well they communicate. Separate may be equal but it is not together. As children grow up and choose partners of their own, they lack this central image of the intact marriage. In its place they confront a void that threatens to swallow them whole. Unlike children from intact families, children of divorce in our study spoke very little about their parents' interaction. They hardly ever referred to their parents' behavior at the breakup. By and large their central complaint is that no one had explained the divorce to them and that the reasons were shrouded in mystery. When reasons were offered, they sounded to them like platitudes designed to avoid telling what really happened. Their parents said, we were different people, we had nothing in common. Children of divorce hardly mentioned their parents together except to express their disdain when the parents continued to fight or behave badly with each other at the birthdays of grandchildren and the like. Indeed, the parents' interaction was a black hole—as if the couple had vanished from memory and the children's conscious inner life.

This need for a good internal image of the parents as a couple is important to the child's development throughout her growing up years, but at adolescence, the significance of this internal template of man–woman relationships rises. Memories and images from past and present come together and crescendo in a mighty chorus of voices at entry into young adulthood when the young person confronts for real the issues of choice in love and commitment. In the old Yiddish folk song, the marriage broker asks the maiden, "Whom will you marry?" and her first words echo the contemporary theme of Karen and her millions of sisters and brothers. She replies, "Who will be true to me? Will he take care of me? Will he leave at the crack of dawn when we have our first fight? Will he love me?"

But children of divorce have one more strike against them. Unlike children who lose a parent due to illness, accident, or war, children of divorce lose the template they need because of their parents' *failure*. Parents who divorce may think of their decision to end the marriage as wise, courageous, and the best remedy for their unhappiness—indeed, it may be so—but for the child the divorce carries one meaning: the parents have failed at one of the central tasks of adulthood. Together and separately, they failed to maintain the marriage. Even if the young person decides as an adult that the divorce was necessary, that in fact the parents had little in common to begin with, the divorce still represents failure—failture to keep the man or the woman, failure to maintain the relationship, failure to be faithful, or failure to stick around. This failure in turn shapes the child's inner template of self and family. If they failed, I can fail, too. And if, as happens so frequently, the child observes more failed relationships in the years after divorce, the conclusion is simple. *I have never seen a man and a woman together on the same beam. Failure is inevitable.*

Courtship is always fraught with excitement, yearning, and anxiety. Every adult is aware that this is the most important decision of one's life. Fear of making the wrong choice and of being rejected and betrayed is certainly not confined to children of divorce. But the differences between the children of divorce and those from intact marriages were striking beyond my expectations. The young men and women from intact families, along with their fears, brought a confidence that they had seen it work, that they had some very clear ideas about how to do it. They said so in very convincing terms.

No single adult in the divorced group spoke this way. Their memories and internal images were by contrast impoverished or frightening because they lacked guidelines to use in muting their fears. Indeed, they were helpless in the face of their fears.

Gina, a forty-year-old successful executive in an international company, told me, "I grew up feeling that men are unreliable, just flaky, that like my dad they only really want to play with toys. I know that I've gone out with men who seemed reliable and wonderful, but still, putting all my eggs in one basket with one man is totally frightening. I'm better off relying on me."

Growing Up Takes Longer

When Karen came to see me in 1994 on the eve of her marriage, she was bursting to tell me everything that had happened since our last visit. I remembered her crying her eyes out, complaining about Nick, and here she was, glowing with happiness and optimism. What happened to her between the ages of twenty-five and thirty-four?

First, she described her decision to leave Nick, a journey that took her to a new life in Washington, D.C., where she stayed with a close friend from college and examined her options. "I realized that I wanted to help children but that to make a difference I'd need a degree, I'd need some expertise," she said. Working her contacts, Karen soon heard about a masters of public health program at Johns Hopkins that would allow her to combine her interest in child welfare and community organization. Drawing on student loans and what remained from her grandmother's inheritance, she applied and was accepted into the three-year program, moved to Baltimore, and worked part-time in a pediatric outreach program while attending school. Karen, at last following her own desires, was an outstanding student who soon caught the attention of senior professors who mentored her as she negotiated career opportunities. "I have the best job," Karen informed me. "I work with severely handicapped children in five southern states where I run a rural outreach program. We're based in Chapel Hill. I love my work, Judy. I make it my business to spend a lot of time out in the community working with the children. People ask how I can stand it but I don't find it depressing because I get a lot of gifts from the children. They open up and share things with me, their hopes, their dreams, the things they want to do, and the many things they fear. I realize from being with them how precious life is and how you only have this day."

"Karen, you've been helping other people ever since I met you, when you were ten years old. But now it looks like you decided to take a chance on what you want. Maybe the dice will fall your way."

"That's right. I decided to take a chance and I discovered what I want. And I finally figured out what I don't want. I don't want another edition of my relationships with my mom or dad. I don't want a man who is dependent on me."

"And you do want?"

"I want a lover and a husband. I'm no longer frantic to find just anybody because if I have to, I can live alone. I can stand on my own two feet. I'm no longer afraid." And then the sadness around her eyes returned. "But it's not really all behind me. Like I told you, part of me is always waiting for disaster to strike. I keep reminding myself that I'm doing this to myself, but the truth is that I live in dread that something bad will happen to me. Some terrible loss that will change my life. It gets worse as things get better for me. Maybe that's the permanent result of their divorce." She leaned forward so that she was almost doubled at the waist, as if holding herself in one piece. "Gavin teases me all the time about being afraid of change. But I think I've learned how to contain it. I no longer wake up in terror when I go to sleep happy." She paused to think about what she meant. "But it never really goes away, never."

On hearing her story, I realized that Karen's journey into full adulthood required several more steps. Leaving her first serious relationship was only an overture. The Karen who graduated in public health and who had helped establish a successful regional program to help crippled children was a different person altogether. She had acquired a new identity as a competent and proud young woman who could if necessary manage by herself. Over and beyond her professional achievements, Karen was finally able to relinquish her role as the person responsible for her parents and siblings. This was a slow and painful process. The turning point was her realization that her brother and sister were adults who were exploiting her generosity. "I had to move on," she said. "I'd done enough." With that she closed the door, a free woman. Having achieved intellectual and emotional growth, she was ready to be the part ner of an adult man who wanted a lover and a wife, not a caregiver. In loving a man who loved her and treated her as an equal, she felt safe for the first time in her life and was able to vanquish her fears. Although residues of her early fears did not disappear, they faded into the background. Within this relationship, Karen completed her struggle to reach adulthood.

In hearing story after story like Karen's about how difficult life was during their twenties, I realized that compared to children from intact families, children of divorce follow a different trajectory for growing up. *It takes them longer.* Their adolescence is protracted and their entry into adulthood is delayed.

Children of divorce need more time to grow up because they have to accomplish more: they must simultaneously let go of the past and create mental models for where they are headed, carving their own way. Those who succeed deserve gold medals for integrity and perseverance. Having rejected their parents as role models, they have to invent who they want to be and what they want to achieve in adult life. This is far and beyond what most adolescents are expected to achieve. Given the normal challenges of growing up—which they had to accomplish on their own—it's no surprise that children of divorce get waylaid by ill-fated love affairs and similar derailments. Most are well into their late twenties and thirties before they graduate into adulthood.

My analysis may not seem to match the pseudomaturity exhibited by many children of divorce who often appear on a fast track to adulthood. Compared with youngsters from more protected families, they get into the trappings of adolescent culture at an earlier age. Sex, drugs, and alcohol are rites of passage into being accepted by an older crowd. At the same time, they're independent and justifiably proud of their ability to make their own decisions and to advise their parents.

But let's not be fooled by the swagger. The developmental path from adolescence into adulthood is thrown out of sync after divorce. Many children of divorce can't get past adolescence because they cannot bring closure to the normal process of separating from their parents. In the normal course of adolescence, children spend several years in a kind of push and pull pas de deux with their parents, slowly weaning themselves from home. But Karen hardly experienced this separation process. By the time she left for college at age eighteen, she was still tied to her parents by her needs and theirs.

And she was not alone. By late adolescence most children of divorce are more tied to their parents and paradoxically more eager to let go than their peers in intact families. Like the folk story of Brer Rabbit and the Tar Baby, the divorce is as sticky as the tar that held the rabbit. The young people want out but can't move on because of unfinished business at home.

Children of divorce are held back from adulthood because the vision of it is so frightening. From the outset, they are more anxious and uncomfortable with the opposite sex and it's harder for them to build a relationship and gradually give it time to develop. Feeling vulnerable, bewildered, and terribly alone, and driven by biology and social pressures, these young men and women throw themselves into a shadow play of the real thing involving sex without love, passion without commitment, togetherness without a future. (We'll explore what happens to children of divorce who marry impulsively and early marriages in Chapter 14.)

The fact that Karen and others were able to turn their lives around is very good news for all of us who have been worried about the long-term effects of divorce on children. It sometimes took many years and several failed relationships, but close to half of the women and over a third of the men in our study were finally able to create a new template with themselves in starring roles. They did it the hard way—by learning from their own experience. They got hurt, kept going, and tried again. Some had relatives, especially grandparents, who loved them and provided close-up role models for what was possible. Some had childhood memories from before the divorce that gave them hope and self-confidence when they felt like giving up. Only a few had mentors, but when they came along they were greatly appreciated. One young man told me, "My boss has been like a father to me, the father that I always wanted and never had." Men and women alike were especially grateful to lovers who stood by them and insisted that they stick around for the long haul. Karen's husband undoubtedly played a major part in her recovery. Finally, a third of the men and women in our study sought professional help from therapists and found, in individual sessions, that they could establish a trusting relationship with another person and use it to get at the roots of their difficulties. It helped that they were young because it meant they had the energy and determination to really change their lives. Clearly people enter adulthood "unfinished," which means the decade of the twenties lends itself to personal development and change.

FOUR

What If They'd Stayed Together—and What If They Can't?

Most people tend to believe that if a husband and wife are unhappy with each other, their children will also be unhappy. This opinion is based on the notion that unhappy parents will inevitably engage in overt conflict and that their children will find this very distressing and frightening. What's left out of the equation are the many families like Gary's where the parents refrain from fighting to maintain household peace and the integrity of their parenting. Gary takes us into the heart of growing up into adulthood within this kind of family. What is it like? How does an unhappy marriage that stays together for the sake of the children shape the lives of those children as they become adolescents and adults? How does parental commitment to maintaining a marriage play out in their lives?

Gary had described with gusto his happy memories of childhood play but had not revealed what he meant by the indoor version of his family. He obviously preferred the good memories. I wondered if the "indoor version" he mentioned would entail stresses similar to those I saw between Karen's parents or in other couples who decided to divorce. Gary was hinting strongly that his parents marriage, while intact, wasn't all that great.

"You haven't got to the indoor version," I reminded him. "What was that all about?"

Gary sighed, locked his hands behind his head, and looked out their large front window. "My folks are a complex subject. I used to think Mom was the cause of their problems. But as I get older, I realize that a marriage consists of two people and both are responsible for what happens in that relationship."

"How did it seem when you were younger?" I wanted to understand what he had felt and thought when he was growing up and before his mature adult experiences had changed his perceptions.

"Mom was a really intense person," he began slowly. "She'd get upset and lose her temper over what seemed like to us was nothing. Things had to be perfect, and perfect her way. I remember Mom racing downstairs with a crowbar telling us she'd put it through the television if we didn't do what she wanted. She was a stickler about doing homework and getting good grades, which we didn't appreciate when we were younger but which paid off later. She'd get really wanged out when people were coming over. Every tiny little thing had to be in its place and every detail of the dinner had to be accounted for. It was like royalty was arriving. What an ordeal."

Gary looked at his parents' photo. "I always felt sorry for Dad because it seemed like Mom just didn't let up. They're just so different. My dad loves people. One reason the store has been so successful for so long is that the customers liked to go in just to schmooze with Dad. He was too good a businessman to give away his merchandise, but he was really generous with his time. I remember once seeing him spend fifteen minutes with an old customer who just wanted to buy a light switch cover."

"You strike me as being a lot like your father," I said, remembering how diligently Gary had tried to find a time for our meeting.

"Thanks! I know now that Dad played his part in their marital problems, but when I was living at home I secretly took his side. In fact there were times when I wished that he would leave her. Of course I had no understanding of the reality of what that would be like for us or for them. I should tell you that it never occurred to us that they would stay together just for our sake. That was a kind of adult thinking that we came to later."

"Could you fill me in on what it's like for children in families like yours, where the parents had problems but they ended up staying together? That's exactly the information that people need and that we don't have."

He swallowed hard. "It's not easy to go back in time," he said, shaking his head.

"Should I withdraw my question?" I was torn between not wanting to upset him but wanting very much for him to respond.

He smiled at me. "Thanks. I appreciate your offer. But I'll try." As it turned out he was more than candid. He opened the door wide and let me in.

"Mom was always on him about things. She was real critical of what were really his best qualities. He wanted to go out to dinner with friends and have people over to dinner. She worried about money and babysitters. When they did have people over, she'd get so tense that she'd often have a migraine by the time the company arrived. If they had a good sex life, I'd be surprised." Gary paused and thought it over. "Let me restate that. I'd give odds that they had very little sex, if any. When I was younger I remember Dad coming home from work and trying to kiss her but she'd always be busy getting dinner on and she wouldn't stop and greet him. After awhile, he didn't try anymore."

"Did they have arguments or fights?" I was trying to see the interior of this marriage as Gary had experienced it.

"No, they didn't have that many actual fights. Or at least we never saw many. They were pretty restrained in what they did or said in front of us kids."

"How did their being restrained affect you kids?" I asked.

"There was this feeling of tension that you could cut with a knife," Gary replied. "As things got worse between them, there were fewer words and more and more tension. My brother and sister and I spent as much time out of the house as we could." I was again struck by the similarity between Gary's household and households like Karen's where parents decide to divorce.

"Things got pretty bad when I was in junior high school," he said. "This is when I wondered if Dad would leave. Mom had always been possessive of Dad—keeping track of where he was and how he spent his time. But then she started getting real jealous. It seemed like she went out of her way to interpret what he did in the worst possible light. And then she'd blame him."

When I asked for an example, Gary told a detailed story about a birthday party he attended with his family. As they were driving home, Gary's mother accused his father of flirting with other women. She said he only cared about pleasing himself and about being everybody's best friend. When they pulled into their driveway, she jumped out of the car and ran into her bedroom. Gary's father told the children to get to bed and took off in the car. He didn't come back until late the next morning. The parents didn't speak to each other for days.

"Was that the only time this happened?" I asked.

"No, the same sort of thing happened again, although this was the only time Mom really lost it in front of us. But after that incident I started to notice more and there were plenty of times when Dad would get home late or he'd talk about a customer, particularly a female customer, and I'd see Mom start to get tense. Later, I'd hear them in their room arguing and there were some mornings when Dad wasn't there and Mom would be in her room with a headache. Once I asked her why she was crying and she told me it was because she had a headache and hadn't had her morning tea. That's when I started to bring her tea in bed on the weekends. I couldn't understand why she was so mad and suspicious of Dad, but I couldn't stand to see her so unhappy."

Children cannot stand to see their parents cry. When a marriage is in trouble, youngsters are eager to rescue an unhappy parent even though they cannot fathom the cause of adult troubles. Gary had no ability to connect his mother's headaches with her emotional distress or depression. Her effort to explain her illness by relating it to "not having morning tea" confused her son, although it did give him something to do to help her. What's interesting about Gary's story is the detail of his memory. Whether he understood adult feelings is moot. But everything he saw was indelibly etched into his memory, and this became the template of his expectations of family life.

"I see now what you mean by the indoor version of your family. Do you think there was any real basis for your mother's suspicions?"

He nodded, as if he had been waiting for me to ask. "One morning, after I knew Dad hadn't been home the night before, I was feeling really low. I guess I was seriously worried that he wouldn't come back. Mom had been all teary-eyed and silent during breakfast. I got on my bike to ride to school but I just couldn't face going. So I rode down to Dad's store. I thought I'd just peek in to see if he was there. He saw me looking and must've sensed something was wrong because he just left off helping a customer and came straight out to me. I remember he looked tired but he also looked kind of alarmed. He asked if anything was wrong at home and looked relieved when I told him there wasn't. So we went back into his office and we talked. He said he didn't know why Mom was so angry and suspicious but that sometimes he had to leave because it got to him and made him angry. He pointed to the old leather couch in the office and told me that when he did leave, this was where he slept. That was when I asked him if they might divorce. I'll always remember this part. His face went all saggy like he was going to cry and he reached out and hugged me hard. 'Let me tell you something, Sport. Marriage is like a roller coaster. It has real highs and real lows. The lows have been worse than I thought and the highs have been better than I thought. The big picture is that I love your mother and you kids are the high point of our marriage. The picture right now is your mother and I are in a slump, but we'll work our way out of it. I know we will because we love you kids so much. Our marriage has been challenging, but it's been a good ride and I'm hanging on till the end.' "

Gary was choking up as he recalled his father's words and blinking back tears. We smiled at each other.

"Your father gave you a great gift. Very few dads talk that way to their young sons."

He nodded silently, unable to speak. Finally, he said, "That was one of the most important conversations of my whole life."

When a Marriage Is Unhappy— What Should a Parent Do?

The conversation that Gary described in such moving detail is one of the most valuable legacies that a father could provide his child. It's worth examining closely because it was so absolutely right, and there is so much to be learned from this remarkably honest, loving, and obviously unhappy man. The first important principle is for the parent to take the child's concerns seriously and to acknowledge that his observations are valid. "Yes, we are having trouble and I'm glad that you are bringing it up" is the best response. The temptation is to brush the child's worries aside, to plead being busy, to postpone, or worst of all to deny that anything is amiss. But all of those would be serious mistakes. They can do the child a great deal of harm. Most children will sooner or later perceive that parent's behavior as cowardly or dishonest or both. He will learn that he cannot trust the parent to provide a straight answer or to help him. Brushing aside a child's accurate perception of trouble increases his confusion, misery, and disenchantment with the parent as someone he can turn to when he is distressed.

As important, parent and child will have missed an opportunity for a meeting of hearts and minds that may never reoccur. When a child expresses concern or worry about his parents' marriage, he needs and deserves priority over other concerns of the day. At that moment the child is absolutely open to what the parents have to say and they may never have another chance like it. Handled properly and treated with respect, the conversation that ensues can be one of the most important conversations in the lives of each adult and child. Parents need to speak honestly and from the heart. This is their time to tell the child the moral principles that they believe in, not abstractly or in fancy language, but as simply as they can. They should say what they believe and show him how they're acting in accord with these principles. First they need to tell him honestly that his perceptions are on target, that each adult is indeed in trouble, that they're both worried and sad about what's happening. Both are giving it their full attention. They need to explain that marriage, like all human relationships, has good times mixed with difficult times, laughter as well as tears. They should make absolutely clear (assuming it is true and it usually is) that children are one of the joys of marriage. And they can tell him that whatever the deficits are at this moment, balance is what matters. Each parent hopes and fully expects to pull through. That was the substance of Gary's father's important and long-remembered message to his son.

Please note that a good parent doesn't criticize the other parent. Quite the opposite. They go out of their way to protect the child from feeling he needs to take sides or that there are sides. Nor do they tell the child that mom and dad are staying together to protect him and his siblings. Such martyrdom is not a gift. They'd be giving the child a painful and heavy burden; imagine feeling responsible for your parents' years of unhappiness together just because you were born.

As an aside here, I should mention that the "don't criticize" rule of behavior given to parents after divorce—for example, if you don't fight in front of the children, they will be spared further harm—is good advice but insufficient. It certainly helps children to *not* see their parents act out like marionettes in a Punch and Judy show. But fighting and taking sides after a divorce has a fundamentally different quality than fighting and taking sides within an intact marriage. After a divorce, open disagreements are normal and expected. The marriage is over and presumably you divorced because of serious differences. People need to try to get along, but tensions are inevitable. And the child has a right to know why his parents divorced. In an intact marriage, disagreements are also normal, but the structure of the marriage itself contains them and makes them safe. Arguments have a beginning, middle, and end—because the important goal is to protect the marriage. It's a critical part of the child's education to learn firsthand how arguments can be resolved without threatening the integrity of the family.

By being honest with his son, Gary's father presents the picture of an adult of high integrity who has struggled with an unhappy relationship and made the decision to remain in the marriage because of his remaining love for his wife and his commitment to his children. He conveys a world in which the values of honesty, patience, working at life's problems, love, and loyalty shine like beacons. Gary is doubly blessed. He's offered a candid picture of a marriage in crisis but overall mixed with sorrow and joy. And he's offered the model of a father who struggles to protect his children and his wife despite his own serious disappointments. This is courage. There is no denial of the trouble, no sugarcoating of the recurrent crises. He levels with the boy in a way that is unforgettable.

When one of the parents (or sometimes both) cannot maintain his or her adulthood and abdicates responsibility to protect the child, then the child is exposed to many serious risks. This can happen in both intact and divorced families. The ambience within many intact marriages is no different from many wretched postdivorce families I have seen—one adult pulling the children into alliances against the other adult. As in divorced families where this happens, the children usually wake up to the injustice of these insults and turn against the accuser. Ill-founded accusations have built-in ways of self-correcting as the child matures. The chief danger is that the children are not given a moral compass by which to steer through problems in their own marriages. They are seriously misled about the nature of the man-woman relationship and the responsibility of a parent to his or her children. We know that this happens after divorce, but it is also common in intact families. I have seen it a lot in my clinical experience. Whenever tensions arise, the urge to scapegoat is powerful.

The Decision to Divorce—Telling the Children

Now let's ask a critical question. Suppose you choose to end your marriage. Taking Gary's father as a role model of a good parent who understands how to speak to his children about very painful issues, how should you conduct yourself? Here, too, there are clear do's and don'ts that are rarely followed because parents are poorly informed, raging, or overwhelmed by the demands of life at the time of the breakup. Typically, they have reached a point of no return in a marriage that is intolerable to them. The situation is unlikely ever to improve. Individual histories vary. Divorce at a young age is different from divorce after spending half or a whole lifetime together. But most divorces reflect a dream that was shattered because of profound disappointment, suffering in the relationship, and the end of hope for a better future. Most of the time people with children take this step reluctantly. Many do so after intense conflict within themselves. It's a terrifying decision because there's no way back as you step across the Rubicon onto an unknown continent.

But as much as divorced couples may want to wipe the slate clean as parents, they cannot. Children are a permanent legacy of the marriage. If anything, a parent's responsibility for them is greater than before. The children have a right to know why their parents decided to divorce and what changes the divorce will set in motion. This is what they will take with them as they grow up, working and reworking every nuance of every message you send. At each developmental stage children of divorce reassess their understanding of the divorce. They rehash it when they're grown and have children of their own and face their own crises. Conversations done fully and well will protect your child, just as Gary's father protected his son. If these discussions are done poorly or don't happen at all, the child is left to figure everything out on his own. Being left in the dark with a problem that is too big to understand increases a child's anxiety profoundly.

In my many years of working with divorced families, I'm sorry to say that few parents have such conversations with their children. Most youngsters are told essentially nothing about the parents' struggle and reasons to decide on divorce—no explanations of the inner struggle, no mention of the reluctance, sorrow, and inability to tolerate any more. It's as if the divorce came out of the blue. No one says a word. This means that the child, especially the preschool child, often learns about the divorce in the most traumatic way possible when she wakes up one morning to find that her father and his belongings have vanished into thin air.

It doesn't have to be this way, but it takes thoughtfulness and time for divorcing parents to help their children. Let's assume for the moment that you are the one getting divorced. What should you do? First, gather the children together and tell them that you have decided to separate and what that means and when it will happen. Talk simply, slowly, and keep in mind that they will remember forever what you are saying. They'll also remember what you don't say. Choose a quiet time when you and the children have plenty of time, that is, not when homework is pending or when you are flying off in the morning on a business trip. Turn off the TV and the computer and make clear that you expect to stay home and be available for the rest of the day and evening. Tell them why this is happening and how sorry you both are for you and for them. Explain that when you got married you loved each other and hoped to live together for your whole lives. Go out of your way to talk about the dream you had when you married and how happy you were when the children were born. Why? Because you want the children to feel that they were born into a loving family and that they were wanted. You want to offset their notion, which can gnaw at them over time, that they were born in anger and are leftovers from a marriage no one wanted. Speak to their self-esteem and keep in mind that you're talking about the relationship between a man and a woman that will shape their lives. Tell them honestly how reluctant you are to call it quits, how hard you tried. If you went to a therapist, minister, or rabbi for help, say so. Don't deprecate or scapegoat each other. Because you and your spouse cannot make the marriage work, and things between you can only get worse, say you've decided to divorce for everyone's sake. You don't want them to grow up with the wrong view of what marriage is. You don't want to live a lie or mislead them into thinking that your failing marriage is the best that marriage provides. It isn't.

Then ask what they understand about divorce. Ask about their friends' experiences. Let them speak. Let them tell you about their worry of losing you, about their strange ideas of having to be put in a foster home, about children not having funds to go to college. They may be full of bad information and you can correct them gently. Some children will be frozen into silence. Try to help them say what they're scared of or relieved about. After all, you know them well. Remember that whether or not they speak, every child will have a mind that is spinning fast forward. They will all be worried, some realistically, some exaggeratedly. Keep in mind that there are no empty spaces in their minds. Even when they say "I don't know," they can have ideas that are too scary to articulate. Keep in mind that they'll try with all their might to protect you, that they're just as worried about you as you are about them, and that they may happily lie to you about what they feel if they think it will comfort you.

Then tell them what plans you are making and ask for response and input. Leave it open and tentative. Be sure to give them some real choices. The worst is when they feel like inanimate objects that are just distributed between two homes. This feeling of having no choice can lead to a combination of anger and powerlessness that has long-term effects on their initiative later in life. Tell them soberly that adults who divorce one another continue to love and care for their children until the children are grown. Talk about good plans and what you'll do together. But don't get carried away. Schedule another meeting to discuss future plans after everyone has had a chance to think, so you can mutually explore what's possible.

Most of all, you need to tell your children that divorce is very sad for both of you and that you are very sorry. Keep in mind that this is one of the saddest days in any child's life and nothing will save you from having to face it. Level with them that things will be discombobulated for a while, but that you promise to keep them informed. End by saying how much you all need to help each other. Talk about courage, that you all need to try not to be cranky, but it's okay to cry and be angry. You may all slip, but it's important to try.

At the next meeting tell them what's happening and when things will be settled. Talk about plans for the future and how you will implement them. At this meeting tell them that sometimes children blame themselves. They think that they're responsible for the breakup and that if they weren't here Dad and Mom would get along fine. Say that the trouble is between you, the parents, and that they didn't do it and that they can't fix it. Assure them again that they are still a very good part of the marriage. Tell them again about plans for parents and children—where you and they will live, changes in parents' schedules, changes in theirs. Make sure you talk about your concern for continuity in their interests in teams, after-school activities, staying close to best friends. Be honest about disruptions and moves. Make a date to show them where Dad and Mom will be living and plan the first visit together. Obviously, this kind of talk should stretch out over time. Many parts will need to be repeated because children can't hear everything the first or second time. And of course, the style, language, and timing of all these messages should be matched to the child's age and capacity to understand.

What will you accomplish? Like Gary's father, you will be providing an example of moral behavior in which every family member receives full consideration. As you and your spouse express your sorrow, the children will not feel constrained to disguise their angry and frightened feelings. They'll learn that parents in crisis can be trusted not to disappear but to be reliable and available as before, perhaps even more so. They'll feel that their interests and concerns have not been forgotten and they will have received permission from both of you to love you both, to be angry at both, and to cry.

Will this or any intervention counteract the effects of divorce or the years spent in a troubled marriage? Of course not. But it will go far in muting the children's fears, suffering, and loneliness at the crisis. It will set the stage for a new relationship in which parents protect their children by conveying that they continue to be in control, that the children continue to be protected, that the parents have made a difficult decision for which they take responsibility, and that no one in this family is a helpless victim of bad luck or the behavior of a villainous spouse.

Parents taking either path—those who decide to stay together in a troubled marriage and those who decide on divorce—will both convey to the listening child how much they value marriage and family. In both circumstances, they will have shown their capacity to deal honestly and bravely with life's problems, sharing the hard-won wisdom that human relationships are both bitter and sweet. Most of all, they will have made clear to the child and future adult what family is about. All of us need courage and the will to keep trying.

Are all divorcing parents capable of this? Of course not. No one knows better than I how difficult this assignment is for angry, unhappy, even tormented people to do. However, I'm repeatedly surprised by how much parents are willing to do if they're convinced that it's in their children's interest. I have no doubt that many parents can have honest conversations with their children, whether they decide to leave or stay in a troubled marriage.

To Stay or Go

I LOOKED BACK at Gary. "Tell me, do you think your parents were right to stay in the marriage or should they have divorced? How would it have been different for you?"

"Wow, that's a humdinger."

"You mean you haven't thought about it?"

"As a matter of fact I have. For me it was definitely better that they stayed together. But that's because they were great parents. My brother, sister, and I had a good home. We never doubted that they loved us. I'll never really know if Dad was unfaithful. My mom was lonely and, as I look back, probably depressed, but she continued to be very interested in us and our schoolwork and our activities. We never doubted that we'd go on to college with substantial financial support or even to grad school if we opted for that. In other words, our world was protected. But if they *had* split up, I'd lay you bets that my father would have been remarried in a flash. And maybe had a couple more kids. We would have definitely lost out."

"How?"

"I can imagine that if my dad had a new wife and kids, he wouldn't have been around for me. I doubt that my mom would have remarried, although who knows? Maybe she'd have been happier with a different guy. I imagine she would. So to answer your question, of course it was better for me and my brother and sister to have a stable place and good parents, even if our folks missed out on some goodies of life. I know that's selfish of me."

"Why do you say that?"

"Because I have no idea how unhappy my parents were or whether they had regrets. After all, there are a lot of other things in life besides kids. I would have liked to see them both happier with their lives. Now that I'm an adult, I feel terribly sorry for both of them."

Gary makes a very important distinction between the competing interests of parents and children in unhappy marriages. When people stay together or decide to split, what do children gain or lose and what does each parent gain or lose? These are not abstract questions. They translate differently for each family depending on a variety of circumstances. If parenting has been poor, the household is in shambles, and the marriage is hopelessly unhappy, there seems little advantage to anyone to maintaining the status quo. The only way children will be helped is if one parent uses the divorce, over time, to rebuild his or her life with a good home and gives the children the role model of one who finds courage to make a better life. But if parenting has been good, as in Gary's family, children stand to lose enormously from divorce. Clearly they are better off if the unhappy parents stay married and learn to accept their mutual disappointment. Ideally, parents will find a way to patch their relationship enough so that good parenting is maintained. If children had the vote, almost all would vote to maintain their parents' marriage.

What do parents gain or lose from divorce or staying unhappily married? Obviously, no one from the outside can tell people what to do. This is one of the most important decisions a person can make. No one has the right to tell an unhappy woman to give up her chance at love and sexual fulfillment because motherhood is more important, nor does anyone have the moral right to tell a troubled man, living with a woman who demeans him and breaks his heart, to stay put because his children need him in their daily lives. But we can tell men and women how demanding parenting will be in the postdivorce family. We can document that the postdivorce years for most adults are far harder than anyone ever anticipates. Remarriage with children brings advantages and new problems that boggle the imagination. Most of all, we can tell them that parenting takes a lot more time, energy, and devotion in the postdivorce family and that they had better be prepared to undertake it along with rebuilding their own lives.

The most important take-home lesson from Gary and others raised in troubled intact marriages is that the children feel protected and relatively content if the parents are able to maintain good parenting. This finding speaks directly to parents who are thinking about divorce. Are your children doing well despite your unhappiness?

FIVE

When There's No One to Set an Example

As I reached more of the adult children in the study and had a chance to talk to them, my thoughts kept drifting back to Karen. After all, she had prompted the whole project with her visit to my home on the eve of her wedding. And so when I was invited to be the keynote speaker at the annual meeting of a nationally known child treatment center in Chapel Hill, North Carolina, in the fall of 1998, I jumped at the chance. This would give me a golden opportunity to look up Karen, who had settled there with her new husband. Her Christmas cards had kept me up to date. The wedding and honeymoon had gone perfectly. Six months after the wedding she sent me a somewhat cryptic note—"Dear Judy, So far so good! Warm regards, Karen." As I puzzled over it, I figured that it reflected her characteristic caution about expecting good things to last. Her job was going well, her husband, Gavin, had been promoted, and they'd bought a house. The next year she wrote to say that she was pregnant. And her last card contained a picture of her baby, Maya, who would now be two years old. Karen also included a couple of lines about her decision to quit work full-time and how she had struggled with the change.

I drove to Karen's house with questions racing through my head, the kind that can only be asked by having seen her life unfold for a quarter of a century. What happens to a caregiver child when she finds a healthy relationship in adulthood? Are there residues from her early experiences? Can she ever break free of that role? Have Karen's early fears of betrayal affected her marriage? Has she learned to be less serious and more light-hearted or is her grave demeanor a permanent aspect of her personality? I was especially interested to see Karen as a mom. To be honest, I was surprised by her decision to have a child so soon after her marriage. After all, she had spent so many years of her life bringing up her mother's children. She could have said, "Been there, done that."

As soon as I pulled my rental car into the driveway, Karen came out the front door and ran over to greet me. She looked different—more settled, a tiny bit heavier, still stunning. She was wearing jeans and a loose green pullover and straddled a little girl with ash-blond hair on her right hip. We embraced and then Karen threw her free arm out in a huge arc. "Look at all this. Can you believe it?" "This" was a sprawling ranch-style house with three bedrooms, large front yard, shade trees, a swing set, and a two-car garage filled with bicycles, camping gear, and other paraphernalia of a family that enjoys the outdoors, plus a spectacular garden.

As I expressed my admiration for the beautiful flowers, Karen smiled, "This is the one thing I was glad to inherit from my mother. She gave me my green thumb." A little later, after putting Maya down for a nap, she said, "You know, I hope, in fact I pray every day, that this is the only way I'm like my mother. All the years that I was growing up, I said to myself, 'I don't want to look like my mother, I don't want to think like my mother, I don't want to be angry like my mother.' " She smiled. "I guess you could say that goes double for my father. He was always finding some woman to take care of him."

"Sounds like you've been thinking a lot about your parents."

"It's funny, Judy. I didn't expect this, but my getting married makes me think about them all the time. It didn't begin so much on my wedding day but almost immediately after, even on our honeymoon, it was like parts of them came floating around in the back of my head."

"What were you thinking?"

"Well, it worries me that when they got married, they loved each other. They were both reasonably suited to each other. And then, for reasons I'll never understand, the marriage went down the tubes." Karen's face showed pure frustration. "I never did understand why they divorced. It never occurred to them to discuss what happened with any of us. Sometimes I think they were just howling at the moon. The whole thing made no sense whatsoever. I'm thirty-eight years old and it's still incomprehensible to me. Who was the divorce for? I have friends whose parents divorced and none of us understands why. Everyone shrugs and says, 'Well, guess they never should have gotten married in the first place.'" Karen's voice took on a tinge of anger. "But that's a cop-out. Fact is, they did get married and they probably were in love at the time and then things just changed." She shrugged.

Karen's reaction to her parents' failure to explain the divorce is understandable. If her parents were in love, well suited to each other, and their marriage failed, what's to keep Karen from following in their footsteps? She can't help but feel anxious. The problem is that children of divorce grow up not having learned anything from their parents' experience that might be useful to them in their own marriages—except that marriage is a slippery slope and people fall off it. Without any guidance and family history, their own marriages begin without an internal compass for telling them which way to turn when difficulties arise. They lack the template I described earlier of how a man and woman live together and solve their differences.

Karen explained it this way: "I haven't the faintest idea how to settle an argument without panicking. First, I've never seen how it's done. My parents were always fighting. Mom was a shrieker and Dad would just walk out. That's how they solved things or I guess you could say didn't solve them. And now, whenever Gavin and I disagree, whether it's about Maya or whether I think he's working too hard or if it's about a big decision like what I should do about my work, the one and only solution that occurs to me is that he's going to leave or that I'll have to walk out of here. And I panic. And then I pull myself together and act like an adult."

I asked Karen for an example.

"Sure. It happened just last week. Gavin was very tense because the economics department was having a meeting and he really cared about the decision they were going to make. I should have known better but just as he was leaving, I started to chide him about not spending enough time with Maya. Judy, he just blew up. As he was walking out the door, he turned on his heel and said, 'Damn it, Karen, are you never satisfied?'

and he slammed the door." Karen bit her lower lip as the stress of the situation came back. "And I sat there, Judy, in a state of absolute terror. I tell you, I thought to myself, 'This is it. This is where it ends. This is what happened to my parents.' And I even went further, I'm ashamed to say. I thought, should I call a lawyer? What should I do about our joint bank account? I even spun out in my head that Gavin would support Maya but probably wouldn't give me a dime if we got a divorce. I worked myself into an absolute panic and sat there frozen, for hours. And then Gavin sailed through the door and kissed me! He had completely forgotten our quarrel. It never registered on his radar screen. He must have realized that I was upset because he took me in his arms, hugged me and kissed me, and told me that he loves me more than he thought he would love anybody. And then it was over."

"How often do you have these panics?"

"You mean how often do we quarrel? We fight very little. It's just that when we do, it takes me back to a place in my life where I don't want to go and I freak out. And I hate that in myself because it's when I become like my mom or my dad. And that terrifies me."

The Terror of Conflict

A CONFLICT-FREE MARRIAGE is an oxymoron. Every married couple must learn how to deal with differences in ways that suit their style, values, and particular relationship. This is a major challenge of modern marriage. Disputes are no longer settled by the father who knows best, a council of elders, or folk tradition. Women hold equal power and not all differences can be compromised, mediated, or settled by taking turns. If he wants no children and she wants one, you can't have half a child. And you can't walk away from the conflict. Someone has to prevail or you have to find a way to agree. You can't live in his hometown in California and your hometown in Boston and be in the same household. Nor is it a solution to live midway in Chicago. You have to face the issue squarely, contain the anger and the disappointment that follows, and solve it peaceably to maintain the marriage. And you have to face the fact that this or another conflict will reappear. It's an ongoing, challenging process that can be the key to a good marriage or the road to divorce.

We learn our most important lessons about conflict at home, while growing up. Every day, children observe how differences and anger are resolved or not resolved in their own families. The lessons are constant, ingrained, permanent. All adults draw on experiences from childhood and adolescence to guide them in knowing how to manage conflict in their close relationships at home, at work, everywhere they turn. This is a never ending struggle because all close relationships—between friends, work or recreation partners, parents and children, or lovers—hold the seeds of repeated conflict. All need to be resolved or the relationship is on the rocks.

Children of divorce have trouble with conflict because they grew up in homes where major arguments were not resolved but were surrendered to. Conflict evokes painful memories and feelings of terror from long ago. The quarrels they remember are not those that got worked out but those that spun out of control, escalated, and exploded. Karen's panic following her husband's fairly mild rebuke is typical of how adult children of divorce can react to simple disagreements. For them any conflict spells danger, a devil that threatens to tear the fabric of family life, destroy their marriage, and break their hearts.

Because children of divorce don't know how to negotiate conflict well, many reach for the worst solutions when trouble strikes. For example, some will sit on their feelings, not mentioning complaints or differences until their suppressed anger blows sky-high. Others burst into tears and are immobilized or retreat into themselves or into the next room and close the door. But the most common tendency is to run away at the first serious disagreement and wrestle with unconscious demons. This is because from the perspective of the child of divorce any argument can be the first step in an inevitable chain of conflict that will destroy the marriage. It's easier to run away. One thirty-two-year-old woman left her marriage when she concluded that her husband gave priority to the wishes of his daughter from a previous marriage. She didn't try to discuss the situation before bolting. Although she was otherwise content with the marriage and fond of the man, she never stopped to consider that the stepchild was an adolescent and would soon be out of the home. When I asked about it, she shrugged. "I'm used to being pushed around. It's not worth fighting about. I'll manage." Then she confessed to me, "I realized when I packed that I had no place to go."

This kind of behavior totally baffles spouses like Gavin who were raised in intact families. The major and minor battles of their parents' marriages were unpleasant but not terrifying. Fights do not, in their minds, threaten the marriage. They are storms but not hurricanes. The Gavins of this world do not enjoy conflict, but their anxiety is muted by an understanding that marriages just don't spring into being. Resolving differences and recovering from anger and hurt simply goes with the territory. They've been present at family crises and seen their parents struggle with serious issues and survive. They understand that marriage requires dedication and hard work. They expect high points and lows. And they expect that two people who love each other will deal rationally with conflict and resolve it. When their partner who is a child of divorce panics after a minor quarrel like the one Karen described or threatens to leave, their reaction is utter bewilderment.

What should people in this situation do? First, couples need to learn to recognize brewing storms and realize that one partner may be badly frightened. The goal is to maintain the relationship, not win the fight. Gavin's instincts were exactly on target when he came home, saw Karen in a panic, took her in his arms, and told her how much he loved her. It's useful at such times to back away from the immediate issue and take time out. As I learned from my research on successful marriages, it's also useful to have rules for handling differences. One very useful rule is never to go to bed angry with each other. This doesn't mean that the problem will be solved. It does mean the passions will be allowed to cool and not continue to the next days. There are other useful rules. For example, all grievances must be aired within twenty-four hours or they're history. Never fight in front of the children. Never bring up past grievances; solve them now. This is especially true for children of divorce. Sulk if you must. Throw things if you have to. But don't leave the scene. Problems in a marriage are meant to be solved, not ducked or avoided. Running away is unacceptable. Rules are useful in every marriage, but they are essential in a marriage involving a child of divorce because rules make it safe to be angry and disagree. Making it safe for anger also strangely enough makes it safe to be honest and safe to love.

Happy Ever After Marriages

As Karen poured us a fresh cup of tea, I said, "Tell me about Gavin. What's he like?" I wanted to know more about the kind of men who make good husbands to the women in my divorce study.

"Well, for starters I love him very much. He's a generous man. And

I finally believe that he really wants me to be happy and that his happiness depends on feeling that I'm happy and that we're good together. When I think about our marriage, I realize that he makes me feel safe. Maybe that's more precious to me than it would be to somebody else because I didn't expect it."

Karen then told me more about Gavin's family. His parents are happily married, live in the same house where Gavin grew up, and enjoy good health. They adore Maya. Family reunions at Christmastime are filled with fun and laughter. It seemed important to Karen to be part of such a family, as if its magic might rub off on her and her daughter.

Karen could not have given me better news. Her strong marriage is a triumph and should help allay some of the fears about the long-term effects of divorce on children. After zigzagging her way through her twenties, she "made it." She and Gavin enjoy a stable, loving relationship, a sweet child, and a promising future. By any measure, they are a success story for our times.

At the twenty-five-year mark, 60 percent of the adults we interviewed had tried marriage. About half of them walked down the aisle when they were in their early twenties; a few were in their late teens.[1] As we'll see in Chapter 14, many of these marriages were doomed from the start. A large number ended in divorce whereas some are continuing amid great unhappiness, with no expectations for change. More on this later.

For now I want to discuss adults like Karen who have entered into what appear to be good marriages later in their lives. Many of these thirty-somethings have been through the hard knock school of relationships. Some have had brief first marriages that ended in failure or they lived with another person or a series of other persons through their twenties. Others had a long run of one-night stands. A few were heartbroken by a lover's rejection and for years felt too discouraged to try again. But then, in tentative but courageous steps, each of these children of divorce found someone whom they could love, trust, and cherish.

It's too soon, of course, to say how many of these good, later marriages will last. Most have only been in place for a few years and, like all marriages, they are not immune from strife. A few were shaky, and some had already come apart. But in the twenty-five-year interviews, I saw many happy, loving couples who were devoted to each other and who had clearly vanquished the fears that beset them in the early days of their relationships. One of the reasons I selected Karen as a main character for this book is that her story illustrates the troubled path that many follow before achieving a splendid marriage. Her mixed feelings of triumph and disbelief are emblematic of many in her generation.

What distinguished these happily married people? After years of trial-and-error, they finally acquired the judgment to choose a mate carefully and wisely. And then they mustered the courage to pursue that person for a long-term commitment. This was a major achievement that reflected their greater maturity and increased self-esteem. As these same men and women entered their twenties, most were terrified of being alone—a feeling directly related to their fear of being abandoned or lost during the turmoil of their parents' breakup and divorce. But as every young adult needs to learn, the only way to reject an unsuitable lover is to be able to face being alone. This is a hard lesson for everyone, but it's especially difficult for children of divorce. Several of the women in the study told me candidly about their first breakthrough in therapy: they were finally able to go to a party and return home alone, without panicking. In another milestone, they also managed to loosen their ties to their parents. Instead of running home to help their moms and dads deal with every minor crisis in life, they were at last able to separate emotionally. Only then could they give up the expectation that they were doomed to share their parents' fate. Only by separating were they free to look forward to a better marriage than their parents had achieved. Of course, it helped that many of these young adults were doing well in their careers and in other areas of their lives. They had learned that they really could trust themselves to get what they wanted.

Karen's story shows these many steps in poignant detail. For most of her childhood and young adult life, she refused to consider her own needs. She took care of her parents, siblings, and a lover who disappointed her every single day. Then, in an act of supreme courage, she broke away from them all and began a journey toward independence and an increased sense of self-worth. Once she stood on this new foundation, Karen was able to call an attractive young man a few days after they met and open the door to a relationship. Smiling happily, she told me, "I finally figured out what I wanted." Like the others, she said, "I decided to take a chance." This triumph over her fears was the key to Karen's success as she reached her mid-thirties. She was able to gamble because she fully realized that her chances of success were at least fair. Because she was no longer afraid, she could take a chance on love and commitment.

Children raised in intact families also spend time in trial-and-error relationships to hone their judgment in choosing a life mate. But they enter these early relationships without the fear of failure gnawing at their heels. Thus, while the external behavior of both groups looks similar—lots of twenty-somethings living together to test the marital waters—they are driven by different expectations. Until they can break free of the past, the Karens of this world expect failure. For the most part, those raised in good intact families expect to succeed.

Once children of divorce are able to put their fears aside and choose a life mate, I was surprised to discover that they often go in search of partners who were raised in stable intact families. This was a top agenda in their courtship. Apparently a stable family background provides a sense of safety to the child of divorce who wants security along with love and commitment. They say proudly, "He comes with no baggage. There has been no divorce in his family for generations." Or, "She's a rock. She makes up for all that I never had from my parents. I was looking for a woman from a stable intact family and I found her." These adult children of divorce tend to cultivate close ties with their spouse's family and distance themselves from their own parents so that their children can share the sense of stability and safety they find so reassuring.

I was impressed by how many women in the study eventually found kind, caretaking husbands who truly loved them and were willing to put up with excitable behavior in their young wives. Several women said that their husbands were challenged by their moody restlessness and enjoyed setting boundaries in the marriage. Marie, who had been wild during her early- and mid-twenties, described this interaction in vivid detail. "He just wouldn't be drawn into my stuff," she said. "He wouldn't let me manipulate him. He tolerated it but he remained himself. He was a center for me. I danced all around. He was on to my tricks. I tried everything I usually do with guys, but it didn't work. He said 'Forget it lady, I'm here for keeps.' That was ten years ago. We've been married ever since."

The men, too, sought calm and kindness rather than passion in their wives. They valued the woman's ability to create a comfortable home. They said that they wanted a woman on whom they could depend. Being older, they were much more aware of how to assess a woman's moods and how to repair the relationship when necessary. Several spoke of their wives in romantic terms, describing their beauty and caring qualities. But they also mentioned their long work days and concern that their wives might be lonely. They worried they might lose their love and fidelity. While this ongoing, subsurface tension was more a residue of their parents' divorce than a current reality, it made the men eager to be good husbands. They tried hard to please their wives and felt blessed by unusual good fortune when they felt loved.

Waiting for the Other Shoe

EVEN IN MARRIAGES as loving as Karen's, there are residues from the divorce. We discussed her problem with handling conflict but now she described another: "Whenever Gavin's late, when he has a faculty meeting, when he has to be out of town for a consulting job, my first thought—and I hate myself for this—is that he's going to leave me. He doesn't really love me."

"Is that what you mean by waiting for the other shoe to drop?"

She smiled wryly. "If you're asking me whether I'm still afraid, the answer is yes, even though I'm married to a man who truly loves me. I've finally come to accept that my fears won't go away. It's like they're imprinted in my head. They're not as strong as they used to be and Gavin tries to teach me to laugh them away." Her serious expression had not faded. "It works some of the time."

Karen's story is fascinating because it illustrates how even a happy marriage carries a residue of the past that can ricochet into the present at any time. Such triggers can be an unexpected absence, a moderate disagreement, or a flash of anger. The child of divorce thinks, "This is the other shoe dropping. Here it comes. I always knew it couldn't last. The man is gone. The marriage is over. I am alone and abandoned, just like I always knew I would be."

Karen's logic is impeccable: if you're afraid of loss, you're safe only if you have nothing to lose. But if you have a happy marriage, a loving man, a beautiful child, then you're in danger. One young woman stated it plainly: "No matter how much I love someone, no matter how much I trust him, no matter how good and trustworthy he is, there is a tiny corner of me that does not believe he will stay. I will never believe it."

Many grown children of divorce ask me: Why do I feel the way I do? Why am I having so much trouble finding someone to love me and someone I can trust? What's wrong with me? Why am I so afraid of change? Why am I so afraid of loss? If my wife is thirty minutes late, I wonder who she's with. Why, if my husband is delayed, do I panic and think I'll never see him again? Why does getting close to someone I love and having sex seem so scary?

I get anguished letters from all over the country every week that pose the same questions, asking for advice. One that came yesterday is typical. "Dear Dr. Wallerstein, I am a child of divorce. I'm thirty-nine and have a loving husband and two wonderful sons. Yet I go to bed every night worried that when I wake up, they'll be gone. Can you help me?"

I think I can. The key phrase they all use is, "I am a child of divorce." I hear it repeatedly when I talk to people in their thirties, forties, or even sixties. What exactly does it mean? Divorce in childhood creates an enduring identity. Because it typically occurs when a child is young and impressionable and the effects last throughout her growing up years, divorce leaves a permanent stamp. That identity is made up of the childhood fears that you can't shake despite all the successes and achievements you've made as an adult.

These are the consequences of the broken template I talked about earlier. You were a little child when your parents broke up and it frightened you badly, more than you have ever acknowledged. When the family split, you felt as if you were splitting in two. When one parent left, you felt like there was nothing you could ever rely on. And you said to yourself that you would never open yourself to the same kinds of risks. You would stay away from loving. Or you only get involved with people you don't care about so you won't get hurt. Either way, you don't love and you don't commit. You would trust no one since you could not trust your own parents to be faithful to you. You would stay free of emotional entanglements. Your fears and your ways of responding to your fears, which were eminently sensible and logical at the time, became a part of your character and have stayed with you up to this day.

There is more. Some of you went another route. You turned on your own feelings. Since feelings are so painful, you damped them down. Because you were a child, you could convince yourself that you don't feel. Feelings hurt, you said to yourself. So I won't have them. It worked for many years. Bad news or good news, you felt invulnerable.

And still more. The divorce disrupted your life. It came suddenly, unexpectedly, but you realized it was caused voluntarily by the people you loved best and trusted the most. You concluded again, logically and sensibly, that nothing is stable. Anything could happen and change is probably for the worse. Since your parents assured you that things would be better but they weren't, you drove your feelings underground even more—where they became more powerful. Like most children, you kept all these terrifying conclusions to yourself because you loved your parents and you didn't want to upset them. They were so upset already. And finally, like a child, you blamed yourself for the breakup. You must have done something bad to drive them apart. You thought you were the most powerful villain responsible for the family disaster. If your parents were fighting over you and if you hadn't ever been born, then they wouldn't have quarreled. You don't deserve to have good things happen. You certainly don't deserve to love or be loved.

There is a remedy for these feelings. It may not extinguish the fears, because they are too firmly rooted in your mind, but it can surely mute them. Try your best to understand that what you felt was right for a small child to feel. You were an intelligent and loving child who was trying to protect your parents and yourself. You didn't want to burden them with your anger or your fears so you kept them all to yourself. But what was sensible then makes no sense now. You're an adult who is able to handle all the things that frightened you as a little child. You're no longer helpless in the night. Of course love is always chancy. But not loving is worse. Trusting is always risky. But not everyone will betray you. Some changes may bring disaster but some storms pass over or never arrive. An adult can cope with feelings that may overwhelm a child.

There are other remedies. Knowing that you aren't alone is helpful. You're one among millions. It can be helpful to meet other children of divorce in groups or to seek individual therapy. Living with these inhibitions and fears is very serious. It cuts deeply into your life. But it does not have to be. With self-understanding, you can close that door almost shut.

Children of Divorce Having Children

As I GLANCED out the window, I caught a glimpse of Maya in her bright purple sweater happily playing with another child. Karen followed my glance and smiled. "We decided to have a child right away because I'm not getting any younger. I was thirty-four when we married and happily it only took a year for me to get pregnant. She's been a delight from the beginning. Gavin's a wonderful father. He does a lot more than most men I see. He comes home and plays with her several evenings a week. I get a break and he loves it. It's been very important for me to have a child."

"You mean important in some very special way?"

"Yes, I do. It was like having a child gave me another chance—for me and for Maya. I have a lot of expectations for her and you might say they are based on what I didn't have. I want her very much to have a childhood that was not like mine."

"Like how?"

"What I want for her is not to be worried about her mom the way that I worried my whole life about mine. I don't want her to take care of me. I want to take care of her. I want to give her all the love and security that I never had. I want for her to have everything I never had. I want her to play. I want her to have time to spend with her friends in school without worrying about what's happening at home. I want her, unlike me, to think of things she enjoys for herself. When she grows up, I want her to think back on her childhood and to know what it was like to be a happy child."

As I listened to Karen, tears welled in my eyes. I looked at this caregiver child as she talked passionately about her own daughter. "You've really put your heart into mothering."

"Yes, as a matter of fact, it's linked to one of the biggest decisions of my life. I decided after she was born to leave my job and to work part-time. I want to take care of her myself. I want to be home with my daughter. I'm not sure for how long, but definitely until she gets into elementary school. My career means a lot to me, but I felt I had to make a choice. The truth is, and I had to face it, that if I wanted to stay and play the game at the top, I would have had only six weeks leave after Maya was born and then I would have had to go back to work full-time. So I bit the bullet and got off the ladder. I'm working half-time."

"Will you be able to get back where you left off? I know how important that program was and how you built it yourself."

"No. Judy, there's no returning for me. It's a major life decision. I've decided to do it because of all that I want for Maya and for another child. I'm trying very hard to get pregnant again."

"It took a lot of courage to make that decision."

"Yes, it sure did. It was hard and it made me sad but it was right. Lots of my friends have held on to their jobs, and I respect that. But this is what I want for me. You might say I also remade my marriage decision. Working half-time means that I absolutely rely on my husband, and as you know, that's not easy for me."

"And how did Gavin feel?"

"Judy, I lucked out. He said, do whatever makes you happy."

Most children of divorce think long and hard about parenthood before taking the plunge. At the twenty-five-year mark, only one-third of the people in our study had children.[2] A small number said that they were planning to have children in the future once their careers were more established and they could afford it. Both men and women were extremely proud of their sons and daughters. They were grateful for the good fortune that had finally come their way. They spoke movingly about how a baby has the redemptive power to undo their past suffering. By having a child, they could erase old tapes and run new episodes in which the new child is protected. As if in unison, they said, "No child of mine is going to experience what I went through." Their unanimity in saying this was probably the most telling statement about their past. As they talked about plans for their children, all the seemingly small parts of a child's world that they had missed came tumbling out—swimming lessons, time to ride a bike, free play after school. All of the pleasures that had been absent from their past were apparently long remembered and were endowed with new importance. Recalling their many moves, they wanted to raise their children in one stable home in one neighborhood. Mostly they wanted their children to have protected years, which as loving parents they could relive with them and through them and enjoy vicariously.

Children were also welcome because, despite their own experiences, the women and men felt that children would strengthen the marital bond. Women who missed their fathers while growing up treasured watching their husbands care for and interact with their children. Their yearning for the "dad I never had" was vanquished in part by seeing the smiles on their children's faces as Daddy walked through the door and by the squeals of laughter that accompanied games of horsy or piggyback.

For women, the decision to have a child was also mixed because it brought up again the issue of whether or not they could trust their husbands to be there. In fact, a fifth of the children were born out of wedlock, and none of the women in this group was in a stable or even a good relationship during the pregnancy. Most of these single mothers are having a very difficult time. Only a few have found stable partners and they are not working in jobs that pay well. After one or more abortions, they had decided to bring the child to term. Most had wanted a baby since early adolescence to offset their loneliness. These women spoke about their children with great love, and the ones I saw were well cared for at great sacrifice by mothers who had only a little help from their families.

For the women who had children within a marriage, several obsessed about whether they should take their husband's name because in the case of divorce, they reasoned, he might be more likely to provide support for a child that bore his name. The decision of some women to quit work full-time was also colored by their fear of relying on the continued presence of their husband to provide for the family. They also struggled with how many children to have. Most opted for one or two. A few had three. Every part of their lives—in love, marriage, and parenthood—evoked new promises and old disappointments.

The men spoke of their growing wish to become fathers in the context of their relationships. One young man told me, "I think I'm finally ready to be a doting father." Unlike men from intact families, they did not take fatherhood for granted. They had weighty agendas for their children, loved being fathers, and took great pride in their children. "My greatest joy is to see my children grow and develop and overcome the hang-ups that I had as a child," one man told me. "My hope for me and for them is that the deleterious effect of the divorce and the pain that I endured as a child would someday stop. And that they will succeed in things I was never able to do." Another spelled out his pleasure in his son's achieving where he had failed as a child: "When I see Thomas do the things that I could never do as a child, I can't explain how gratifying it is. He's five years old. He has on his backpack. He's raring to go. The bus comes and he gets on, ready for camp. No crying, no hesitation. I just couldn't have done that. I was too insecure. I'd have said, no, no. And he just doesn't have any of those fears. To see my son so well adjusted, to see him succeed in things I was never able to do, is the most rewarding thing that has ever happened to me."

It may be that having a child was a deterrent to divorce, especially among men in divorced families. In this study very few such men divorced.[3] For example, one man, whose wife walked out on him, was struggling financially, attending school, working all night long, and paying child support in full. It was very important to him not to behave like his own father, who left him stranded economically and emotionally when he was six years old.

Most of the women in the study who divorced had no children. But among those who did have children and went on to divorce, all left violent or addicted men. The decision was never easy and they stayed in the marriages as long as they could. They told me at length how hard they tried to avoid divorce. No one wanted their child to experience the same losses that they had endured. Years earlier, these same people had told me that they approved of divorce "when necessary," but most were against divorce if there were children. Their attitude changed when they felt that they or their children would be physically or emotionally abused in the marriage. Several decided to remain in very troubled marriages because they had young children and didn't want to disrupt the children's lives.

In our conversations, parents reported that their children were happy and well adjusted. Most are still young, including many babies and toddlers. Those I spent time with looked very good and well cared for. In watching the parents with their children, I was impressed with their consideration and kindness. Those who were stepparents extended the same interest to their stepchildren. Several said it's important to treat all children in the family alike. One man with three stepchildren spoke with me earnestly about his grave concerns about the children's relationship with their father. Having been abandoned at age ten by his own father, he wanted to help them not feel rejected by their father.

How Can I Be a Parent?

TWO OUT OF three adults in our long-term study of children of divorce have decided not to have children.[4] National surveys are turning up similar results. Childbirth is down everywhere, but children of divorce who choose not to have children specifically cite divorce as the main reason. Of course, these people are still relatively young and may change their minds if the right person comes along. But our data are unique in that these men and women are telling us very clearly why they don't want children. "Kids?" they say. "No way. Out of the question." Married, divorced, or single, they say things like, "I never want to hold a baby or to raise one." Others insist they'd be poor mothers or fathers so why undertake a role for which they have neither interest nor talent nor good experience in their own childhood to draw from. They said, "How can I be a parent? Look at the upbringing I had." Or, "My life is too insecure to think about having a kid." They had little confidence in their ability to bring up a happy child. Others were afraid that a child might destabilize their marriage. No one cited a demanding career as a reason not to have children.

I found it fascinating that children of divorce who want children and those who don't want children draw on the same experiences to arrive at different conclusions. People who want kids seek to rewrite their history by providing the children with what they missed. Those who don't want kids have no interest in looking back at their history and find little to inspire them about becoming parents. They seem to doubt they could do any better than their parents and have no interest in trying. But in looking closely at their upbringing—amount of contact with fathers, levels of child support, anger between parents—I could find little that distinguished the two groups. They are similar except for the fact that those who don't want children were more distant from their parents, either angrier or less involved. One important, though usually unconscious, motive for having a child is a sort of payback, to express appreciation for having been brought into the world and to provide your own parents with a child who is a symbolic lien on immortality. It's natural for new mothers to present their newborns to their moms and dads with a great sense of pride and interconnectedness. I was interested that so few children of divorce seemed interested in their own parents' desire to become grandparents. It was a theme that came up frequently among those raised in intact families. It may be natural for children who are still angry about divorce to refuse this gift as a way of keeping their distance from their parents. If this is true, it is an exceptionally sad legacy of our divorce culture.

The Caregiver Grown Up

As Karen described her life and all that changed, I remembered a question I'd asked myself four years earlier: what happens to caregiver children in the long run? Mental health professionals generally assume that this role can only be detrimental to the child's development because she loses out on both schooling and play and sacrifices her own interests to the needs of the family. The answer is more complicated than that. Yes, she loses important pleasures and activities of childhood and adolescence. But she also gains a great deal that serves her well in the long run. After talking to many of these children and watching them grow to mature adulthood, it may be time to revise our view of what this experience does to children.

Many caretaker children become admirable adults. Karen is a sensitive, moral person whose altruism and capacity for loyal devotion are rooted in her childhood role. Her early experiences left her with a responsiveness to other people and a high moral sense that helped her to achieve loving relationships as an adult. Talking with Karen was easy and rewarding because she caught my meaning and interest so fast. Her career is undoubtedly grounded in the empathy and compassion of her childhood. Karen understands the give and take of true love and friendship. She has freed herself from being a martyr. Her relationships are no longer a one-way street and she expects full return on her loving investments in others. Despite her painful experiences, Karen loves her parents and siblings wholeheartedly, and grows to adulthood understanding that love entails loyalty and sacrifice when necessary. She never became cynical or bitter. She did not turn on her parents, accusing them of having robbed her of her childhood and adolescence (even though she sometimes felt so). She's glad that she did what she did as a child and adolescent. And she's also very pleased and aware that she was able to break free of her self-sacrifice and guilt, which had become a bottomless pit. Her experiences as a daughter laid the groundwork for her ability to participate fully in a loving relationship with a man and to be a sensitive and devoted mother.

There are, of course, children who never break free from caring for their parent, husband, or other needy person. There are many dangerous traps along the way for the caregiver child who places others' interests far ahead of her own. Karen could have remained in her unfortunate cohabitation with a man who needed her ministrations and stood in for her needy parents. Several caregiver children went on to marry men who were dependent on their caregiving, and, in fact, that was their appeal. Karen, too, might have remained at home sitting in the cinders like the well-known fairy-tale child waiting to be rescued by a fairy godmother and a prince. So the role of caregiver imposes a corollary task of freeing oneself and moving out and up because there is no one to rescue or even help her.

Inarguably the role of caregiver is tricky. If it lasts during adolescence, it provides the young person with a sense of pride and satisfaction, of having been a virtuous person who helped her family. If it extends too far and there are no limits, then the child begins to feel responsible for keeping the parent alive. It becomes an impossible burden. And if it extends into adulthood and becomes the dominant pattern of relating to people, it's a serious detriment to enjoying one's own life. The other great hazard is that the child forever feels deprived of her own childhood and as an adult tries to make up for the playtime she has lost or for the nurturance she never received when she was young. Whether a caregiver child can shed her role as she reaches adulthood or remains tied emotionally and sometimes physically to her parents or to her own unsatisfied needs is the single most important key.

As our meeting ended I realized that Karen had provided me with an intimate portrait of what it's like to grow up in a divorced family where parenting collapses and the child takes over adult responsibilities. She had shown me how she finally broke free of the demanding caregiver role and went on to create her own family. And she had been remarkably candid about divorce-related residues that she struggled with almost daily. As I drove away from her house, I marveled that she was upbeat not only about herself but also about the future of her generation. She said, "Divorce makes you grow up very fast. I resented this when I was young, but as I grew older, I realized it could be a good thing. Some kids were so angry at their parents' divorce, all they could do was get into drugs and an unhappy lifestyle. Even now I know people who have not recovered. But I have. And I'll tell you why. Somewhere in my twenties I stopped wanting a lost childhood. I think that's the secret. I began to realize that it's now, not then, that matters. And I realized that I'm me, not them. I can do what I want, not what they did. I learned to take responsibility for myself and my life."

Then she said, "I know we live in a culture of divorce and that many people have given up on the idea that you can find a partner for life. But I still believe that marriage can be a wonderful thing. I like to think that mine is. But to make it work, you need the right understanding and the right tools. I hope that Maya and the children in her generation will be able to marry for love with no hang-ups."

In expressing her hopes and fears, I believe Karen speaks for us all.

SIX

Setting an Example

In Chapter 4, we saw that despite his parent's personal unhappiness, Gary was raised by a mother and father who were good parents. They provided love, protection, and a moral compass to their children. Not only were they able to give priority to the children but they were able to work together on their behalf. When one of their sons got into trouble in high school, they went hand in hand to the school counselor for advice. They devised a plan where each took turns waiting up at night for the errant boy until his acting out subsided. Despite their anger and distrust of each other and disappointment in the marriage, they presented their children with a united front. Gary's parents are like millions of American couples who have serious, hurtful problems with each other but who nevertheless give priority to their children. So we can ask: Did their many problems affect Gary when he went in search of a life mate? Are there residues from their unhappy relationship that Gary brought to his own marriage? Or did their shared commitment to parenting make a more powerful impression? How did the tensions of his parents' marriage affect Gary's identity as husband and father? And what is his relationship like today with his parents?

Gary had hinted that his parents' marriage influenced his own. It was time to hear more about his life with Sara. I leaned toward him and said, "Talk to me about your marriage."

"Meeting Sara really turned my life around," he answered, warming to the change of subject. "But first let me give you the full perspective. I'd graduated from college and spent two years in the Peace Corps. When I got back, I was thinking of going into business with my dad but I wasn't enthused about it. So I started working for a friend who started a small software business. I was living at that time with Tanya. She was a beautiful and passionate woman. We fell madly in love and things were just great until I got to know her better. I couldn't believe it. She turned out to be an awful lot like my mother at her worst." Here Gary gave a reminiscent shudder. "She was possessive and jealous and she was pushing me to get married. I wasn't ready and after about a year, I wanted out. I learned a lot from that experience. I learned that I wanted a woman who could think for herself and didn't look to me to be everything for her. And I wanted someone a lot calmer. I didn't want a playback of my dad's life."

Gary had gotten himself deeply involved with a woman who was tempestuous like his mother. She was exactly the kind of person he promised himself he would avoid in relationships. Many of the adults we interviewed from intact families reported similar episodes. They had love affairs with partners who were exciting but bad news. Most got terrified and escaped by the skin of their teeth. Later they credited these near mistakes as rites of passage that were important to their maturation. They then used these experiences to help define what they wanted in their life partner, so by the time they were ready to marry they had in their mind's eye a fairly realistic portrait of what they wanted and needed. Even more important, they had found out what they did not want no matter how exciting it was and when to turn away. The portrait in their heads was a composite of their perspective on their parents' marriage, lessons from their own earlier experiences, and their lifelong hopes and yearnings. In the process of searching for love and sexual intimacy, they had learned a lot about themselves as well. It was a journey of self-discovery as well as discovery.

But children of divorce, as we saw in Karen and others, did not undertake a similar search for the kind of person they wanted. They lacked the self-confidence to think of the choice as theirs. Although some had many relationships, these did not lead to a better understanding of themselves or of the kind of partner that would be a suitable choice. They were too beset by fears of loneliness and too needy to reject an unsuitable lover and move on. They didn't dare. Nor did they enter marriage or cohabitation with a portrait in mind. Rather, their ideas of an ideal mate were sketchy or very modest, built largely on fears rather than forethought. Mostly they wanted someone nice and caring who would not betray them. Instead of actively choosing, they settled for whatever was there. They moved in with lovers who had serious problems and got stuck for years with only a dim awareness of what had gone wrong.

This is a serious distinction between people raised in divorced or intact families, and Gary had led me right to it. Arguably, the most important step in marriage is the first step, choosing the right person or someone who comes close to being right for you. Some people know intuitively what they want and need. My husband has told me throughout fifty years of marriage that he decided to marry me the day we met. He was twenty-one. I have no reason to doubt him or others who say the same. But most people follow Gary's course of gradually finding out what they need, and then when they find it, going after it. People raised in good enough intact families who feel loved by their parents rarely doubt that they have choices and that they will be able to choose when the time is right. The reason for so many failed marriages among children of divorce may be in the forlorn, haphazard way that they begin.

"Tell me what made Sara different. How did you know she was the one?"

"That's a good question," Gary said. "I knew I wanted an independent woman. But I also wanted someone who was gentle and loving and not saccharine. I liked that she was emotionally even and constant, which was also what I wanted. No super histrionics. I had had it with that from my mom and other ladies. Sara offered me an alternative way to be with a woman. Also, it didn't hurt that she was a very attractive lady."

His expression clouded. "But when it came time to setting the wedding date, I did get cold feet. Images of my parents fighting, my dad walking out, and my mom crying came flooding back. I hadn't thought about those things in years and I felt panic. What if Sara and I were headed for the same? I really wanted my marriage to be different from my parents' marriage. And then I had a kind of epiphany. I realized that there are no guarantees in life and that if I wanted a good marriage, I'd just have to work damned hard to make it happen."

As Gary spoke, I could see before me the similarities and differences between him and children of divorce. Like all young men and women, Gary stood at the threshold of marriage with trepidation. His anxiety was increased by his awareness of his parents' unhappiness, and it is no accident that he was flooded with images of their troubles at a time when he was ready to commit to Sara. He loved her but was scared by his parents' lifelong unhappiness. But he stopped in his tracks only briefly. He also had a competing image that was equally powerful of his mother and father working closely together as a team on behalf of their children. He had a storehouse of memories of both parts of his parents' marriage. Their unhappiness frightened him. But he also knew a lot about the skills and compromises that they made in order to keep the marriage afloat. These observations underlie his resolution, which he called an epiphany—that if he wanted a good marriage it would take hard work.

School for Spouses

Adults raised in intact families have been to "marriage school" alongside their academic learning. By the time they reach adulthood, they figure they're as prepared as they will ever be to build their own family. They have watched their parents carefully, observing them in many moods, in different settings at different times, in sickness and in health. They have seen them use humor in tense situations to tide them over and watched them read each other's moods and body language to distinguish a minor upset from an incoming storm. One colleague, Paul Amato from Pennsylvania State University, has proposed that the main difference between adults raised in intact families and those in divorce is that the latter lack social skills. But it's more than social skills. Those raised in an intact family understand the marriage's context. They know that to make a marriage work amid today's pressures, you have to keep it front and center in your mind at all times. Nobody wanted a marriage just like their parents. There are big generational differences. All of the men and women in the comparison group wanted a freer, more equal relationship than their parents had, even if it meant more arguments. They all expected that the wives would work, which made a huge difference in their roles and especially in their parenting. But the children raised in intact marriages used their parents' marriages as a model that they could shape to their liking. They did not doubt the very existence of a happy marriage, even if their parents failed to attain it. The lack of observations and memories of a working marriage is a serious handicap for children of divorce in learning to live closely with another person and striking the balance that both need. It's like becoming a dancer without ever having seen a dance.

Adults from intact families have two other advantages over those raised in divorced families. They had a sense of continuity with their families. They felt that they were part of an important tradition with a history and that they had a responsibility to their parents and children to maintain this continuity. This sense of being part of a family tradition gave them a perspective that helped to stabilize their relationship and influenced their desire to have children. They also had a realistic sense that marriages change over time. They did not expect their twenty-five-year-old brides to look and act the same at age thirty-five. They knew that having children would alter their lives. They were aware that the road ahead would be sometimes rocky and sometimes smooth. They didn't expect or even want serenity or perfection. They did expect that their relationship with each other would influence them as individuals. Finally, they were open to change from the day they embarked on marriage.

Gary surprised me when he explained that one of the many things that attracted him to Sara is that she's from a very close-knit family. I didn't expect that people would give a hoot about the marital status of the parents of the person they fall in love with. I was wrong. A number of people from intact families said that they took a good look at prospective in-laws before getting too involved. Some claimed that they could always tell on a date if their partner came from a divorced family—the women were edgy and too eager to please, the men confided their history too quickly. I doubt that this perception affects the numbers of people willing to marry children of divorce, and I don't know of any engagements broken because of it. Nevertheless, many young people admitted that the pedigree of coming from a happy intact family is reassuring. They boasted, "My husband comes from a large family with no divorce. He's got no demons." Their attitudes reflect the general anxiety in our society about the fragility of marriage and the fear that children of divorce may have less of a commitment to marriage.

I was impressed with the self-confidence of so many of those raised in harmonious intact families. Despite the high incidence of divorce among their friends and schoolmates, they said that they never doubted they'd marry a good person and have a stable life with children. This was not true of the adults like Gary who were raised in troubled marriages that stayed together. They came to marriage with serious concerns that they would repeat their parents' behavior along with a firm resolve to keep that from happening. Despite their passionate hope for a good marriage, children of divorce came with a much higher expectation of failure and only a sketchy sense of how one goes about protecting the relationship.

In contrast, like the other adults who did not want to emulate their parents' marriage, Gary had a clear agenda. One of the lessons he drew from watching his parents was that he wanted to have better communication in his own marriage. "That wasn't hard," he quipped, "because my parents hardly talked except about us kids. Communication isn't talking baseball or even children. It's solving problems. I had this notion that admitting to problems meant that you'd end up in a big, screaming fight feeling misunderstood and angry for days. But I've really learned from Sara that it doesn't have to be that way, that you can discuss your differences and actually have the tension get less, not bigger. That's been a huge relief to me."

In his anxieties over dealing with conflicts, Gary sounded a lot like Karen. The difference is that Gary eventually learned how to argue without feeling the world would crash down on his head. Karen never could. Gary had the enormous advantage of having seen his parents cooperate consistently over many years in situations involving the children. Their cooperation made it easier for him to learn from Sara how to deal with differences directly, without fear that they will rock the marriage. He was also greatly reassured by Sara's firm belief that problems in a marriage are meant to be resolved.

The multiple parts of Gary's legacy from his parents were evident in two marital crises that Gary described. The first reflects Gary's legacy from his father of a steely resolve to fight for the marriage and the belief that one has to give it priority over other relationships.

"The first showdown in our marriage came because Sara was so close to her family. Early in our marriage she had a bad fall on a ski run and got a compound fracture in her right leg. That's extremely painful and she had to be on drugs, in a cast, and on crutches. Anyway, during the first week of her injury her mom came and took her home to take care of her. I got home and Sara wasn't there. Instead I found a note from her mom saying that Sara would stay with her folks until she got better and that they hoped to see me often. I was so mad I could have torn the place apart. I called Sara and said, 'What the hell is going on?' She said her mom had insisted and she had agreed. I said to hell with that, I was her husband and she was married to me and this was her home. I called my dad to help me run the store for a few weeks so I could run back and forth and take Sara her lunch and check out how she was feeling. Let me tell you, I got Sara back so fast she didn't know what hit her. She was very quiet when I brought her home. A few days later we had a long and very useful talk in which I made it clear that she is first a wife and only second a daughter. She belongs with me just like I belong with her. Whatever care was needed we would provide for each other. She was subdued but didn't raise a single objection. Actually I think she was pleased that I fought for her. I think she knew that a separation from her family was overdue. Anyway, I won that battle hands down."

I think it would be fair to say that Gary's battle established the marriage as the top priority for himself and Sara. He understood the importance of what he had done when we discussed the episode. "I was fighting for my marriage," he said. "These are exactly the values I got from my folks. They taught me that marriage comes first. I realized that if I didn't do something drastic, our home would end up as a satellite to her parents' home."

It is, of course, impossible to compare particular incidents in one marriage with what occurs in other marriages. But in looking through the stories of children of divorce, I noted with dismay how passively these young men and women addressed their marital difficulties. During crises in their relationships, the men typically waited on the sidelines for the woman to make a decision. They'd accept her behavior as a given, essentially unmodifiable by anything they said or did. It was as if the trouble they dreaded had come to be and there was nothing they could do to change things.

The second crisis in Gary's marriage reflected conceptions he had unconsciously internalized from his parents' marriage. The inner template of family relationships that we each carry within is only partly known to us. Much of it emerges only when it is kicked off within a particular interaction.

Gary told me the story about the biggest fight he ever had with Sara. Their youngest child was having chronic earaches that kept them both up at night. Their son was having tummyaches in kindergarten. "I was worn out and disillusioned with everything," he said. "Sara and I were stale on each other. We were stuck in a child-centered rut with no time for us. I wanted to go away for a few days on a ski trip with the guys. That went down like a lead balloon. I caved in, grumbling not too tactfully about how she was forcing us into the mold of her parents who really never did anything separate from their kids. She said, with no attempt at tact at all, that it had nothing to do with her folks' marriage. The trouble was that I was always taking my direction from what I thought wouldn't upset her. She was sick and tired of being treated like she was a fragile doll who was too tired to go out and too worn out to have sex. Wow, she really let fly. After I picked myself up off the floor, I realized that she was absolutely right. I'd no idea that I'd gotten from my folks the notion that a woman is fragile and that you have to tiptoe around or she would explode. I didn't realize until that afternoon that my dad really had been very passive, always watching and waiting to see how my mom would fault him, or get a migraine, or go to her room depressed. Everything Sara said was right and it hit me like a ton of bricks.

"But it was a body blow with a good ending," he said. "Since then we've been dating once a week. Our sex life improved. We got rid of my parents' ghosts who were coming between us. You might say that we both set each other free."

Sara of course had put her finger on exactly what Gary had come to expect in his family and was unconsciously reenacting—namely the notion that a woman is fragile and easily upset and a man's job is to anticipate the storm by continued vigilance. As a result, Gary kept checking every move, to be sure not to upset her. This infuriated Sara because she was being treated like she was on the verge of exploding. Finally she did, and they came face-to-face with the hidden expectations of her that he had brought into the marriage.

Each of us brings conscious and unconscious expectations, hopes, unfulfilled wishes, and fantasies from long ago into marriage. Each of us then comes up against the other person's conscious and unconscious agenda as we evoke their hopes, fears, and fantasies. The secret of a good marriage is to arrive at a good enough fit so that each person feels that the relationship is uniquely satisfying, sometimes uniquely annoying, but probably irreplaceable. People who have been raised in good marriages have an easier time. They have clear models in their head and know the effort required. They've seen it work and don't give up easily.

Those who have been raised in an unhappy marriage that stayed together bring more guarded hopes and expectations. They may have a harder time deciding to marry. But they also have an extraordinary model of people who have been able to triumph over their anger at each other to protect their children. After a long journey, both Karen and Gary and many others like them were able to protect their marriages because they were willing to change. On balance, their stories are hopeful and encouraging.

Being a Parent and the Legacy of Intact Families

CHILDREN CARRY symbolic meaning for all parents. Just as they embody our aspirations and dreams for the future, they inevitably evoke the past, including vivid images and memories of our own childhoods and passionate feelings about our parents when we were young. Thus for Karen and other children of divorce like her, the decision to have a child brought up feelings of sorrow, anger, and deprivation. When Karen considered motherhood, she was beset with concerns. Could she trust the marriage to hold? Would Gavin be a better father than her own father had been? Could she trust herself as a parent to give her child a more protected, happier upbringing than she had experienced? She was determined to do so. Like parents since the beginning of time, she wanted her children to have all that she had missed. Unlike her peers from divorced families who took the opposite route of avoiding parenthood, she had confidence in her ability to be a good mother.

For Gary, however, the decision to become a parent was never in serious question. His mother and father had presented a united front as parents, and Gary had an excellent role model for how to be a loving, sensitive father. In this he was unquestionably better equipped than any of his peers who had been raised by part-time, divorced fathers. By becoming a father, Gary had the opportunity to refurbish happy memories of his childhood. Those children of divorce who were close to loving stepfathers also had good role models to draw on and could look forward to reliving happy experiences with their own children.

"Having kids had a huge impact on our marriage," Gary said with satisfaction. "I love being a father. I like the newness of my kids' lives.

I love reading the books to them that my folks read to me and playing the games I played as a child. Those were happy times and my children give me the double joy of sharing the parts of my life that I loved with them and replaying these precious experiences in my own mind. Both Sara and I are committed to spending as much time as we can with our kids. We have this crazy schedule that's all about maximizing our time with them." As he told me the details, I felt exhausted just listening.

This is the story I hear these days from all parents with children. They come home from their busy, demanding jobs to pick up children at school, take them to their playdates and their music lessons, sports, and a zillion other activities plus hours of homework that by second grade require the presence of parents. Fathers in general are more present in the lives of their children. It is one of the better changes in American society over the last few decades.

Unlike Karen, who wrestled over the decision to have a child, Gary took marriage and fatherhood totally for granted. The fact that his mother and father had troubles in their marriage in no way affected his decision to have children of his own. Indeed, this is one of the major differences between those raised in good or "good enough" intact families like Gary's and children of divorce.[1] Gary and his peers felt that becoming parents was a natural step and discussed having children as part of their courtship. They knew that their parents wanted to be grandparents and were happy to oblige them.

But in another respect, Karen and Gary were very much alike as parents. Their children were central to the marriage. They wanted what was best for their children and were willing to make sacrifices on their behalf. For example, Gary explained that he got an offer from a national chain to buy out the family hardware store. The deal meant he'd make a lot more money, but he'd have to relocate the family to company headquarters in Seattle. "That's a very nice city and a really good offer but I said no," he explained. "It wasn't because of me or even Sara. We would have enjoyed a big rise in our standard of living. And we would have stayed close enough to my folks and hers to see them pretty often. But I wanted the stability for my children that I enjoyed as a child. I want them to feel that they have roots. I still feel like I have two homes—ours and my folks'."

I heard several similar stories from children of divorce who turned down career opportunities if it meant moving the children away from their familiar surroundings. For example, Jonathan was a rising star in cancer research who turned down an offer from Harvard University because his school-age children were well settled in their California suburb and he didn't want to disrupt their lives. "You have to know your priorities," he told me.

In thinking about these stories, I realized that the family home is a symbol for both children of divorce and children raised in intact families—but for different reasons. For one it's a symbol of continuity. For the other it's a symbol of what has been lost.

For those raised in intact families, the childhood home is a symbol of family history. It's the storehouse of good, bad, funny, and bitter memories—a place children can leave when they feel ready and know it will be there when they come back. Considering how much Americans move around, it's interesting that the family home has retained its traditional meaning for these young people and that a couple like Gary and Sara were willing to make sacrifices to preserve it. I found it interesting that adults raised in intact families recognized the importance of stability for them and their children.

For children of divorce, especially those in their teens or older, the family home also carries great meaning and they mourn its loss for years after the breakup. The home is the repository of the family they lost and the sense of continuity with their childhood that ended with the divorce. Some poignantly go back to the neighborhood where they grew up, gazing at the house from the outside, and sit there for hours with tears in their eyes. One young woman whose parents divorced when she was a senior in high school made regular pilgrimages during her college vacations just to see the family home and renew her memories.

Will You Still Need Me . . . When I'm Sixty-four?

THE FAMILY AS symbol of continuity plays yet another role in the lives of adults whose parents have stayed together. When I asked Gary how he got along with his parents these days, he spoke about how much closer they had become in recent years. He said, "I guess I've come to appreciate that my dad and I have stayed close. We talk several times a week. It's not so much father-son as man to man. It's a precious relationship to both of us and it gets more so as the years go by."

I was interested in Gary's response because it was different from what children of divorce were saying. There were very few father-son relationships among the adult children of divorce that grew to have the emotional richness that many sons in intact families described with so much pleasure. Rather, there was a widening gap between the generations. (Because this is so important, I will describe it in greater detail in Chapter 15.) But men like Gary became close friends with their dads, even when those same fathers had not been around all that much during their childhoods. They said, "He's changed, I've changed. We have more time to ourselves together." It was a time of mellowing. What did they talk about? They talked shop, politics, sports, and grandchildren. This was a welcome second chance, which both men treasured, to become good friends.

Those raised in intact marriages have a ringside seat at the changes in their parents' relationship over the years, and this, too, helps them cope with vicissitudes in their own marriages. They understand that adults can treat each other differently at turning points such as when children leave home, a crisis hits, work schedules change, or their roles shift. They witness gradual changes as their parents reach middle age and retirement. As a result, they come to their own adult relationships with an understanding of how a couple maintains a balanced relationship, of how that balance fluctuates over time, of how partners protect each other. Moreover, they enter their own marriages with the sense that change is going to happen and that they have power to influence the direction of those changes.

When I asked Gary about his parents' current relationship, he said, "I think that they're happier. They went through a serious crisis a few years ago when my mom got breast cancer, and we all worried that she'd die. But she's in remission and their whole life has changed. He's more attentive, and when they're together he sticks by her instead of going off and making the social rounds. They've worked on finding activities that they both enjoy doing together. Mom is more relaxed than she's ever been."

As I thought about what Gary said, I realized that we have not appreciated the importance of an intact marriage in guiding the expectations and behavior of the younger generation. Adults whose parents have stayed together through thick and thin say that they deliberately use their parents' example in the early years of their own marriages. One woman said, "Whenever my husband and I quarrel, we look at our parents, who have been together for so many years, and we say if they could do it, so can we. It makes it better and easier for us." It is deeply reassuring for young adults to have an external model of stability at this juncture in their lives. We've tended to think that people complete their growing up by the time they enter adulthood, but most of us are still in need of parental examples and symbolic support. The vision of a stable marriage in which two people have weathered small squalls and major storms is of critical importance to young people as they start out on their journey, especially in today's unstable world.

The sheer power of this symbol is revealed when much older parents decide to divorce. One might think that the grown children of such couples might feel sad but not devastated. After all, they're adults. They're not losing the protection of an intact family, familiar surroundings, and other supports. But when we talk to them, they're profoundly distressed. In addition to their concern over the suffering of one or both parents and their resentment at having to take care of a grieving or angry parent, the divorce sends shock waves through their world. Suddenly they are propelled into examining their own relationships and into wondering and worrying what and who they can rely on and for how long. This is another way that the high incidence of divorce affects us all. In the absence of a long remarriage, children of divorce don't get to see married people struggle over the life course. Most have no experience in observing their parents as a couple reacting to illness or helping buffer each other from the stresses of work and home or the changes of getting older. It is an additional loss that is hardly ever noted.

I AM GRATEFUL to both Karen and Gary for sharing their stories with such honesty and integrity. By telling us about their lives for the last twenty-five years, they paint a vivid portrait of what it was like to come of age in America's crazy divorce culture. The fact that both are in stable marriages, raising children as a priority in their lives, bodes well for a society that is so often worried about its future. As we are about to see in coming chapters, other children of divorce and others raised in intact marriages have had very different experiences from Karen's and Gary's, with very different outcomes.

PART TWO

The Legacy of Violence: Larry and Carol

SEVEN

The Wages of Violence

People commonly think there is a "his" divorce and a "her" divorce—two versions of the same events that hardly seem alike. But there is a third version, as valid and divergent as the others. It's the "child's view" of divorce. The child's experience would astonish both parents . . . if they knew.

Larry remembers the last night of his parents' marriage in violent fragments, as if the memories had been cut into sections with a sharp knife and inserted deeply into his brain. He was not quite seven years old, small enough to crouch under the stairwell but big enough to realize what was happening. His father, who was drunk, followed his mother from room to room, slapping her across the face and upper body, screaming at her for sins Larry could not comprehend. The beatings had been going on for three years until that night, when his mother decided she had had enough. After her husband stomped out, she scooped up Larry and his younger sister and went to spend the night at a motel.

Before that night, the Litrovski family had all lived in a green clapboard house in a middle-class section of Monterey, California, where Larry's father, who had learned four languages from his parents, taught Russian at the Monterey Language Institute. He was a disturbed, angry man whose violent outbursts stemmed from early life experiences that neither he nor anyone close to him knew much about. Larry's mother taught Spanish at the public high school, speaking so softly that her students often had to strain to hear her.

Like many abused women, Larry's mother was ambivalent about her decision to file for divorce. "Children need a father," she said, with tears falling down both cheeks. "I gave him children and a purpose, it was a shared dream." Her voice faltered as she struggled to explain herself: "I hope I was important to him at one time." With that, she began to cry openly.

Larry's mother was heartbroken but her children were furious. Like most young children in the abusive families that I have seen, they made no connection between the violence and the decision to divorce. Their mother told them that she was ending the marriage because their father "drank too much," but this explanation made absolutely no sense to them. Drinking what? Milk? Soda? Orange juice? How could they know what "drinking" meant or how it affected their father's behavior? Nor did they link the drinking with his violence. They were aware that their father hurt their mother, and they were very distressed at her pain, but they did not understand his taunts or the depth of her humiliation.

Larry was especially enraged at what he considered his mother's outrageous decision. Shortly after the divorce, he told me that his father always said that women and girls were stupid and worthless. In his view, he had been left with an inferior being. Whenever Larry's father visited, he told the boy, "You are my favorite." He pointedly ignored his little daughter who tagged behind hoping, as she later told me, that she would at least be allowed to pet her father's dog, Ivan.

After the separation, Larry donned his father's tie and marched around the house shouting obscene insults at his mother. He threw himself into the role of filling his absent father's shoes, representing his father in the household and identifying with his attitudes and behavior. Years later Larry confessed to me, "I was infuriated with my mother and I wanted my dad to return home. I would regularly compile a list of my grievances against her and call up my dad on the phone and tell him what she had done wrong. He would then call her and yell at her and she would cry."

Larry continued to lead the charge against his mother for all kinds of real or imagined misdeeds, with his father acting as silent partner and sometimes coach. Sometimes Larry took the lead. At other times his father was chief inquisitor. Larry's mother continued to feel as helpless as she had throughout the marriage. Indeed, all three protagonists—Larry, his mother, and his father—kept the interactions of the marriage alive as the boy assumed the father's role and dominant influence in the home. In this way, the father's departure from the home was symbolically undone. It was as if the divorce had never happened.

At the same time that Larry filled the household with rude yelling his teacher told me that he was "an inhibited, anxious, withdrawn, sad child who had trouble making friends. He is a bright boy," she reported, "but his capacity to learn has been impaired by his preoccupation with the divorce." Larry's academic and social learning came to a standstill for several years. His psychic energies were fully spent in frantic efforts to restore the marriage.

But now, twenty-five years later, I am face-to-face with a young man who in no way resembles the furiously angry little boy who attacked his mother so relentlessly. At age thirty-two, Larry is calm, self-assured, and—as he tells me—outrageously happy. He is married to a woman "who brought love and laughter into my life." They are expecting their second child and he has a good job as a structural engineer, which he enjoys. As I think back to our periodic visits through the years, I am frankly amazed at his turnaround. Here was a child who set out to become a carbon copy of his abusive father and who fell into every trap that violent, dysfunctional families can set for their children. And yet he is a survivor—a child of divorce who drew on his own inner resources in adulthood to break the mold established by his unhappy parents.

The Scars of Violence

Unlike most children in the study who don't remember events around the breakup, those adults who remembered these events in vivid detail had all witnessed violence in their homes when they were very young. The images of those episodes did not fade away decades after the divorce. We have only recently begun to understand the awful, lasting influence of seeing one parent hit or hurt by the other, the suffering that it causes to the child and how detrimental it is to mental health.[1] Many judges who deal with such families do not understand that merely *witnessing* violence is harmful to children; the images are forever etched into their brains. Even a single episode of violence is long remembered in detail. In fact, there is accumulating scientific evidence that witnessing violence or being abused physically or verbally literally alters brain development, resulting in a hyperactive emotional system.[2]

But on the hopeful side, Larry's experience shows that even the worst kinds of marriages and divorces do not condemn children to a life of everlasting misery. Dramatic turnarounds happen, especially in the latter part of the third decade of life, among youngsters who appear for many years to have been failing in their schooling and social adjustment. Larry's struggles with the long-lasting effects of both the marriage and postdivorce family take us to the heart of the challenges that the child faces in growing up.

Perhaps most strikingly, Larry's experiences reveal that divorce is not the quick solution to a bad marriage that many people understand it to be. High-conflict marriages often lead to high-conflict families after divorce. Postbreakup, the children are not better protected and the bitter fighting continues. Ironically, despite the recent proliferation of legal and mental health experts, the divorce has the effect of leaving the child to find his own way in a treacherous labyrinth in which he can easily become lost and harmed.

Of the 131 children in this study of children from educated middle-class homes, 32 heard or saw evidence of violence during the marriage or breakup. Although there are homes where women are violent or where both parents hit each other, in these families the women were victims. The typical pattern was for the woman to sue for divorce and for the father to protest, deny the violence, or admit to only one episode. It is also common for such men to sue for joint custody. At age thirty, Joy still has nightmares twice weekly in which she sees her father enter the house with a loaded gun. He aims the gun at her mother and fires, but fortunately he is drunk and the bullet hits the sofa. The police come and take him away. She had just turned four years old when this happened. The memory remains so powerful that although she has no conscious memory of it during the day, it continues to terrorize her dreams. John told me how, at age six, he sobbed and banged his head against the wall while hearing his mother being beaten in the next room. Marsha cannot forget screaming over and over, "Daddy don't! Daddy, please stop!" when her father pinned her mother to the floor and put bobby pins up her nose. Marsha was eight at the time. Many others say that they were mute in terror and recall being too frightened to feel anything. Twenty-five years later, the children who saw or overheard such attacks say that they felt someone—their mom, their siblings, themselves—might be maimed or killed at any given moment.

After seeing Larry doing so well at the twenty-five-year mark, I went home and pulled out the family's record and studied it in detail. There are lessons for us all in what divorce means to children, why some youngsters react the way they do, and how we might better protect children from violent households.

The Child's Mind

One of the major themes of this book based on my findings—and I cannot stress this enough—is that divorce is a different experience for adults and children. To an adult, divorce is a remedy to an unhappy relationship. Yes, it's a painful remedy, especially when children are involved, but every adult hopes to end an unhappy chapter and to open the way to a better life that will include the children. Naturally, parents worry about their children when they decide on divorce, but they expect that the children will understand and support their decision and that they will adjust quickly and well to new family circumstances. They do not realize how little the child shares their view and how much help the child needs to even begin to accept the changes that divorce brings.

For children who have not reached adolescence—which means most children of divorce since demographers tell us that 80 percent of divorces occur by the ninth year of marriage—splitting the family to solve family problems makes no sense at all. For them, it's a bizarre and terrifying idea. Few children are aware that their parents are suffering. Even if they have seen one or both of their parents crying or yelling or hitting, they do not make the connection between the parents' behavior and the breakup of the marriage. Among younger children, such a connection is an abstract idea far beyond their ability to understand. It's well known that young children cannot cope with what they don't understand. Moreover—and this is particularly difficult for adults to grasp—children do not understand about recurrent patterns of behavior. The fact that Daddy hit Mommy several times and then said that he was sorry in no way signifies for them that this behavior is likely to reoccur. So the divorce makes no sense to them as a necessary protection for their mother.

Thus children do not think of divorce as a remedy. Similarly, when they are ill they do not distinguish the pain caused by the illness from the pain of the treatment. Divorce for the child is the root *cause* of the trouble that follows, not the solution to the troubled marriage. They do not want to adjust their lives to the divorce. They want to make the divorce go away and restore the marriage. And they continue to hope and even expect for many years that this will indeed happen. It is hard for children to distinguish their powerful wishes from reality. I have had many discussions with children about their reconciliation hopes in which I have patiently pointed out that both of their parents are remarried. Their equally patient response has been, "If they divorced once they could again." Parents would be surprised to learn that many children cling to their reconciliation hopes well into their teens.

The wide gulf between the adult mind and the child's mind is the same in high- and low-conflict divorces. Children in the most abusive families are often very worried about their parents. But unlike adults, they do not conclude that they or their parents would be better off if the parents separated. To the utter despair of mothers who, like Larry's mother, have to mobilize all their courage to leave the marriage, children in violent marriages want their parents to stay together. They want the fighting to stop but they want the marriage to continue. In his campaign to bring his father back and reunite the family, Larry engaged in behavior absolutely typical of children his age and even much older. Being children they fully believe that they can rescue the family. Often they think that it is their moral duty to do so.

Because children in most divorcing families are not given explanations of the breakup that make sense to them, their anxiety and confusion increase. Many children like Larry and his sister are told that one parent was drinking, and they have no idea what this means. Or the explanation is provided when the child is engaged in some other activity, like having friends over to play. Or they are told so hurriedly that they have no chance to absorb the message. (Half of the young children in this study first heard about divorce on the day their parents separated.) Some are not told at all. I remember one terrified third grader who learned about his parents' divorce in the carpool on the way to school. When he entered the classroom, his face was ashen. Although the child was in agony, the teacher waited until school was out to call the father so he could pick up his son and avoid the carpool to his home. Typically children hear a real estate explanation of divorce: "Your mother is going to live here and I am going to live there." Violence as the cause of the breakup is hardly ever mentioned, even though it is a central issue in many divorces. Mostly mothers assume that the children know and understand the connection because the child saw or overheard the fighting, or the mother feels too ashamed to discuss it with them. Mothers fail to realize that young children do not make the connection.

No End to the Anger

LARRY'S ANGER AT his mother for the divorce continued throughout elementary school. Every weekend his father visited for three hours, during which time he played chess with Larry, taught Larry the Cyrillic alphabet along with how to insult his mother in Russian, and brushed off his daughter, calling her vulgar names that she fortunately did not understand. Larry and his father talked about their living together, but these conversations never materialized into realistic plans. Larry's attachment to his father grew even more passionate and intense because of the ever threatening possibility of loss. Once, as Larry and his dad drove past some high-powered electric wires, Larry asked questions about the voltage. After hearing the answers, he turned to his father and said, "Dad, I would grab that dangerous wire for you. Daddy, I would die for you." This dire declaration of love and willingness to sacrifice his life for his father reflected Larry's growing sense that his father was slipping away. Their bond grew more fragile as time went on.

At the same time there were growing cracks in Larry's armor against the women in his family. As his father's insults continued, Larry felt increasingly uncomfortable with his sister's pain at being ignored while he was praised. "I feel guilty and very sorry for her," he told me when we met shortly after his tenth birthday. But he did not pity his mother, who was haggard with worry and overwhelmed with the care of two young children. She had made every effort to stay at home during the postdivorce years and came home directly from her job at school so that she could provide a secure base for them. But this meant that she herself led a very lonely, isolated life. Moreover, her little girl had developed a range of serious somatic and psychological symptoms that required a lot of attention.

Putting lives together after the breakup is hard for everybody, but especially so for women like Larry's mother who played a subservient role during the marriage. For her and for others like her, the transition from a submissive role to taking full responsibility for all decisions is overwhelming. These women are not used to being in charge and they have to learn to do it at a time when their children are acting up in new ways. Fathers in such families are often the ones who set the rules for the household routines, making the big decisions about where and how the family will live. They set discipline and mete out punishment. Larry's mother, like many newly free women, at first felt helpless in undertaking so much by herself and cried often. But gradually she learned how to cope, and like others, she succeeded. It can take a very long time for women like her to trust their own judgment, though. Larry's mother was especially fearful because her former husband, aided by his son who called to complain about her rulings, criticized her at every turn. Caught between her fear of making a mistake that might be detrimental to the children and her fear of the father's criticism, Larry's mother felt hamstrung. It didn't help matters that her tendency to be overprotective in bringing up the children directly conflicted with the father's macho image, which loomed large in Larry's eyes.

Larry's family illustrates a finding that can emerge only from long-term studies of divorce—the fact that in high-conflict marriages, the fighting rarely stops with the divorce. On the contrary, unless one adult disappears from the scene, it continues and even escalates. In my experience with high-conflict marriages, the divorce is a way station rather than a termination point for serious conflict. Whether fought out in the courts or among themselves (and most anger is not litigated), the fury of one or both parents continues. This was the experience for both children in Larry's family and in a great many others. Although the parents no longer live together, their psychological relationship rages on for many years until the mothers gradually find their independence and break free of their husbands' hold on them. Children who live in an atmosphere of ongoing accusations and counteraccusations feel little relief with divorce. It's not until adulthood, as Larry's story will show, that they come to understand the dynamics and divorce themselves from the chaos.

But why, when he was living at home, did the boy behave so badly? Why did he buy into his father's seduction at the cost of losing his mother? Understanding Larry begins with understanding what it's like for a seven-year-old boy when his parents' marriage breaks up. At seven, children who have been raised in an intact family rely on having both of their parents around. The divorce terrified Larry and his sister. With irrefutable logic they figured that if one parent could leave the other, both parents could surely leave them. They were preoccupied with the fear of being abandoned. And since it was their understanding that daddies come with families, they feared that their own daddy would soon replace them with "another mommy, another dog, another little boy or little girl." That was a prospect that broke their hearts.

This fear is the key to understanding the initial changes in Larry's behavior. Overnight Larry became a replica of the delinquent aspects of his father. He took on his father's brutish role with his mother, and by donning articles of his father's clothing as magical talismans, he set about representing his father in the family. As he said later, "I became my alcoholic father."

What was his behavior about? There is no question that he hoped single-handedly to restore the intact family. He said so many times. Like countless other children, he was on a serious mission, committing himself to what he viewed as a just and noble cause. He had no idea that what he portrayed was a caricature of his father's worst attributes. Larry thought of himself as the emissary of the powerful hero he envisioned his father to be. But he was not the envoy that the courts and mental health professionals might presume. He was not receiving his instructions from headquarters. He realized pretty soon that he got his mother's full attention with his obnoxious behavior and that he was able to reduce her to a quivering victim. This reinforced his fantasy self-image of power. He also enjoyed his father's full approval and rewarded his role model with frequent conversations and compliments. They engaged together in "man's talk" about how inferior and awful women are—irresponsible behavior in the father but not in the eyes of the enchanted seven-year-old. For Larry, it was a glorious role with a noble cause. Moreover, it provided a fantasy escape route from the frightening prospect of having been left with the inferior being, his mother, and losing his still shaky identity as a young man. But the true driving force was the child's own campaign to restore the family that was breaking apart.

Before the breakup Larry had not been an aggressive child. He was quiet and withdrawn, a loner at school. His favorite activity at home was to spend long hours lying on his parents' bed watching TV together with his father. Undoubtedly he missed this close connection and mourned the loss of his father's companionship. For Larry, his father was an admired and beloved parent and he did not see the serious flaws that led to the divorce. He could not fathom his mother's experience in this violent marriage. But the appeal of his role as stand-in for his departed father had roots that extended beyond his fear of abandonment and his genuine longing for his father. At age seven a little boy is in the process of identifying with his father and is still engaged in separating from the protective mother of his preschool years. Larry's longing for his father as a little boy was not only built on his relationship with his father during the marriage but was also rooted in his own developmental need for his father at this time in his life. When the divorce happened, he was still an at-home little boy who had not yet entered the rougher world of play with other little boys. Had his father stayed, Larry would have been able to move gradually into this bigger, more dangerous realm. But the abrupt loss of his father pushed him forward before he was ready. Larry was not comfortable on the playground, but he could not go back to a more childish relationship with his mother. Although there's never a good time to lose one's father, it's especially perilous for six- and seven-year-old boys who still have their footing in the home and are just beginning to feel comfortable in school and on the playground. It wasn't until adolescence and adulthood, however, as I was to learn, that the destructive elements of Larry's identification with his father clearly emerged.

It is also hard for many people to understand that young children cry for wonderful loving fathers and they cry equally hard for fathers who hardly know of their existence or fathers who beat them. Larry's sister cried all the way home after her visits with her father because he hurt her feelings so much. And then she sobbed bitterly after he left her because she was afraid that she would not see him again. At age fifteen Anja recalled, "I used to cry so hard when he drove away. I wanted my brother to run after his car and bring him back. It wasn't till I got older that I realized how mean my dad was. I was very upset as a little girl when he always called me stupid. But that did not change my feelings. I wanted my dad at home." The longing of children does not reflect whether the father is a beneficial influence or a destructive one. It does reflect the child's fear of losing the parent at that developmental stage.

Carol, the Prisoner

WHAT IF a child is brought up in a marriage in which the parents are cruel or violent but choose not to divorce? Does an intact family—even a chaotic one—confer any de facto protections to children? Can we assume that high-conflict families are inevitably unhappy? When is divorce likely to rescue one or both adults? And from the perspective of this work, when is divorce likely to rescue the child? These are some of the questions people ask in deciding to divorce, but the answers, as Carol's story shows, may surprise them.

In recruiting adults from intact families to participate in the study, we simply asked, "Would you be willing to talk about your family and your experiences in growing up?" I was frankly worried that we would attract only those who had happy stories to relate. Why else would they come forward? Fortunately, I was wrong. People have complex motives for wanting to be heard, and we were presented with a wide spectrum of life histories, including some far worse than I had ever seen among divorced families.

Carol Kincaid and I sat in the breakfast nook of her tiny home with a side patio and garden overlooking a creek in San Mateo. Carol has a good eye for design, so the space felt colorful and warm. She served tea and butter cookies on Italian majolica set against a dark red tablecloth, with flowers arranged in the middle of the table. The ambience struck me as peaceful, calm, and comfortable until, minutes into our interview, I discovered that Carol's story is one of the most harrowing tales I have ever heard about growing up in an intact family. In decades of working with divorcing families, I have rarely encountered worse situations than those described by this pale, blue-eyed, forty-year-old woman who works as a buyer for a major department store in downtown San Francisco.

Carol handed me the cookie platter and asked with a gracious smile, "Where would you like me to begin?"

I always begin with an open-ended question so that the person I am interviewing will feel free to guide me in understanding the past and present. I simply said, "Carol, I'm interested in what it was like growing up in your family. What do you remember about being a child and a teenager?"

Her expression hardened. "Let me put it straight. I come from a family where children were not the center of anyone's interest. My mother's favorite statement, which I heard many times and continue to hear in my head, was 'I'm the mother and I can do anything I want!' "

"What does that mean?"

"Well, let me tell you what life was like in our house. Every day at five o'clock sharp my parents sat down for cocktail hour. My brother, Steve, and my sister, Claire, and I always had to be home at five so Mom could get things ready. If we were doing errands and even when we were away on trips, we had to be back by five so they could start drinking."

"Why did they want you home?" I thought this was an odd demand to make of children.

"It was part of the ritual." Carol fought to keep her voice steady, unemotional. "I still remember Mom saying 'only alcoholics drink before five,' though she'd start to get edgy at four. At home, Mom would take a shower and change and put on perfume. She'd take out the pitcher and the shaker and the ice and put them on the coffee table. When Dad would walk in the door he'd give her a kiss on the cheek, head straight for the liquor cabinet, make the martinis, pour them, lift his glass, and say 'cheers.' It was usually after the first or second drink that the fighting started." Carol hesitated, seeming unsure how to continue.

"What did they fight about?"

"About nothing. They'd get into heated debates about some strange point in art or maybe politics. The topic didn't matter to either of them. They'd get so involved by the end of their second or third martini that Mom would forget all about dinner. My brother and sister and I would take turns being the one to remind them that we hadn't eaten, but only if the argument they were having was not dangerous. Because I'm the oldest girl, I'd often help Mom put dinner on the table. It makes me cringe to remember how she'd stumble around the kitchen, banging pans and dropping things. Once we sat down, Dad would sober up and drill us on our understanding of a political situation and he'd taunt us when we didn't know enough. He really picked on my brother, although he could turn his sarcasm just as easily on my little sister or me. Sometimes Steve would be driven to tears. If he tried to leave the table or argue back, Dad would lose his temper and roar at him—'You are not ex cused!' " Carol sighed. "Those were the good days. That happened about half the time."

"Those were the good days?"

"You haven't heard anything yet. My brother and sister and I knew it was going to be bad if they started in on each other during the second drink. My parents would begin to taunt each other with hurtful names like stupid and worm. Dad usually took the lead but Mom could rise to the occasion. She'd whisper insults and end up screaming at Dad. He'd wait and goad her on. Mom was usually the first one to get violent. She'd throw a glass at him or kick him. He'd get this horrible grin on his face and say something like 'Now you've got it coming.' Mom would back away and he'd grab her and slap her and she'd scream. On the better nights she'd cry and it would end there. He'd back off and tell her to get dinner. I'd help her in the kitchen and then we'd all sit there and pretend nothing had happened. Mom would act very aloof and distant. Daddy'd ignore her but he'd be nicer than usual."

Carol shook her head. "But some nights they'd really go at it. There'd be a lot of screaming and yelling and hitting. That was a sort of once-a-month routine. It would end with them disappearing into their bedroom or with Daddy storming out of the house and staying away for the rest of the night. We hated it when they went to their room because then their yelling would change into sounds of them having sex. We could hear them. Later, Dad would come out and tell us to get our own dinner. He'd take something to eat and disappear into his study for the rest of the night. We'd put ourselves to bed. It was so lonely and awful."

As Carol described these scenes, a heavy sadness fell over her small frame and her spirit seemed almost crushed. But she was not finished.

"The worst times," Carol said, crumbling a cookie on the plate in front of her, "was when they'd go for us. I was the favorite target. It only happened a few times a year but I remember every detail. They'd spot me or hear me in the kitchen making dinner and then they'd call me into the living room. Dad usually started it with a question about dinner or school that then escalated into a verbal attack by both of them. Before you knew it, they were hitting me. If I tried to say anything in self-defense, they hit me harder. I remember one time being chased into my bedroom, where my dad held me down and my mom slapped me over and over like she couldn't stop." Carol's voice trailed off.

I was stunned by her story. "And no one protected you?"

"My little sister used to come in my room and lie down beside me on the bed. She'd wrap her arms around my neck and pat my cheek. We'd lie there and hug each other. We were frightened our whole childhood. We never knew what to expect or when it would get real bad again."

Carol fell silent as the memories flooded her body and caused her throat to constrict. Unable to speak, she stared vacantly at the flowers, holding back her pain. I waited a good thirty seconds for her to regain her composure and leaned closer, "Carol, what an awful way to grow up."

She was stone still as the next words came out in a slow monotone, stripped of inflection because her emotions were on the brink. "The worst part wasn't being hit." She rocked slowly with each word. "It was the wishing and hoping that things would change and especially that my mother would become another person—a mother who loved her children and cared for them and protected them." She put her face in her hands. "I longed so desperately for the parents that I never had."

We sat in silence for another minute until Carol recovered enough to say, "I've been in and out of therapy since I was thirty years old. And I've thought about this and know now that they couldn't change. All my life I wanted a mom or a dad or someone I could rely on even a little. I've tried to stop hoping for what I'll never have and I've tried to get some comfort from being a better mother someday—if I ever have children."

"You've had so much pain, Carol. Do you have any happy memories?"

"A few when I was little. I remember that my mom used to read me *Winnie the Pooh.* And I remember that one Christmas we had matching black velvet dresses. I was so proud that I could look like her—we even had matching headbands and shoes with bows. I have a picture of us then—Dad's holding me on his shoulders and he has his arm around Mom and we're all standing in front of an enormous Christmas tree."

Carol stopped abruptly, fighting tears. "I used to have that picture in my dresser drawer when I was older. When it was bad with Mom and Dad, I'd take it out after they'd left and stare at it. I couldn't believe it was the same parents and the same daughter. They looked so kind in the picture."

• • •

CAROL'S NOSTALGIC MOOD snapped. "My parents never should have had children. I never understood why they did. They were *terrible* parents. They never helped us with anything. We served at their pleasure. They told us what they expected and told us what to do and what not to do. We were there to be used. If we didn't comply, we were out. You know, it's funny about the mix of the good and the bad. I remember being really cared for was when I was sick. Mom would fuss over me and bring me sherbet and soda. But at five o'clock, she'd be out in the living room getting the drinks ready for Daddy."

I asked Carol if she could describe her parents' marriage in a few words.

She shot back, "Codependent, dysfunctional, and passionate." This is a topic she had thought about for years. "I know this sounds crazy, but my parents really do love each other and are committed to their relationship. They're both in their late sixties now and they still do things together every day. They don't ignore each other. They sleep in the same bed. But since Dad had a series of heart operations, he had to curtail his drinking and Mom followed suit. They still have cocktails but they stop at one or maybe two. And there's no more violence, although they still get into heated arguments about nothing. They still call each other nasty names. Go figure." She shook her head. "It's simply how they relate."

"What if your parents had divorced? What would have happened to you and your brother and sister?"

"I remember wishing they'd divorce. My sister and I would talk every night about escaping. But when we talked about divorce we couldn't figure out where she and I would go. How would things be better if we were with my mom or with my dad? They were both such bad parents. I spent eighty percent of my time imagining that I'd have a magic button that I could press and make both of them disappear."

She smiled wanly as she sat back and remembered. "I never played much with other kids on my block because I was so lost in my fantasies. I'd watch them but not join in. Instead, my sister and I had our own private games. Our favorite was that we lived on top of a high steep mountain and saw our parents once a month, maybe less. All we had was magic, a fantasy, a dream. From the time I was very small I knew that they would never divorce. I knew I could not make them disappear. And I knew that I was trapped with them forever. I spent a lot of my childhood thinking, When will I be old enough, when will I be big enough, when will I be strong enough to leave? Those were my wishes."

As we sat in silence, I thought to myself, "go figure" indeed. According to our demographic questionnaire, Carol's father had made it big in the corporate world, rising to vice president in one of the largest West Coast engineering firms. Carol's mother was a successful fund-raiser and had been on the board of numerous nonprofit organizations. They had a nice house, good clothes, expensive cars. The children had been sent to the best private schools. Yet life at home had been one long nightmare for Carol and her siblings. When did she begin to question the normalcy of her family life?

"All through my growing up, I knew in my bones that I was supposed to keep what happened a secret," she said. "Had you interviewed me then, I would never have told you about our rituals, about what was going on. I had no one to talk to. Only my brother and sister and I knew and we didn't dare let it seep out. Maybe the hardest thing of all, which I still haven't told you, is that we kept our secret so hidden, making sure no one found out. It was like I had two identities. It was a heavy thing for me to carry. I know that after awhile I began to feel sort of dead inside. I went into treatment years later because I was afraid that I was dead or empty."

The Castle Secrets

FAMILIES LIKE CAROL'S rarely come into public view because they are so normal-looking from the outside. Had I met this couple at a party, I would have found them to be cultured, respectable members of the community. The children were never hit so hard that they had visible bruises or needed to be taken to an emergency room. Nothing about the family's behavior in the public domain—in business, social, or school life—would have given any clues as to what happened from five o'clock on. A man's home is his castle. It is surrounded by a moat and outsiders are not invited in.

But if you could cross the moat, guided by a child who lives in the castle, you would see a capricious inner sanctum where anything can happen. Sometimes the parents are benevolent and kind. Carol lovingly remembers the velvet dresses she and her mother wore and the sherbet and soda when she was sick. These memories strengthened her yearning for loving parents. But more often, family life was terrifying and destructive. Carol and her brother and sister lived in constant fear as they watched their parents engage in a perpetual cycle of drinking and violence. The children's presence was required because the parents needed spectators and an escape valve for their anger. Everyone in this family was caught in an ineluctable web of mutual destruction. All were committed to keeping it hidden from the eyes of the world.

The key to understanding such families is to realize that the parents are committed to each other. The nightly rituals of drinking, violence, and sometimes sex reinforce their powerful ties. But the children, who live in fear of being ejected from the home, have no power, no bargaining chips, no champions. Instead, they are swept into a conspiracy of silence. Everyone participates and no one ever breaks the rules. It's hard to know at what age children become aware of the conspiracy, but I've seen it in four-year-olds. What transpires within the family is never to be divulged. The result, of course, is that the children are isolated from outside support. They cannot talk to their friends, teachers, minister, or even close relatives. The dreaded secret increases their shame and, oddly, makes them loyal to their parents. The loyalty is based on a sense of inclusiveness—we are separate as a family and we are in this together. One sad result is that the children have very little opportunity to enter into the social world of their peers or to learn about other families. This affects their childhood relationships and later adult relationships in almost every domain.

If we look at the reasons given for why people should divorce, violence usually tops the list. Even people who oppose divorce allow for it as a solution to violence in families and certainly all would agree that Carol's childhood was horrendous. But the view that conflict makes people wretched is not true of everyone. Many couples find conflict pleasurable and an exciting overture to sex. It can even occur within a framework of mutual love and concern. So the expectation that divorce will always be welcome to violent families is built on sand. Within their castle, divorce is not on anyone's agenda. In families that do divorce, at least one parent wants out because he or she is not happy with the marriage or with what's happening to the children. But this does not describe Carol's family.

To understand why people create this kind of a marriage, you will need to watch the nightly enactment of the parents' two-act play from their point of view. In act one, husband and wife are the star actors sitting in the floodlights, martinis in hand, discussing the world. The children are placed strategically around them, in the dark, watching and listening. The play is passionate as each protagonist delivers new lines, adrenaline flowing. Soon the sparring begins as the dramatic tension rises, new martinis are poured, and the actors flail at one another in excitement. This is not a dull family. The children observe, saucer-eyed, mesmerized, terrified, and also excited.

Act two has various endings. In one version, dinner is served and the children are verbally attacked. In another version, the fighting escalates and takes on a tone that drives one actor offstage, perhaps to sulk. In another scenario, the physical fighting becomes sexual foreplay. The actors fall into bed to make passionate, even violent love.

Such people really do need and want each other. They derive a tremendous amount of gratification from their relationship in which drinking and fighting are center stage. The children are peripheral, their needs sacrificed on behalf of the parents' desires. Moreover, no one is ever seriously hurt. Physical injuries are superficial. Sex does not turn into rape. The endless drama has careful boundaries in which violence is acceptable and the secret never gets out.

It's important to realize that in chaotic homes like this, fighting is not over substantive issues. They usually are not arguing about where to live, whose job comes first, how to discipline the children, and so on. They fight over nonissues because the content of their quarrel is irrelevant. The quarrel itself is what they find exciting and pleasurable. Karen's parents had similar interchanges, but their fights were not used to keep the marriage going. Carol's parents were different in that they fought for the erotic excitement generated while they drank martinis. Again, many people including professionals are often under the impression that quarreling reflects conflict or that it can be resolved rationally, if only the two people would come to the table. But in families like Carol's, no table would work.

For children, this kind of family is disastrous. First, they grow up fearing that they or a parent will be hurt. They are hypnotized by the continual portrayal of a man-woman relationship in which intimacy and pain are intertwined. And they internalize a lasting view of adult love as lacking in kindness, tenderness, friendship, gentleness, and a sense of morality. The template of intimacy that they carry to adulthood is uniting to hurt one another, albeit without inflicting serious injury. The passion is in the danger.

In these families, the children hardly matter to their parents. Instead of existing as real people separate from the parents' wishes or sudden whims, the children are shadowy figures who hover on the periphery of their parents' lives like courtiers or slaves in the sultan's palace waiting to be summoned. In Carol's family the parents are themselves the children. They are astonishingly self-absorbed, acting out their own impulses while being completely unaware of their children's suffering. They don't understand or care that their immoral bchavior will warp the developing conscience of their children and harm the children's future relationships.

It's fashionable in some circles to claim that people who divorce are more selfish or, as the saying goes, more "narcissistic" than those who stay married. But it would be hard to think of any couple more self-centered than Carol's parents and others in this group of very troubled intact marriages.

EIGHT

Our Failure to Intervene

Larry entered adolescence like a hungry tiger. He became involved in every drug known to teenagers and went to school every day stoned. He stayed out late and came home sick from drinking booze. With a vengeance, he violated every rule that his mother or the school laid down. Finally, in despair, his mother called her ex-husband and asked if he would take the boy because she could not control him. She reminded Larry's father that he had offered many times to take his son into his life and that this was the time to follow through on his promises.

The next day, Larry was in his room packing his clothes when the phone rang. It was his dad who hemmed and hawed and finally said, "This is not a good time for you to come live with me." Instantly Larry understood the deeper message: there will never be a good time. Feeling totally betrayed, he turned on his mother and began beating her with his fists. She managed to escape into her bedroom and, terrified by her son's behavior, called 911. Larry was taken to the local police station and spent the rest of the day in a marathon session with a specially trained officer and his mother. For hours, he howled in anger and despair about how much he hated his father for rejecting him and how his whole life had been ruined by his parents' divorce.

Although the image of a child beating his mother is startling, and indeed should shock us to the core, it is reliably reported in a 1980 national study that 18 percent of children below age seventeen engaged in acts of violence toward their parents—usually their mothers.[1] Other recent studies show that this brand of violence is higher in divorced families;[2] I saw several serious instances of it in the families we studied. Such teenagers tend to be extremely angry and are not constrained by the protective presence of their fathers. I was badly frightened on behalf of the women whose youngsters attacked them with a savagery that looked identical to the father's loss of control. Sometimes the older violent child would attack younger siblings. Moreover, the behavior lasted several years. For example, Larry beat his mother seven years after his father left home. One thirteen-year-old girl pinned her mother to the wall with a ski pole after an argument over a curfew.

Larry's crisis provided a major break in his skewed understanding of the divorce. After years of planning how he and his father would live happily together, his father backed off abruptly when it headed for reality. Driven to utter despair and realizing that all his expectations of his father were built on sand, Larry turned on his mother. Luckily, she now was able to call for help. As it happened, the hours they spent at the police station were a nodal point of change for Larry. For the first time since his parents split up, he began to face the loneliness and sorrow of his loss, to cry instead of rage. But it took several more years for this change to work its way through his twisted world view.

Adolescent Anger and Adult Burdens

Compared to intact families, parents and children in divorced families share a different kind of history that throws a long shadow over their relationships during adolescence. In many homes, structure disappears for years because no one has the time or the energy to enforce routines and discipline. As we saw in Karen's family, young children can take responsibility for raising themselves or are cared for by slightly older siblings. But not all of them move into this role with grace and compassion. Some resent every moment, infuriated by the burdens placed on them. This anger can translate into trouble for single or remarried mothers who want to set disciplinary standards for their teenage children. They have less capital to draw on because their earlier absence and the child's lasting anger stands in the way. The child feels that the parent has not earned the right to lay down rules. "Where were you when I needed you?" becomes a battle cry between them. The child's anger at the parent for particular past deprivations is reignited by the adolescent's resentment of parents in general.

All teenagers need to separate from their parents and identify with peers, but children of divorce carry out this natural rejection with special intensity. One young woman, who led a wild adolescence, captured the fusing of past and present feelings when she said, "My mother has never been there for me. She reacts to what she thinks is my bad behavior but she just feels bad because she fucked me up. How can I respect what she tells me? Why should I?" In many of the divorced families, girls did not receive the special protection we saw in intact families. Few had curfews or special regulations to report in. If they did, these were honored more in the breach than in the practice.

In our comparison group, the boys were rebellious and used nearly as much alcohol and drugs as boys in divorced families. The two groups looked a lot alike with one important difference: boys in the intact families were keenly aware of their parents' expectations. Their acting out was muted by their plans to attend college and their recognition that they needed their parents' help. All this placed limits on their misbehavior. Most of their wilder acting out ended by their second year of college.

The girls in intact families, in contrast, had a different kind of adolescence than their peers from divorced families. They had strictly enforced curfews that they mostly obeyed. Their weekends were carefully monitored. Right or wrong, parents were much more controlling. Although the parents did not expect their daughters to be virgins at high school graduation, they did insist on knowing their whereabouts and they expected to be kept informed of any changes in plans. Boys and girls were both expected home for dinner every night unless they had been excused by a parent. They were expected to call when late. In brief, there was a structure in these middle-class homes that the young people could butt up against and defy. Many did, but there were consequences when they broke the rules. (It's important to bear in mind that the youngsters in the comparison group had been neighbors of the families that divorced, making the differences in the families all the more striking.)

The same kind of rule-based structure exists in remarried families, but the moral authority of stepparents is almost never equal to that of a biological parent. When push comes to shove in adolescence, as it so often does, the boy or girl is likely to shout, "Who the hell are *you* to tell me what to do?"

Little Boy Lost

MY THIRD INTERVIEW with Larry took place shortly after the episode in the police station when he was seventeen years old. The little master of the house had grown into a tall, slender young man with reddened eyes and a sallow complexion. Chain-smoking Marlboros, face fixed in a scowl, he spat out his feelings: "The last five years have been a total bummer. My mom gets on my nerves just like she always got on my dad's nerves. She wants me to be responsible." He threw back his head and laughed. "Christ, I come home every night bombed out of my head. I drink more than my dad did when he was a kid. Except for all the Russian crap, I think I'm going to live a lot of my life just like my dad. It helps me solve my problems to drink. A couple of weeks ago I hit my girlfriend in the face." He seemed proud. "I guess I'm going to live my life like my dad."

I was deeply dismayed by his words and hostile manner. "Tell me," I said, "how much do you feel in control of your life?"

Larry's shoulders sagged as he answered truthfully, "About three-quarters. I'm maybe three-quarters in control." And then he described how disappointed he was in the father who seemed no longer interested in him. "Do you know that when my dad got remarried, I didn't find out for four months! When I talk to him, it's always by phone. I guess he's pretty busy." Then Larry hastily pulled back, regained his scowl, and returned to the familiar theme. "My life is a lot worse because of their divorce. Not having a father was hard on me. My mom pushed him out. I'll never forgive her for that."

After I left Larry sitting at his kitchen table that day, I had the sense of seeing a lost child who had advanced in years but who had hardly matured since his mother took him and his sister to a motel in the middle of the night. It was as if he had remained fixated developmentally from that time on. As an adolescent, he was just beginning to face the pain of his increasing distance from his father. He continued blaming his mother for all his suffering. I was reminded of a sketch Larry did for me at our first meeting, showing a little gunboat bristling with cannons. It had been prophetic but not, I'm happy to say, fated.

DOMESTIC VIOLENCE IS often alleged in divorce although real figures are hard to obtain. In 1991, Murray A. Strauss, a leading sociologist who studies family violence, reported that every year ten million children may witness abuse in their family—slapping, hitting, yelling, screaming, and other forms of recrimination. Half of these children may, along with their mothers, also be victims of outright physical abuse.[3] In my study described in this book, a quarter of the fathers were physically violent toward their spouses some or much of the time in the years leading up to the divorce. (Although women can be violent—giving as good as they get or taking the lead in abusive acts—none of the mothers from this group were violent. Very few of the children were hit by their fathers.) However, when the final crisis arrived and the parents decided to divorce, some form of physical violence erupted in over half of the families in this study. Such acts were an aberration, but every slap in the face or hurled object was meant, in the heat of the moment, to injure the other adult.

At such times, children really do fear for themselves and for their mother's safety. But here again is where the difference in the "child's mind" comes into play and confuses adults. Using the skewed logic of an immature mind, children blame themselves for their father's rage and for their inability to rescue their mother. Young children have a limited capacity to understand cause and effect. They try hard to understand what they see, but they tend to think in terms of blame—specifically *who* is to blame. By analogy, when a child is hurt or falls ill or disappears, parents tend to blame themselves for not protecting that child. Using the same logic in reverse, the young child feels that she is to blame if her mother or father is suffering and that it's her responsibility to rescue that unhappy parent. She would much rather blame herself than get angry at her parents. And so, she says to herself, "I did it"—hoping in this confession to retain some measure of control by promising to be good. But if the omnipotent parent is evil, no place is safe. Mother and child are both in great danger. Paradoxically, the child who blames herself feels less helpless because it means she is not at the mercy of a powerful, capricious, and cruel parent. This is one reason that telling the child "you are not responsible" often falls on deaf ears. Children hold on to their first explanation because it's less frightening.

Adults need to understand that a child's explanations for divorce are deeply rooted in the child's psyche and cannot be overridden by complex adult explanations. In fact, adult explanations often push the child's real feelings and thoughts underground. Children know exactly what adults expect of them. They're eager to comfort their troubled parents and are well schooled in supplying answers that grown-ups want to hear. I stress this aspect of a child's response because current popular educational programs for children whose parents are in the process of divorcing assume that children willingly believe what they are told. Well-meaning adults think that children will modify their thinking because a kindly teacher, counselor, or parent explains that they are wrong. I know of several court-sponsored educational programs where the children march around chanting, "I didn't do it." But the explanation that "no one is at fault" is far too abstract and absolutely beyond the comprehension of the young child. The truth is that many children believe for years that they caused their parents' divorce regardless of what they are told. When the parents quarrel, the children's view that they are the root of the difficulty is confirmed. They conclude: if I were to disappear, the rift between my parents would mend. No explanation to the contrary can undo this observation. Of course, children need to make rational sense of this central event in their lives. But any explanation of divorce needs to be told and retold in accord with the child's unfolding capacity to understand as she grows up. There is no quick way to accomplish this.

Like children in other violent families, Larry and his sister witnessed their father's assaults on their mother. No attempt was made to hide the violence or to protect them from seeing or hearing everything that transpired. If the children tried to intervene and protect their mother, they were in danger of being hurt—and so they stopped trying.

Yet I am always surprised at how little these same children understood about their mother's plight and how, like Larry, they tried to rewrite family history. Many of them spent years trying to restore the abusive, violent, dysfunctional family. It makes you wonder whether their eyes were ever open. One boy who was physically beaten by his father said, "All I can think of was how much she hurt my dad by leaving him. She probably feels like a conqueror." How did he get it so wrong? Another child said, "My mom is such a bad person. She is so cold-blooded. My dad was so upset." And another told me, "Divorce upset my dad real bad. He lost much more than my mom did. It was unfair."

The Need for Intervention in Violent Families

At the time of divorce much can be done to help children who have witnessed violence. But before we get to suggestions, let's first consider what happened to the families in our study in the years following the breakup. Every child from a violent family continued to visit his or her father after the divorce. Men sought to co-opt their children as allies, to help bring the woman back. Often these men found a receptive audience for their pleas. Children tend to sympathize with the parent who wants the marriage restored. They identify with the father's distress and come to feel that he is the aggrieved one, even when they have witnessed their mother being hurt or were themselves beaten or kicked. When a father begs his children to help bring his wife home, the children can be greatly moved by the transformation of the powerful man to the sad woebegone daddy. In this they are not unlike many abused women who take the man back again and again, out of pity or love, saying, "He didn't mean to hurt me. He needs me."

Courts typically regard a child's relationship with the father as being entirely separate from any assaults on the mother. Husbands who beat their wives are not barred from visiting their children. In most states they can still obtain joint custody, although in an increasing number this is no longer possible. The dominant perspective of the courts and mediators is that the child should have access to both parents after the breakup and that parent-child contact should resemble their predivorce relationship as much as possible. Basically it's assumed that if the father attacked the mother, such violence is irrelevant to the child's conscience formation or any other aspect of his future development. So following divorce, the woman no longer comes into contact with her ex-husband, except when children are exchanged within visiting arrangements, but the children are in regular contact with the man who beat her.

According to the children when they were young and after they'd reached adulthood, no single father discussed or bothered to explain his past violent behavior during the visits. Nor were they instructed to do so by the courts or the mediators. Many didn't even admit that they had been violent. Some said that maybe they had hit the children's mother just once. Others denied it completely. Not one father said that he was sorry. No single father admitted that his behavior was wrong. Not one tried to convey any moral principles to his children. This vehement or blanket denial of events that the children had seen with their own eyes was terribly confusing. As some told me later, their pitiful confrontation—"But Daddy, I *saw* you!"—was met with ice-cold stares. Such children were unable to trust their own observations and withdrew in anguish with an impaired sense of reality and conscience. Since the mothers often did not discuss the violence either, the child's traumatic experience was never touched. To compound matters, this conspiracy of silence was reinforced by court policy. Judges and mediators are often hostile to allegations of domestic violence, which almost always come from the mother. They may consider these accusations vengeful or manipulative strategies to withhold the child. So who is left to help the children who deep down know what they witnessed and are thoroughly confused, distressed, and lost? They have no say in proceedings that presumably center on their best interests. Who speaks for the child or to the child?

The courts have a window of opportunity to help children deal with issues of morality and controlling aggression, yet, incredibly, they turn away from what may be their most important task.[4] There is no mechanism for bringing domestic violence to light except in a custody battle. How many judges instruct violent fathers to help their vulnerable children? How many magistrates tell women how important it is to advise their daughters how to avoid the perils of abusive relationships? A small number of courts require perpetrators of abuse who sue for custody or unsupervised visitation to complete classes in curbing violent impulses, but such courses rarely address how parents should or could help their children. The children, alas, are lost in the shadows.

I'm not suggesting that children should be barred from visiting fathers who were violent in their marriages. We know this kind of ruling can boomerang. A father who is a forbidden figure can become, in the child's heart and mind, an epic hero or martyr. But I am suggesting that we should undertake programs to counsel children and parents in these issues *before the visits are allowed.* When violence occurs behind closed doors, as we know it does, it is very difficult to reach these families. But when a divorce occurs, violent families including these children can and should be given help. (I'll discuss providing help to violent families further in the conclusions.)

The Mother's Role

In leaving violent marriages, many women manage to escape. Unfortunately, their children continue to be trapped by internal images and memories of violence. Direct intervention with such children is critical. Here a mother has a very important responsibility in helping her children understand why she is leaving the abusive relationship. Her tender loving feelings will go far in soothing the trauma that they have witnessed. But even this is not enough. After she musters the courage to leave and faces the rigors of reconstructing her life, she owes her children the story of what really happened. It is their history as well as hers. Through telling it, she needs to convey the moral message of why violence is not acceptable. Most of all, she needs to help her children understand what love between a man and a woman is about and how it can go awry, how it can lead to hurt and eventually to destruction. Hard as it is, she needs to explain to her daughters, when they are old enough to understand, how she was misled. Many women who marry violent men are aware of the behavior during courtship. One of the wives in our study was beaten with a whip during her engagement and married the man anyway. She hoped that her love would change him and help curb his violent temper, but of course it did not. He carried the whip into the marriage. Other women have warning signs—glimpses of a violent temper, paranoid jealousy that seems flattering during courtship, details of a family history of violence—but they fail to listen to their intuition and brush away their doubts. Mothers also have an important obligation to their sons. One woman made the serious mistake of saying to her son, "Your father beat me and you will beat your wife." This message haunted him for years, casting a dark cloud on all his relationships with women. What if her prediction came true? Sons need special guidance from their mothers that says violence is the opposite of true manliness. It destroys the relationships that people want and value. Most of all, mothers need to tell their sons and daughters that they are not fated to follow in violent footsteps, as abuser or victim, and that they are free to make better choices for themselves. (We'll see how Larry and his sister dealt with their violent past in terms of their future relationships in coming chapters.)

Unfortunately, many women in this position run into the "don't criticize" policies of our legal system and are constrained from giving their children the moral guidance they need. Most judges prefer "the friendly parent" who encourages frequent and regular contact with the other parent. If a parent complains about the misbehavior of the other, attorneys argue that the offending parent is deliberately trying to alienate the children against their client. One woman whose husband held a loaded pistol to her head during the marriage was faulted in the custody report for not encouraging her child to have a friendly relationship with her father. A serious unintended result of the "don't criticize" rule is that it's very difficult for a parent with serious grievances to tell the child what really happened or to defend the child's interests in court or with a mediator. As a consequence, children are kept from learning the moral implications of the breakup and they are unprotected. These policies, which reflect the court's giving priority to parents' rights, are further damaging to already traumatized children.

Alliances

One other scenario can play out after divorce in families where there is high conflict or where enmity overshadows good sense. In these cases one parent and one child form an alliance, with all their energy and criticism aimed viciously against the second parent. Larry and his father formed such an alliance. They were bound by their shared feeling that Larry's mother had betrayed her family capriciously and that she, like all women, was a fool. What brings these parent-child alliances about? How long do they last? How much harm do they do to the child? I have seen many alliances like the one between Larry and his father. Typically these coalitions are formed during or after the breakup with the goal of punishing one of the parents. In these situations, the child is usually a preadolescent or young adolescent and the targeted parent is the one who sought the divorce. The ally parent, like Larry's father, has presumably been hurt and humiliated by rejection. The child, like Larry, feels himself to be the family guardian—a gallant Horatio standing at the bridge who seeks to restore the family or help the sorrowful parent.

At the breakup, one-fifth of the children in this study formed such alliances on behalf of one parent against the other.[5] They were very talented nabobs of negativism, often provocative and very rude. It was as if they had been granted a hunting license by the powerful authority of one parent (the ally who was teaching them to be good) to destroy the wicked parent in their sights. Pull your skirt down, you're a whore, God will punish you, and so on. The mischief wrought by presumably well-bred children was astonishing.

These bizarre alliances crop up like mushrooms over the postseparation landscape. They are powerful because they assuage the loneliness and hurt felt by one child and one parent. By becoming each other's trusted companions-in-arms, they support one other. To their credit, children tended to make such alliances with the parent who seemed to be suffering most and needed help. Those children who participated were likely to be more insecure than the siblings who refused to get involved. Often the best candidate was a child like Larry who prior to the divorce was a loner with few friends and outside interests. Such youngsters find the parent's attention dazzling.

In following these alliances over the years, I find that the vast majority are short-lived and can even boomerang. Children are capricious allies. They soon become bored or ashamed of their mischief. Not one alliance lasted through adolescence and most crumbled within a year or two. Larry's alliance with his father lasted somewhat longer because his mother was easily cowed by his father and it took her several years to find the strength to control her son. Until she called the police, she had not been able to punish or restrain his bad behavior. In any case, most children find their way back to age-appropriate activities as they enter adolescence, and this, as the co-optive parent finds, turns the tables. With time they are likely to turn against the parent who encouraged them to misbehave. As one sixteen-year-old girl, who had attacked her father five years earlier for all kinds of sinful behavior, told me, "I don't want to make my mom sound rotten but she was very persuasive. We were terrible to my dad. I'm still surprised that he was willing to forgive us after all that we said and did to him. I really appreciate all that he did for us."

There is great advantage in allowing natural maturation to take its course and to avoid overzealous intervention to break these alliances, which are usually strengthened by efforts to separate the allies. In this, the alliance may be akin to a moderate case of flu that mobilizes the immune system and generates antibodies. It is not a fulminant cancer requiring radical surgery or limb amputation, especially by poorly trained surgeons.

However, where violence is concerned, children do need help in understanding what is wrong with such behavior. They need to be told that violence not only hurts the victim physically but hurts people's feelings and that the damage can last a lifetime. This is not self-evident to a child who has been raised in a family where a parent has been violent. After all, children model their own behavior after the model their parents provide. They need guidance in learning alternative ways for resolving conflict. Indeed, there are many ways that these ethical ideas can be taught. A good curriculum would include games and videos that help children learn how to deal with their own anger and how to control their impulse to hit people or destroy property. The important thing to remember is that the divorce itself has no impact on these critical issues for the child. Moreover, it's difficult for parents to deal with these issues during and after the breakup without professional guidance. Parents and children both need help. We as a society have an obligation to provide it.

When There's No Escape

BEFORE GETTING TO Larry's adult life, I want to return to Carol and her adolescent years to help hammer home a major point about being raised in chaotic intact families. As we have seen, divorce was never an option for this family. The parents had no desire to stop their destructive behaviors. And if they had divorced, nothing would have changed for Carol and her siblings. Divorce is only a "solution" for people who want and have the ability to change. For the Carols of this world, there is far less opportunity to escape from the madness that surrounds them because there are no true adults to give them a helping hand.

Carol's voice was low and angry. "When I was a teenager, my mom would listen in on my phone calls and she'd go through my stuff. She'd ask nosy questions about me and boys. She accused me of hanging out with a bad crowd at school. All she could think about was that I was in trouble."

"Were you?"

"Not really. Certainly not in the way she thought. Compared with some of my friends I wasn't bad at all. I didn't use drugs and I didn't drink. I was afraid of being thrown out if I got involved with guys. I knew that's what she was waiting for when she listened in on my calls." As Carol described her adolescence, I was struck by her assertion that she had stayed away from sex and alcohol, both of which were prominent in her home. Because these activities were so familiar to her, it would have been easy for her to adopt the same behaviors.

"Why didn't you drink, especially when many of your friends were doing it?"

As Carol considered my question, she flushed slightly and got a distasteful expression on her face. "I think it was because of my mom. It was so disgusting when she got drunk. And she always ended up in a weak position, usually crying in her room. I figured alcohol would do the same thing to me. See, I didn't want to look like her, think like her, or be like her. But I might as well get it all off my chest. I became something else. I figured either you're a victim or you're the winner. You take advantage or someone else takes advantage. I didn't want to be a victim so I became the class bully. I was a real wiseass, always cracking jokes and making fun of people. I was the leader of a band of girls—all of us from really disturbed families—and we targeted people we could torment."

Carol saw my involuntary reaction to her words and looked down at her hands. "I'm really ashamed of it now but I remember how thrilling it was to be able to reduce some person to tears. I'll feel guilty for the rest of my life for what we did to one poor fat girl who we drove out of the school."

Her expression of shame then turned to excitement. "We also loved to shoplift. That was the best. We'd go in a group to a store and someone would make a disturbance and when the authorities went to see what happened we'd take expensive cosmetics and other things that looked good. Once, we even took some cameras. I remember the feeling—my stomach would be all knotted with fear and I'd be light-headed and almost dizzy because I felt so exhilarated. We were almost caught several times. Getting out and running fast even made it better. I didn't need the camera. I never needed or even wanted anything that we stole. What was important was the excitement."

"Did your folks find out?"

"Never. I knew I was there on sufferance and I was very careful. That's probably another reason I didn't do the things they were watching for. One wrong move and I'd be out. They kicked my brother out of the house when he was seventeen. They found him smoking pot in his bedroom and that was it."

"Did you have lots of boyfriends in high school?"

"No, not so much then. I didn't get into sex in a big way until after I left home and my parents had less control over me. I didn't have a steady boyfriend until I was a freshman in college. I met Ian the summer before my junior year. We smoked a lot of dope together and had a good time. But one night we got caught just like my brother, and my folks threw me out of the house. I had nowhere to go, except to Ian's, and so I moved in with him. This threw us together before we were ready and then everything went downhill. We spent the next three years in a repeat of my parents' relationship except with marijuana and speed, not alcohol."

Because her parents cut off all financial support, Carol dropped out of college and went to work as a waitress. "I was completely dependent on Ian for almost everything, including a place to live, a car, and money. This put me where I least wanted to be, feeling vulnerable and powerless. It wasn't long before things got really ugly. We broke up several times, got back together several times, and fought like tigers. It usually ended with Ian hitting me and locking me out of the apartment. I felt like he had a hard hold or a spell on me because I just couldn't leave him. I'd collapse outside the door and cry and whimper and beg him to open the door, just like a dog, and let me back in."

Just then a shadow fell over Carol's face and her voice strangled. "I wanted so much to talk to my mom or my dad about what was happening with Ian and hoped they would tell me what to do. I desperately needed to talk to someone, anyone. I remember crying, and the image of my mother's face would come up. Even though she threw me out and did all sorts of terrible things to me, I still needed her. It's crazy, but the more she hurt me the more I desperately longed for the kind of mom I never had."

She took a deep breath. "Well, I finally got rid of my oppressor. I'd love to tell you that I did it on my own but that's not what happened. After three years of no contact, my mother sent me a check for enough money to cover my last two years of college and living expenses. She wrote that they were still angry at me and didn't want to see me but that I was their daughter and they wanted me to finish my education. I still remember what a cold letter it was. She started it 'Dear Carol' and signed it 'Mom,' not 'Love, Mom' or 'Sincerely, Mom' but just plain 'Mom.' That's all. It made me so sad, I just sat down and cried and cried. But having that money made a huge difference. I went back to U.C. and started taking classes. It felt like I was coming out of a black hole. I was meeting new people and really studying hard. I felt so much better and less passive. You see, all my life my parents had told me that I was stupid. I didn't try hard in school because I believed them. But now that I was on my own, I wanted to get on with being an adult. I wanted a sense of control over my life."

There was very little that distinguished Carol's adolescent behavior from what I saw in teenaged girls raised in chaotic divorced families. Carol was able to avoid promiscuous sexual activity in high school, but she more than made up for that after she left home. All these girls had to manage on their own from a very early age. They felt that their parents didn't care what happened to them. For both groups, adolescence was a wild, desperate time dominated by hungers for nurturance and long-standing anger at parents, aggravated by powerful aggressive and sexual feelings.

One subtle difference between the two groups is that girls raised in violent intact families are often trapped by their overwhelming need for parental love. It's something they can't relinquish, whereas girls from divorced families are more able as adults to walk away from destructive relationships once they recognize how dangerous they are. They have a model for how to exit their plight. Despite repeated rejection and disappointment, women like Carol do not give up hope that their parents will change, and so they maintain a passionate tie to their parents despite their suffering. Carol's response to her mother's check after three years of silence was to turn the letter over and over again, looking for "affectionately yours," or even "sincerely yours." Seeing no such words, she almost tore up the check, as though her whole life depended on a crumb of affection from her mother. She still couldn't believe it. She continued to want what wasn't there. She keeps hoping and she keeps getting disappointed.

Paradoxically the hope and longing—the expectation that things can't be all dark—are also what kept Carol emotionally alive and eager to be a good person. She always maintained the sense that she could do better. But as we'll shortly see, her move into adulthood was beset with troubles. Unlike Larry, she did not receive a wake-up call from seeing her parents in a new light. Nothing at home changed.

NINE

Order Out of Chaos

When I saw Larry five years later, he was twenty-two years old and showed signs of turning his life around; he was struggling to assume a new identity as a fair-minded, responsible adult. Had we stopped our conversations just a few years earlier, I would have pegged him as a lost boy who would become an angry young man likely to install violence in his relationships. But I was oh so wrong. On this visit, I got my first glimpse of his turnaround, which, like Karen's conquest of the caretaker role, gave me a whole new perspective on the long-term consequences of divorce on children.

Along with working at night and going to school during the day, Larry had begun to rework his relationships with his father and his mother, essentially coming to grips with their divorce. For me, this remains one of the most interesting interviews in the entire study. I still feel privileged to have seen this process unfold before my astonished eyes.

We met in a sandwich shop down the street from the gym where Larry now worked out regularly. I hardly recognized this stocky, muscular, and blatantly handsome young man. The red eyes and sickly complexion were gone, along with all drugs, cigarettes, and alcohol. "By drinking and carrying on, I was trying to be the man of the house," he said matter-of-factly. "I was my alcoholic father." I listened with amazement as he said, "I'm proud to look back with a different perspective. I finally realized how much my mother has done for me and I now appreciate how hard she works. I feel very bad about the way I've treated her. She's had a very difficult time. I was very selfish."

"What caused this great change?" I asked, wondering to myself whether to believe him and if he was talking to impress me.

His answer was straightforward. "I didn't have any great vision all of a sudden. No religious conversion. I didn't wake up in the middle of the night screaming or sweating. A few years ago, when I was nineteen, I just stopped. I looked at my friends and saw what was happening to them and I dropped them. I looked at myself in the mirror and I hated what I saw. I don't know how to explain it, Judy. I guess I just did it from within. I decided I wanted to have a family and kids and I wanted a good job, so I applied to a community college and got back into school. I didn't want to ask anyone for help, not my mom and certainly not my dad. There was no one. I've been working my way through college, paying for everything by myself."

I tried to keep from rubbing my eyes in disbelief as Larry went on to talk about his father in a more balanced way than I had ever heard. "You're talking very differently about your dad than you used to, Larry."

"When I was younger," he said, "I used to see him on weekends. In the beginning it was fun, but after a while I began to realize it wasn't really a father-son relationship. We never really talked." With a sudden flash of anger Larry said, "And finally I realized that he had been leading me on about everything my whole life. Suddenly I knew that I meant nothing to him, just nothing. What an asshole I had been, a goddamn monkey on a string. When I calmed down, I suddenly saw him for the pathetic creep that he was, a drunk who hits helpless women, who picks on my little sister her whole life, and who lies to his son. That's who he really is. And that was who I was becoming. And I hated that."

Larry's words were now spilling out nonstop. "Do you want to know what's getting me through school, working seven days a week, going to work every night at midnight at the most boring job in the country, and coming back at six to get ready for school, earning minimum wage? Sometimes I'm so lonely I feel like I could die. But every time I think of quitting, I see my dad's face and I say, 'If you quit, that's how you'll end up.' And that keeps me going."

As I listened to the changes in his words and way of speaking and saw how different he looked, it occurred to me that in all our previous conversations Larry had disclosed only one side of himself and his history. He'd told me a hundred times over about his anger at his mother and how little he had gotten from her, how heartsick he was at the divorce. But it was now becoming clear to me that there were reserves of strength and resilience that I had not seen.

"I understand, Larry, why you've given up on your dad and what a terrible blow it was for you to be turned down when you had pinned your hopes on living with him. But where did your plans come from? You're going to school to study for a profession and to have a better life for yourself. Where did that idea come from?"

"It came from me. I decided that I had to be my own father and take control of my own life, that I couldn't rely on anyone, that I was the only one who was responsible for me."

"What does that mean, 'be your own father'?"

"Just that! I realized that I had no father. It was up to me to do it for me. Or else sink." He grimaced. "I decided not to sink!"

Larry's statement was stark, clear, at once chilling and inspiring.

"What about your mom?"

"I feel sorry for my mom. I used to watch her cry and I would yell at her to stop crying and she couldn't stop and I knew it but I kept up. When I gave up on my dad I began to see my mom in a different way. You could say that I began to see her as she really was."

"How is that?"

"What I finally understand is how my dad rewrote history. I knew it before but I didn't pay attention. My mom had a good dream when she married my dad. She wanted a husband and a happy family. She wanted her children to have a stable home. When I realized that my dad had bullshitted me, I took another look at what a sad life she had and I realized that he had almost destroyed her—and that I had helped him." Larry's face was very sober. "I'm thoroughly ashamed of myself for how mean I was to her for years. I've apologized and tried to make up by being helpful when I can. She's a decent, honest, kind woman. But she's not a strong person, and it's taken her a long time to get the strength to get rid of my dad. She was beaten down."

"And now?"

"She's better, but she's had a tough time. I see her more these days."

"Do you find a lot in common?" I was somewhat skeptical, knowing his mother's tendency to hover.

"My mom still doesn't get it that I'm an adult. She's a worrier and her life has not made things any easier. But she does her best. She tries to help me with my tuition, but she earns very little money teaching Spanish. Also my little sister is running up a lot of medical bills. But she got me my first computer. She also sends me small sums of money from time to time. It means a lot to her and it means a lot to me. Because every time she gives me something, she goes without something else that she needs."

I asked about women.

"I'm pretty cautious in my relationships," he said. "I don't pick up women at bars and I don't plunge into relationships." He gave a shy smile. "I've had girlfriends but no great love of my life. Actually my time is limited what with school and working to support myself. I did so poorly in high school that I almost didn't graduate, so I've had a lot of catching up to do."

As Larry left that day, he surprised me by asking about the other young people in the study. (I wasn't used to his showing interest in other people.) I explained that several others had turned their lives around after a bad start. Larry said, "You know, I really didn't want to participate in this study, but now I'm glad I did. Maybe I can help some little kid who has the same problem with his father that I did with mine."

Larry had come a very long way entirely on his own.

Stories of Transformation

LARRY HAD GONE FAR in explaining his baffling overnight transformation from an angry, violent delinquent into a law-abiding, decent young man. His striking phrase—"I had to become my own father"—encapsulated his passionate rejection of his father as role model and his understanding that he had to grow up fast if he was going to pursue another kind of life for himself. Ironically and tragically, Larry's early identification with his violent father was greatly strengthened by the divorce. It took him ten troubled years to break that tie and set his own course.

The first step in the transformation was Larry's despair and rage. After several years of disappointments, he began to realize that his father's promises were built on shifting sand. This man was not the idealized hero erected in his fantasies. Somewhere along the line Larry realized that he was not central to his father's life. His discovery that his father had married without telling him and then had no time to see him broke his heart and forever ended his fantasy of restoring the closeness of the relationship that he had enjoyed as a young child.

Larry provided me with another missing piece. He confessed that his sister's and his mother's suffering had been apparent to him for many years, but his alliance with his father had blocked his ability to see straight. He had been unable to acknowledge his mother's tears, or his father as the violent agent of her pain, or his own role in tormenting his mother. Freed of his subservience to his father, he could finally acknowledge his complicity and make amends. As he corrected his misunderstanding of his parents' violent marriage, he was at last able to accept the divorce and agree that it was necessary.

The last piece was his own courage, his persistence and conviction that he was finally doing what was right. For the first time in many years he felt good about himself. It was comforting for him to feel that he was a good man after so many years of being ashamed.

Other young men and women in the group drew a similar conclusion and turned their lives around just as Larry did. They, too, had been headed on a steep downward path. And they broke away dramatically from their identification with a delinquent or emotionally disturbed parent, finding other images to guide their lives. Jim, whose parents fought savagely and ignored their children for several years, at age sixteen burned down a million-dollar church building. The district attorney wanted him to be sentenced as an adult. An enlightened judge sent Jim to a correction center for youth instead of prison, and now, at age thirty-eight, he is a respected headmaster of a prestigious school and a happily married man with three children. He overcame drug use and a criminal record that included robbing houses, car theft, and arson. Like Larry, he accomplished this feat by revising his view of his parents and of his place in society. As he reported it, the central image that triggered his turnaround was the sight of his father sobbing at the arson trial. Before that, Jim had been unmoved by anything his father or mother said or did. Standing before the judge, waiting for sentencing, he silently concluded that his parents had joined together to help him. Despite their conflicts with each other, they had not—as he fervently believed—forgotten him. Most of all, he concluded that despite what he had felt for years, his father really loved him. At that critical moment, he resolved to turn his life around.

There are many other stories. Children who had been drinking or taking drugs since age eleven quit by their early or mid-twenties, sometimes before. A whole group who had witnessed violence and been either victims or perpetrators of more violence during their adolescence fell into this category of turnabouts. They were able to transform their lives when they reached a particular crossroads, without direct intervention from therapy or family.

All were in their twenties or early thirties when the transformation unfolded, which may not be a coincidence. Many people this age seem able to mobilize large reserves of physical and psychic energy to implement the change. Although it takes them longer to grow into adulthood, they often do so with spurts of self-determination. Think how hard Larry worked for at least six years to establish his new life and how much effort Karen expended in her twenties in entirely revising her career, her relationships with her family, and the relationship in her marriage.

As children and teenagers, Larry and the others did not stand out as being resilient or special in any regard. It may be in fact that these very impressive changes for the better are made possible by the divorce, which provides a window of escape. But the young person must have the will and strength to climb through this window, something I'll say more about later.

As I left Larry that day in the restaurant, I realized with awe that I was witnessing a transformation in almost every aspect of this young man's personality. But I left him still wondering what lay ahead in his relationships with women; he had not yet seriously addressed this part of his life.

No End in Sight

CAROL'S STORY IS instructive because it shows what happens to children from chaotic families when there is no turnaround. The children live in turmoil whether or not their parents get divorced. Without some intervention—help from a parent who recovers, a sudden self-realization that life could be better, or anything else that prevents a young adult from following in the shoes of their self-destructive parents—the entry into adulthood is fraught with problems.

After graduating with a B.A. in psychology when she was twenty-five, Carol spent a couple of years working in mental health settings but found herself unsuited for the work. A job at a shelter for abused women and their children overwhelmed her with sad memories. A friend got her a job in retail, selling a line of popular cosmetics. Here, Carol's flair for organization and her people-pleasing skills shone. She quickly rose to becoming a buyer for a major department store in downtown San Francisco. She had some difficulty from the outset in working with her supervisor and other people in authority, but her talents outshone her problems and it was assumed that she would improve as she matured. These were glory days in Carol's life. She loved the glitter of the elegant stores, the traveling, and the huge trade shows. She spent long hours working and released pent-up energy going out with friends to discos at night.

"I must have gone home with over fifty men in those days," she recalled with a mixture of pride and shame. "I liked attracting them. I knew it was dangerous but it was thrilling to go home with someone who's last name I didn't even know. There was something about that atmosphere of attraction and danger and not knowing that really turned me on. I'd say now that I was almost addicted to it. But I always kept the upper hand."

Carol sighed deeply. "But I hit a low point after awhile. It was when I was turning thirty-one and I was tired and strung out after living in the fast lane for so long. I was feeling empty and jaded and it took more and more drinking and partying to make me feel high. Plus, my judgment was slipping. I was getting careless, and that frightened me. I'd gone home with a couple of guys who wouldn't let me leave when I wanted to. They threatened me, and one even beat me up before I could get out. And my job that I'd formerly loved was getting frustrating. I wanted to be promoted to regional buyer and I got skipped over. It was a time that nothing fit."

We had several families in our divorce study who were just like Carol's family—the only difference being that one family split up and the other stayed together. The divorce brought no psychological change or serious expectation of change to either adult and had little effect on the children's lives in both groups. The drinking and drug abuse that were codependent during the marriage continued during the postdivorce years, sometimes solo and more often in new relationships. Children continued witnessing addiction or violence in the remarriages or subsequent cohabitations.

In fact, conditions for the child often got worse after the divorce. Whatever structure the marriage provided was further weakened by the turmoil of the postdivorce years. After the divorce, sexual activity sometimes escalated shockingly. One ten-year-old in our study returned home from school and found her father and one of her teachers having sex on the living room floor. "Daddy," she cried, "couldn't you have picked someone I don't know?" The limited care offered the child within the marriage diminished further. Whereas during the marriage one parent tried to make sure that the child got up in time for school and had food in the pantry and clean clothing to wear, with divorce the chaos spread so that often there were no family routines, no order in the household, no family dinners, no one in charge. Money became a serious problem in many homes. Less money for the child translated into the loss of important supports that the custodial parent could no longer afford, like private school, music lessons, special medical care, and tutoring when needed. So from all sides within the chaotic families the supports for the child were further weakened after the divorce. The bad relationships that the child witnessed during the marriage worsened after the divorce. Of course, for Carol, the availability of private school and money didn't help.

Brenda's story is an example of how divorce does not rescue children from chaotic families when the adults are unable or unwilling to change their lifestyles. I first met Brenda when she was ten years old and had written a satirical story about her parents' divorce for the school newspaper. After the breakup, she was entirely unparented. Sometimes she went to school, but if she felt like it, she stayed home. Her mother and father drank as much as before and each had a series of lovers. Brenda never knew where she'd sleep at night because she wasn't sure which house would have more strangers in it. Both of Brenda's parents had multiple sexual relationships that they did not hide from the child. Brenda's father was a famous television executive who married five times and hit each of his wives. Brenda's mother owned a travel agency so she could take off on trips whenever she liked. Money was not a concern in this family, but no household help was arranged to provide for the little girl's care when her parents were otherwise occupied.

After the divorce Brenda saw her mother maybe twice a week. Her father came to visit her sporadically, depending on who he was with at the time. Money for food was left on the kitchen table at both houses so Brenda could buy her own food and clothes and other things she wanted. She was never hit. She was ignored. It was as if she had disappeared along with the terminated marriage.

Because neither parent took responsibility for the child after the breakup, divorce put Brenda at more risk. Living in a highly charged sexual environment with no help in growing up, she became a call girl at an early age and commanded several hundred dollars a night. She snorted cocaine. When I saw her at age thirty-one, she had just moved into a small apartment in Oakland, by herself. For our visit, we both sat on boxes. And then I noticed that she had unpacked only one item—a framed photograph of herself as a little girl, standing with her mother and father, all smiling and happy. This is all that remained of the intact family, with Brenda struggling in her mind to hold on to some unity, some sense of affection, some hope. Even though her parents had in effect abandoned her, she, like Carol, talked about them with a longing that was utterly heartbreaking.

Thus we are left with a troubling but very important finding that highlights what divorce can and cannot accomplish. Children who grow up in chaotic families—divorce or no divorce—have similar lives. The divorce by itself provides no rescue unless at least one parent changes and shows real concern for the child by establishing a stable household and responsible parenting. Sometimes, as Larry's story shows, the child can rescue himself by finding mentors or summoning the inner strength to become his own parent. Both groups of children enter adulthood with low self-esteem, a hunger for love and human closeness, and badly skewed views of man-woman relationships. Women who are exposed to the sexual acting out of their parents are more likely to become promiscuous starting in their early teens and continuing into their twenties. But in what may be a silver lining to this dark cloud, their promiscuity tapers off as they reach their thirties. Some decide to just stop because they're afraid of getting hurt or becoming ill. Others find that sex no longer relieves their depression. Still others are lucky enough to meet men who, as one woman put it, "refused to be just the next guy in line." Two women in the divorced group joined churches with strict standards for moral behavior. "It took the church to keep my legs closed," one told me seriously.

The men raised in chaotic marriages and chaotic divorces also suffer low self-esteem but it's not usually manifest in promiscuity. Rather, they turn to alcohol and drugs. Unlike their sisters who give up reckless sex, the men's addictive behaviors overall do not wane as they reach their late twenties and early thirties. Nevertheless, a few of these men and women—six in all in our study—turned their lives around when they joined mainstream churches. None had gone to these churches as children, but here they found the moral guidelines they had been missing as children. They found spouses and a community that provided the support they had always longed for.

I left Larry in his early twenties full of admiration for the progress he had achieved in rejecting the alcohol and violence that were the ideals of his adolescent years. But I had more questions than answers about what lay ahead for him. After years of rage in childhood and adolescence, can a young man fully turn his life around? Can he set new goals and sustain his progress by his own efforts? Can he decide to be his own father and carry it off? Larry had been propelled far by his disappointment and anger at his father. His decision to adopt his father as a negative image had energized his grueling work and school program and kept him going. But how would that affect his future relationships with women and in making the important life choices that lay ahead? Considering the view of man-woman relationships that he had experienced in his family, would he be able to become the good husband and father that he aspired to be? Although the lives of all these young people were full of unexpected turns, Larry's history so far was baffling. I also had many concerns about his younger sister, who had been so demeaned by her father. How had she negotiated the transition to young womanhood? Had her mother been able to rally enough to really help her? I looked forward eagerly to seeing her as well, but I was worried about the long-lasting impact of her father's efforts to humiliate her.

TEN

Family Ties

When it came time to locate Larry for the twenty-five-year interview, I had no trouble finding him since he was listed as a licensed structural engineer in several public directories. I was very curious to know, now that another decade had gone by, if his transformation had stayed on course. Had he continued to turn his life around without help? Did he completely break the identification with his violent father? Or, as is so often the case, did he go on to repeat his father's bad behavior despite his conscious wish to be different? What kind of relationship did he have with his mother? And most intriguing, what kind of relationship would he create with a woman, given the wretched model his parents had provided?

The first time I got Larry on the phone, he was reluctant to talk, explaining that he was far too busy with a new project at work. Life at home, with a three-year-old and new baby on the way, was just too hectic. He was polite: thanks (for calling) but no thanks (for catching up on his life). I wasn't at all surprised. There was nothing in Larry's past that he should want to revisit. I decided that the only way to win Larry over was to tell him straight why it was so important that we meet: "Look, I don't want to talk to you about the distant past. That's long gone. But I do want to find out what happened to you after you decided to change your life. It would be very useful for other young people to know what worked for you and what didn't, where the minefields were, where you compromised and where you succeeded most. They have nowhere else they can find out."

Larry was dead silent. Apparently I had struck a nerve. As he hesitated I reminded him of something he had said ten years earlier. "Larry, you once told me, 'When I decide to marry, it will be until the day I die.' Do you still feel that way?"

"You remember that?" He was genuinely surprised. "How could you?"

"Larry, I remember most of what you've told me. That's my job. I'll meet you anywhere, anytime, at your convenience. Because your experience is important."

A week later we met in the San Jose office that Larry shared with two other structural engineers. He came straight out to greet me, shook hands, and led me into his office. He had a stocky build, short brown hair, direct blue eyes, and a somewhat harried look about him. His office was thickly cluttered with blueprints, government reports, periodicals, newspapers, and countless stacks of loose papers. Larry grabbed a set of blueprints off a chair near his desk so I could sit down and then brought his chair around so that the desk didn't separate us.

I looked around admiringly at the professional surroundings. "You've come a long way. Congratulations!"

"You mean since the first time we met? I was what, about seven?" He laughed.

"That's exactly how old you were."

"Those were not good years. I was a brat."

"You were a very unhappy brat."

"You're right. I was a pretty miserable brat for a long time." Larry looked around his office. "Lots of times I can't believe that I'm sitting here." He relaxed a little and smiled. "Do all the kids in your study agree to see you twenty-five years later?"

"Since you're an engineer, I'll give you the numbers. So far, one hundred percent."

"What will you do with your conclusions?"

"Publish them for people to read. If you want, you'll be among the first to see them. I promise to send you a copy."

"Will anyone be able to recognize me?"

I assured him, "If they do, then I will have failed badly. I promise that I'll protect your privacy. Your identity will be carefully disguised."

Larry nodded and turned brusquely to the business at hand. "What exactly do you want to know?"

"I want to know how you got from where you were at twenty-two, which is the last time I saw you, to where you are today. What were the steps along the way?"

Larry frowned. "Well, it was no piece of cake. I'll start with the easy part. I got married four years ago. My wife's name is Grace. We have a son, Alex, who is three and another baby is due in September. Grace is a school psychologist but she'll probably take a year off after the new baby arrives. We figure we can afford it now. As for this," he said, waving his hand at his paper-strewn office, "this is a new firm started by two young guys. I had just graduated from engineering at San Jose State and landed my first job here. That was three years ago and it's been great. I may stay here forever." Larry smiled briefly and then his mood turned somber. He had decided to tell the full truth. "I got this job through a lucky break and not because I was some kind of whiz kid. When I graduated, I didn't have any self-confidence. I had to put myself through school and started out with a D grade point. So much for M.I.T. But after a while I did better at community college and finally transferred to San Jose. It's a good school but not in the big leagues. So every time I went for a job interview the guy from Berkeley or Caltech or wherever was first choice. They had the connections. I felt so low, I almost sank through the floor. And then I decided to contact one of my professors who had liked my work, to see if he had any ideas. That was real tough for me because I never expect anyone to come through for me. He asked me lots of questions about how I had been able to go to school during the day and work all night and why it had taken me six years instead of the usual four. Bottom line, he said he liked my work, said I had talent and grit, and recommended me to another former student who was starting a new company. The rest is history."

"That's a very nice story. And it's a tribute to you."

Larry looked at me soberly and said, "That's the only time in my life that I've gotten help from a man."

"I take it your dad didn't help with your education?"

He hooted. "Not a cent. The only good thing is that I didn't expect any help. My dad is a taker, not a giver. He's never thought of anyone in his life except himself. He's a smart man. He can be a charmer when he puts himself out. He has a good sense of humor. But he has never made sacrifices for anyone. He's selfish through and through. I used to think he was a hero, a great man. I even thought that he loved me. He kept telling me, 'You're my favorite.' If that's true, hell must have a special place for those who are their father's favorite child."

I was taken aback by Larry's bitterness. "What's your relationship now? Do you ever see your dad?"

"I see him rarely. Once or twice a year. We talk on the telephone. We chat about work. About the weather. We tell each other dirty jokes. But that's the extent of it. We don't communicate on a deeper level."

"Do you miss not having a closer relationship?"

"I don't really care to be close to him now," Larry said evenly. Then, more gently, he added, "Sometimes I feel bad. Like I heard recently that he was diagnosed with prostate cancer and I'm sorry. But the truth is that my sister and I can't be there for him. We're still angry at him, even after all this time."

I wondered whether Larry's father was aware of these feelings. "Tell me, did you ever try to tell him how hurt you were feeling or to talk about having a different kind of relationship?"

Larry looked away and then stared down at his hands, inspecting his fingernails. "I did try. I tried to tell him about the issues between us that hurt me. I told him that I felt cheated out of a father. I reminded him of the awful night that he left after hitting my mom a whole lot of times. I said to him, 'You could have dealt with things a little better.' " Larry looked up with a pained expression. "He hardly heard me. He just didn't get it. You know, it still makes me sad not to have had a father in my life. I know I still have a lot of pent-up anger. I try not to think about it."

Larry sat back and then responded to my unspoken question. "I don't really see a road for me to be able to work through all of the anger and hurt from my childhood. It comes up now because of my own children. I want to do for my children everything that my dad didn't do for me."

This last remark rang familiar. Karen had said the same. These young people do not want their children to have a childhood like their own.

They want something better and are willing to fight for it. I was also very interested that none of the adults who had felt rejected or misused by their fathers as children rejected their importance or denied their long-standing wish to have had a loving, concerned father.

How Fathers Rate

After decades of minutely recording mother-child interactions as if they existed in a "daddy-less" world, researchers have finally discovered fathers and how important they are to a child's development. Today's answers to the question "What good are fathers?" would fill a small library. Children with sensitive, involved fathers surge ahead in their cognitive and social development as they explore their environment and play with other children. One important study that followed children for twenty-five years showed that those who were closely involved with their fathers at age five were more empathic as adults and were happier as husbands and as parents than those who had not experienced close relationships with their own fathers a quarter of a century earlier.[1] And just to dispel the strange notion that fathers are more important to their sons than to their daughters, a study of young women who excelled in their academic studies at Stanford and Berkeley revealed that they attributed their high ambition to their father's long-standing encouragement.[2] In my own work on good marriages, I found that women who maintain a passionate relationship with their husbands throughout many years of the marriage had a healthy, loving relationship with their fathers as children.[3]

But in divorced families, father-child relationships run a different course. Because the child lives only part-time or even half-time with her father or sees him according to a set schedule, their interaction is not a given. Coming and going as they do, father and child don't take one another for granted (this is true for visiting or joint custody arrangements). Instead, their relationship must be created from the more limited interactions they enjoy or, if things are not going well, do not enjoy. The potential for disappointment and hurt, or for misunderstanding on both sides, is omnipresent. The opportunities for making up after a quarrel, for doing better, are more limited. It's as if the myriad daily interactions of the father-child relationship have to flow through the narrow end of a funnel. Relationships feel constrained by the clock because they are being interrupted constantly.

Even more important, as the child gets older the symbolic significance of the divorced father changes. He's no longer the commanding presence in his child's life—the loving protective figure who makes sure everyone is cared for. Because he's no longer responsible for the welfare of the household, his image inevitably diminishes. Daddy may be good company or a bore, he may be loved or resented, but he has lost his big job. Henceforth he is judged by what transpires between himself and his child, not by virtue of his traditional role as father in situ. Whatever relationship father and child create, they must do it by themselves without the structure of the family to support either of them, without the comforting presence of just having each other around, and without the help of the mother who, in a good intact family, encourages the father-child relationship to take off and to grow.

The average child in a functioning intact family turns to each parent as he wants or needs their attention or help. Children are very astute in figuring out what each parent is better at providing emotionally as well as in other spheres of knowledge. When children get hurt, they often call for their mothers. Even older children want comforting and holding when they're in pain. When the same child feels lively and eager to do something new, she may well turn to her father. When my twelve-year-old daughter was hit by a car, she wanted her father to ride in the ambulance because she had greater confidence in his ability to take charge. Later on in the hospital, she wanted me to sit at her bedside all day to comfort her. What could be more natural?

I'm reminded of Alice in Wonderland, who held pieces of a magic mushroom in each hand. One side made her smaller and the other taller. She could nibble away at will and change her height. Similarly, the child in an intact family is free to turn alternately to each parent to meet her changing needs and wishes as she grows. Young adolescent girls typically turn to their mothers. Six-year-old boys want to be with their dads. But in the divorced family the child has to tailor her needs and wishes to the parent who happens to be scheduled in her life at any given moment. Many children complain that when they're with their moms they miss their dads and vice versa. Indeed they do. They cannot postpone their needs to fit the custody schedule until they're much older.

Being a father in a divorced or remarried family is a lot harder than being a father in an intact family. A part-time or even half-time father has no counterpart in the intact family. It's an entirely new role with no rules. How much authority does a visiting father have? Does he set rules for conduct, for homework, for allowance? When if ever does he override the mother or the stepfather? And who will listen if he does? What does he do with a nine-year-old and a four-year-old on Sunday afternoon in the city? What will they do in his one-room or five-room apartment? But aside from the logistics, how important is he? All men worry whether their children really want to be with them. Will my daughter prefer to spend the weekend with her best friend? (She surely may.) Will my son prefer to go off on the rock climbing expedition with his class? (Answer: you bet.) What should a good father do under those circumstances? Should he insist on his time? Should he grin and bear it? Should he promise the children the moon, load them with gifts like Santa Claus, and bend to their wishes?

The father-child relationship in a divorced family is thus unconsciously negotiated month by month, year after year, forged from countless interactions, until the son or daughter grows up. By the time they're adults, children of divorce have set opinions about how well their fathers did, whether they're worthy models to follow. Central to their judgment is a nest of feelings and questions that the children formulate over time. They ask themselves and their siblings: How faithful were you to me and my brothers and sister? Were you willing to give up anything to be my father? Did you make sacrifices? How hard did you try? What have you done with your personal life that I might want to emulate? Have you been civil with my mother? These are the children's yardsticks. Some, like Larry, use them to do the opposite of their father's behavior.

I'm happy to say that within this study there is a group of fathers who made the grade. They were loved, admired, and appreciated by their adult children. These men gave priority to the relationship with their children from the first marriage and expected their wives to join them. Sometimes this commitment generated a lot of tension in the remarriage but the men insisted. These fathers had invested a great deal of love and effort into parenting before divorce and had no intention of changing their ways after divorce. They helped all their children and stepchildren financially through college and made sacrifices to do so when necessary. When they could, they helped their adult children find first jobs. One father of modest means sent a check to his son for the down payment on a house; the young man was flabbergasted. He had not asked for help and was everlastingly grateful for the thoughtfulness and generosity that prompted it.

On the other end of the spectrum, we saw fathers who abandoned their children outright. One man adopted his stepsons and stopped seeing his own children (who were the same age as his stepsons) even though they had been close during the first marriage. Others saw their children once a year and felt it was adequate. Some violent husbands continued to be violent in their second marriages and did not see their behavior as being detrimental to their children. The sons and daughters of such men struggled for years to break away from the powerful model of such immoral behavior. As adults, most angrily rejected their fathers and have little compassion for them when they're in trouble. When Larry learned that his father had prostate cancer, he felt bad but said, "I feel sorry for him but he was never there for me. I can't be of help to him, either."

Most fathers in this study fall in between. They intend to maintain frequent contact with their children but gradually visit less as the difficulties of maintaining a relationship loom larger and as they are caught up in second marriages with new children and stepchildren as well as new jobs, new communities, and new concerns. These men are regarded by their children as selfish and insensitive to the consequences of their failures as fathers. "My dad loves life but he has no heart for others," said one young man. "He never wrote, he never called. He didn't understand that getting a message from him would change my life." Most young adults do not blame their stepmothers or stepsiblings for these shortcomings; they blame their father. They often speak of their fathers with affection, even with compassion, but they make no attempt to hide their disappointment or anger. They say, "I love him but I don't respect him."

Many people believe that children learn to dislike their fathers because mothers say bad things about them, but that has not been my experience. The children that I have talked with make their own observations and draw their own conclusions. They ask, Has he been a faithful father? Is he a loser in love and marriage? Can he be trusted? Only eight men and women in the entire group said they would seek their father's advice about any aspect of a personal relationship or a family problem. A large national study reports that young adults in divorced families, very much in accord with my findings here, are angry at their fathers and are unlikely to be helpful to them as they grow old. This is a very serious issue for the future, considering how long people are living and how much they will need to turn to their children for loving care and support in their old age.[4]

ALMOST ALL THE young adults from divorced families in our group knew their father's address at the twenty-five-year mark, but unlike Gary and his dad, most were not close friends. Their relationship was very different from those in the good intact families where fathers and adult sons grew closer and both valued the relationship more as the father aged. Few divorced fathers were good friends with their adult children. Fathers and sons did keep in touch and come together for important family events, such as the birth of new children, birthdays, holidays, and sometimes regular visits with grandchildren. A few fathers and sons played golf or tennis regularly. Over the years, fathers who had disappointed their children were observed from afar for any sign of increased interest in their adult children. "I think he's beginning to mellow," they reported. The way that adult sons were able to hold on to their hope and compassion was very moving. Some went in search of fathers they had seen only rarely and tried hard to find points in common. One thirty-year-old man remembered the airplane models that he and his dad had built together when he was a little boy. He purchased several model sets and invited his father to join him in model building in the hope that they could go back and retrieve their old ties. Sam, a thirty-one-year-old photographer, said, "I keep in touch with him. He's getting older now and maybe more reliable. He abandoned me, I know that. But there's no point getting sad or pissed off. People do what they have to do."

Here I'd like to point out a strange phenomenon that baffles many observers of our divorce culture. I have met men who were good, loyal, decent fathers to the children born in a second marriage or to stepchildren from the remarriage. If you asked those children about their dad, they'd say he was the best in the world. Yet this same man a few years earlier walked away from the children in his first marriage. They'd say he was the worst dad in the world. How could one person behave so differently?

One such father in the study explained his behavior when he said, "I wasn't happy in my previous marriage. I never felt that my first wife belonged to me. The marriage was so terrible, I became disgusted, and after a while I didn't try. It ended. I had two children. My son was seven when I left. So he doesn't think much of me. I literally packed and left in front of him, which is very hurtful to a child. I know that. Whatever feelings he harbors toward me to this day I understand. They are still my children. I don't know them and they don't know me. I paid child support and their college tuition but I didn't go to their weddings or to any other events in their lives. It would have been too stressful for everyone. I want them to be happy. But when I met my current wife there was just no way I was going to spend the rest of my life without her. I never thought you could love somebody that way. Out of that bond we had two children. They are the best thing that ever happened to me and I would give my life for them."

I think it's reasonable to say that this father lives with the guilt of having deserted his children but he feels that maintaining ties to his past is more than he can tolerate. Although he is a man with a modest income, he paid child support and college tuition. But his feelings for his children are tied to his feelings toward his ex-wife, and that is a door he cannot stand to reopen.

We need to come to terms with a great deal of variation in postdivorce parent-child relationships. The notion that these relationships are entirely separate from marriage and are self-sustained during the many changes in the postdivorce family is not supported in this work. There is no universal pattern. Some fathers are eager and able to continue parenting after the breakup and willing to shape their entire lives accordingly. Others cannot maintain loyalty to two families or have no wish to do so. Others find that continued frequent contact with the children of the failed marriage makes them unhappy. And still others continue to be driven or tormented by lifelong angers at their ex-wives. There is no dominant pattern that we can use to guide our policies and interventions for all or most families. Yet in part because of the demands of the legal system, our search is for a one-size policy that fits all.

Effects of Witnessing Violence on Girls

I HADN'T HEARD much about Larry's sister during my previous interviews and now seemed like a good time to ask. I remembered her well from our first meeting at the breakup when she was a very pretty, shy, gentle four-year-old child who cried when I asked her to draw her family. I had thought about her on several occasions during my interviews with Larry and had long been distressed by her father's statements to the child that she, like her mother, was inferior to men. I also remembered how the mother had wanted to cut back on the little girl's visiting with her father because the child was brokenhearted after each visit but that the child had insisted on going despite her pain.

I asked Larry to tell me about Anja.

His manner softened. "I've been concerned about Anja for years, just as she's been concerned about me. We've looked out for each other. She was almost the only human being I saw when I was working so hard at school. She would call or she had a key to my hole in the wall and sometimes she would bring over stuff my mom had cooked and put it in the fridge. Her visits meant a lot to me."

"What's your concern?"

"The divorce was hardest on her. Dad didn't care about her and she knew it. He insulted her or he ignored her. It really affected her self-esteem. When she graduated from high school, she started to get involved with bad guys. She'd come home with a yellow bruise on her face and a rigid posture, so that I knew her ribs were taped and that the guy she lived with had beat her up again." His tone turned to exasperation. "What can I tell you? For years she lived in a dream world. She'd say, 'I love Danny, or Joe, or Jim. He has so much potential. If I love him enough, we can get through this.' She got involved with violent men who were like leeches. She took care of them, supported them, babied them, did everything and they took advantage of her and hit her. She's a very pretty woman so boyfriends were never a problem. But she didn't understand that. There were three guys who hit her that I knew about. She was always afraid that she would marry someone like my dad. I was afraid that was exactly what she'd end up doing."

"What do you think this is all about?"

"Seeing my dad hit my mom affected her badly. She had nightmares and stomachaches for years after the breakup. Plus she always thought it was her fault that my folks' marriage was falling apart. She was fourteen before my mom finally sat down with her and explained the divorce and the violence. I've really been worried about her getting badly hurt or killed. I've gone to get her twice in the emergency room. Each time I told her she needed professional help, not just getting emergency aid. I think that she finally listened. She's doing better, but it's taken a lot of years and a lot of beatings."

"It sounds like you were able to help each other."

"That's true. That's been one of the good things about our crazy family. Recently Anja told my wife that maybe there was a point to all of that pain and suffering that we had. 'You know what I think of,' she said. 'I have Larry as a brother and that makes it all worth it.' " He smiled. "I certainly feel that way about her." He seemed to be holding a vision of his sister in his head. "Anja finally went into some heavy-duty therapy and it's helped. Now she's married to a decent man and they have a neat child. I think she's finally made it."

Witnessing violence may have a particularly malignant effect on the emotional development of girls.[5] In comparing the young men and women who witnessed violence within this group, I found the effects on women lasted longer and were still evident in their relationships in their thirties. This is very different from the young men who hit their girlfriends in late adolescence but who years later were not violent with their wives. Many of the daughters appeared to have internalized the father's denigration of women and accepted the view that women are inferior, ugly, stupid, and deserving of suffering. These women were surprisingly similar in how they viewed their parents, themselves, and their own adult relationships. One after another they entered into exploitative relationships in which they supported the man emotionally and sometimes economically, in which they nursed him tenderly during periods of drunkenness, drug addiction, or depression, and in which they were hit and insulted for their pains. And then they went back. One of the most vivid and chilling images in this study is of a woman in her thirties who grew up in a family in which the father got drunk every weekend and hit the mother but did not hurt his children. I will always remember her standing with her three young children, planning her escape to her mother's home while her husband who had been arrested for battering her was temporarily out of the way. She looked exactly like her mother had looked twenty-five years earlier when she was on the lam from her husband with her three children. She said to me, unforgettably, "Now for the *first time* I understand what happened to my mom. And I was so angry at her then."

There are numerous roots to domestic violence. In many families, the perpetrator suffers from paranoid jealousy. We have many Othellos in modern America. In others, violence is a brutal method of establishing and maintaining control. A common pattern in the marriages and divorces that I have seen is for a man to hit his wife while desperately needing her and despising her and himself at the same time. These dynamics are more visible during times of unemployment, when violence, alcoholism, and divorce typically rise. The man's threatening stance and raised fists often reflect his own underlying insecurity and almost childish dependence on the woman to hold him together. Many a woman becomes trapped by the vain and foolish hope that she can rescue the man from himself and uncover the prince in the frog's skin.

Some women are able to escape this trap when they divorce. It may take them many years to extricate themselves from their rescue fantasy as they gradually and reluctantly give up the hope of changing the man. It often takes them years after divorce to regain their perspective and to overcome the stark fear and humiliation they lived with.

Their daughters, however, are at risk for remaining trapped in relationships that echo the violent marriage. Tragically, toxic elements in the marriage endure after the breakup. Larry's father did not hesitate to make abundantly clear to his little daughter his views about the inferiority of women. He insulted her openly on visits, calling her "little bitch" and "stupid." There's almost no way a little girl hearing this can escape internalizing the view that she's an inferior being. Moreover, the violent father is often a seductive and charming man who doesn't hesitate to court his sons and daughters in the hope of enlisting their support. This combination of power and helplessness is very appealing to a child. It has strong erotic overtones. The child internalizes the image of a man who is overpowering, needy, and appealing. She buys into and internalizes a view of herself as an inferior being who needs a strong man to hang on to because, as several of these sad young women said to me, "Without a man I am nothing." As she matures, this image is built into her expectations of men and her relationships with men. The man is supposed to hurt her and she is to remain the helpless victim. Her job is to rescue him. When he fails to respond, it is her fault.

Unfortunately, the mother's transformation from victim to independent woman often comes too slowly and too late to be built into the psyche of her daughters. It may be years before the child is able to see her mother as a person worth emulating, with the strength to stand up for herself. The view of the mother as weak and helpless is a lasting and powerful one. Little girls do not for many years see their mother's courage in breaking free. Only as adults did the young women in this study begin to understand the wisdom of their mother's decision.

Most of the women raised in violent families in this study were able to break out of the pattern by their early thirties—but only with great difficulty and only with individual or group therapy. Some who escaped violent relationships ended up in lasting unhappy marriages or remained caught in demeaning long-term relationships without marriage. (I'll talk more about this group in Chapter 14 when we examine early, impulsive marriages.) Anja was helped by the encouragement of her mother and her brother plus several years of psychotherapy. She was eventually able to find a man who loved her and was not abusive. But when I saw her at age thirty, she was extremely worried about the future. Her self-confidence was still poor. Although she had graduated from college, her career plans were shaky. Compared to Larry, she was floundering.

Siblings

LIKE MANY SIBLINGS in divorced families, Larry and Anja were very helpful to each other during the postdivorce years. Larry's first awareness of his father's flaws as a parent came from watching his father treat his sister so unfairly. He felt sorry for her at an early age and suffered at the unfairness of her treatment. Anja in turn leaned on her brother in her many sad experiences with violent men. He was the one who took her home from the emergency room. And he was the one who encouraged her to leave abusive men and seek professional help.

After divorce, siblings are often drawn closer together. Amid the shifting moods of troubled parents, they turn to each other for safety and warmth. After all, they share a special history that binds them together. Unlike only children after a divorce, they help each other every step of the way. As adults they say things like, "My brother saved my life" or "Because of my sister I kept my sanity." Only children often have a much harder time and are more likely to feel lonely, isolated, and overwhelmed by their parents' problems. Siblings after divorce often form small subcultures within the family, creating a united front vis-à-vis their parents and the adult world. They lie awake at night discussing their parents and trying to make sense out of what they observe. As adults, many continue to share their concerns, including opinions about each parent and his or her significant other, with a candor and openness unto themselves. Their sense of camaraderie—of "we-ness"—does not end with childhood but extends into adult life to their mutual benefit.

In an interview, one young man made sure that I understood the importance of his sister as his champion. "She helped me all the time," he said. "She's two years older and didn't feel the impact of the divorce as much as I did. She was already free, more able to risk my dad's anger. So she fought for both of us."

A young woman referred repeatedly to how she and her brother were caregivers for their parents. She said, "And still whenever there is a crisis in any part of the family, we get back into sharing the guilt and into deciding who will take care of what, as if we were a permanent nine-one-one ambulance team."

Some siblings maintain the family's moral standards. One young woman told me, "My brother and I have been incredibly close. We have always adored each other. Mom was nuts. Dad was gone. Whenever they got together, there would be mayhem in our house. When my dad came home it was like a time bomb. They would scream and throw things. Mom would hide or disappear and my brother and I would go find her. Things were so crazy, we tried to make it safe between us. Other kids thought we were strange. If my brother and I had a disagreement, we would sit down and discuss it calmly. We are very proud of how we helped each other. We are still very close."

ELEVEN

Undoing the Past

While he was telling me about Anja, Larry got an urgent phone call from one of his partners about an emergency on a job site. He listened attentively, quickly assessed the situation, and offered a solution to be implemented in three phases. I was impressed by his decisiveness and ability to plan—and told him so after he got off the phone. This clearly struck a chord. His eyes became very bright as he replied, "I believe in planning. I'm always thinking about ten years ahead. It's the best way I know of to make your life turn out the way you want it to. All the important things in my life—my education, my career, and even my marriage—have turned out because I've figured out what I wanted ahead of time. Sometimes it took me a while. I was pretty dumb about the marriage part, but after a while I caught on."

I decided to tease him a little. "So, you tried to plan your love life? Tell me about it."

Larry flung himself back in his chair and laughed. "I figured we'd get to that." He settled himself and thought for a moment. "It really goes back to my mother. She told me that she knew, after one year, that her marriage was wrong but she ended up staying for ten years anyway. She felt it was morally wrong to divorce and to deprive her children of a proper family, so she stayed and got abused and beaten down until she couldn't take it anymore. It took me a long time to see it this way but I absolutely think she made the right choice in leaving." Larry sighed and went on. "But out of that I formed in myself a promise never to get a divorce. You remembered when you called me that I had told you, 'When I decide to get married, it will be to the day I die.' That was exactly my view. But the result was that I just avoided the whole issue because it seemed too much. To be truthful, it was terrifying. I asked myself, How can anyone be sure? There's no way for that. Anyway, I was working so hard that women had no place."

"You mean you didn't date at all?"

"Sort of. I wasn't too interested in wasting my time. Young, ditzy women with no goals or focus never attracted me. I remember that what impressed me about Grace was her serious manner when I first met her."

"What was she like?"

Larry's eyes grew bright as he described meeting the woman who would be his wife. "I met her at Kinks where we both worked through the night. She was a psychology major at San Francisco State and was putting herself through college, just like me. After I got to know her a little, I found out she worked two jobs and went to school. She'd had an early marriage that had been a disaster. After that she hadn't dated much. In fact, she was kind of shy with men."

"How did you get to know each other?"

"One night I gave her a ride home and we began to talk. We liked each other and we got into the habit of stopping for coffee a couple of days a week on the way to work. Then we started making dinner together at her place. Well, she did all the cooking and I'd do the chopping. I remember one night she brought out an apple pie for dessert. I told her she shouldn't have bought a pie and she said, 'I didn't buy it, I made it because I remember you said apple pie was your favorite dessert.' That's how she is—just really thoughtful and giving and going the extra mile for you."

I thought to myself how much this consideration, that so many would have taken for granted, must have meant to this lonely man.

"Our relationship started as a friendship over those dinners," Larry said. "We shared things about our lives. She told me about her marriage—how she left when he wouldn't quit smoking pot and he got violent. I told her about my parents and my dad's violence. And even about me and how I'd started to hit my girlfriends and how ashamed I was of that part of me. I was afraid that would put her off—and I wouldn't have blamed her. But she understood how hard I was trying to get that behind me, and she actually said that she appreciated that I'd seen the dark side, as she called it, and that I'd come out a better person for having confronted some of these things. Talking about this with her and getting her reaction was the first time that I'd felt whole, like I could accept all of who I was and even be kind of proud of everything I'd been through. We're still each other's best friends. I can tell her anything. It's incredible. I never thought I'd be able to say this, but I trust her with everything."

"How did the romantic piece get added into your friendship with Grace?" I asked.

"I guess it was about a year after we met. Grace went to Arizona to visit her folks for a month and I really missed her. I realized how much we had grown to share with each other and it also hit me how much lighter and more fun my life was when she was there. She's a really optimistic, positive person and she has a great sense of humor. I started to think then that she might be the one for me. When she got back it turned out she'd missed me, too, and so we started to date more seriously. We were inseparable for about a year and then we moved in together."

"How did it come about that you decided to marry?"

Larry's response confirmed my expectation that commitment is really hard for these young men. He said, "It took a long time. There was no way I was going to take getting married lightly. And that caused some of our earliest friction. I realized I loved her and that she was important to me but I was unable to make a decision. I was afraid because of the divorce. I was afraid of being left and I think that is why I was afraid of making a commitment to her. Somehow that brought up the sadness I felt when I was seven. That same sadness came back every time I was about to say 'Let's do it.' It just stopped me cold." He looked chilled as he described these events. "What happened was that we'd been living together for about three years and Grace gave me an ultimatum. It was on Valentine's Day. She said, 'Are we or are we not getting married? I don't feel that we are getting anywhere.' I just sat there, tongue-tied. I couldn't say a word. So she packed her stuff and moved out. She was right. She wanted to get married, and if I wouldn't, she needed to move on with her life. But that didn't make a difference. I just wasn't ready. And frankly, I was resentful about being put on the spot like that."

"What happened?" I was engrossed in the drama of their coming together. I knew the ending but the twists and turns were astonishing. How long would the testing of each other go on? How much could these young people stand? What kept them from tragically going their own separate ways?

"I told her to give me another year and then we'd decide for sure. But Grace wouldn't go for this anymore. She decided to take a job offer in L.A. and she moved south."

"And so you lost her?"

"Almost. Within a week I knew we'd made a terrible mistake. I missed her more than I could stand. So I flew down, got on my knees, and begged her to marry me." He smiled broadly. "And she accepted."

"Were you sure after all your waiting?"

"To be honest, no. I was still hesitating. I was more certain than I'd ever been but I knew that I'd lose her if I kept this up. I wanted to be sure but finally understood that there are no guarantees in life. By then I was ready to take the risk. I thought to myself, 'I've got to take a chance on love.'" These were Karen's words exactly. Larry and Karen had to bring themselves to take a chance, whereas both wanted an iron-clad guarantee. Who doesn't? But these young people are terrified at the start.

I shook my head. "What an ordeal for both of you."

Larry nodded his assent. Here was a courtship that had lasted seven years. First they establish a friendship and learn to trust each other. Within that friendship they tell each other about their past and their mutual trust deepens. Having passed that hurdle, they become lovers and live together. But they are still miles away from commitment. It's only when Grace insists that Larry is able to overcome the last obstacles to his decision. Think how great his fear was for it to have taken seven years to make this decision, knowing how much he loved her. Think how much patience and love Grace had to give in letting Larry have the time he needed. How easy it would have been for one or both to quit in frustration—for Larry to give in to his fears and run or for Grace to turn elsewhere.

Fear of Commitment in Children of Divorce

THE TWO CENTRAL tasks of adulthood are loving and working. Most of the young men in our study did reasonably well or very well with the second task. They understood about supporting themselves and took it seriously. Some had excellent careers and made plenty of money. Others worked steadily at moderately or poorly paid jobs But the first task was a giant hurdle that caused a tide of heartache. As we've seen, young men and women from divorced families enter young adulthood anxious about love, commitment, and marriage because they are so afraid of failing and being hurt. One way this anxiety plays out is to avoid commitment altogether.[1]

We've already seen how the fear of commitment played out in Karen's story and her delay in saying yes to marrying the man she loved. But as the findings of this study shows, these young men have an even harder time than the women. Many can't even begin to play the courtship game. Their fear of rejection runs so high that they spend years running away from women or standing still, waiting to see who wants them. Many lead solitary lives and suffer in isolation. Casual dating is not an option. Most lack the dash and self-confidence to enjoy it or do it well.

Why is courtship so important and why is it going out of style? Courtship, be it short or extended, is a necessary overture to a loving relationship. It's the process of selecting who is right and deciding who is wrong. As we saw in Gary's story, during courtship each of us asks, Do we fit? Are we good together? Is what we have in common good enough to stay together for one night, one year, a lifetime? For building a family? Courtship is that critical time early in a relationship when each person learns about himself and about the other and decides whether they match each other's needs, wishes, and fantasies well enough to pursue the relationship further. The goal of courtship is to find someone who comes closer than others in meeting one's realistic expectations for love, intimacy, and friendship.

Unfortunately, our divorce culture has fundamentally changed the nature of courtship. Its goals are no longer clear because commitment is feared instead of expected. Young and not so young people want lasting love and companionship as much as ever. Given the loneliness of modern life, the bleakness of offices, and the stress of commuting and traffic, they need it more than ever. They want to come home to someone who loves and appreciates them. A pet won't do it. Sometimes people try to avoid facing the fears of commitment by moving in together right away and then pretending it's not for keeps. Cohabitations like this can last for years or a lifetime (more on this later). As Larry's story shows, the young men's fears are not simply part of a general discouragement in our culture about marriage. Rather, their fears are deeply rooted in their own memories. They grow sad when talk turns to marriage. As a result, many young men from divorced families are immobilized. When the woman says "now or never" many stand silently at the door, waiting for a push, or they close their eyes in terror and jump. Sometimes they run away or play for another delay, trying to keep open an escape door for as long as they can.

I was intensely curious about Larry's marriage and decided to be blunt: "Tell me about your marriage. Is it working out as you hoped?"

"If I tell you about Grace, you'll think I've gone soft in the head."

"Try me."

"She's a bright, caring, and sweet woman who has made us a home that I never dreamed I would have. It amazes me every day that something like this could come from a family like mine. Or that it even existed anywhere. She goes out of her way to make me park my work at the door, to calm me when I come home frazzled when this or the other structure is not going to hold and the foundation we okayed is going to come crashing down into the canyon. She has brought love and laughter into my life."

I was very moved by his poetic description and marveled once again at his transformation. "What kind of husband would you say you are?"

"Certainly not a perfect husband. We have our ups and downs. I have a temper that can flare. When it does, I'm stubborn and mean. I have a terrible habit of getting caught up with work and forgetting to call. Look, you know what I have to go on. I keep saying to myself, 'Do it better, do it right, don't mess up.' I try. I try every day." He smiled. "She's a generous woman and she makes allowances for dumbness."

"What would you like to change if you could?" I realized that this blunt question might throw him off balance but decided to take the chance.

Larry looked out the window for a full minute without speaking. Turning to face me, he gave an answer that I will long treasure, one that captures the continuing emotional constriction and fear that so many of these young men feel but have a very hard time talking about. They are ashamed and lack the words. He said: "I have a difficult time showing love to my wife, even telling her that I love her. She complains that I don't show her enough affection. I'm aware of that. And I try to change it. But I can't because of my parents' marriage and divorce. I feel almost cursed. Sometimes when Grace comes to meet me here at the office, I want to jump up and hug her—but I can't."

Of course, women have complained since time immemorial that their men have trouble expressing tender loving feelings. Obviously this problem is not confined to children of divorce. But it's fair to say that the men in divorced families are conscious of this difficulty long before any woman brings it to their attention. They've known for years that they have inexpressible feelings and that their anxiety stops them from reaching out. They have rehearsed in their minds a hundred times the things they wanted to say to their parents. And then they couldn't do it. I would venture to say that many of the men raised in divorced families were conscious of their inhibitions and badly disappointed in themselves when they failed to break out of them. Some said they mastered the ploy of silent withdrawal because they had to protect themselves from becoming their mother's confidant as young adolescents. Used to a life of pulling away and hiding feelings, they could not break the habit even within a loving marriage.

Residues of Violence

WALKING BACK TO Larry's office after lunch, I asked a question that had been bothering me since the interview began. "Larry, how gone are the memories of your dad's violence?"

His steps slowed, the pain returned. "The fact that my folks got a divorce does not erase those memories. Not in the least. I try not to think about what happened between my parents but it's there, inside me. It's not really buried. And then I think about how close I came to being just like my father." He sighed deeply. "It's something that haunts me."

"Explain to me how."

"Violence is like hard wiring. If I don't keep fighting it, it can take over. Every time I lose my temper, I have to remember to keep my hands at my sides. Sometimes I walk away or leave the room. If I don't, I might explode. It's a silly thing but I used to wrestle with Grace for fun and I stopped because if we got into a certain clutch, I would worry that I would go too far. Like here's a woman I adore and I might hurt her. I would die before I hit her but I have to be careful. So to answer your question, it never goes away. I have to stay on guard." He came to an abrupt stop on the sidewalk and caught my arm. "Which reminds me. Grace made me promise to ask you about my teasing Alex. She's worried that I get too rough."

"She doesn't like you to tease Alex?" I asked, a little bewildered.

"It's one of the few things that Grace and I haven't been able to resolve between us. Grace wants me to ask you about it. Alex is a sensitive kid. I don't want to ridicule him or punish him for being sensitive so I tease him, to teach him to fight back. I have to admit I think it's pretty funny because the little guy does get angry when I tease him. He throws himself at me and starts to hit me with his fists and he sobs. He really gets out of control. He's been in trouble at preschool fighting with other kids."

"Does that concern you?"

"What concerns me is that I don't seem able to stop the teasing. I think I do get much too rough and excited. But I'm not able to control it, either. It's like a shadow play that happens between us. Alex is really so much like I was as a kid that it's scary."

I was very troubled with the interactions that Larry described. I struggled over whether to tell him that his continued and uncontrolled teasing of his son is a reenactment of his own violent relationship with his father. It could have grave consequences for the child, who at age three is already having trouble controlling his own aggressive impulses at preschool. This violent, teasing interchange, under the guise of play, obviously humiliates and upsets the boy and drives him to hit his father back. It reinforces Alex's own sense of helplessness. My dilemma, which has come up before in other interviews, is that I am not Larry's therapist or teacher. Throughout this study I've tried very hard to maintain an objective stance and not offer advice or even a referral for help unless there's a real emergency. At the same time, I knew that Grace was concerned and wanted my help. I also worried about the child. So I decided to support Grace's concern.

"This is a hard call, Larry. I agree with Grace that the child is becoming too upset with what should be pleasurable and lighthearted play. I think you should listen to her intuition and just play with Alex so you both enjoy laughing and being together. He's really too young to understand that you are teaching him to fight back. He probably thinks that you are really fighting with him and he loves you and can't stand that."

Larry looked at me for a long minute and then said a quiet, "I gotcha."

I thought it interesting that the residue of Larry's violent boyhood should show up in play with his son. He had been able to master his impulses in relation to women, but unbeknownst to him, the violence had crept into his relationship with the child he loved. I realized how little we know about human behavior and about the insidious legacy of family violence. On every questionnaire, Larry would have answered honestly that he had been fully able to escape being a violent person with his wife and his children. Who would have thought to ask him how he plays with his son?

A Window of Opportunity

I HAVE TOLD LARRY'S story in detail because it's a remarkable account of the mind of a boy who slowly, painfully, and successfully extricates himself from his violent origins. Larry shows us how divorce can provide a window of opportunity through which the child can climb to freedom—with the proviso that the growing child must provide his or her own energy, resourcefulness, and courage to make it happen. The divorce by itself won't do it. Larry's moral and emotional evolution from delinquent boy to loving husband, father, and responsible citizen captures the psychological steps needed. Like Dorothy in *The Wizard of Oz,* who relies on the help of the Scarecrow in search of a brain, the Tin Woodsman in want of a heart, and the Cowardly Lion in search of courage, a child growing up in a violent family needs the full use of his intelligence, capacity to love, and courage to climb out of the lower depths to which he has been exposed. He has to put together for himself a value system that rejects violence, respects women, and places decency and human kindness at the core. In his personal relationships, he has to achieve the capacity for love and intimacy without exploitation, loyalty to his family and friends, and responsibility to his professional community and society. Counter to the system in vogue in family courts that emphasizes the importance of continuity in parent-child relationships after the divorce, the child has to find the strength within himself to reject the violent parent and the values and attitudes that that person represents. If the child continues to embrace those values, he will repeat the ugliness that he was exposed to during his most impressionable years.

Although Larry rescued himself, he was helped by his mother's decision to divorce and her love for him and her dignity during the post-divorce years. She set an example of courage and faithfulness to her children that strengthened her son's ability to leave. The divorce that she undertook despite her fears and misgivings showed him that getting out was a better, braver way, and he learned from her example and found within himself the power to follow her lead and to leave behind the identity that he might very well have embraced had she remained trapped.

An Escape Hatch Blocked

WHAT ABOUT THE Carols of this world? Without one parent to help her escape the craziness of her family, what's in store for her?

At the end of our interview, Carol eagerly told me how she'd met Tom, a pilot for a major airline company. She recalled in great detail how their acquaintance progressed from smiles and nods to short conversations, to dates in New York and San Francisco, to their present arrangement in which Tom stays with Carol whenever he has layovers in San Francisco.

Then, as Carol chatted on, sounding for all the world like an enamored twenty-three-year-old instead of a forty-year-old who'd slept with over fifty men, my newly optimistic mood took a nosedive. "The thing is that he's married and he has two children. His family lives in New York and he's waiting for a good time to break up with his wife. Their marriage hasn't been good for years and he'd have left long ago if she hadn't had a second child. I do appreciate how careful Tom's being. He wants to make sure no one's hurt or left hanging. I know that when we do get married he'll be faithful to me. It will be such a relief to live together openly instead of having to keep our relationship secret and feel like we're sneaking around."

I struggled to keep the dismay I felt from showing. What Carol was describing so blithely was, of course, the oldest story in the book. A man with full family commitments making empty promises that he'd never keep. As long as Carol believed him and tolerated their arrangement, he'd stay. When or if she got too insistent or too unhappy and demanding, he'd probably leave her. The scenario was ancient and obvious. The trouble was, Carol didn't seem to have a clue.

"When did you learn that he was married?"

"You know, that's one of the few things we disagree about," she replied, still in the same upbeat, chatty tone, as if we'd been discussing shopping for shoes. "He says he told me right away, four years ago when we first met, that he was married with a little boy and a baby girl. But I don't remember that at all. It wasn't until two years later when we were so involved with each other that I first suspected, but I didn't want to ask. He made such an effort to spend all his free time with me and we were so happy, so I told myself that he couldn't have a wife or a family to go home to. Finally I did ask if he was married and I remember he told me 'kinda, sorta.' Well, I probably wouldn't have allowed myself to get so much involved had I known, but by then we were hopelessly in love, so what could I do?"

As I said earlier, parents in these chaotic intact marriages wreak untold havoc on their children who grow up terrified and miserable with a legacy they can't seem to escape. There is no window of opportunity for them to use because there is no one parent who is willing and perhaps able to put in the extraordinary effort required to bring about change for the child. As mature adults in their late thirties and forties, the men and women are still prisoners of warped expectations and profound needs. Their distorted sense of relationships and hunger for love combine to seriously affect their judgment. Some were in therapy for many years trying to close the door on their unhappy history and eventually succeeded in establishing a happier life. But others, like Carol, settle into a familiar place where the child watches from the wings, a bit player in someone else's drama. Utterly lost, drifting from relationship to relationship, or remaining stuck in unhappy marriages of their own, they settle for crumbs in love and life.

PART THREE

The Parentless Child: Paula

TWELVE

Growing Up Lonely

People ask me all the time if there's a best time to get a divorce. Isn't it easier, they wonder, if the child is still very young and won't have strong memories of the intact family? Or is it better to wait until children are nearly grown, with one foot out of the nest? Does the age of a child matter and should people contemplating divorce wait for a better time?

The answer, of course, is "it depends" on a host of factors, including the quality of the marriage (is it violence or boredom that's behind the decision) and the quality of the postdivorce family over the long haul. That said, it is clear from my work and others that in our divorce culture the youngest children tend to suffer the most. At an age when they need constant protection and loving nurturance, these young children have parents in turmoil. In many families this includes infants or toddlers who may have been tenderly cared for and suddenly experience a drastic change in that care. Their mothers go back to work and to night school to improve their financial status. Their fathers are less available. And they suffer.

Paula is the classic example of such a child and I have chosen her story to convey the experience of millions of children like her. At least half of the children in this country whose parents divorce are under the age of six when the breakup happens. Too young to understand the sudden changes in her family, Paula grew up brokenhearted and very angry. Her life story captures her continuing rage and the dramatic, self-destructive ways she found to express it. As we follow her life, we get a close look at how court-ordered visiting plays out from the child's perspective. In Paula's adult life, we gain a view of how children of divorce handle divorce with their own children.

PAULA STRODE INTO my office, sat down, shrugged her heavy backpack to the floor, and grinned. At age thirty-three, she looked fitter and healthier than she did at our last meeting ten years ago in Seattle when she was borderline anorexic, pale, chain-smoking, and ignoring the salad she had ordered for lunch.

She also looked considerably older, with weathered skin and deep lines in her forehead.

"Do you remember our last visit?" I asked, wondering if she was aware of how much she had changed.

Paula startled me by throwing back her head and laughing in a throaty, smoker's voice. "I don't remember it at all, zip, nada. You should erase everything and anything I said back then because I was probably high on cocaine. I've been in recovery for two years now and things that were numbed out are starting to come back . . . but that time in my life is still a total blur."

I looked more closely at Paula. She still retained vestiges of the tough street kid she had been—a tenseness in her jaw and squared-off shoulders that could carry any burden you'd care to toss at her—but she was softer now, less cocky, somehow less strident. Her backpack was filled with college textbooks, her green eyes were bright and direct, and she was plainly eager and able to tell her story.

Even as she began to talk, I could feel a sigh of relief somewhere inside me. Paula was one of those children who, after her parents divorced, literally and unceasingly had to raise herself. Watching her grow up from afar, there were times that I despaired for her well-being, wondering if she had any chance of ever attaining a normal adult life.

There is no comparison for this situation within intact families. We heard about families in which the father lost his job, the mother fell chronically ill, or a fire destroyed all the family's possessions. But none of these sudden losses or setbacks within intact families matched what happened to little Paula, whose whole world collapsed in less than one month's time. The closest comparable experience for children in intact families is the sudden death of a beloved parent. Fortunately, unlike divorce, death of a young parent is uncommon in this country.

Paula and I settled in for a heart-to-heart talk that lasted three and a half hours. She told me that her memory of the postdivorce years is "a blur," but I remembered this little girl and her family quite clearly. The younger of two children, Paula was four years old when her young parents separated. Her father, a handsome, charming man from an affluent family, had been a pharmacist who owned three drugstores. He had been a devoted husband, proud of his pretty, lively wife, and close to his daughters, who resembled him in their looks and gestures. He delighted in the likeness and loved to take them both to the local playground where people admired the children's high spirits and friendliness. Unfortunately, he made some very bad investments in the market on the advice of a friend who deceived him, and trying desperately to cover his losses and keep the information from his wife and parents, he got deeper into debt. By the time Paula turned three, he could no longer hide his financial ruin. Forced into bankruptcy, he had to sell the three stores and have his other assets frozen. Overcome with guilt, he could not bear coming home to his wife and children.

Soon Paula's parents began to fight, often and loudly. Paula's mother, a cheerful woman who enjoyed taking care of her home and her children, became increasingly desperate as her husband spent more time away from home. The marriage ended when Paula's father came home one Christmas Eve too upset and depressed about his financial problems to go to the family party given by his parents. When Paula's mother accused him of not caring about her and the children, he exploded—hitting her for the first and only time. The children were standing three feet away, eyes bulging in terror. After their agitated father ran out of the house, the children watched their mother as she sat heavily in a chair, her head buried in her sweater, rocking back and forth. Paula wedged herself into the chair beside her weeping mother. "Are you scared of Daddy, Mom?" her mother remembers Paula asking. When her mother nodded, Paula silently took her "Blankie" and wrapped it around her mother's shoulders.

The story of Paula's family is all too common. Most people are familiar with the fact that nearly half of all first marriages end in divorce. But what they don't know is that each year an estimated five hundred thousand children under the age of six find themselves in Paula's shoes—small, uncomprehending, frightened, and vulnerable.[1] As they grow up, they retain very few memories of life before the divorce with two parents at home. Most of what they know and remember stems from being raised in the postdivorce family. The family that created them simply vanished.

As happens to so many children of divorce, life changed radically for Paula and her sister after the separation. Their mother had left college after her freshman year to elope and had spent her married life involved in child-centered activities around her home. She had been active in both children's nursery schools and had ferried Joan and then Paula to friends' houses, to swimming lessons, to the park to play, and out for ice cream afterward. After Joan started kindergarten, this at-home mom became involved in the PTA and was often at the elementary school, helping in the classroom and organizing school events. She drove for every field trip and was present at every class event and party. She fetched Joan and Paula to and from school and had snacks for them at home afterward. A teenaged girl who lived down the street always babysat on Saturday evenings when the parents went out. The only other times Paula and her sister were separated from their mother was once a year when their parents went away for a long weekend together and they were cared for by their paternal grandparents.

For Paula, divorce meant that she lost the three things that had always anchored her—her mother, her father, and the comforting routines of her life. Only now, at age thirty-three, can Paula put the magnitude of these losses into words: "I don't remember anything except living together and then not. I don't remember anybody explaining anything to me. Suddenly, there was no one there. I spent so much time alone that I tried to become my own company. But how can you do that as a four-year-old child? I would go for days without saying a word."

No More Security Blanket

After the separation Paula's mother was in dire financial straits. The bankruptcy left both her and her ex-husband destitute. He could not afford to pay alimony or child support. For a while, the young mother's only financial support came from her husband's parents, who sympathized with her plight and sent money each month to help pay for food and health insurance. Without marketable skills, she went to work full-time at what was then minimum wage. At the end of each month, after she had paid the household expenses and the babysitter, she had sixty dollars left over. In the space of just a few months, this cheerful, chatty, always available young mother whom Paula and Joan had known and counted on was transformed into a strained, quiet, driven, desperately tired stranger who came home only to scream at her daughters and the babysitter for not cleaning up the mess in the house or to sit, silent and resentful, eating the TV dinners that had replaced home-cooked meals. Every night she stumbled directly to her bedroom after ordering her daughters to bed without the stories and cuddling they had always shared together.

Paula's mother is one of an army of women for whom divorce brings economic nightmares. The statistics are well documented.[2] Divorced mothers as a group earn a lot less than divorced fathers do, and child support does not make up the difference. Studies show that women and children who were in the upper economic group prior to divorce suffer the most precipitous decline in income. In 1991, 40 percent of all divorced women with children were living below the poverty level. The situation was even more desperate for those women with children below the age of six, like Paula's mother. Over half of these mostly younger women with young children were living below the poverty level. Divorced women are not only poor after divorce but remain poor for many years.[3] This is because, despite improved collection of child support, the average amount that they receive, when it is paid, is much less than the cost of raising a child. Moreover, when the women seek employment, many, like Paula's mother, are handicapped in the marketplace. They lack the requisite skills to begin with or they have spent the years prior to the divorce taking care of children and working part-time or working full-time as homemakers. After the divorce they are faced with the double burden of acquiring a new education or updating their former skills and simultaneously supporting their children and themselves. Many take night jobs, shift jobs, temp jobs, or real estate jobs that keep them away from home all weekend. They are physically exhausted and emotionally depleted as they run in place, like the Red Queen in *Alice in Wonderland*—the faster she runs, the more she stays in one place. Their valiant efforts to feed, clothe, and house their children tragically diminishes their availability as parents. As Paula told me, "I have no memory of her sitting down and reading to me or playing or just hanging out. It still makes me mad and sad to think about this."

Of course, in the flesh-and-blood world of a child living in a post-divorce family, economic issues are not separate from psychological issues—a fact that is rarely talked about. After divorce, the drop in income carries other losses that cannot be measured in dollars and cents, like being forced to move away from friends in a familiar neighborhood to less expensive housing, like being exposed to the violence and chaos of a bad neighborhood, like being sent to a more crowded school with overwhelmed teachers. The extras that make life comfortable for a child are lost. Special weekend activities, movies, summer camps, swimming lessons, piano and ballet lessons, uniforms for athletic teams, and other after-school activities, not to mention private schools, are the first to go. Later on, there is the real possibility that children from a father's second marriage will receive more resources and be given greater opportunities than the child of divorce whose mother does not remarry. The narrowing of educational opportunities and usurping of their place within the family have a chilling effect on children of divorce. Why aim high when you've been pushed to the bottom of the ladder with others blocking your way?

Loss of Structure

I VIVIDLY REMEMBER the first time I saw Paula six months after her parents had separated. A small, wiry child with unkempt, dark curly hair and vivid green eyes, she roamed my playroom restlessly, too anxious to settle down and play. As she picked up and threw down toy after toy, I tried to ask her about her life, her house, her parents, her school, and her sister. Instead, she talked endlessly about her pet dog, Daisy, and ignored all my questions. Then she startled me—for the first of many times—when she suddenly stopped her anxious wandering and said clearly, "I'm going to find a new mommy."

Here was a child overwhelmed with anxiety. The world had changed overnight into an incomprehensible, unpredictable place in which her central, all-important, caregiving mother had disappeared and was replaced by a series of hastily chosen, low-paid babysitters and a person who resembled her mother but who had little energy or time left over for Paula. Paula's father, while largely absent from the everyday routines during her early childhood, had brought presents and had played with Paula and her sister when he lived at home. After the separation, his absences grew longer, and after the first year, he disappeared for several years. Paula had lost her place in the world from being a cherished, well-cared-for, protected child who was the centerpiece of the family life to being a child who felt she was a leftover from a failed marriage and a burden around her mother's neck. At age four these losses cannot be put into words. They are felt and expressed in overwhelming internal panic. Trust and spontaneity, which are the outward manifestations of feeling loved and nurtured, disappear as panic and anxiety give way to disappointment and anger.

Realizing that their daughter-in-law would never be able to earn a larger income without more training, Paula's grandparents offered to pay her mom's tuition if she went back to school. Summoning a steely resolve and reserves of determination that previously had not been evident in her personality as a mother and homemaker, Paula's mom enrolled in college seven months after the separation.

Although she was intent on forging a better life for herself and her children for the long haul, their mother's return to college resulted in further losses for Paula and her sister. She left the house at seven o'clock to attend classes five mornings a week. She worked from noon to six o'clock and then all day on Saturday to maintain her full-time paycheck. At night, she would study. Paula, still a preschooler, was cared for twelve hours per day at a babysitter's house with five other young children. Nine-year-old Joan walked herself to school and then came home to an empty house.

After Paula started school she was in day care before school and then went home with Joan, who was expected to look after herself and her little sister until their mother returned home after six-thirty at night. Joan was resentful and overwhelmed with the responsibility of caring for Paula every day and for making sure the house was picked up and that dinner was in the oven by the time her mom got home. Both sisters remember turning off the TV and racing around tidying the house as their mother's car drove up the driveway. Both sisters also remember numerous times when Joan, angry and frustrated, threw things at Paula and locked her out of the home. They learned, early on, to keep silent about their conflicts and resentments since meeting their mother at the door with their troubles resulted in sharp, cutting remarks and punishment for both sisters. Increasingly their mother would say that she had no time to deal with them and would simply go into her bedroom and shut the door. The price of maintaining their mother's presence and some semblance of family harmony was to hide their feelings and to pretend that things were fine. When this happened the mother and daughters would eat dinner with little conversation and then their mother would study while Paula and Joan did their homework or watched TV. When quarrels did break out or tensions escalated into whining and fighting, Mom would leave.

Gradually, Paula's memory of having a mother who took joy in her children's everyday ups and downs and who thoughtfully anticipated her children's needs and gratified their wishes simply faded. In the hard times and strain of the postdivorce years, the image of her mother was recast and with it Paula's image of herself. Again, it takes years for these transformations to be understood and to be voiced. All of the children in our study who experienced the divorce when they were preschoolers, except a few whose parents maintained two well-functioning households, felt abandoned and neglected as little children. They lost their mothers to full-time employment, her return to school, and the mother's efforts to establish her social life. They also felt abandoned by their fathers, who worked full-time and similarly got caught up in dating. These years remain very painful memories.

With divorce, preschool children lose the benefits of a structured childhood, which has serious consequences for their development. Children need regular routines—bedtimes, naptimes, mealtimes, playtimes. Even adolescents need household routines. Such stability gives teenagers the freedom to test their aggression and to learn self-control from observing that life has uniformity and rules. But after a divorce, households are typically disorganized. Mealtimes are helter-skelter, children make their own lunches, bedtime is haphazard. This is almost always true at the time of the breakup, but the chaos can continue for many years if, as in Paula's case, the mother embarks on a new, demanding schedule and cannot restore the previous routines. The fallout has many faces. Without a regular bedtime, a child wakes up tired and cranky and won't learn well at school. Older children given the task of caring for younger siblings feel angry and resentful. The responsible parent looks and feels exhausted, pressed to the limit of human endurance.

Parents need to know that it's extremely important to restore routines as quickly as possible after divorce. This structure helps children resume their regular school activities, learning, and friendships. These are the rungs of their developmental ladder. Actually, many divorced parents know this but are too pressured to put their knowledge to work. Also, as they soon find out, rules established in one home can be undone in the other. Routines and bedtimes vary in each parents' home. In some parents' homes the preschool child sleeps with the parent regularly whereas in others the child has her own room. So-called junk food and unlimited television are permitted in one home and forbidden in the other. Nudity is the mode in one household and frowned on in the other. (In one family the five-year-old child returned from a visit to her father's home full of excitement about the tattoos on his new girlfriend's upper thigh.) These seemingly small differences can become major issues that are never settled and contribute to the difficulty of stabilizing the life of the preschool child in the divorced family.

The Loneliness of the Youngest Children of Divorce

When I asked Paula-the-Adult to tell me the memories of Paula-the-Child, she said, "I remember that I was in trouble and I remember anger. I was always angry with somebody. I don't think the divorce itself really affected me. What affected me was that my mom wasn't around. I missed that we were not a regular family. I had nobody to talk to. I didn't have any guidance. I know that Mom turned herself inside out to support us and I'll always be grateful to her, but I remember her as absent. There were times when Mom would come home late from work and I'd need help with something for school. She'd get really uptight because she'd have an exam the next day and she needed to study. She'd tell me I'd have to do the best I could on my own for my school project because she needed to study. Then she'd lock herself in the bathroom. I remember sitting on the floor outside the bathroom door, listening to her turn the pages in her textbook."

Although Paula's material needs for food and shelter were taken care of, she felt abandoned. Years later, Paula and other children who are very young when their parents divorce remember one thing most: a vast, unsoothable sense of loneliness. They're angry about being left so much to themselves. They know that their parents were overwhelmed by their own changed circumstances, but that's not grounds for forgiveness. Those who shuttled back and forth between two homes complain of going from mommy's sitter to daddy's sitter without spending enough time with either parent.

Little children who cannot comprehend their parents' dilemmas conclude that they're left alone because they aren't important, particularly valued, or interesting to any adult. They blame themselves for being naughty to explain why their mothers go away. They blame their mothers for being faithless. When they're older, they tend to linger at their playmates' homes, hoping that they'll be invited to stay for supper or maybe for the evening. Some have the very secret fantasy that they'll be invited to join the other child's family.

Children at very young ages learn to be sensitive to their parents' moods. In some of our heartbreaking videos of families going through a divorce, a toddler can be seen climbing onto her mother's lap and stroking her cheek to comfort her. While grateful for attention, children learn not to expect or demand it. Some resourceful children learn to entertain themselves by watching many hours of television, but others are too little or too sad and sit listlessly, waiting for the parent to return or to get her attention. Others turn to animals for companionship and reciprocity of unconditional love.

Recent scientific findings show that these little preschool children are right to feel seriously deprived.[4] Young children need continuous interaction with caring, nurturing grown-ups to learn about human emotions and to develop their capacity to think. Being fed and put to bed is a tiny fraction of what they need. Parents must provide time and energy to talk, play, read, and pay attention to their young children. But where will the overwhelmed recently divorced parent find the time and the energy for this?

In comparing the overall adjustment of young adults in our study with how old they were when their parents divorced, we found that the youngest looked the worst off and had the hardest time growing up.[5] Nearly all lost their mothers to the workplace and the stresses of single parenthood. Their feelings of loneliness and anger at both parents carried over into later school years and adolescence. At the twenty-five-year mark, now between twenty-eight and thirty-two years old, they are doing less well in the workplace and in relationships compared with children who were older at the time of the breakup. They have a lower level of confidence about their chances of marrying successfully and are more worried about being betrayed. Only one of the preschool girls in our study is now in a happy, stable marriage while one other is living happily with a man without plans to marry any time soon. Another, who seemed happily married, suddenly left her devoted husband to live with a former high school lover and took her own preschool daughter with her. Most of the girls in this group have not found good jobs or satisfying careers. Several operate small and rather chancy businesses out of their homes. A few are cleaning houses to support themselves. Those who had good educational support have found rewarding careers but are having trouble with men. The boys are in similar straits. Most of the men in our study who led lonely, isolated lives came out of this group.

In looking over the records of these youngest children of divorce, I was mystified by the fact that good remarriages did not seem to help them overcome the trauma of divorce. Because their mothers were relatively young and found new husbands within a few years, many children soon regained the protection and financial advantages of an intact family. Several had loving stepfathers and stepmothers who cared for them tenderly and were central figures in the children's lives from very early on. But I finally realized that, for most of these children, stepparents remained secondary figures compared to their attachment to their biological parents. Relationships with stepparents generally lack the passionate commitment that children feel about their parents. It was as if they had a slot in their minds for parents and another for stepparents and the two were kept permanently separate. They liked their "steps" a lot and appreciated their kindness and interest. Sometimes they loved them and clearly respected and admired their stepparent more than they respected their biological parent. But they did not worry about their "steps" or pity them or cry for them in the same way they did for their "real" moms and dads. They were not as vulnerable to feeling rejected by a stepparent. One young man in his early twenties who had a very loving stepfather from the age of seven and who rarely saw his biological dad said it clearly: "My stepfather could be Saint Francis or Saint Anthony. He could walk on water. But he would not take away the hurt I feel about my father." Children are remarkably faithful to their parents in their love, anger, and suffering throughout their lives.

The Motherless Child

At our meeting five years after the divorce, Paula, then age nine, was engrossed in her pet rabbit, Racer. She spent hours every day feeding and taking care of Racer. She told me that she liked her friends but she didn't like her teacher. She said soberly that she didn't like her mother or her sister. She refused to talk about her father. It was at this interview that Paula startled me again with one of the most upsetting statements I've ever heard from a child. "I don't want to be anything when I grow up. I don't like the idea of growing up. I just have to grow up." In the notes I wrote after this interview I recorded my impressions of nine-year-old Paula: "She doesn't see family life as ever getting better. Her fate is that of difficulties. She couldn't elaborate; she was just wary of the future."

Paula's third-grade teacher also reported her impressions to me: "Paula is a quiet and cooperative child in the classroom. She doesn't relate well to adults and prefers to avoid connection and interaction with adults. Her affect is bland. She doesn't show interest in any subject or activity. She never talks about her family. She's scarcely animated in class." Paula's teacher was describing a depressed child.

By now, Paula's mother, by dint of heroic effort, had graduated from college with a degree in hotel management and had secured a much higher-paying job as an assistant manager at a downtown hotel. Her daily commute to the city meant that she had to leave by 7 A.M. and she often didn't return until after 7 P.M. Her new job conferred higher status and vastly improved her self-esteem. The job also demanded more of her time and energy. To be considered for promotion to manager, Paula's mother started working toward a master's degree, which meant taking classes two evenings per week. Still an attractive and now poised and self-assured young woman, Paula's mom started dating a man she met at work. Feeling desired and being treated romantically was intoxicating to her after so many years of strenuous, unrelenting work. She acquiesced to being whisked away overnight and for getaway weekends with her new lover.

It is one of the cruel paradoxes of this and many divorces, especially for the preschool children, that the more the mother gained the more her children lost. The mother's advances in education and in employment and her very human need for adult love and play all enhanced her life and took her more and more away from the lives of her children. While highly valuing education and strictly demanding that her daughters do well in school, Paula's mother was rarely there to oversee or to help with schoolwork. She did not notice, and her daughters didn't tell her, when they were having problems or difficulties. Notes from the school were left crumpled in backpacks. This mother was present so little at the school that several teachers reported that they barely knew who she was. Paula and Joan were not encouraged to participate in after-school activities, nor would their mom have been able to attend extracurricular events. While friends were driven to piano and ballet lessons, Paula and Joan continued to walk home to an empty house. Being bright children, they got passing grades in school and learned to get by without getting into trouble that would call the teacher's attention to them. (A depressed child often goes unnoticed in school, especially if she is doing passing work.) What was missing was the feeling that their efforts were noticed and valued. Lost was a sense that their progress as children—learning to study, acquiring an excitement in learning, developing special talents and having talent appreciated and fostered—really mattered. They learned to comply with adult demands but without a growing inner sense of confidence and direction.

When their marriages fail there is no way most mothers can maintain the same level of physical and emotional involvement with their children. As Paula and every other young child of divorce told me, the biggest loss they faced was the loss of their mother. One day she was there, giving hugs of encouragement, fetching and carrying as needed, and the next day she was out the door, giving orders as she exited. For young children, the sudden loss of mommy's attention is unimaginably traumatic—akin to slowly freezing after being plucked from a warm, balmy climate. Your mother is your whole world. She provides food and comfort. Under her watchful approval, you experience growth and joy in your own development. And then you're placed in the care of strangers. Tragically, in their thankless task of providing everything to keep the family afloat, mothers often lose the ability to keep their primary emotional investment in their children.

The focus of divorce policy and intervention has centered on the loss of the father, which is profound for many divorced children. But the loss of a mother pervades and forever changes the way a child, especially a young child, experiences the world. For the preschool children in our study the loss of their mother was central and their suffering was enduring. Twenty-five years later they cried as they remembered, "My mother was really not there. No one was there." Talking to these children at that time and as they recalled their childhoods made me think of the song "Sometimes I Feel Like a Motherless Child." This emotional cut-off—from feeling that you are the center of your mother's attention to feeling that you are a peripheral appendage—remains an enduring part of mother-child relationships in many divorced families. While mothers desperately struggle to raise their children alone, many enriching parts of their shared lives must change. Mothers no longer have the time to witness and participate in their child's everyday life. They don't have the luxury to plan playdates and have friends to the house. Baking and cooking are abandoned for convenience meals. There is no time to monitor a child's small ups and downs, their worries and achievements; there is no other parent with whom to share and to strategize the child's future. Budding talent and potential trouble areas are overlooked in the mad rush to get out of the house and to get to bed in order to have the energy to meet another day. Overseeing table manners and teaching the niceties of life give way to making sure clothes are washed and the house is presentable. Fatigue and anxiety consume tolerance, softness, and cheeriness. There arises a harsher, stricter personality in which smiles are often forced and irritability reigns. The transformation of one's mother and the loss of her availability is abrupt and, for many children of divorce, permanent. It is the hidden but most significant loss for young children following divorce, and we have almost completely overlooked its impact.

Paula's wonderful care of her pet rabbit reflects this loss. In mothering the rabbit, she rediscovers and resurrects the loving mother she has lost. By identifying with the mother she loves, she rehearses the memory, keeping it fresh and alive. She is in her imagination the well-cared-for rabbit, and she is also the loving available mother whom she loved and lost when she was four years old.

Of course, there are many millions of married mothers of young children who work full-time, but they have a husband to help them with the job of parenting when both return home in the evening. This joint support is critical for those who want or need to work while raising young children. Two parents can spell each other in daily routines and when children fall sick. Recent studies show that compared with fathers a decade ago, fathers in today's two-income families spend more time with their young children. There really are four hands rather than two. Intact families with two people working also have higher incomes than single-parent families and can spend more on child care and other kinds of help. I recall one divorced mother who, having done one too many loads of laundry at 3 A.M., decided to hell with sleep, she would just stay up all night every night to get everything done. She pulled it off for three days and then collapsed. The parent who shares responsibility with the other parent works very hard but is not on permanent, continual overload with the full responsibility for making every decision alone, with taking care of every bill, with worrying about every needed repair. She can take time out even after a busy tiring day to sit on the floor and play with her toddler. She can enjoy the child, replenish her own emotional reserves, and allow herself a few happy hours to herself even once or twice a week. In our comparison group of intact families, most of the women reduced their work hours when their first child was very young. If they had more children, more than half dropped out of the workforce for a few years and went back when the youngest entered grade school. Unlike the single parent striving alone, these were choices they could afford to make.

THIRTEEN

Court-Ordered Visiting, the Child's View

Shortly after her eighth birthday, Paula's father reentered her life. Like many men after divorce, he eventually used the crisis to pull his life together and was now feeling chipper about himself and recovered from his financial debacle and humiliating betrayal by a trusted friend. Now he genuinely wanted to spend time with his children, to get to know them again, to be given a second chance.

How much or how often fathers should visit their children is a matter of endless public debate and friction between advocates for mothers' rights and fathers' rights. Many judges, mediators, and mental health professionals who work in divorce believe that the amount of visiting by the father fluctuates with the level of anger between the parents. They assume that the mother's anger at the father is to blame when the father's visits lapse or significantly decrease. This may be the case immediately after the breakup but in the years after divorce many other influences affect the frequency or infrequency of visiting. A major study of father visiting in eight states showed hardly any links between the mother's anger and the father's visits.[1] Courts don't generally see these fluctuations because they are focused on the period of the marital breakup.

In Larry's story, we talked about fathers and how their role changes after divorce. Here I want to focus more deeply on one aspect of that change—the nature of visiting and how it can both help and hinder parent-child relationships.

One important influence on a father's visiting pattern over time is the attitude of his second or third wife and her interest in the children of the first marriage. I'll describe the stepmother's role at length in Chapter 20, but for now I just want to note that generally the man is eager to please the new woman. He has sustained one failure already and is likely to yield to his new wife in setting rules for the children's visits. In many homes, she calls the shots that determine whether visiting is a happy or dreaded occasion.

Another factor in visiting patterns is the father's overall sense of well-being. When a man changes his life and increases his self-confidence, his desire to visit his children can skyrocket. This is what happened with Paula's father, who reentered her life after a four-year absence. Like so many other men who are physically ill or psychologically depressed during and immediately after divorce, he was uncomfortable about visiting. "I felt I had nothing to offer them," he said a year after the breakup. But when he felt better, he wanted to initiate contact. Such factors also explain the tremendous instability and fluctuations in how many fathers visit their children in the years after divorce. In short, as the man goes up and down, the visiting goes up and down.

When Paula's father reappeared, both the children and their mother were surprised. Their lives had been based on his absence, and now, like Lazarus, he was back. The children missed him but they had given up expecting him to be an important part of their daily lives ever again. In some families, the father returns after the mother has remarried—and this poses a threat to the emerging role of the stepfather. Whatever the circumstances, the father's reentry opens a new chapter in family life, which is plagued by an unhappy question in the children's minds: since he disappeared once, will he disappear again?

Paula's father was now managing a large variety store and living in one of his family's apartment buildings in Santa Rosa, a city about an hour to the north. Almost immediately the two parents resumed fighting. They could not agree on a visiting schedule, and years of unpaid or poorly paid child support remained a bitter, unresolved issue. Anger arose with new vigor. When Paula's mom threatened to block their visits Paula's dad took her to court, whereupon a judge set child support and a visitation schedule. Paula's dad was to have the children for two weekends each month, from Friday after school until Sunday night at six o'clock. Holidays would be rotated every other year. The children would reside with the father during the full month of July. For the next three years Paula and Joan, despite their many protests, were held to this schedule as if they were factory workers punching a time clock.

The visiting schedule was set up on the basis of a compromise meeting the demands of both parents. The wishes and needs of each child—now eight and thirteen years old—were never consulted or considered. It's shocking to realize how often this goes on throughout the country. Typically children are not asked to participate in formulating court-ordered or mediated plans that make for radical changes in their lives. Neither parent asked either Joan or Paula how they felt about it. After their day in court, each parent retreated into an entrenched position, rigidly adhering to court orders and communicating with each other as little as possible.

After his long absence, the children hardly knew their father. Paula, in her characteristic blunt manner, retreated into a sulky silence. For her part, Joan wailed, "Where is he going to take us? What will I do there? What should I tell my friends? Why do I have to go?"

Joan and Paula were excited at the prospect of having a real-life dad like other children but they couldn't understand where he had been the last few years. They didn't know how to ask this and he did not explain. They were also frightened of being left alone with a strange man in an unfamiliar place. Joan, as a young adolescent, was especially embarrassed about having her first menstrual period at her father's home. She worried sick about how she would tell him.

In this family and many others, no one talked about how the children would spend time with their father. No one thought to help the man or the daughters figure out ways to get to know one another after such a long absence. The parents never met alone or with an adviser to explain the children's interests or their natural concern about how the visits would cut into their social lives and friendships. The court made no provision for a gradual implementation of the new schedule. Basically the children were treated like objects and sent off on the assumption that of course everything would work out for the best. Paula's mom arranged for a neighbor to take the girls to the bus station for the trip up to Santa Rosa every other Friday afternoon. Their dad met them at the depot or, if he was working late, had them take a cab to his apartment.

Unaware of his children's anxieties, the father did what he remembered doing when they were young. He took them to the playground. When this bombed, he took them to the movies. But with a limited selection of G-rated films in Santa Rosa, he finally resorted to the video store. As time wore on, the girls spent their weekends watching television or videos or tagging along with their father while he did routine errands. Occasionally, he would take them to an amusement park, especially if he had a girlfriend along. Sometimes he helped with homework. He tried his best to be a good father and there was no question that he loved them and looked forward to their visits. But he was at sea. The four-year absence plus the sullen resentment of the children at the disruption of their social lives were very hard for him to overcome. The hardest was when he went out on dates in the evening and Paula and Joan were left alone in the apartment complex. There were few other children to play with. Neither girl liked to venture out alone. Once they tiptoed down to the small swimming pool near their apartment, only to be set upon by a group of older boys who teased and frightened them. They never went back.

At first, Paula and Joan were allowed to call their friends in Marin from Santa Rosa, but when their mom refused to share in the long-distance bills, telephone calls were barred. When play invitations and friends' birthday parties fell on a Santa Rosa weekend, they could not go. Joan, now in junior high school, had many weekend projects that involved working with an assigned group. She was told that she could only work with her group after six o'clock on Sunday evenings, after she got back from Santa Rosa. When other parents offered to have Joan or Paula stay with them so that school projects could be facilitated, their dad refused. This was, he claimed, his only time for seeing his daughters. Having regular time with them was important to him in that it helped him stabilize his life and develop his sense of being a responsible person and father. But he really didn't know them as individuals. He didn't ask and no one helped him catch up with the important years of growth that he had missed. Having little experience in the daily life of children, he was not aware of their interests or needs and fully expected that they would conform to *his* life. He was content with the arrangement and only vaguely aware that they were not.

Joan's perspective on the visiting was entirely different from that of her father. She felt increasingly distressed at losing out on school and friends and was intensely angry at her father and at the court for intervening in her life without warrant. When I spoke with her on her fourteenth birthday, she asked me with great urgency, "How old do I have to be before I can refuse to visit my father?" She explained, "I feel like a stranger at his place. I don't feel comfortable there. I have no friends and there's nothing for me to do."

"Why do you go?" I asked, trying to find out what she had been told and what she understood about the purpose of her bimonthly trips.

"Because I have to," she replied.

"Why do you have to?"

"I don't really know," Joan said. "Some silly judge said that I had to. I have to go two weekends every month and all July."

"Does your father want to see you?"

"I don't think so." She frowned. "He doesn't love me. People who love people respect them. He never asks me whether I want to come or what I want to do. He never gives me permission not to come. He was different when he lived with us."

I admit that I found her protest both rational and convincing. Since she had been given no say over her free time, how could she think differently? She was keenly aware that none of her friends had such obligations. I was also concerned by the strength of her feeling that her father and "some silly judge" had treated her unjustly. As a young teenager, she was trying to establish her own ideas and values, yet the adults who held authority over her life set a questionable example.

"What happens when you ask him if you can go to a weekend school activity?"

Tears welled in Joan's eyes. "He won't let me change. I tried. He says that's his time." She shook her head sadly. Then in a rush she added, "When summer comes, all the other kids in my class look forward to it. I dread it. I hate July. It's terrible for me. Last July I cried the whole month and thought, why am I being sentenced? What crime did I commit? I was so lonely and I missed my friends. Paula and I would cry ourselves to sleep every night. I felt like a second-class citizen."

After this interview, I worried about Joan. Surely her conclusion that she was being sentenced by the court, like someone who had broken the law, to spend lonely summers with her father was hurtful to her and would not contribute to her loving or respecting him then or in the future. Her phrase "second-class citizen" reverberated in my mind.

For her part, Paula's mom quickly came to appreciate the new freedom offered by two childless weekends per month. She could spend Friday nights in the city with her boyfriend and long weekends catching up on work, sleeping, and reading the Sunday paper. She became as protective as her ex-husband about keeping the schedule as planned. She turned a deaf ear to Joan's and Paula's complaints that their social life was being disrupted, that school projects weren't getting done, and that Santa Rosa was boring. The girls' initial excitement at seeing their father quickly faded to grumbling, resentment, and protests. When neither parent showed a willingness to listen or to change the arrangement, complaints gradually subsided into sullen acceptance and apathy. Paula displayed a rare moment of animation when I asked her about her visits with her father during our five-year follow-up visit. Her cheeks growing pink with indignation, she burst out, "Racer can't come on the bus and Daddy won't drive down to get us. Mom doesn't take good care of Racer while I'm gone and sometimes he doesn't even have water when I get back!"

Years later, Paula said, "I hated it there. I don't think it's good for children to spend two weekends with one parent and then go back to the other home. It's really hard. When you're a child, you're trying to discover who you are and to have friends. Their plan was totally disruptive to me. My friends got so they wouldn't even invite me on the weekends I was home. Dad tried to connect with us but he didn't."

"How did you manage?"

"Do you really want to know?" said Paula, smiling in recollection at her sly behavior as a child.

I nodded.

"I would pretend all weekend to myself that I wasn't really there."

I smiled, too, thinking to myself how little we credit children with being able to defeat our best-laid plans. Undoubtedly Paula's father and the judge thought that the court order granting regular visiting had established the groundwork for a good father-child relationship. But all the king's horses and all the king's men failed to put the relationship together again. Little Paula managed to trump all these grown-up plans by resolving that she "wasn't really there."

Sadly for all children in this study, court-ordered visiting failed in its very important purpose of bringing father and children together in a renewed loving relationship. The goal was laudable. But the abruptness of the visits and a schedule that was never shaped to fit their needs sabotaged this ideal. How could it have been done any differently? For starters, the father and children would have benefited from an overture, beginning with shorter visits that gradually increased in time so that Paula, Joan, and their dad could have made mutual plans. Obviously, this father didn't have a clue of what to do with young girls and *no one helped him.* Like many fathers we saw at our center, he would have been very responsive to advice about what to do during visits with his children. Undoubtedly he loved his daughters. Most fathers are eager for advice if it is offered tactfully, and when they test it out, they find it helpful with their children. They especially don't want to play Santa Claus. Handled rigidly and without help for parents and children, this kind of visiting is a lost opportunity for all.

In good intact families, children are not ordered to spend major blocks of time with one parent or another on a rigid schedule about which they have no say. Why treat children of divorce with less consideration?

The outcome for Joan was more serious. I talked with her shortly after she graduated from college.

"Tell me about your dad," I said.

"I haven't seen much of him since I graduated from high school," she replied with a shrug.

"Did he help with your college tuition?"

"Well, not much. He sent me money from time to time. But he never really helped with tuition." Joan was bitter. "My mom had to mortgage our house."

I was not surprised at her anger but I wondered if other feelings lay buried under the surface, especially feelings of love, disappointment, or regret. "Did you ever make any attempt to get closer to him?"

She answered angrily. "I remember forever those dreary weekends and those lonely Julys without my friends when I cried my eyes out. I have no reason in the world to be in contact with him and so why should I bother?"

There was no mistaking Joan's anger and sense of having been treated unjustly by powerful forces over which she had no control. As we talked, I had a sad sense that both father and daughter had missed a unique opportunity to get to know and cherish each other. Their spontaneous interest in one another had been blocked by a system that could only antagonize an adolescent and discourage a father from having to make the effort to find points of mutual interest with his daughter. By relying on his "rights," he lost her. What a pity. How foolish we are to think that we can legislate or direct the human heart.

When Joan was twenty-eight years old I asked her about her social life. "Oh, I go out a lot," she said. "And I get hurt a lot. Maybe it has to do with my being dominated all those years by my dad and the court. But it's hard for me to stand up for what I want. I never learned to fight for myself." Joan clearly made a connection between the powerlessness she felt as a child and her current relationships with men. If she is right—and I believe she is—then our interventions are not only misguided but may have harmed an entire generation of young people who grew up under similar circumstances. How many are still reacting to their feelings of having been bullied and made to feel powerless?

Two Wrongs Don't Make a Right

THE AMERICAN LEGAL system is under the impression that its activities and decisions are geared toward safeguarding children after divorce. But I have rarely met a child who felt protected by this system. On the contrary, most children would be very surprised to hear that any judge, attorney, mediator, or anyone else had their interests at heart when setting up court-ordered visiting. Many do not feel protected by their own parents in the planning of visiting or custody. Instead, they feel silenced. The visiting schedule, which the children deem arbitrary and oppressive, is made without their interests and wishes in mind.

When they were preschoolers, how the time was parsed out was less of an issue. But as they grew up, went to new schools, made new friends, took up sports and other organized activities with their peers, the court-ordered visiting that worked when they were little became a major burden. The children in this study whose lives were governed by court orders or mediated parental agreements all told me that they felt like second-class citizens who had lost the freedoms their peers took for granted.

They say that as they grew older and craved independence, they had even less say, less control over their schedules, and less power to determine when and where they would spend their time—especially precious vacation time. Joan, like all teenagers, valued her weekends, her yackety-yak time on the telephone, parties, and other social events. Paula adored her pet rabbit and worried about it every weekend she was away. Would the order of the world have changed if each of these children had been consulted about what they wanted?

Our court system is strangely at odds with what we experience in our own families. Most households welcome input from children. Although the home is not governed by the child's wishes, Americans tend to listen to their children and value their opinions. They are seen and heard and consulted. But the "court-created child" is a passive vessel—like a rag doll that stays put in whatever position it is placed. Children are regarded by the legal system almost as nonpersons, strangely lacking in preferences or opinions based on their own observations and experiences. They're expected to go along contentedly and silently with whatever arrangements have been made by respective attorneys or their parents or the court. They are given zero opportunity to express their preferences among plans made for them, and if there is a court battle, their development is expected to come to a complete halt. A visiting schedule established for a six-year-old is expected to meet the needs of a thirteen-year-old. Why not issue flexible orders that could be reopened for assessment and increasing input from the growing child as she reaches each new developmental stage?

The real children in this study did not remain silent about the system's unfairness. They complained that they were being bullied by the courts or by a parent backed by the court. They cajoled, conspired, and cried—but no one listened. They begged to be consulted about visiting because they, and not their parents, knew what the visiting was like. They wanted to be consulted about dual residence because there, too, they—not their parents—knew what it was like. They wanted to feel safe and yet they were afraid to travel unaccompanied. They worried themselves sick when they had to fly in airplanes alone. What if the plane crashes? They worried all through the journey, what if no one is there to meet me? Do adults really believe that the thousands of children, some as young as five years old, who fly alone across country each week are pleased with a visiting plan that makes them do this? Do people think these children feel loved and protected and are sure that there will be a joyful parent waiting at the gate to toss them into the air and catch them happily? Many of these children are deeply frightened and remember their fear and confusion for many years.

One woman, who from the age of six shuttled back and forth between Denver and San Francisco, recently told me, "I felt like a piece of garbage being put on the plane."

"Did you complain?" I asked.

"Yes, all the time," she replied. "I said to my mother, 'How can you do this to me?' I remember her telling me, 'This is what the experts think is good for you.' "

I have become increasingly concerned about children traveling unaccompanied on airplanes. It's bad enough when five-year-olds are put on planes by themselves clutching teddy bears for company. But it's just as bad when nine- and twelve-year-olds are sent through major airports and expected to change planes. One nine-year-old I know was ordered by the court to travel from Flint, Michigan, to Philadelphia twice a month to spend a weekend with his father. The judge determined that he could not lose any time at school so he had to leave after school was out on Friday and board the plane to Chicago in the late afternoon or early evening. In Chicago, he changed planes by himself and boarded another plane to Philadelphia. He arrived at his destination after ten at night. The child got to bed after eleven or sometimes closer to midnight. He was terrified of changing planes in the giant Chicago airport. On several occasions, he got lost when planes were late or changed gates. He was afraid of flying during rainy or cold winter weather. He would return after a weekend with his dad and sit in his room silently holding his dog, refusing to see his friends. He became increasingly withdrawn at school and reluctant to leave the house. His mother called me to ask what, if anything, she could do. She explained that her attorney had told her that any complaint on her part would be interpreted by the courts as another example of her anger at her ex-husband, which would only have made matters worse; she'd be seen as angry and unstable. So her son was left without any advocate. She could not speak for the boy because the court would assume that she had an ulterior motive. The attorney also warned her that going to court would cost a ton of money. The mother was frantic. She had lost the power to protect her child. Under the present system, where parents are silenced, no one protects the child.

During any given week in this country there are thousands of unaccompanied children flying to see their parents.[2] Their number is unknown because no one keeps a record. It's hard to believe that the courts are protecting the interests of children when we have no idea how many are flying, how frequently, at what distances, and at what tender ages. Rather, the courts are acting blindly. Neither the judge nor the mediator have any knowledge of the child's state of mind before, during, or after the flight. Once the order is made, there's no follow-up plan to assess the impact on the child at the time and during the months that follow. Some children can travel with poise. Others panic. How can the court or the mediator or the parents be so sure that the child's suffering is outweighed by the value of the visit?

New and better solutions that protect children, or at least do not further traumatize them, are badly needed. The system is flawed. For starters, as children mature they want their concerns heard. They don't want to be bullied. They don't want to cry alone. They want a say in how their schedules are determined. In this, their complaints are absolutely in accord with their best interests and with their wish to grow toward greater independence and more self-regulation. Few people emerge full-grown like Athena from the head of Zeus. We grow up slowly and gradually, taking step after step toward independent judgment and adulthood. Older children and adolescents especially want a say in how they spend their vacations—a time they want for pursuing emerging interests and spending summers with friends at home or at camp. Yet we continue to penalize children of divorce by insisting that they spend every summer with one or the other parent so that the calendars of each adult will balance the other and the parents' legal rights to their children will be protected.

There are powerful lessons in these findings. When they reached adulthood, all of the children in this study who had been court ordered or mediated to visit a parent on a schedule that remained rigidly fixed and unmodified were angry at one or both parents. Most were very angry at the parent they had been ordered to visit. All rejected the parent whom they were forced to visit when they got older. They said things like "I don't care if I ever see him again," or "We have nothing in common because we never really talked in all those years." Sometimes they said, "I feel sorry for my father but that's all I feel."

We have to wonder why the legal system fails to acknowledge the fact that children change or that they should have the right to participate in planning their own lives. Imagine ordering a twelve-year-old to wear the shoes that fit her when she was six. When she complains that the shoes pinch or cries because she limps or whimpers that she can't walk at all, we ignore her. We turn her objections aside because we must zealously uphold the parents' right to select their children's clothes. Unfortunately, returning to court to change such orders is not a real option for most people because it's emotionally and financially too costly. What's more, most courts would not hear the child's voice but instead assume that the parent who speaks on behalf of the child is acting out of anger at the other parent. Essentially there is no place within the court or the mediation system or elsewhere in society for children like Joan or Paula or the thousands of others to make their plea for justice or compassion when they are young. They have no rights. They have no voice. When they reach adulthood, however, the power is all theirs and the parents whom they regarded as bullies when they were minors are rejected in anger and disdain. Is this really what we want?

I was presented somewhat unexpectedly with another solution by a father who told me about visiting his eleven-year-old daughter. We were driving in his car to a conference center in upstate New York. Divorced three years earlier, the father, who was a busy pediatrician, traveled a thousand miles twice a month to visit his daughter. Typically he called during the week, made plans for the weekend, and then took two rooms at a residential hotel. When his daughter had her tenth birthday, he thought that it might be hard or boring for her to spend the weekend alone with her father so he invited her to bring a friend. The child was very happy to do so. I asked the father whether he had ever thought of asking his daughter to fly to his home. He said sharply, "I don't want my little girl alone on an airplane."

I was very impressed with his sensitivity and concern and so I said, "Your child is very fortunate to have you for her father." As I glanced at the man, I was startled to see tears rolling slowly down his cheek. "Doctor, you're crying!"

"You're the only person in the whole world who has ever said that to me," he said. "Everyone else tells me that I'm a fool."

There may be many sensitive, loving fathers or mothers who would be willing to make the necessary sacrifice in order to fly to visit their children. Perhaps no one ever asked them.

FOURTEEN

Sex and Drugs

In Larry's and Carol's stories I talked a bit about drug and alcohol abuse during adolescence and the astonishing rise in sexual promiscuity among many of the young girls from both chaotic intact and chaotic postdivorce families. But we still have not delved into the heart of these destructive behaviors and what the child gains from them psychologically. Paula shows us the inner logic of running out of control.

The next time I saw Paula she was fifteen and looked about twenty-five. She was thin, very attractive, and very, very precocious. Her green eyes, lined with heavy black eyeliner, were bloodshot, whether from her incessant smoking or from some other drug I could not tell. With her black, short, sleeveless dress artfully falling from one shoulder and her legs encased in high red leather boots, she was the picture of what her exasperated mother had warned me of a week earlier: "Don't be surprised, Judy. She looks like a slut." With bravado, constantly tossing her long, curly hair into and then out of her eyes, she told me of her numerous boyfriends and of her adventures partying and evading the police and the school authorities. She boasted about being high every day and of the huge quantities of alcohol that she and her friends drank. In describing a confused mixture of sexual exploits and physical fights, she told me, "I give as good as I get." She looked very tough and seemed utterly lost.

I remember being saddened and very troubled by Paula at this time, but I wasn't surprised. Her mother told me that the trouble started the summer after sixth grade when Paula turned twelve. In the next two years, Paula accumulated a police record for possession of drugs, disrupting the peace, and drinking in public. She had been suspended from school several times for possession of marijuana and for stealing from and harassing other students. She was on her final probation. One day, Paula's mother unexpectedly came home early from work to find her thirteen-year-old daughter in bed with two seventeen-year-old boys. Screaming, pleading, grounding, and taking away privileges had no effect. Paula stomped out as soon as her mother left for work and returned when she felt like it. At age fifteen, she took her sister's car and totaled it. Paula was on a tear and out of control.

Paula hit adolescence filled with anger about having been abandoned as a little girl. She craved love, attention, and above all, she wanted to be noticed and taken seriously. At the same time, she had long-standing and growing doubts about her value and desirability as a person and as a woman. She was afraid of being alone and had little or no internal sense of direction, confidence, pride in achievement, or ability. She was singularly vulnerable to the dangerous temptations of sex and drugs. She had no reason or resources to resist their lure.

Sex was a sure ticket to being noticed and sought after. Screwing boys provided the illusion of being held and loved. Drugs and alcohol numbed troubled, empty feelings, inflated shaky self-esteem, and made her feel confident and powerful. As a young teenager Paula was intoxicated with feeling important and powerful for the first time, and she resentfully pushed away any doubts about her behavior. At the end of that ten-year interview, she responded to my genuine concern about what she would do if she got expelled (as she was sure to be). "I'm just confused most of the time," she admitted. "I don't know why. I don't like to think about things unless they happen. If I get into trouble again, I guess the police will solve it for me. Most of my trouble is during the day when Mom's away. Coming home to an empty house got me into drugs and alcohol. I couldn't stand the emptiness."

I continue to be struck by the poignancy of this statement. She was indeed confused. She had absolutely no sense that she had any control over herself. She assumed that control had to come from the outside, from the police if necessary. She did connect her trouble to years of having no parent really being there for her, but her attachment to her parents wasn't rich enough or strong enough to keep her safe—and she remained angry at both. Very early Paula crossed the boundary from childhood into pseudoadulthood. She became attached to and increasingly dependent on sex and drugs as ways to feel better, to express her anger, and to feed her loneliness. Their power over her was irresistible, and she was on a dangerous and potentially fatal path into her future.

Rebellion

ONE IN FOUR of the children in this study started using drugs and alcohol before their fourteenth birthdays. By the time they were seventeen years old, over half of the teenagers were drinking or taking drugs. This number compares with almost 40 percent of all teenagers nationwide. Of those who used drugs, four in five admitted that their schoolwork suffered badly as a result. A majority used these substances for more than five years and several were seriously addicted by the time they reached their twenties. As I pointed out in Larry's story, teenagers in the comparison group were no angels and also used drugs and alcohol as part of their rites of passage. But only a few started this behavior before age fourteen and only a quarter ended up as heavy users by their senior year in high school.[1]

Early sex was very common among girls in the divorced families and has been described in several national studies.[2] In our study, one in five had her first sexual experience before the age of fourteen. Over half were sexually active with multiple partners during their high school years. In the comparison group, the great majority of girls postponed sex until the last year of high school or their early years in college. Those who engaged in sexual activity did so as part of an ongoing relationship that lasted an average of a year.

Intense sexual activity serves many purposes for girls from divorced families, as it does for those in chaotic intact families. Some combine promiscuity with drugs and drinking as a way to deaden feelings. They go to bars and spend the night with the first guy who catches their fancy. The sex rarely ends in orgasm for the women, but it does bring excitement and comfort in being held and wanted. Others are more aggressive, and I have come to think of them as female Don Juans. They take dominant roles with men, getting pleasure out of seducing, conquering, and then abandoning partner after partner. "Love them and leave them" was the script. These young women are anxious to turn the tables on what they understand to be the natural pecking order between men and women. One said, "From age eighteen on I was a man. I was being like my dad. Men use, they're powerful and they're smart. Women are stupid and want men. I get a kick out of being sexy, smart, and using people." Several told me that they enjoyed seducing their girlfriends' lovers. These young women were motivated by a frank vengeance against men that was startling in its passion.

Such behavior seems hard to understand in attractive, intelligent young women, including some who were in graduate programs and professional schools. But they were driven to use sex as an arena for playing out unfinished business with their parents—especially anger and longing for their fathers and defiance of and competition with their mothers. Some had watched their mothers struggle to make it alone while their fathers enjoyed relative wealth and got away scot-free. Others had been abandoned by their fathers but were also locked in conflict with their mothers. Sex is a way to get even with both parents—to get what their moms couldn't have (a man), to get what they missed growing up (a man), and to vent their anger and disdain (onto that same man). It's doubtful the women learn much from these experiences since the men, as they describe them, are mostly indistinguishable. Many of these women show poor judgment in terms of protecting their own health and safety. Sexually transmitted diseases and unwanted pregnancies are common; abortion left them depressed but was preferable to raising a child with a man they did not want. Young women who follow this path are relatively unsupervised during adolescence and have the abiding sense that they are accountable to no one. There's no harm in doing whatever feels good at the time, they reason. These are also the girls who were privy from childhood to the many details of their parents' sexual love affairs and escapades plus accusations and counteraccusations of infidelity during the marriage. They may very well have been stimulated by what they witnessed and overheard. One youngster age eleven told me, "Every time I go to my mom's parties I get so excited I want to swallow my tongue."

Taking the Leap

I REMEMBER AWAITING my interview with Paula six years later, when she was twenty-one, with both anticipation and trepidation. I wasn't disappointed. Now engaged and living with her fiancé in Seattle, she attracted attention when she walked into the restaurant overlooking Puget Sound where we had agreed to meet. Thin to the point of emaciation, dramatically dressed and heavily made up in black lipstick and nail polish, she chain-smoked and barely picked at her salad. She spoke glowingly of her boyfriend, whom she had met a few months earlier during a dance rave while high on Ecstasy.

"What attracted you to him?" I asked.

"He was the best-looking guy on the dance floor," she answered proudly. "I was determined to get him for myself. At two A.M. we were both at the bar. I had a few drinks and we started talking. We ended up in bed and that was that."

Knowing Paula over the years as I had, I ventured another question. "I know you've had a lot of boyfriends, Paula. What made Brad different? How did you decide he was the one you'd marry?"

This was another time when Paula startled me by the frankness of her reply. Throwing herself back in her chair and regarding me from beneath long, hennaed bangs, she lit another cigarette. "You really want to know?"

"It's important that I understand," I told her seriously.

"He's not really different from the others. He loves me, he's kinda hyper, and he likes to party. He's good in bed. He's a really cute Italian guy. I think I was just ready to settle down. We were out to dinner and I said to him, 'It's my birthday, marry me.' And he said, 'Why not, let's do it!' So, we're getting married."

"But you're barely twenty-one," I ventured again. "Why do you want to settle down? Many women feel they're just getting started when they're twenty-one."

Paula raised her eyebrows and snorted derisively. "Most women haven't had the kind of life I've had. I've been sleeping with men since

I was twelve. I've probably been with over seventy guys. I've hardly ever been without a boyfriend. Lots of times when I'd get the man then I'd be mean and they'd be nice and I didn't like that. I'd end it if they were spineless jellyfish." Paula grinned and raised a tightly clenched fist. "I mean, I'd hit them, not slap."

"Does this include Brad?" I asked.

She nodded. "Yup, but he's not spineless. He's ambitious, he likes to work. He pushes the business. And he's cute!" she finished triumphantly.

I reminded Paula of our last meeting, when she had been in so much trouble in high school. Shortly after her interview with me when she was fifteen, Paula did get expelled. She went to an alternative school but dropped out when she was sixteen. She worked at part-time jobs—a gas station, a convenience store, and a number of restaurants. At age seventeen Paula's mother offered her a new car as a reward if Paula went back and finished high school. Paula was able to follow through on her end of the bargain, although it took her several years. She got her diploma when she was nineteen and marriage license at age twenty-one.

Many children of divorce take up with people they hardly know and, like Karen and Paula, impulsively marry them or move in together. Unions like these feature virtually no courtship and certainly no exploration of shared background, goals, or values. Such marriages are almost doomed before they start. In looking over the cases, I recalled that only sixty children of divorce (out of the ninety-three we followed for twenty-five years) had ever gotten married.[3] I was dismayed to learn that of those who did marry, half made the decision the way Paula had—on the spur of a moment during their late teens or early twenties. "Marry me," she said. "It's my birthday." His response: "Why not?" One nineteen-year-old married a trucker who was driving through her hometown. Many of them married people they met in bars and bedded after a few drinks.

The girls who married in their early twenties had much in common. (We'll talk about the young men who married early in Chapter 19.) They acted impulsively because they had no idea of what to look for and no expectation of getting anything special anyway. They convinced themselves that it really didn't matter who you marry. And yet it did matter. Deep down they knew this, but as they told me so often, they were afraid to fall in love because falling in love means you can get hurt. They were also afraid that if they hesitated or said no, they would never get another chance. So to avoid getting hurt, they threw themselves into relationships that they knew might not last. "I broke all my nevers with him," said one young woman. "When we got married I thought, Well, if it doesn't work, I can get a divorce. No big deal."

But then these women discovered it *was* a big deal. Leaving a troubled man who needed them turned out to be intolerably painful. It reopened old wounds. Anna said, "Every time I decide to leave John, who is an alcoholic and can't hold down a job, he cries and then I can't go. I get helpless because I flash on my father walking down the front path of our house crying after my mom threw him out when she discovered his affair." Anna was eleven at the time. Many young women like her are trapped because it's more painful to leave a bad marriage than to stay in it. Close to half of these poorly conceived marriages continue to this day despite their unhappiness. It was even harder to leave after children were born. But they mainly stay because they still don't expect to do better if given a second chance. And they have no place to go.

I was shocked to discover that many of the lasting bad marriages in this group were as troubled or more troubled that the marriages their parents had escaped. Their problems may have been different but their unhappiness was not. If the goal of the parent who had left the marriage decades ago was to safeguard the children, then I'm sorry to say they failed. Many of the still married but unhappy couples were mutually addicted to drugs and alcohol. There were sexual difficulties and some violence. We saw both infidelity and serious sexual inhibitions. One young woman who stayed in her marriage cut off all sexual relations after the birth of their two children. Apparently her husband accepted the ban. Another woman told me, "We don't talk to each other. We don't tell each other anything personal. We don't make demands on the other." One unhappy wife allowed her husband to bring his lovers into their bedroom. There was never any mention of divorce in these homes. The man and woman decided to settle for what they had.

Who were the women who stayed in these poor marriages? I can't put my finger on any one trait but I can say that they all shared low expectations of themselves and of marriage. Several grew up in chaotic, violent families. Some maintained the caregiver role they'd learned in childhood; the husband was a stand-in for the mother or father or both. One woman from a seemingly stable postdivorce family who maintained close contact with both parents married a man who criticizes her constantly for her sexual frigidity and humiliated her for "doing nothing right." Her mother told me twenty-five years earlier that these were her husband's complaints. A few of the women had devoted stepfathers, but somehow this did not brighten their expectations of marriage. Many had been very young when their parents divorced and grew up like Paula, feeling lonely and driven to sexual frenzy.

The women who married early and then divorced tell similar stories about drug and alcohol abuse, low expectations, and anxieties about leaving the marriage. At their core, the bad marriages that lasted and those that ended in divorce all looked pretty much alike. But the women who did leave finally said "enough." The decision to divorce was fraught with anxiety because these women had few resources and little money to start over again. They did not expect to get child support. Paula will shed more light on this aspect of the story in the next chapter.

In talking to the women from divorced families who married young, I thought a lot about our comparison group. Many of the women from good and "good enough" intact families told me that they were often drawn to losers in their late teens and early twenties. The guy in the motorcycle jacket was exciting and fun to play with. Men who used drugs and drank hard were wonderful party boys and excellent lovers. But they did not go on to marry such men. As they told these stories, I heard time and again how their parents' concern played an important role in not choosing such men for life partners. "I knew my mom wanted me to be taken care of and respected," said Donna. "I didn't always follow her thinking and I lived with one guy who drove her up the wall. But I didn't marry him. In the end, I listened to my mom's advice about men." Another woman told me, "I knew all along that my folks disapproved of my lover. But it took me five years to dump him. It was a narrow escape." By contrast, few of the divorced parents tried to intervene in their children's poor choice of marriage partners. I don't know of a single father who sat his daughter down to warn her about what was ahead of her. The few mothers who tried to intervene found that their daughters ignored them because the girls didn't credit their moms with wisdom in relationships.

Like Gary, the young women raised in good intact homes entered adulthood expecting that their future relationships would work, not fail. By their early twenties, they were in no rush to select a life mate but did have notions about the kind of relationship they wanted. Most postponed serious commitments, including marriage, until after they began to establish themselves in the workplace. But when the time is right they are reasonably confident, although admittedly also apprehensive, that they will choose well and settle down to raise a family. They feel that they have a good start and fair chance to make it on their own.

It is interesting to note that there were a few women from divorced families who married early and went on to establish happy, lasting marriages. Like those raised in good intact families, they went in search of men who would be good providers and caring parents. They knew that a good marriage takes commitment and hard work. Where did their understanding come from? I think it helped that they had attentive fathers or stepfathers who kept a close check on them, albeit sometimes from a distance, following their progress in school and their social relationships. The father's standards made a difference in the woman's expectation of herself and of the men in her life. The experiences of this small, select group who made appropriate choices and were happily married calls attention to the enduring importance of a father-daughter relationship in which the young woman feels cherished and valued. These bonds exert a powerful protective influence on the young woman's adult choices and relationships with men.

FIFTEEN

Evolving Relationships

To find Paula for our twenty-five-year interview, I called the only number I had: her mother's house in Berkeley. To my surprise a very young voice answered. "My grandma can't come to the phone now. Can I take a message?" Taking a chance, I offered my name and that I was an old friend of the family. Then I ventured, "I'm really trying to get hold of your grandmother's daughter, Paula. Can you tell your grandma?" After a short hesitation, the child said, "Paula's my mom. She's here. I'll get her."

Paula's voice was strong and straightforward. "Sure I'll see you. I can come any day after my classes. A lot's happened since our last meeting. I'd like you to meet Racer, too. He's doing okay, I think. But then sometimes I'm not so sure. I'll tell my mom you called. See you on Tuesday."

The woman who walked through my door was a new person. After we got settled and I brought her up to date on the project, she brought me up to date on her life.

"Well," she began, "I married Brad and our son Rand, who I call Racer, was born five years later." (The nickname sounded vaguely familiar, and then I remembered that Racer was the name of her beloved pet rabbit.) Paula's marriage had been filled with nightly partying and alcohol abuse. "Brad didn't want kids. He was against me going to college. He basically wanted me to stay messed up. That was our marriage. Nine years of being high on alcohol. Yeah, and a lot of fighting. I hit him as much as he hit me. We would party all night, get two hours of sleep, and be chronically late to work. I wanted to stop but I couldn't—not with everyone else into that scene. I tried going to Alcoholics Anonymous, but Brad wouldn't go. So I quit going. We were all out of control. I got more and more desperate. I wanted somebody to see what we were doing but nobody saw."

"Was there nothing happy or good for you in this marriage?"

"If you mean like loving or caring, not much. Maybe six months at most. There was sex but even that got old pretty soon. I wasn't exactly an amateur at that and his performance went way down with drinking. I know you're thinking why didn't I leave right away if I really hated it."

"Yes, I was thinking that. What kept you?"

"I probably thought about leaving every day after the first year, but," she said with great earnestness, "the last thing I wanted to do was divorce. I know all about divorce. I know my mom's life like the palm of my hand. I didn't want that for me. Especially after I discovered that I was pregnant. Brad wanted me to have an abortion but I refused. I'd already had three abortions and didn't want another. I stayed for two years after Racer was born. I knew it wasn't good for Racer or me but I wimped out every time I tried to think about leaving. I'd immediately go to how angry and unhappy I'd been growing up in a divorced family. I didn't want Racer's life to be that and then I'd get paralyzed. I stayed because I was so afraid. Also I had no place to go."

She couldn't stay and she couldn't leave. "What happened so that you did leave?"

Paula looked down, then squared her jaw and looked directly at me. "Here's the whole story. I'm not proud of it but it's really what happened. I went right back to drinking after Racer was born. Of course, Brad had never stopped. There were times, more than once, when I just lost track of Racer when we were partying. Then I'd remember through the haze that I had a baby and I'd sober up fast and try to figure out where Racer was and what he needed. But it wasn't pretty. I was getting more and more upset at myself and Brad. And we were drinking more. Our fights escalated to really nasty. One day when Racer was two Brad was baby-sitting while I was at work. Both of us had partied all night. Brad fell asleep, and Racer wandered outside. He tootled down the street right into a busy intersection. The police found him and somebody told them who Racer was. This cop came to the store where I was working, carrying Racer. I'll never forget Racer's face. He looked so lost and so scared. 'Lady, is this your little boy? You're lucky he's still alive.' That cop looked at me like I was dirt. I freaked out." As she told me the episode Paula twisted her hands together and her voice thickened.

"My God, Paula, what a nightmare." She nodded, hardly able to speak.

"That did it. That night I told Brad that we both had to stop drinking because our son's life was in danger. He tried to laugh off what had happened, like it was no big deal. I couldn't stand that. So I grabbed the baby, took my purse and his diaper bag, got in the car, and left. I called my mom from a gas station and told her that Racer and I were coming. Thank God she didn't ask for details. We arrived at midnight. She took one look and put us both to bed. We've been here ever since."

Paula's face was strained and withdrawn. "So there I was—no money, no training, no job, no home, no nothing, with a child to support and raise. I was just where my mom was when I was four. All that I had sworn to avoid had happened in spades."

Social critics have been quick to say that children of divorce have more divorces because they are less committed to marriage. I see no evidence of that. They fervently want to avoid divorce in their own adult lives, dreading it even more if they have children. Yet despite a conscious resolution to not follow in their parents' footsteps, many do end their marriages amid great suffering. It's the arrival of the nightmare they feared. Like their peers from intact families whose marriages don't work out, they are often devastated. Recovery is slow because the divorce confirms what they've always believed—failure is inevitable and cannot be prevented.

"How has it been living with your mom? Is it working out for you and Racer?"

Paula shook her head sadly. "It's not permanent. My mom has a lot going on. She's remarried. Dan is a nice guy but we don't know each other and I can't expect that he would have the same feeling for me as my own dad. I can tell it's a strain on him and Mom having Racer and me living there. The truth is Racer and I have no home of our own.

Anyway, the first thing I did was to get sober. Mom paid for me to see a counselor. From there I went into AA. I've been sober for over two years," she said, adding with grim humor. "High for almost twenty years and sober for two. Not much of a record."

"It's a great victory. You've been drinking since you were twelve. Tell me, how were you able to stop?"

Paula lifted her chin and stared out my window for several moments. "I was always ashamed," she started slowly. "But I guess what happened with Racer was a wake-up call. I can't tell you how degraded I felt when that cop brought Racer back. Right then I knew I needed to take control or really awful things would happen to me and to my child."

One of the encouraging findings of this study is that nearly all of the women who abused drugs and alcohol in their teens and twenties gave up this self-destructive behavior by the time they reached their early thirties.[1] Moreover, they did it on their own. "I started to black out after the third drink," one woman told me. "I wouldn't remember driving home, where I parked the car, or how I got myself to bed. Sometimes I'd wake up in some stranger's bed. At first it was kind of funny, then real quick it became frightening. I had to stop." The decision to end the addiction was typically part of a major change in relationships that included the decision to end their promiscuous behavior or a decision to leave a bad relationship or a bad marriage. It heralded a change in lifestyle and a change in values. It was an important crossing and they knew it.

There is no one stimulus for these major changes. For some women, the birth of a child in or out of wedlock jump-starts their emotional development. As they grow into the role of parent and gradually take responsibility for the infant, toddler, and young child, they realize they cannot continue their adolescent acting out. Others become badly frightened by somatic symptoms or simply wake up to the fact that they have been on the wrong road for too long. They don't make a big deal of whatever it is that triggers their decision to change. At the same time, they realize the importance of their transformation and have no illusions about the difficulties ahead. They've seen friends go to jail or die from overdoses. Their decision to quit cold turkey or with a brief assist from self-help programs reflects their powerful wish to control themselves. It's an amazing feat that is in some ways parallel to the change we saw in Larry, who finally learned to stop identifying with his violent father. But in this instance, the girls learn to stop waiting for their parents to rescue them and instead rescue themselves. After years of self-destructive behavior, they decide to join the world of adults and accept its standards. Their stories are honest, startling, and inspiring as they shoulder the responsibility of becoming their own parents. As I suggested earlier, their extended adolescence finally drew to a close.

Enter the Grandparent

PAULA CONTINUED. "Racer's really the reason that I decided that I had to get my life shaped up. After I got sober I took a hard look at my life and decided that I wanted to give him stability. And, as I started to think, I decided it was important to go back to school but not the way my mom did it. I wanted to take classes and work toward a degree and have time to be with Racer—to be there when he got home from school and to see him off in the morning. Then I kind of got stuck because I couldn't see how I could work and have time for Racer and go to school. Mom was already paying for Racer's preschool and she was babysitting in the evenings so I could go to AA meetings. I was barely getting by on welfare and some yard jobs. And then a miracle happened! You'll never guess."

Paula looked at me quizzically and said, "Dad showed up. He was out of touch for a few years but now he's back and he's changed for the better. He called me and said, 'Paula, I hear that you have a son.' I said that I did and he asked about him in a very grandfatherly way. And then he blew me away. He said, 'Paula, you have to go back to school. You have a child to take care of. You need a college education.' Sure, I said, expecting nothing. But was I surprised. He said, 'If you go to college, I'll pay for your tuition and your books. You can stay on welfare for your living expenses and I'll buy you a car. I'll pay for clothing for you and my grandson and reasonable other stuff for him and you.' "

Paula took a deep breath. "So, I did it. I went to Laney Community College and took remedial courses until I made up my high school deficiencies. Then, my first real semester, I took English, psychology, and political science and I got an A in everything. You have no idea how that felt. Next fall I'll be transferring to Hayward State, which is a four-year university. I'm going to get a degree in landscape architecture."

"Did your dad do what he said he'd do?"

"Oh, yes. We've been getting along better since he came back and helped out. He came through with shining colors. He was not always a good father but he's a very good grandfather. Dad loves spending time with Racer. He's making up with my child for all that we missed doing together. They go fishing, see movies, eat at Racer's favorite restaurant, which is the Red Lobster." Paula laughed and then grew serious. "I love my dad now all over again and I'm grateful for what he gives us. I say to him, 'I love you now but I can only try to forgive you for the past.' "

"Should you forgive him?"

"I don't know. I used to love him a lot and I think he loved me. People do things. I don't know whether you can hold them responsible. I've learned to accept a lot of things and I've stopped being upset so much. Dad's finally acting like the parent he was before they broke up. He was a wonderful father when I was a real little kid. He wants Racer and me to go live with him but I won't. I need to stand on my own two feet."

As children of divorce move into their late twenties and thirties, relationships with their parents can change unexpectedly. Both generations have another chance to reexamine their interest in one another, to do things differently. Each developmental stage in adulthood offers the potential to grow as a person, to enhance one's closest relationships that have gone awry, and to correct past mistakes and poor judgment. Several of the fathers came through with new interest and money for college when their children, especially their daughters, were still drifting in their late twenties. Sometimes it was in response to the birth of a grandchild in or out of wedlock and sometimes it reflected the stabilization in the older man's life. It was not that they had more money. They never denied that they could have supported their child's higher education. But their own life had become more stable in a second or third marriage or in their own decision to give up drinking. These funds made a huge difference in the lives of their children, several of whom were able to turn their lives around after wasting almost the whole decade of their twenties.

There's a clear message here about the plasticity in parent-child relationships and the ability of both to recast their relationship to everyone's advantage. Some young adults go in search of their fathers, looking for ways to establish an adult relationship. One thirty-five-year-old woman called her estranged father out of the blue. "I didn't want to go to his funeral someday and not know anything about him," she said. Some of these efforts at rapprochement seem related to a new awareness of the finiteness of life, a sad sense that the parent will not live forever and time is running out. Such efforts to reach out can go awry, especially if the young adult is trying to magically restore the father she had wanted but never had. Some men do not welcome their child's interest. They've put that part of their life far behind them. But other fathers are very responsive. The father-child relationship takes off on a new and better basis as long as the older man doesn't expect to rewrite history. One of the men in our study was elated. He told me, "My daughter finally asked my advice about something. I can hardly believe it." His daughter was thirty-four.

Building a Bridge

I WONDERED IF Paula's relationship with her mother had also improved. "How do you and your mom get along these days?" I asked.

"It's like we're finally becoming friends after all these years. I've grown up and she's mellowed. She's happy with Dan, he loves her, and she's finally being able to relax a little. We've talked about stuff that happened when I was growing up. I told her how angry I was and how alone I felt. She actually listened. And she told me some of what it was like for her. We never did that before."

"Did you just start talking? Did something happen to open both of you up?" I wanted to know.

"Well, I wrote a paper for my English class called 'The Single-Minded Mom' about our life after they divorced. I read it to her and that started us talking. I know I blamed her for their divorce. At the same time, I now understand what she had to go through. I understand her now, like I couldn't before Racer was born."

"And does she understand you better?"

"I hope so. She told me she did notice the bad things I was doing but she just couldn't do much about me. She was doing the best she could and hoped that her kids would do the same. She even told me that she spent years waking up in the middle of the night with her heart pounding, worrying about us. But she had to get up and get out early in the morning so she learned to shove those feelings aside and put on a no-nonsense attitude. That attitude I remember real well. It's helped me a lot to know now that her coldness was a cover-up in order to get her through the day. I began to clue in to how hard life had been for her when I was around eighteen. I realize now that she hadn't meant for me to have been so unhappy and lonely when I was a kid. I'm beginning to realize, too, that she was really happy in her marriage until Dad fell apart financially, but then she was really trapped after the divorce. I was trapped with her. And then I trapped myself when I married Brad." With grim humor she said, "I'm an expert on traps."

Few relationships are as complex as that between mothers and daughters in divorced families. The strands from both sides include love, longstanding anger, compassion, and guilt. But the fact remains that mothers and daughters in divorced families are more conflict-ridden than their counterparts in good intact families. Their relationship is less stable, fluctuates over the years, and reflects more ambivalence on behalf of both generations. The postdivorce relationship is complicated by the undiluted intensity of these feelings and each woman's reciprocal need for love and approval. Fathers can buffer the mother-daughter relationship, helping the girl separate from her mother and move on to create her own career and new family. The stepfather can also serve this function in a divorced family. But if there is no one to play this role, the two women often engage in a prolonged push-pull, going from too much closeness to too much distance. While profoundly distressing to both, this situation also fails to help the girl resolve her conflicts and get on with her adult life. Paula spent her whole childhood and adolescence locked in conflict with her mother, which did not cool until she divorced and returned home at midnight with her child and was taken in. The two women then had the opportunity to reformulate their relationship. The mother took on an important supportive role as grandmother and the child consolidated the new bridge between mother and daughter.

In general, the arrival of a baby drew mothers and daughters of divorce in this study closer together. Daughters who had kept their mothers at bay now welcomed any and all help with the child. As new mothers, they finally began to understand how much sacrifice is required to care for a baby and young child. Perhaps their mothers were not as bad as they thought. Maybe they had had good mothering before the breakup. As their anger at their moms receded, the daughters' compassion emerged more strongly. The result was a greater understanding from which both women benefited.

The perspective of this long-term study has enabled me to observe an incredible amount of fluctuation in parent-child relationships in the postdivorce family. Of course, all families change as parents age and children grow up, but the changes in divorced families are more dramatic. It starts with the breakup, when children feel abandoned by their parents, continues with the changing cast of characters that come in and out of the family, and moves into phases of reassessment when children grow up, sustain their own disappointments, and decide that maybe they had judged their parents too harshly. Parents, seeing their children struggle as adults, are newly worried and want to help. As a result, families that are estranged for decades may come back together during a serious crisis. As both generations mellow, they can turn to one another and discover what they had lost. This finding, which is just now emerging after twenty-five years, bodes well for our divorce culture. It means that forgiveness is possible—and that it's never too late for parents and children to regain mutual love. That's the encouraging side of our story.

But there is an equally powerful discouraging side. Researchers now say that elderly people with a history of divorce will get less care from their children than people who have never been divorced. They will get even less care from stepchildren. People who have been divorced are much less likely to reside with a child in their old age and less likely to receive care from a child, even if they are disabled, compared with the elderly who have never divorced. When divorced parents get help from their children, it is more often in the form of cash and not personal attention. The trend is true for mothers and fathers, especially for those who remarried. However, widowed parents receive more than twice as much financial help as divorced parents.

Who will step in when the Baby Boomers reach old age? In the generation that ushered in our divorce culture, the safety net traditionally offered to aging parents is not likely to be in place. Society may well pick up the tab through higher taxes to pay for Medicare, but that will not be commensurate with the sense of abandonment and loss that long-divorced parents are about to experience. This we surely did not anticipate.

SIXTEEN

The Custody Saga Continues

After Paula had finished telling me about her relationship with her parents, I decided to delve into a topic that I was very curious about. As a child of divorce who had gotten a divorce, how had Paula dealt with custody and visiting decisions? I remembered how angry she was at being ordered by the court to visit her father because it interfered with her friendships and school activities. Did Paula think that the popular solution of joint physical custody, in which the children go back and forth between two homes, was an improvement over her childhood? What was the situation with her own son, Racer, and was she able to bring special knowledge from her own childhood in protecting him from being hurt the way she had been hurt?

After Paula filed for divorce, Brad shocked her completely by requesting that Racer live with him half the time in joint physical custody. In relating this to me Paula shook her head in disbelief. "If anyone'd told me that Brad would want his kid half-time I'd have said they were completely in left field. His idea of a quiet evening at home is to get loaded, order pizza, watch the sports channel, and fall asleep. When we lived together it'd be me who remembered to give Racer his dinner and put him to bed. Yeah, Brad would play with him when he felt like it. He'd let Racer watch TV with him and he'd explain about baseball and who the players were. But anything having to do with really taking care of Racer—forget it!" Paula snorted and tossed her head. "Then I figured out why Brad wanted Racer half-time. You pay a lot less child support, that's why. The court counts nights that the child spends in each home and that's how they figure child support. I guess they think you rent out the room when the kid's away. They really are a bunch of jerks. Anyway, that's the law. I was real worried about this half-time custody of Racer, but Brad was adamant. He said he wouldn't party and would stay home or get a babysitter when Racer was with him. Fat chance!"

In California, when divorcing couples are unable to mutually agree on a plan for their children's living arrangements, they are referred to a court mediator. After hearing each parent's side, the mediator helps them devise a shared plan. Most parents can do this with the mediator's help, but if they cannot agree, the case goes to trial, and after ordering evaluations of the mental health and parenting of each of the parents the court decides for them. Brad and Paula could not develop their own plan for custody of Racer so they were assigned a mediator. In many states parents have no alternative and have to go to court.

"I couldn't let it get to trial. Hell, I was on welfare. Trials cost a fortune. Only very rich people can afford snazzy attorneys. I knew we were going to have to agree on something with the mediator. Anyway, I learned a lot."

"What did you learn?" I was curious to hear this from Paula's perspective, Paula having had a chunk of her own childhood arranged by court-ordered visitation. "Well, the mediator was very pleasant and very professional. She would only see us together. She had about an hour and a half for the whole works. Can you imagine planning for my child's whole growing up in an hour and a half? Hell. She never asked anything about Racer. Anyway, she explained that Brad and I should draw up a plan and that it was important for fathers to stay involved with their kids and that was the law.

"Brad isn't dangerous according to their criteria," Paula said. "He makes good money painting Victorian homes. People from all over the Bay Area want to hire him because he's so talented. He never hit anyone in his life. Mostly he passes out. I tried to tell the mediator about the drinking and the parties. I tried to tell her about the time Racer was almost killed when Brad fell asleep. I told her I was trying to stay sober and that I'd be happy for Racer to live half-time with Brad when and if Brad cleaned up his act. Brad of course denied he had a problem with anything. He still has his big brown Italian eyes and he can be real sincere sounding and convincing." Paula rolled her eyes and shrugged.

Then her face hardened and she looked away. "The bottom line is that nothing I said made a damn bit of difference. She said the only thing that mattered was the present. The past was history. So we ended up drawing up a schedule that gave Brad the maximum time between Racer's beginning kindergarten here in Berkeley and Brad's work. So Racer spends every other Friday through Monday morning with Brad and Wednesday from after school until bedtime. And six weeks in the summer. We alternate holidays. I asked what happens if Brad is out of it when Racer is there, but she would not hear that. She said that I should stuff my criticism of Brad and pretend for Racer's sake that everything is wonderful. So I figured that was it and I gave up. And we had a mediated agreement."

Mediation and Public Policy

In many states mediation is fast becoming the primary method for settling the disputes between divorcing couples. The goal is to keep their differences out of the court's adversarial system, which all too often makes people angrier and reduces their desire to cooperate in the postdivorce years. Mediation is rooted in several principles. First, conflict between parents is harmful to children and should be actively discouraged. Second, parents know more about their children's needs than any judge whose job it is to know the law. And third, parents are more likely to cooperate with a postdivorce plan if it is mutually negotiated versus being imposed against the will of one parent. Mediation proposes that both parents should emerge feeling that they have won. Basic to the working of the process is the notion that the past history of the marriage should not intrude on the present unless it is shown to be relevant in specific ways. These "intrusions" have been narrowly defined by most courts as those that pose a direct hazard to the physical well-being of the child.

There is no doubt that mediation represents an advance over the adversarial process, which not only is dreadfully expensive but often angers and humiliates one or both parents. Mediators are specially trained by senior practitioners and have backgrounds in either law or mental health. Overall, most parents find the mediation helpful and reassuring. Parents who have gone through mediation are indeed more likely to abide by their agreements than parents who have been involved in traditional adversarial proceedings.

But does mediation protect children? When mediation began to emerge as an important alternative method for settling disputes, proponents claimed that children would benefit enormously and that it would significantly improve their psychological adjustment. This has not happened. Long-term studies show no significant differences in the child's adjustment at home or in school whether the parents use lawyers or mediators to settle their differences.[1] A child's present and future are not shaped by the method of negotiation used by parents and courts.

Mediation doesn't help children because the child is hardly present in the planning—either in body or spirit. Mediation brings together the contesting preferences of the parents. But the mediator is not charged with developing a plan that will suit the child's developmental or emotional needs. Nor is the mediator charged with inquiring into the child's interests or wishes or preferences. The extent to which the parents are able or willing to speak for the child is not asked. And the merit of their conflicting claims for the child's interests are not weighed on behalf of the child. Mediators have very limited training in child development, especially when it comes to the needs of very young children. The law does not instruct or require them to consider different developmental needs. Moreover, the mediator is not an independent agent. He or she operates within the legal framework of the court and in the shadow of its policies. If the prevailing court policy is extended visiting or dual residence, it's not incumbent on the mediator to ask whether the infant or the two-year-old child has ever been separated from the primary parent. Mediators do not have to ask about the child's reaction or whether the plans were ever discussed with the child. Nor do they offer advice to parents for preparing the child to handle the transitions that she will be called upon to make.

It appears, in fact, that the mediation outcome continues many of the disadvantages of court judgment—locking children and parents into rigid agreements that ignore how children change as they grow up. Parents are told that they can return to mediation if the arrangements are not working. But that is not the same as giving an older child a place at the table and recognizing her voice as a participant. Nor is it the same as building in a review process that, after an appropriate time interval, would see how the child is faring.

Another difficult issue that I mentioned earlier bears elaboration. The central model of public policy as implemented by the courts and mediation has been that the child's relationships with both parents should be continued and if possible strengthened. Courts distribute booklets to parents with the slogan "Parents Are Forever," by which they mean that parent-child relationships in the predivorce family are expected to endure. The moral dilemma is that many people divorce because they have come to abhor the lifestyle and values of their partner. They leave because they don't want their children to be subjected to the toxic influences of the other. Men and women alike leave marriages because of their partners' dishonesty, manipulative relationships, violent behavior, drinking, infidelity, or overall irresponsibility. They divorce for serious reasons to escape a delinquent or demeaning life only to find themselves in a system that reinstates and even strengthens the values and lifestyle they fled from.

I don't have an alternative solution short of enabling the courts or the mediators to play the role of moral arbiter—an idea I strongly reject. Nor do I think we should conduct prolonged investigations of every alleged misdeed. We would create a witch-hunting society that would probably be worse than the present system. But I do want to point out that the courts' neutral position has serious consequences. It does not rescue the child or even purport to do so. On the contrary, it rescues the parent. As we saw in Larry's continued adoration of his violent father, it can and often does lock the child into troubled and immoral relationships. As a result, it imposes on the child the task of rescuing herself from identifying with a troubled or an immoral parent. This can be an enormous burden. Many divorced parents are preoccupied with these issues for good reason.

Joint Physical Custody

I ASKED PAULA how the joint custody was working out and she gave me a soliloquy on how frustrating the situation was in her eyes. Racer has a hard time making transitions between the two homes—hers in Berkeley, his in San Jose. She and Brad are not talking about it. She still feels like a pawn, bending to other people's interests. But, she said, Brad's new girlfriend is a decent person and that's helping. Above all, Racer wants to see his dad. She said, "In spite of Brad's problems, which worry me a lot, I have this gut feeling that Brad and Racer have a good connection. They have a whole thing going about baseball. Racer knows all the teams and he has this incredible baseball card collection that he lugs back and forth. Racer wears his Giants cap sideways, just like Brad does. And he's starting to roll up the sleeves on his T-shirt and whistle between his front teeth. Guess who does the same thing. Brad must be doing something right because Racer loves him. I have to say that's one thing that mediator got right. Racer definitely feels that he has two parents."

But what does Racer say about all this? Paula asked if I could talk to Racer directly. She pointed out that her family had been coping with divorce for two generations and she was worried. She wanted my opinion about how the child was doing. I agreed to an informal meeting and saw Racer the next day. Paula ushered him into my office, introduced us, and said she'd be back in an hour. He was startlingly like a male version of Paula as she'd been as a child, with her unruly, curly black hair and bright green eyes. His Giants hat was sideways, just like Paula had said it would be. With wonderful poise, he sat in the chair facing mine, crossed an ankle over the opposite knee, and said, "What's up?"

Quickly adjusting myself to Racer's grown-up tone and attitude I said soberly, "Your mom brought you to see me because I'm trying to understand what divorce is like for children. You'd help me out a lot if you could tell me what it's like for you, especially the part about living some of the time with your mom and some part of the time with your dad."

Racer fiddled with his cap. "You mean you want my advice?"

"I sure do. You're an expert on seven-year-olds. I know some seven-year-old kids whose folks are divorcing and the kids want to know what's best to do. What's it like for a seven-year-old kid when his folks break up?"

"It's okay. Except not all the time." Racer shifted the cap again. "Tell them they'll wish they could see both of their parents more."

"If you could make it any way you want, how would you arrange how you live?"

Racer didn't miss a beat. "I'd have them move closer. I don't like

Dad's house but I like being with him. I wish that he and Mom would move into the same house."

"Do you remember when they were married and all of you were living together?"

"Sure. If they were together I wouldn't have to take the bus so much and I would see them every day. It's a long, long, long bus ride. I like seeing them both but this way's hard because when I'm at my dad's I miss my mom and when I'm at Mom's I want to see Dad. Half the time I feel okay and half the time I feel bad. Every night I miss someone."

"What advice would you give someone your age who's going to start living part-time with each parent, like you do?"

"He'll be tired," Racer admitted, "because you have to keep on telling people where you are and you have so much to remember, where you are going and where your favorite stuff is. And it's hard because, like, I have friends at my school but they can't come to my dad's house. And there are some kids I play with when I'm at my dad's but I only see them when I'm there. And a lot of the time they don't remember that I'm going to be there and they've made plans to play with someone else. So I don't have anyone to play with when I go there. And when I'm at my mom's the kids have made plans I don't know about. Sometimes you feel like a rubber band. And," here Racer looked very solemn, "if this boy likes to play baseball tell him he'll probably miss some games and maybe some practices—that's what happens. I hope his coach understands."

"Your mom told me you play baseball. She said you liked to pitch." (This was an understatement. Racer is passionate about baseball but his parents have trouble getting him to practices and games with one home in Berkeley and one in San Jose.)

"Yeah, I like to play a lot," Racer told me. "Our team has the best record. We're going to be in the championships. And the coach told me that I could pitch in the play-offs. But only if I'm there for the rest of the season." Racer looked worried.

"Have you talked to your parents about this? It's so important to you."

"They said they'd try to work it out to get me to all the rest of the games, but I don't know." Racer scowled. "They say that a lot, but things don't work out."

"If you could change something, what would it be?"

"Going back and forth bugs me. Like me and my friends are playing and then it's time to leave right when we're into a game. And I have things I really want to do on weekends, like baseball, and I miss important stuff."

"Could you be on a baseball team in San Jose, where your dad lives?"

Racer looked at me as if I'd taken leave of my senses. "That wouldn't solve anything." His tone was a mixture of condescension and irritation. "It'd just make everything worse. Then I'd have two teams that I couldn't make it to the games for and two coaches who'd be mad at me."

"Of course; I see exactly what you mean." I hastened to regain lost ground. "It's a problem."

"A big problem," Racer emphasized. "Their houses are too far apart. I wish they would get together."

As Racer walked out the door, I thought to myself that this was certainly a mixed review of joint custody by the young expert I had consulted. He complained of fatigue, which is unusual among children his age. Could Racer be describing the strain he's under as fatigue? Was he having trouble sleeping? He was very open in describing the trip between his two homes as "a long, long, long bus ride" and how hard he found it to maintain playmates and playdates because of his constant comings and goings. He's an outsider in both communities. How many children can comfortably maintain two sets of friends going back and forth? Racer was worried about being allowed to pitch if his coach was not assured of his attendance. Obviously coaches want a winning team and players they can count on. The same is true of school play directors or Cub Scout leaders. Racer is appropriately worried about losing out in important events because of his spotty attendance. He also told me poignantly that he misses his mom when he's at Dad's house and misses his dad at bedtime in his mom's house. I hear this sad complaint from almost every young child in joint custody. At the same time, many children adjust to their new circumstances reasonably well and are firmly attached to both parents. Their self-esteem is good and their anxiety is not out of control.

But is Racer trying to tell us something we don't want to hear? He doesn't seem so happy about the joint custody script and the transitions he's required to make. He doesn't describe a happy, protected childhood. He has serious complaints. But he provides a very good picture of a competent little boy—the kind we call resilient—who understands the high price of keeping up with two parents after divorce. He's doing his best. He's managing. Racer is a poster child for a lot of children in joint custody who keep wishing for one home but keep going between the two because that doesn't rock the boat.

When this study began in 1971, joint custody was little known. Although some parents arranged to share their children's time, the law provided only for sole custody. The parent with sole custody, who was almost always the mother in those days unless she was physically or mentally incapacitated, had legal responsibility for the children. They lived with her full-time. She brought them up, deciding their schooling and attending to their physical care, including emergencies. The other parent, or father, had visiting rights. A schedule was worked out in which the children spent time with their father that might include overnights, alternate weekends, shared holidays, and summer vacations. The majority of the children in our study started out in this arrangement. Eight children were raised in the sole custody of their fathers. In all the rest, mothers were primary parents and fathers visited. Although children raised by mothers and those raised by fathers had different experiences in growing up, I saw little difference in the psychological adjustment between children raised in the two groups. This was also true of a much larger group of children, raised by either a father or mother, who were seen at our center.

Starting in the early 1980s this model of custody changed radically. California passed legislation in 1980 that added joint custody to a number of custody arrangements after divorce. Judges and attorneys interpreted this new option as being preferable to other configurations, although the laws did not say so. Many states quickly followed suit in allowing or prescribing joint custody. The number of divorcing families with joint custody arrangements rose in California from 5 to almost 20 percent.[2] By the late 1980s the California legislature officially clarified the status of joint custody by saying that parents could choose freely among different custody arrangements. About 20 percent of families today still choose this option. Elsewhere in the nation, the incidence of joint physical custody varies. Large states like Massachusetts report only 5 percent of children in dual residence. Everywhere, the pros and cons of this way of sharing children is being debated, especially among newly organized fathers' and mothers' groups.

Before I proceed, let's get straight some terms and legal definitions. Joint legal custody means that the parents share legal responsibility for major decisions about their children. This includes decisions about religious instruction, education, medical and health issues, and sometimes place of residence. In some joint legal custody arrangements, the areas requiring parental agreement are clearly spelled out. Other arrangements contain a more general agreement to share legal custody and leave the specific areas of decision up to the parents. Unless there are unusual circumstances, the majority of divorcing parents in many states share joint legal custody of their children after they divorce. In many courts, all divorcing parents are assigned this type of custody routinely unless they object. It's argued that although the legal arrangements may not directly change the daily life of the child, they carry symbolic meaning in that fathers may be induced to increase child support and see their children more often. There's a difference of opinion about the relationship between child support and joint custody. The issues are hard to unravel because more affluent families are likely to select joint custody to begin with. But research shows that neither child support nor father-child relationships are notably changed by the legal wording of custody orders. Child support varies much more with the ability of the father to pay and the methods of enforcement.[3]

Joint physical custody or dual residence is the newest form of custody. Usually when people talk about joint custody they mean joint physical custody and I will follow this convention. Joint physical custody refers to both parents having substantial and significant physical time with their children. The most common way families carry out this form of custody is when each parent maintains a household and their children divide their time between each parent's home according to a prearranged time-sharing agreement. The central tenet is that both parents continue as primary influences in their children's lives. They share the major decisions about their children's upbringing and the smaller day-to-day responsibilities as well. Seen from the child's perspective, being in joint custody means that the child has two homes, travels regularly between the two homes, and spends substantial time in each. Although other forms of joint custody have been attempted, the most common model by far is that each parent maintains a separate house and children shuttle back and forth. I find it amusing that an alternative form of joint custody, called birdnesting, in which the children stay "home" and the parents go back and forth, is too taxing for most adults. After an initial flurry of parental interest, this option has been largely abandoned.

Each divorcing couple custom-designs their own joint custody plan, usually with the help of their respective attorneys or a mediator. There are no legal requirements spelling out how much time or the patterning of time each child should spend with each parent. But in California child support is calculated by the amount of time that the child spends in each home. This linking of money to time introduces another agenda into custody negotiations, one that is unrelated to the child's interests but often very important to parents and their advisers. An attorney would be seriously remiss if this economic difference were not discussed with his or her client. Bluntly stated, the more time you can get the child to stay at your house, the less child support you'll have to pay.

In most states, however, child support is not tied to the child's time clock but is calculated according to each parent's respective income and how much it costs to raise a child. Factors in the calculation include each parent's job requirements, distance between their residences, children's school hours, extracurricular activities, availability of day care and after-school care, other money issues, and individual considerations. In today's complex world where both parents have jobs and children have after-school activities, time-sharing schedules can be complicated. Variations in the patterns of time-share are endless. But once set, arrangements are not as flexible as they might seem at first glance because they are typically based on occupation and work schedules of the two parents and not the interests or needs of the child. Babies and toddlers often go back and forth between homes *more frequently* than their older siblings.

Does Joint Custody Work?

EVERYWHERE I GO, worried parents, mental health professionals, and teachers ask the same question: Is joint custody good for kids? Is it better for kids to go back and forth between two parents than to have a main home base with one parent? What about a one-year-old? A three-year-old? What custody arrangement produces better-adjusted kids? What should I do when my child cries because he doesn't want to go or my teenager refuses to comply? People want answers that will either reassure them that joint custody is helpful or provide grounds for changing our social policy back in favor of sole custody. Parents know this is a new and unproven way to bring up children.

Our courts want rigid guidelines. As we've seen, most judges do not distinguish the needs of children at different ages. Fortunately some enlightened judges do. But in the calculus of most courts a five-year-old should not be treated any differently than a ten-year-old. The nature of a child's relationship with one or the other parent is irrelevant. The notion that children come single file, have different temperaments, and mature at different rates is difficult for courts to incorporate into policy. The central guideline is that both parents have equal legal rights to the child's time.

So what makes for a successful custody arrangement? In a nutshell, it depends on the child, the parents, and how the parents treat each other and their children. It matters whether the arrangements accurately reflect the needs and wishes of the child. It's a complex undertaking. What works for a child at one age may be harmful to the same child at another developmental stage. One size can never fit all children or all families. Joint custody arrangements that involve the child in going back and forth at frequent intervals are particularly harmful to children in a high-conflict family. Children who are ordered to traverse a battleground between warring parents show serious symptoms that affect their physical and mental health. The research findings on how seriously troubled these children are and how quickly their adjustment deteriorates are very powerful.[4] Tragically, the courts often order joint custody precisely for these fighting families if only because the judges are baffled by the ongoing bitterness of one or both parents. However, the same arrangement might be very beneficial for a child of the same age in similar circumstances whose parents get along well. The bottom line that our studies show is that the legal form of custody is *not* what matters in the child's welfare.[5] Nor is there any study that shows the amount of time spent with a parent is relevant to psychological adjustment. The amount of heat generated by these arguments finds no basis in our studies or the work of others. Comparing children in joint physical custody with those raised in sole custody homes shows that the amount of time a child spends with each parent is unrelated to how well that child copes with life in the family, at school, or on any other measure of social and psychological adjustment.[6]

Parents who spend thousands of dollars in legal fees to fight over the merits of joint or sole custody for their child are simply wasting their time and money. No model of custody, no axiom of time-sharing, no principle of greater access governs how well children do after their parents' divorce. Joint custody can work very well or poorly for the child. The same is true of sole custody with visiting. What matters is the mental health of the parents, the quality of the parent-child relationships, the degree of open anger versus cooperation between the parents, plus the age, temperament, and flexibility of the child. What also matters is the extent to which parents are able and willing to have the same routines for their child in each house. A child can't go to bed at eight o'clock in one home and ten o'clock in the other, watch unlimited television in one and have severe restrictions in another, or for that matter sleep with a parent in one house and by herself in the other without serious consequences. Joint custody depends on parents giving priority to the child's changing capacity and need for uniform routines. With older children, it also depends on asking their opinion and taking it seriously.

Infants and Joint Custody

JOINT CUSTODY PRESUMES that babies are able to attach to two primary caregivers and will learn to do so over and over, sometimes every few days. This frequent transitioning and continual disruption of contact may indeed be possible for some or even many babies to achieve, but there's a great deal about the psychological impact of these arrangements that we don't know. Infants need consistent sensitive parenting in order to thrive during the critical first years. When a baby doesn't see her primary caregiver for several days, the child suffers a lot because she is likely to assume that the caregiver has disappeared and that she's been abandoned.[7] But our knowledge about how much absence the infant can tolerate without severe suffering is still insufficient to build regular disappearances of a parent into the child's schedule. Courts have ordered infants into several weeklong stays away from the primary parent.

Over the first year of life the baby needs access to the primary caregiver, whether mother or father, as often as possible, especially at times of stress, which is often during the night when she wakes with a tummyache, or because she is hungry, or because of the many complicated parts of the child's environment to which the baby needs to adjust. The role of the primary caregiver is to provide a steady base of security by consistently and predictably responding to the baby's needs. During the second year, a toddler relying on this solid base of security is ready to venture out and explore the world. It's okay to try the playground slide because the safest lap you know is waiting at the bottom to catch you. The child's interest in the world, her capacity for learning, and her cognitive, emotional, and social development rest on her sense of a solid base.

Very few studies have looked at infants and toddlers who visit overnight in the other parent's home. One very important study at our center carried out by Dr. Judith Soloman shows that these very young children are exquisitely sensitive to the relationship between their divorced parents.[8] If the parents are angry or unable to cooperate or communicate well with each other, the children show disorganized attachment to both, meaning that they don't trust either mommy or daddy as protective figures. They feel insecure everywhere. If the parents are able to cooperate, talk about the child's care together and to exchange the baby peaceably, the baby may thrive. But even though some parents may try to ease the young child into feeling comfortable in two homes, let's face a hard truth. When a marriage fails in the last trimester of pregnancy or a few months after the birth of a child, the man and woman are likely to be hurt and angry. When a court orders overnight visits in these situations, I doubt very much that many parents are able to cooperate about the details of the child's feeding or sleeping or what to do about colic. They are very distressed, sometimes distraught people.

When I'm consulted on what to do about custody of babies I advocate creating a postdivorce environment that's as close as possible to life in a good intact home. The baby should have a chance to form his earliest relationships within a stable environment, to have a sense of a solid routine and predictable care. If the parents can work this out, they can surely consider overnights in the two houses and carefully observe the child's response. Parents often need help in overcoming their fear that the baby will not be safe in the care of the other parent. Babies vary greatly in their capacity to deal with change. As the child grows older, parents can increase the time he spends in each home. The child who is happily attached to one parent is able to deal more happily and easily with the other parent and with other caregivers. Putting the child's best interests forward and honoring what is best for the child is extremely hard to do in many postdivorce families. It requires parents to stand apart from their raw, hurt, jealous, competetive feelings and take an objective, compassionate look at what life will be like for their child. Not every parent can do that, but surely the job of the court is to give priority to the helpless child over the demands of the parent.

How Older Children Cope with Joint Custody

WHAT ABOUT THE school-aged child? Can all children handle living in two homes? Can everyone deal with two sets of friends and the need to engage in activities that don't conflict with their parents' schedules? Obviously there are differences among children that affect their capacity to deal flexibly with changes in daily life. The chief job of the school-age child is to learn at school and to develop socially. For this reason, the child's personality and temperament need to be carefully considered in making custody plans. People are born with different levels of reactivity and arousal, a basic difference in neurological "hard wiring" stays with us through our lives. Some children adjust easily to change and transition, indeed, some seek it out and thrive on it. Others have a much harder time accepting change. It stresses their neurological system and it takes them longer to get used to it. Translating these basic differences into the school and social arenas of children, it follows that kids for whom transition is harder need more protection so that transitions don't interfere with learning and making friends. Some children can spend the weekend with one parent and be dropped off at school Monday morning without missing a beat. Other kids with more sensitive temperaments are not able to do any of this unless they've had a day or at least an evening to readjust. Without a transitional day for reentry they fall behind in school and in play.

As we saw in Racer's story, school-aged kids can also become deeply involved in after-school activities such as sports, music, or gymnastics, to name a few. Friendships as well as ability and talent are fostered through participation in these activities. As children try different activities and schedules change, conflicts with custody arrangements are inevitable. Invitations to friends' birthday parties, playdates, and outings with other families don't fall neatly into established time-sharing schedules. Usually, the farther away the parents live from each other, the harder it is to get the child to all of their activities and events. Racer seems to be a sturdy child who is very aware that he is missing out on some practices and opportunities, but once he's there, he's able to try his hardest and enjoy the experience. Other, more delicately balanced kids worry themselves sick over the possibility of being late, missing a practice, disappointing their dance teacher or coach, or being the only one in their group to miss the slumber party. They spend hours fretting about upcoming conflicts in the schedule. This, too, is detrimental to their development. I have found that their anger at feeling "pushed around" is often lasting.

As in intact families, parents attempting joint custody should pay close attention to how much stress their children are experiencing. There needs to be fairly constant checking in with the child, with each other, and with teachers. Parents should be prepared to readjust their own schedules as the child progresses in critical areas of learning and social development. Mediated agreement or court orders should make provision at the outset for changes based on the predictable changes in the child. Parents in intact families monitor their children carefully for a match between their schedule and the child's response. Surely the child of divorce deserves the same loving care. She needs it even more.

There is no way to generalize about the custody of teenagers. They mature at different rates and they follow idiosyncratic pathways. One principle is clear. In intact families teenagers have increased voices in planning their schedules. The same privileges should be available for youngsters in divorced families. It is absolutely clear that parents will need in most instances to confer even more frequently and help each other during these years if only to keep the youngster from playing them off against each other or going from home to home in order to avoid responsibilities in either place.

I can only conclude that joint custody as a legal presumption for all children is a misguided policy. Although our legal system is mandated to protect the best interest of children, it often makes life harder for them. The emphasis on finding policies that suit all children is unrealistic and detrimental to the individuality of children and their family situations. We need to develop procedures that allow children to discuss their needs and wishes before visiting arrangements are made—and we need to make provisions for monitoring these arrangements through time. Each arrangement should be tailored to individual circumstances.

Repeating the Past

A WEEK AFTER talking to Racer, I met Paula to discuss what I'd learned. The child was obviously frustrated. I couldn't help wondering, shouldn't his mother, who was so unhappy as a child of divorce, have a huge amount of empathy for her son's predicament and take steps to protect him? I asked Paula if she could do more to accommodate to Racer's concern that his interests would get no support from either parent. Her face contorted.

"I've done all the accommodating so far," she said. "If Brad will back off and come to me, then maybe we can talk. But I'll be damned if I'm always the one who explains things to Racer, the one who makes the sacrifices. Racer will have to live with who Brad is and who I am—and he'll have to make the best of it!"

I was troubled at her angry response, which had blotted out her genuine concern for her son. But I had seen this before. I decided to try again: "Paula, is there anything you learned from your own experience as a child of divorce that would make it easier for Racer? He's having a hard time and trying very hard not to show it."

She sat glumly for a moment and then relented. "Maybe during the baseball season, which doesn't last forever, Brad and I can figure out another custody arrangement that would work better for him. Maybe I should call my ex-mother-in-law."

Sadly, children of divorce who divorce are not better at protecting their children. I'd hoped that they might draw on their own experiences and treat their children with more understanding when their marriages failed. But I was bitterly disappointed. Although all those in our study complained that their parents didn't explain the divorce to them and failed to ease their adjustment to the new circumstance, they made the same mistakes with their own children. Nor did they welcome the children's questions or try to understand their troubles. Like their own parents, they were overwhelmed with the demands of their new lives, finding a place to live, making do with less money, and planning for the future. I knew before seeing Racer that Paula hadn't learned much from her own childhood, although she remembered vividly how angry she was at her mother and how she worried that her parents would disappear. Like many parents, Paula assumed that Racer was a resilient child who'd understand what was happening. He was expected to manage. But she didn't see that he might feel as lonely and abandoned as she had as a child or that he might develop the same kind of anger that had shaped her life for many years.

I've come across Paula's attitude many times in my work with divorcing parents. It's common for them to have strong concerns for their children and equally strong, if not stronger, feelings that the other parent is falling down on the job. They know that life after divorce isn't easy and truly want advice about how to make things better and easier. But there are no easy solutions. Things that can make a significant difference in the child's life always involve sacrifice and change on the part of one or both parents. They require flexibility in both parents in deference to the child's concerns. These changes are required at precisely the time when the parents, depleted from the travails of separating and setting up a new life, are at their lowest ebb. Who wants to cooperate at a time like this? Who wants to make more sacrifices? In an ideal world, what's good for parents should be good for children. Happy, successful parents should produce happy, successful children. This is an axiom of our culture, but it breaks down in the complexity of real-life families. Some very happy, competent parents have children who feel excluded from their orbit—forever on the outskirts of deep affection. And when families come apart, the needs of every member diverge. What feels good for the divorced parents may not satisfy the needs of the children at all. It is at this point that many divorced parents draw the line and harden their hearts. Often they lose touch with their children and expect them to be little adults.

"He has to compromise, too," one newly separated mother of a five-year-old told me when her therapist suggested that she not move in with her boyfriend right away.

"I apologized to her for causing her to grow up in a divorced family," a father of a three-year-old told me seriously. "Now we all have to move on with our lives. She has to do it, too."

Although Paula knew firsthand what it was like to grow up in a single-parent household and could fully appreciate her son's feelings, she's constrained like her mother and millions of divorced parents by the economic realities of life. "I try to spend time with Racer. It's not easy. And I'm exhausted. Once I graduate there are no part-time jobs out there that I can live on. So I'm looking at working full-time." She added grimly, "Racer will be lonely and angry just like I was. But what can I do?"

At the end of our interview Paula became reflective.

"I've covered a lot of topics," she said. "When I look back now on what kids need I realize all I didn't have. I was lost for so long and I could easily have just stayed high and self-destructed. There must have been something that kept me going, and maybe it is something I got from my parents. I guess they loved me even though they didn't show it. I always thought they were both selfish. But things are better now and that's what's important. I have a better family now than I had as a kid. I guess there's no way not to have something left over from what's happened to you. As for what I've done, I'm very pleased. I know you're supposed to say your wedding day is the best day of your life. But, for me, the day I graduate from college will be the best day of my life. Because I'll be able to say to myself, I did it. I never thought I would."

At age thirty-three, Paula is finally, painfully, completing her adolescence and becoming a true adult. Her journey is not yet ended and it isn't clear what lies ahead. In her thirties, Paula is working through and trying to understand some of the losses she sustained growing up. Moving beyond anger and disappointment, she's forging relationships with both of her parents in which their shortcomings are neither denied nor dwelt upon. She's finding ways of remaining connected with them. She clearly loves her young son and wants him to share in her newly regained family. After spending eighteen years dependent on alcohol, she's slowly building a view of herself that rests on pride at what she has overcome and accomplished rather than on shame, compliance, and avoidance of pain. Paula is also figuring out how to be a mother. She knows how she doesn't want to bring up her son, but knowing what not to do isn't the same as knowing how to do it better. She still has a lot to learn about how to be independent and how to create and enjoy a satisfying, loving relationship. I leave her and her son at the crossroads.

PART FOUR

The Vulnerable Child: Billy

SEVENTEEN

The Vulnerable Child

The next few chapters concern a group of children who have not been studied in the context of divorce. They are vulnerable children who suffer from a wide range of disabilities or problems, including birth defects, learning disorders, diabetes, cancer, and other diseases. After talking to physicians, teachers, clinicians, and others who treat these children, I learned that marital distress and divorce are high among families with such children. The job of raising a child who needs round-the-clock nursing, frequent doctor appointments, or special classes at school is daunting. Some parents thrive under the pressure, but alas, many cannot cope and find themselves blaming each other or the marriage for the strain they face each day.

Billy's story is about a child born with a congenital heart defect who was protected in his early years by a doting mother. But after his parents divorced, Billy's world collapsed and he was never able to adjust to the changes demanded of him. Like Karen, Larry, and Paula, the divorce shaped his personality, but unlike the others, he grew more and more isolated and unhappy. What happened to Billy is another example of how the divorce experience in childhood can lead to changed lives and different outcomes in adulthood.

I MET BILLY for his twenty-five-year interview at the Berkeley bakery and coffeehouse where he works—a large establishment with hardwood floors, lots of green plants, and skylights atop fifteen-foot-high ceilings. The smell of cinnamon rolls followed Billy as he emerged from the kitchen in a floury apron, his long hair tied back in a net. Billy had invited me to join him for breakfast at nine o'clock, which is when his early morning shift ends and he can begin what for the rest of us would be lunch break. He was almost breathless. "We have a special order just coming out of the oven and I'll be a while. I apologize. Here, Sue will take care of you." A waitress showed me to a table and gave me coffee. "Billy is so conscientious," Sue said to me shyly. "He oversees every order and he's the one they trust to do the really delicate cases."

I pondered her words "the really delicate cases." I first met Billy when he was nine years old and he had certainly been a "delicate case." Small-boned, pale, and seeming to want to make himself invisible, he sat huddled in an oversized San Francisco Giants parka. I remember the sour, miserable look on his face and his refusal to answer most of my questions. His mother complained that he had been rude and jealous of her friends since the divorce. His father told me that Billy was spoiled.

Born with a congenital heart defect that had been only partially repaired surgically when he was six months old, Billy had been on medication all his life and needed extra care and protection. Small, thin, and weak, his activities and diet had to be closely monitored. He was hospitalized several times and missed a considerable amount of school. Throughout his early years Billy's mother was his nurse, overseer, adviser, and closest friend. She took him to endless medical appointments, consulted with doctors and dietitians, and watched over his daily meals and routines. During the long days at home when he had to miss school and rest, Billy's mother was there helping with homework, playing games, and inventing diversions. Her care and attention paid off. From almost being held back in kindergarten and first grade, Billy's academic work and self-esteem steadily improved. Shortly before his parents divorced, Billy was at the top of his fourth-grade class and was an especially gifted writer. Other kids liked him.

Then Billy's world caved in. "I'm tired of full-time mothering," his mom told me during our first interview, five months after the separation. Young and attractive, Billy's mother started dating the minute her husband packed his bags and within weeks was spending all her time with Tom, the man she would later marry. "Billy *adores* Tom," she exclaimed. In fact, Billy and his mother spent most of that first summer visiting Tom in Petaluma where Tom owns a sporting goods store, away from Billy's friends and regular summer activities. "All Billy does is sit home on the couch and mope," she said. "It drives me nuts. The more he demands my attention, the more obnoxious he gets. I've devoted my life to this child," she said earnestly, leaning toward me. "He has to realize that I need a life of my own!"

Billy's mother was a gregarious woman who was an accomplished amateur musician. His father, a native Australian, built a successful restaurant franchise and spent the rest of his time engaged in his true passion, racquet sports. The parents had an active social life but maintained predictable routines at home for Billy. When they went out in the evenings, Billy was cared for by a retired nurse whom he had known all his life.

One of the only times that Billy came out of his shell during our first interview together was when I asked if it was hard for him to miss so much school. He looked at me sharply and then his eyes fell on the bony little hands tightly laced in his lap. In a low voice, he muttered, "Mom made it okay. We used to do things together."

"What sorts of things?"

Billy huddled into his parka. He was silent so long I thought he wasn't going to respond. Then he said, softly, "We had games we played only on those days. We'd use my spelling words and it was really fun to learn them that way. We made multiplication dominos and I knew all the times tables up to twelve even before third grade ended. We read the kid's *National Geographic* and made up stories to go with it. And we had big maps of imaginary worlds that we kept adding to and coloring." His voice trailed off and he looked very sad.

"That sounds wonderful!" I said, glad to have found a topic that evoked some interest in him. Billy looked at me almost angrily and again twisted his hands. "Yeah, but she doesn't do it anymore."

I met Billy's dad a week later at his well-appointed office near North Beach in San Francisco. The entire wall behind his desk was filled with trophies and ribbons from his various sports victories. Constantly interrupted by telephone calls and secretaries, Billy's father had a powerful athletic build and charming smile. He waved an arm at the chaos in his office and apologized. "It's been this way ever since we opened our first restaurant." During one of his telephone conversations, I leaned forward to get a better view of the silver-framed pictures on his desk. Expecting to see family, I was taken aback to see pictures of sports teams and an especially large one of Billy's dad embracing a very young woman, both in tennis whites, in front of a spectator-filled playing field, apparently after winning a doubles match.

"Here's Billy," said the father, noting my examination. He indicated a smallish, dark picture on the wall mostly hidden by the corner of his desk. "Billy's a very lucky kid," he told me. "He'll have the bonus of two Christmases, two birthdays, and probably two daddies."

As in many marriages that become unhappy, Billy's mother turned increasingly to her child as her primary source of admiration and unconditional love. This is one important reason why children are often happy in a marriage that is unhappy for their parents. They have first dibs on one parent's love and attention. The fact that Billy was physically vulnerable, needed her, and depended on her made it easy and natural for his mother to become absorbed in caring for him as long as the marriage lasted. Billy's father grew increasingly preoccupied with his life outside the family, getting more gratification from making successful deals and winning squash tournaments. Truth be told, he was secretly dismayed at having a physically imperfect child who remained small and scrawny-looking, who could not play sports.

The marriage ended with a disquieting lack of feeling. Billy's mother had come to resent her husband's preoccupation with partying and business. After he started an affair and took no pains to conceal it, she asked him to leave. They shared one attorney and settlement negotiations were simple. Both felt it was a fair and compatible divorce. Billy's reaction was deliberately guarded, as are those of many children who are trying to please one or both parents. "Now I can get a dog," his mother remembers him saying on receiving the news of his father's departure. His dad was allergic to dogs.

Many people separate as coolly as this couple did. The marriage fails for any number of reasons but the partners are not particularly hurt or wounded by the divorce. Both believe that their needs have changed or that they find each other boring and that they are moving on to livelier times. This is not the common view of divorce given that attorneys and mental health professionals typically see people who are agitated. Nevertheless it happens frequently. The problem in Billy's family is that no one faced the fact that the boy's special needs had not changed. As we've seen in all the stories in this book, when parents divorce and become preoccupied with reorganizing their own lives, the children are less protected. There's almost never room for extra nurturing. More insidiously, there is far less tolerance for distress, weakness, or protest. Behaviors and feelings that have been treated compassionately as part of a child's vulnerability are now viewed as deliberate, spoiled grabs for attention. Both parents have moved on. Their needs for themselves and for their child have changed. Billy's lifelong problem became that he did not have the internal capability to successfully adapt to the postdivorce situation. He remained a vulnerable, needy child in a world that could no longer give him what he needed in order to thrive.

There are many children like Billy who are born with special needs, including early surgery, medication every six hours around the clock, and regular monitoring of vital signs. It's hard enough to care for a baby, but those born with handicaps are especially challenging for experienced and inexperienced mothers alike. These include infants and children with heart conditions, asthma, cystic fibrosis, Down's syndrome, epilepsy, and a long list of other familiar maladies. In addition, many more babies who would have died from rare genetic conditions, including difficult-to-diagnose metabolic diseases, are now being saved by modern medical treatments. Many will live, but they are afflicted with severe mental or physical handicaps that improve very little over time. Other children challenge their parents with developmental disorders such as attention deficit, specific language impairment, dyslexia, or conduct disorder. Finally, there are many parents who adopt children who arrive with severe emotional problems due to lack of early caregiving or whose mothers have abused drugs and alcohol. Such children often have severe emotional problems, including an inability to form close attachments to parents or siblings. Many of them literally cry and fuss for twelve hours a day, rarely giving the baby smiles that help keep parents sane. All such children need an enormous amount of extra help just to survive and grow.

Social workers, special educators, and medical professionals who work with vulnerable children frequently report that marital tensions and divorce are much higher in such families.[1] It's no surprise that the tremendous need for care, coupled with worry about a vulnerable child, puts special strains of physical fatigue and emotional depletion on the couple. It's understandable that powerful feelings of anger, guilt, and blame intrude into the couple's intimate life—burdens that carry a high potential for disrupting the family. Although everyone in a family may pitch in to help care for a vulnerable child, the major burden of care usually falls on the mother, which can set up serious resentments. Whereas other family members may understand intellectually that their mother or wife is occupied with necessary tasks of caregiving, many can't help but resent her preoccupation with the needy child. Life grows more stressful for everyone. The father may work harder to bring in extra money for the child's care. Siblings quietly decide not to ask Mommy for help that may really be needed. Everyone grapples with feelings of loss, disappointment, resentment, or guilt that this child is not, and in many instances never will be, like other children. These feelings arise not only at the child's birth but repeatedly as the child grows and continues to fall behind other children's attainments.

I have met many people who could not handle these strains and whose divorce was directly caused by the child's frailty. For example, one young couple carried their autistic son to every medical center in America hoping to find a cure. Finally, they decided to institutionalize him and then divorced several months later. She explained, "Every time we looked at each other we saw Jason, and we felt so guilty we couldn't stand it."

One of the women in our comparison group, Debbie, was born with a rare muscular disorder that required daily massage and physical therapy. Her parents and siblings took turns administering her treatment all the time she was growing up. She learned to walk at age five using leg braces and crutches, learned to talk clearly after years of speech therapy, and attended public schools accompanied by a personal aide. She'd elected to attend a small, midwestern college that was her father's alma mater. Her parents had thoroughly investigated the disability program and access at the college and Debbie's mother stayed on campus for the first three months of school to help set up living arrangements and special assistance services. They'd been understanding and supportive of her slow course through college, punctuated by several extended returns home for additional treatment. Prominently displayed in Debbie's living room was a large photograph of herself in cap and gown surrounded by her smiling family. She's now partially self-supporting as a technical writer.

When I interviewed Debbie at age thirty-eight, she was living in a specially equipped apartment in the lower part of her parents' home. Personable, cheerful, and realistic, she told me that other, less fortunate people with her medical condition were wheelchair-bound and lived in full-time residential institutions. "Almost all of my memories as a child are of me together with my family," she said. "I was always with them and they took care of me when I was sick. Anything I've needed, they try to help. I know they'll be there for me no matter what happens."

Debbie said that sometimes she wishes she could be more self-sufficient, get out more with her friends, and maybe even marry and have children. A tinge of rebelliousness surfaces in her voice: "Right now I think my parents are too involved in my life. I see a lot of them. I like having them near, but I think they're too close, and they worry about me and want to know too much. It's hard to feel like I have a real life separate from them."

Aside from her work, Debbie spends as much time as she can with her network of friends. She's had two romantic relationships, one in college and another more recently. Wryly, she told me about her father's pretended nonchalance as he "happened" to drop in on her when she was being picked up by a male friend. "I know they're overprotective because they're so used to taking care of me, but puh-leeze, I am thirty-eight years old!"

When I asked Debbie how she would have been affected had her parents divorced when she was young, she answered, "I imagine almost everything would have been different." She envisioned that she would have lived with her mother and sister and seen much less of her father and brothers. Cognizant of how much her parents supported each other in caring for her, she concluded, "I think Mom would have worn herself out taking care of me and then I don't know what would have happened to her or to me!" Although she saw her parents' marriage "with much rosier glasses" when she was younger, Debbie feels strongly that their marriage was and is a successful union. "You have to expect to take the bad with the good," she said, "to make the most of what life gives you and to make your own happiness."

Realizing that her condition placed burdens on her family, Debbie said, "I worry that having me to take care of has kept my parents from doing other things, especially now that Dad has retired. He plays golf and I know that they'd like to travel more. They make sure there's someone staying here when they do go away, but I know Mom worries about me and she doesn't like to stay away too long. But they've told me all along that I'm a great gift, not a burden. And most of the time I believe them." Debbie's two older siblings, whom I also interviewed, candidly told me that they thought Debbie's disability had strengthened the marriage of two people whom otherwise seemed somewhat distant and formal in their relationship.

This special care does not have to stop because of divorce. In one divorced family, the child lived with the father after the mother left the marriage. But the mother was able to do the shopping and the cooking and to come to the house for several hours a day to stay with her son. Another affluent family hired a housekeeper who went back and forth with the child, who lived in both homes. This arrangement went on for years. When I interviewed the child, who has muscular dystrophy, at age fourteen, he was poised, charming, and well-adjusted. His divorced parents had done a magnificent job.

How to Protect the Vulnerable Child after Divorce

WHAT PARENTS NEED to know is that all vulnerable children have exceptional trouble with rapid or radical change. The gains that parents work so hard to achieve (a baby finally learns to sit up, a toddler can make it to the toilet, the child is able to travel on the school bus) may be wiped out by divorce. Vulnerable children regress with frightening speed and recovery is painfully slow.

Thus families with a vulnerable child who are planning to divorce should carefully plan the transition period. The child's routines should change as gradually as possible. If one parent has been primary caregiver and the other will now have the child in a separate residence, the caregiver should spend two to three afternoons a week in the child's new home. The goal is to overlap the old with the new, to enable the child to become slowly used to the new. Obviously, the child's medical needs take priority, but every effort should be made to maintain familiar interventions, treatments, exercises, and the like so that the child feels comfortable with routines.

If less care is given, as in Billy's case, because the mother is ready for new interests and a different life, parents need to understand that the child will take this as pure rejection. It will break his heart. Like Billy, he may react with depression, anger, or rebelliousness, and there is no reason to assume that his hurt will lessen. His loss is enormous and can be the defining event of his growing up years. This is because every ill or handicapped child carries a double burden. First, he must deal with his own handicap in an often pitiless world. Second, and even more difficult, he must cope with his parents' disappointment in him, for he knows that they had hoped for a healthy baby. He mustn't disappoint them any further. As the vulnerable child sees his parents' struggle to contain their grief, he is likely to feel anxious, ashamed, or depressed. He is likely to be hyperalert to their moods and more likely than a healthy child to feel responsible for any troubles in the family. The vulnerable child needs a double dose of praise and encouragement for every step he takes toward realistic independence. He needs assurance that there is a great deal he can do by himself and that he can master important ways to care for himself. He especially needs praise for his courage in trying.

When the parent of a vulnerable child remarries, he or she needs to proceed gradually. Billy's mother, for example, could have set aside exclusive time with her son in the early months, which would have helped him make the transition. In planning remarriage, a parent needs to work out the complex feelings of love and resentment between caregiver and child. Just as weaning means gradually giving up a dependency for both mother and baby, the vulnerable child and his mother need to respect their relationship and give it time to adapt to new conditions. Boys who are ill and lack stamina usually cannot compete in the world of sports, which in our society is often a major link between fathers and sons. A sensitive father will help his son cope with this loss, finding other ways to bond and real achievements that he can take pride in. In a good intact family, parents spell each other in taking care of their children; when one person is exhausted, the other takes over. This sort of sharing is even more needed in homes with a vulnerable child, where physical and emotional exhaustion are constant undercurrents of daily life.

Most important, people should not use divorce to solve their tremendous distress about bringing a defective child into the world and the overwhelming emotional and financial cost of raising the child. This is a very serious issue. Most people assume that divorce is caused by marital conflict. But we now know how readily stress from another sphere can ricochet into the marriage and lead to an impulsive divorce decision. Vulnerable children evoke strong passions and great suffering. The impulse to run away is potent.

Trickle-Down Happiness

WHEN I SAW Billy eighteen months after the divorce, he was a very sad and troubled child. He told me he no longer liked school. He refused to discuss Tom, his new stepfather. He wanted to see his biological father more often but he admitted that the visits had not been good. It was obvious from his story that his father continued to deny his son's handicap or didn't care. "Dad's girlfriend is a runner and they invited me to run with them," he said miserably. "I tried it once and I got halfway around the track and I had to sit down. I couldn't breathe. They just waved and kept on running. Finally I waited in the car for an hour. Then Dad dropped me off at home."

Billy was also having a great deal of trouble with his mother's remarriage. "It was bad timing for Billy," his mother said, shaking her head. "He adored his fifth-grade teacher but she left unexpectedly in the middle of the school year for emergency surgery. So he had to change teachers. This was a week before our wedding. Her leaving really hit him hard and he was very quiet and withdrawn at the wedding. Everyone else had a great time. We were all kind of annoyed at Billy. He was a real party pooper."

Billy's version of the wedding was slightly different. "The wedding was boring. There were all these people I hardly knew drinking too much and acting stupid. They wanted me to make a speech like Dave did." (Dave was Tom's fifteen-year-old son from his previous marriage.) "But I was too tired. I was sick the night before and couldn't sleep. But my mom was too busy partying with Tom to check in with me like she usually does."

In a mixture of concern laced with irritation, Billy's mother told me about her son's increasing sullenness and withdrawals. "Billy is ten going on eleven. He's too old to play the kinds of games we used to play. Anyway, I don't have the time for that anymore. Tom and I agree that Billy needs to be more independent."

That Billy didn't agree with this assessment of the state of things was all too clear. "She changed since he came," he said sadly, referring to his mother and Tom. "She acts silly and laughs a lot and she even sits on his lap," he said in disgust. "When I talk to her she's always saying 'Wait just a sec, hon' "—this said in a syrupy sweet falsetto voice—"and she's on the phone with him again. He calls from work more than anyone I know. My dad never called from work. He does his work, not play kissy face over the phone!"

Billy's story shows us another way in which changed parent and child relationships can shape a child's personality through the postdivorce years. Like Paula, Billy lost his mother's devoted attention immediately after the divorce. But Paula's mother disappeared because she had to go to work to support the family. Billy's mother did not go back to work. Her devotion to her child in part reflected her dissatisfaction with her marriage. As she moved into a happier marriage, she expected her son to change with her—invoking the trickle-down theory of happiness that so many people believe in and which I questioned earlier. But Billy did not have the capacity to change. Caught between his inability to hope or to give up hope that his nurturing mother will come back, he comes increasingly to believe that he is unloved and unwanted. Like Paula, he's angry but instead of lashing out at the world, he turns his frustrations inward. He withdraws into a sullen passivity. And as we'll see in his later interviews, this passivity comes to dominate his adult life, including his attempts to build intimate relationships with young women—or to avoid them.

EIGHTEEN

The Stepfamily

Billy was almost fifteen when I drove to Petaluma to meet him for our five-year follow-up. Billy, his mom, and stepfather Tom were now living in a Victorian home in an old section of the city with Tom's son Dave. Billy also had a new half brother, Mark, who was two years old. We timed it right, for Billy arrived in a friend's car just as I drove up. Still small for his age, he looked wiry rather than scrawny. I knew from my preliminary phone call to his mother setting up this round of interviews that Billy's health was still precarious. Any physical exertion could bring on palpitations and shortness of breath. He carried his heart medication with him. In high school, as in previous school years, he had study hall when other students had physical education, and he had special permission to rest in the nurse's office when he was fatigued. His mother was worried because his few friends tended to be loners and troublemakers rather than kids in the "in" crowd, which revolved around sports. Nevertheless Billy looked better than I had expected. His scowl and sullen attitude were replaced by a teenage awkwardness and tentative smile. Sitting in the large, sunny kitchen before the other family members arrived home, he was articulate for the first time about the divorce and his mother's remarriage. "All divorces are bad for kids," he told me. "They make kids do things that they normally wouldn't do."

"Like what, Billy?"

And then Billy told me with shame in his face how he had gotten into trouble in the year and a half since the family moved to Petaluma. "I ripped off some stores. I got caught smoking dope. I had a bad attitude toward my teachers. I fought a lot with my mother." He looked at me as if to say, "You want to hear more? I'll give you more."

Instead I asked, "How is this connected with your parents' divorce?"

"I was really angry," Billy said quickly. "I remember thinking over and over, 'If you won't do for me, I'll make life miserable for everyone.' "

"Are you still angry?"

Billy shrugged. "Sometimes I am. Sometimes I'm sad. I wish my parents would have tried harder and maybe they could have worked it out."

"Do you think they might still get back together?"

Billy looked startled by my question. He waited a long minute before responding. "Yes," he said solemnly. "I do think about that, sometimes a lot."

This response didn't surprise me. After their parents' divorce, many youngsters have powerful fantasies that can last well into adulthood that their parents will reconcile.

"How are you and Dave getting along?" I asked, remembering the earlier incompatibility with his stepbrother.

"Well, he's okay sometimes, but it's better since he left for college. He's not here that much. We fight a lot about what's fair and who gets to do things and who should do the chores. Tom gets really mad and Mom won't ever take my side. She just disappears."

"How about Tom? What do you think of him?"

Billy sighed and slumped down in his chair. "He's okay," Billy said grudgingly. "But he's too strict. He's hard on me and he doesn't give me any time to explain." Billy gave as examples a couple of incidents in which he was late doing chores or underestimated how long it would take him to water the lawn. "It's like he's never pleased no matter how hard I try," Billy complained. "He's hard to talk to. Tom always makes deals. If I want to go with my friends it's, 'You can't go 'til you clean the garage,' and then I'm too tired and I have to lie down. So I don't get to see my friends at all." Billy sagged with defeat.

"What does your mom say about things like that?" I wondered if Billy felt supported by his mother in any way.

"That's the whole problem!" he burst out. "She always backs him up. She never takes my side. If I tell her I don't think he's being fair, she just says she'll talk it over with Tom. Then she comes back to me and tries to explain why Tom did what he did or said what he said. Or they both come in and tell me why I'm wrong. It's like they're both against me. I'm sick and tired of it."

I left the interview with a sense of déjà vu. It seemed to me that Billy's family relationships had progressed very little in the five years since our last meeting. It was still just as hard for Billy to adjust to the new family circumstances and it appeared that he still was hoping that his stepfather would disappear. As before, he assessed his parents' divorce as a tragedy that might have been averted if only they had been more mature or willing to try to work out their difficulties. I was impressed by Billy's awareness that stealing and drug-taking were his way of retaliating for the unhappiness he felt his parents had imposed upon him. (Most adolescents who become delinquent after divorce do not make the connection between anger at their parents and their acting out. Unfortunately, many parents don't make this connection, either. If they did, they might reach out to their children who are often lonely and depressed like Billy.)

But I was troubled and somewhat mystified by Billy's attitude toward his stepfather, Tom. From all accounts except Billy's, Tom, a former Peace Corps volunteer and English teacher, had made consistent efforts to be an available, interested, and involved parent to Billy. After nearly five years, Billy respected Tom but still resented him and certainly didn't seem to feel close to him.

I knew from talking to Billy's mother that she felt happier. She was very active in her younger son's preschool, played her cello at community events and convalescent homes, and was very involved with Tom in several charitable organizations. Billy's loyalty to his own father seemed as strong as ever, even as the real-life ties grew weaker. The father had gotten more deeply involved in his work and seemed to have little time for anyone outside the spheres of sports and restaurants. Later he told me that Billy's stepbrother, Dave, was a "great guy" and that he hoped Billy would turn out more like Dave.

The Stepfather

Our latest national reports say that 25 percent of all children will spend part of their childhood in a stepfamily.[1] Moreover, 40 percent of all marriages in the 1990s involve one or both persons who have been married before.[2] So we are looking at new roles for millions of adults and millions of children. For adults, this situation means knowing what it takes to be a successful stepmother or stepfather. For children, it means dealing with the arrival of a stranger who takes up residence in the bosom of the family. Neither job is easy. Both are rife with potential for misunderstanding and misery as well as deep emotional support and unfailing love.

The stepfather–child relationship is usually conceived as a duet that involves only the child and the stepparent. But it is composed of at least four voices, sometimes more, each of which has a major role in the harmony or the dissonance that ensues. The four voices are the new husband, the child, the mother, and the biological father. They are the new ensemble that has to learn to play well together. The background sometimes swells to a chamber orchestra what with stepmothers, stepsiblings, and half siblings, but for now we'll talk about the main players.

It seems that we are comfortable with the idea that each person has only one biological mother in this world (egg donor technologies aside) and that stepmothers, while loved, do not usurp that special position. But fathers are different. We seem to accept the notion that a child can have two fathers of equal standing—a biological dad and a stepdad who share the same slot in the child's mind. Some people think that stepfathers can even replace fathers, as if a father's role is somehow blurrier or perhaps more porous than a mother's role. But in real life this doesn't compute. If a child maintains a close relationship with a biological father, there's no ready role for a stepfather, no traditions to turn to, no scripts. Oddly, the fathers' movement in this country has diminished the stepfather's potential role in his stepchild's life. Who is the stepfather alongside the biological father? A Dutch uncle? A friend? The man who lives with my mom? My parent? Who carries responsibility for the child's life? Who makes the rules? Assuming that fathers and stepfathers disagree, as sometimes they must, whose values prevail? Who helps with the homework and who talks with the teacher? Does every adult in the family attend parent-teacher conferences? There's almost no part of a child's life that is clearly in one domain or the other because there are no rules, legal or otherwise, that lay out a stepfather's role when the father is still around. If mother and stepfather divorce, or if the mother dies, the stepfather has no formal relationship with the child, not even the right to visit, even though the stepfather may have raised her since she was a baby. So there is ample room for conflict, misunderstanding, and competition. By the same token, there's ample room for cooperation and creative solutions.

Most men who are thrust into this role don't understand how hard it is to build a new parent-child relationship. This is one of the many roles in the divorced family for which there is no dress rehearsal. People getting married a second time assume that an interested stepfather will slide smoothly into the shoes of an absent father. The new man arrives on the scene with great expectations and energy. But in my experience, the transition rarely works quickly or easily, especially if the biological father is still front and present in the child's life. There are of course circumstances when a stepfather truly replaces a biological parent and is acknowledged as such—for example, when a child is very young and has limited contact with the biological parent. Compared with cultivating the interests of an older child, reaching out to little children is easier for stepfathers. It's fun to toss toddlers into the air, hold them on your laps, read them stories, or put them to bed. And young children have an easier time responding because they usually don't have conflicting loyalties that hinder their new attachments. But finding common ground with an older child takes a lot more time because it depends on gradually building a genuine friendship, winning the cooperation of the child, and making it clear that the stepfather does not intend to displace the biological father in the child's affection.

Time, patience, and persistence are key components to becoming a successful stepparent and to creating a happy remarried family. Good intentions are important, but that's only a bare beginning. Building a close bond with a child takes as much time as building a close relationship with an adult. It requires sustained effort and most of all genuine affection that can outlast the child's resistance and anxiety about trusting a new adult whom they fear may disappear. Stepparenthood in the child's heart is never a given. It is earned.

Billy's stepfather wanted to be a parent to Billy and made many overtures to the boy during the first year of the marriage. So why did he fail? He was not in direct competition with Billy's father and he did not expect Billy to choose between them. I suspect one reason is that he did not need Billy in his life. He already had a son and very soon he and Billy's mother had a new baby boy. Thus he had little incentive to pursue a relationship with a difficult, angry boy. Essentially, after a few attempts, he gave up trying to build a relationship. To make matters even harder, his son was good-looking and athletic—everything Billy was not. Billy would have loved to be like his stepbrother and it broke his heart when all the family members, including his own father, spoke glowingly of this rival. No one ever seemed to admire Billy.

As a result, tragically but predictably, Billy forfeited his chance for a good relationship with a decent man who tried to befriend him. His stepfather essentially remained "the man my mom married, my mom's husband but nothing for me." For many children and stepfathers, this is a sad lost opportunity. However, given the difficulty of moving into a family midstream, it may represent the best compromise that the family can reach. Certainly it is a very common solution. This kind of relationship was the outcome in a full half of the remarriages in the study. Many stepfathers have little interest in the new wife's children and heartily wish that the woman had come unencumbered. Others resent living with or caring for another man's offspring. It is by no means a given that a man who wants to marry a woman can be expected to embrace her children as well. And in fact, some women recognizing this potential problem sent their children to live with their father when they remarried whether or not the father had indicated that he was eager or able to accept them. There are tensions in remarriage that we did not anticipate.

The Child

From the child's point of view, a stepfather (or live-in lover) is not immediately welcome. After all, he's a mysterious masked stranger who sweeps onstage in the middle of the second act to seize a commanding position. But the first act of the play, which was the child's life before the stranger galloped in, had a full cast of characters, including a mother and father and children in well-defined roles. Why is the stranger here? Is he good or bad news for my sibs and me? Will he take my dad's place at the head of the table and in my mom's bed? Will he try to usurp my dad's place with me? Will he take my mom away from me? Most children don't want the play changed. They certainly don't want new leading actors. They like the simplicity of the first act. The powerful forces swirling around them make children feel fragmented, not whole. This is a major reason why children hold on to the hope that their parents will reconcile. Mom and Dad together represent the inner sense of wholeness that the child is losing because of divorce. But the stepfather's arrival is a powerful statement that the divorce is here to stay. This is unwelcome news for the many children who in their heart of hearts cling to the hope that Dad will walk in the door and resume his place at the head of the table.

On top of all this, there's a built-in conflict of interest between the newly married couple and the children. The couple wants privacy, which means opportunity to be without the children. They want and need time for sex, companionship, and adult play. Children who fear losing what they had naturally demand more time from their mothers. They are endlessly resourceful in getting into trouble, becoming ill, creating emergencies, or simply making mischief. (The many young children who have been displaced by the stepfather from sleeping in the mother's bed are especially outraged.) These inevitable tensions add to the drama of the stepfather's arrival. Nothing about it is easy. Nevertheless, the parents should strive for a balance that fairly allots time to the new couple and to the children. Moreover, they should make the limits of each clear. Many remarried families have found that regular family meetings to discuss various issues can be very helpful in clearing the air. They allow each person to be heard and then give the opportunity to set household rules and future plans firmly in place. It is very important for children to feel that they are being treated fairly but not that they are in control of the family. This is no small feat for the parents to accomplish, especially with older youngsters who often had a big say in the divorced family.

There are important gender differences, especially at the outset, that should also be carefully considered by the adults.[3] Boys may welcome the presence of a man in the household once they are reassured that he will not disrupt or run their lives. He relieves the anxiety of the only son about being the only male in the family. Many school-age boys complain after divorce, "There is no one here like me since my dad left." Girls, in contrast, often enjoyed a close, privileged position with their mothers prior to the remarriage and resent the stepfather's intrusion, fearing that they will lose their access to their mother. It would be very helpful for the mother to think realistically about each of her relationships with her children and consider how each child is likely to feel when the stepfather arrives. Simply setting aside special times to be alone with her son or daughter can be very effective in preventing difficulties later on. It would have been very reassuring to Billy had his mother set aside exclusive time with him a few hours each week.

From the child's point of view, a stepfather is resented if he marches into the home in seven-league boots, telling the mom that she's been too lenient and that the children need a man's firm hand. Taking over the discipline without first earning the child's respect and loyalty is a bad mistake. (My experience is that it is better for child and stepparent if discipline remains with the mother, especially during the early years of the remarriage.) Adolescents are especially offended and angered by this kind of insensitivity and are deeply dismayed when their mothers don't take their side. They conclude that their mother and stepfather have ganged up against them. They can remain angry for many years, well into their adult life.

Billy rejected his stepfather from the outset and was unresponsive to genuine overtures of friendship. Why? Because as far as Billy was concerned, Tom never got past being the interloper—the enemy who had taken Billy's place at the center of his mother's attention and affection. Billy desperately wanted his mother to return to her caregiving role. He wanted his stepfather out of his life, period. Although his anger at the stepfather dissipated over the years, they never became close, and as adults they had almost no relationship. Billy never identified with his stepfather's values. He never shared his companionship or interests. Essentially he never gave the relationship a chance. The boy was too aggrieved to recognize the virtues that the stepfather had as a parent, even though his biological father didn't come close to measuring up. Billy had an agenda with his own father that gave him no choice but to reject his stepfather.

The adolescent-stepfather relationship is particularly hard to navigate. After all, the teenager is busily engaged in breaking free of parental authority. Rules are the natural battleground of the adolescent's struggle toward independence. Few stepfathers realize that their stepchildren are angry not at them per se but because they are caught up in a developmental stage that goes with anger at adults in authority positions. So when the new man comes down on the kid like a ton of bricks, he can only expect further rebellion. This behavior can start a no-win cycle of rebellion and punishment that in one instance in this study led to a sixteen-year-old stealing and wrecking the stepfather's new sports car. The stepfather retaliated by sending the boy to juvenile hall. In another instance, an overly nosy stepfather began to monitor his stepdaughter's conversations with her friends with the excuse that she might get involved with the wrong company. Although these and similar battles occur in intact families, stepfathers and adolescents are in special jeopardy because their bonding is fragile.

Stepfathers and adolescent daughters may feel constrained to keep their distance for another reason. A biological father who changes his daughter's dirty diapers is less likely to think of her sexually at age fourteen than is a man who arrives years later and sees the developing girl parade around the house in bra and panties. Stepfathers and stepdaughters have not built up the kinds of protections against erotic fantasies and behaviors that biological fathers and daughters have naturally developed. Hence, consciously or unconsciously, they keep their distance.

The Mother

MANY WOMEN REMAIN largely on the sidelines, hoping that their new husbands and children will get along and then becoming frustrated when they fail. This is a mistake. I doubt that these women fully understand the importance of their role in encouraging their new husband and child to cooperate. I suspect that Billy's mother never discussed her son's vulnerabilities with her new husband since he paid them so little attention when he demanded that Billy perform his appointed chores. Nor was there evidence that she tried to understand Billy's resistance to forming a relationship with Tom. Had she made that effort to build a bridge between them, the outcome might have changed.

In many intact families, the mother serves as intermediary between father and child, interpreting the needs of each to the other in ways that sustain their connection. Thousands of women say to their tired husbands, "It would mean so much to the child if you could set aside some time for him over the weekend." Or they turn to their busy children and say, "Your dad wants to spend some time with you. When can you do it?" This maternal role is even more important in the remarried family.

If the mother does not take an independent role, the child sees her as siding with the stepfather against him. It's also up to the mother to bring the child into the orbit of the happy couple to offset his observations of the failed marital relationship. Few women recognize this as an unparalleled opportunity to influence their children's future attitudes toward marriage.

The Biological Dad

THE FOURTH MEMBER of the quartet is the biological father, who together with his ex-wife can make or break the child's relationship to the stepfather. Some absent fathers, though they don't directly block the child's attachment to another man, can prevent it from happening by keeping alive the child's hope for a better relationship. Such children are the ones most likely to have a poor relationship with their stepfathers—a fact most adults find hard to understand. After all, a child who is unhappy in one relationship should logically welcome another person to fill that gap. But that would be true only if the child gives up hope for the father's renewed love and interest or rejects the father, as we saw in Larry's story. Billy, no matter how many disappointments he sustained, never gave up expecting that his father would someday love him and value him. To many children, the father's disinterest fuels a passionate attachment in the son toward the father. A close relationship with a stepfather would be a betrayal of the father.

Whether he is nearby or far away, the biological father's attitude toward the stepfather is of utmost importance. He stands symbolically at the entrance to their relationship. If the biological father resents the stepfather or competes with him for the child's affection, it is almost impossible for the child to love the new man. But if the father encourages the new relationship, he helps clear the path for stepfather and child to proceed.

In contrast, children and adolescents who have rejected their biological father, seeing him as a failure or morally flawed or lacking in interest, often turn eagerly to their stepfather as a person they can admire and emulate. Many talked of their stepfather with great affection and praise. "I really love him. He's a good, loyal man." Others said, "My stepfather saved my life." One young man explained to me, "I have no respect for my father. He's irresponsible and self-centered. But my stepfather is just the kind of person that I want to be. I'm lucky to have him." One young woman, who was rescued from a delinquent life with a motorcycle gang by her stepfather's confidence in her, told me proudly, "He told me that I was smart and that I was too good to waste my time with those losers. He said that I should go to college, and best of all he put his money where his mouth was. He is the father I always wanted." I have seen many such transformations when an adolescent turns his back on the morally bankrupt biological parent and looks to the stepfather for guidance and help in the real world. One young man said, "My step is more of a father than my real father. He's the one who took care of my mom, my sisters, and me. He's earned his place with me."

Several of the young adults said they appreciated stepfathers who played quiet, protective roles in their lives and in the life of their mother—in effect taking good care of their moms. This they found comforting. "He was always there for me if I needed him," a successful thirty-four-year-old businesswoman confided about her stepfather. "We'd go to Dad's and it was like a big party. He'd buy us presents and let us do things that Mom and my step didn't allow. We adored Dad. But I was always glad to come home to Mom and my step. He wasn't as exciting as Dad but we needed something solid after chasing rainbows with Dad all weekend." Obviously a happy, stable remarriage has enormous economic, social, and psychological advantages for the couple and the children.

Children raised in good remarriages and who feel loved and protected are indeed fortunate. But they are not in a majority. National studies find no significant differences between the psychological and learning problems of children raised in single-parent or remarried families.[4] It appears that the advantages of remarriage, including having more economic resources, are counterbalanced by the high potential for conflict and emotional difficulties seen in so many remarried families. Not everyone can achieve harmony in a newly formed quartet.

Who Takes Responsibility?

When I called Billy's mother to arrange our ten-year follow-up visit, she told me that Billy had moved out. "I can give you his address and his phone number, but Judy, we haven't seen him in over a year. He left when he was sixteen to live with his father. Well, that was a disaster.

Billy ended up living alone in Fred's new house in Palo Alto and trying to go to high school. I begged Billy to come back here for his senior year, but it didn't help that the baby had moved into Billy's room. After six months Billy moved into an apartment upstairs from the restaurant where he works. He's lived there ever since. I honestly think he's rejected us."

National reports tell us that children in remarriages leave home earlier than children in intact families.[5] Many feel unloved, unwanted, and excluded from the new family orbit. Some are very angry at their mothers and stepfathers. One young man said, "I was a hindrance—the leftover from a marriage that died." The angriest were boys in their teens who were bitter about what they regarded as harsh discipline imposed unfairly by their stepfathers and mothers. I was frankly surprised to find the anger alive among a group of these young men years later. One thirty-year-old man who left home at age sixteen told me, "I was arrested for drunk driving the day after my best friend was killed. It was my first arrest ever. My mom and stepfather came to court like vigilantes and told the judge to throw the book at me. That's when I moved out." He said chillingly, "I'll never forgive her as long as I live."

I met Billy a month later. "I always wanted to get out, *always*," Billy said vehemently as we walked slowly down the road to a bench under a shady tree. Now twenty years old, he was tanned, thin, and wiry, sporting a small mustache strikingly like the one his father had always worn. Since graduating from high school, Billy had worked full-time as a waiter and then as assistant manager in the restaurant that was now his home. His mother told me that Billy had started college at Sonoma State University but hadn't liked it much and had dropped out after a quarter. When I asked Billy what had happened he snorted.

"What did she tell you, that I couldn't hack it, right? What does she know? I was only there one quarter. When I enrolled, Mom told me that she would pay for half the year and that Dad would pay for the other half—tuition and board. So I go to register for the second semester and I couldn't because Dad hadn't sent the tuition check. Then the dorm told me I had to move out because the money hadn't been sent. I called Dad and he told me he'd had some temporary cash-flow problems and that Mom should pay it and he'd pay her back. Mom said she'd pay the tuition but she wouldn't front the money for the dorm. So then I got a job to cover the room, but I was working nights and going to school and I got really tired and short of breath. I got scared about my heart and discouraged because it was hard to keep the grades up. I thought, 'Fuck it—if my going to college isn't important to them then it isn't important to me, either.' I came back here and I've been working ever since."

I had seen Billy's father just the week before and found him as urbane and charming as ever. He thought Billy was doing beautifully. "The reason Billy's okay is that I've never told him to do anything," he said. "I haven't pushed my ideas or my lifestyle on him. I'd say he's off and running. I don't see a problem at all."

"Have you and your ex-wife ever talked about helping Billy if he wants to go to college?" I asked, wondering if "off and running" meant paying one's own way through school. Billy's father looked serious. "There was some idea about splitting his college expenses. I've given it some thought and I don't think it's such a good idea. If Billy chooses to go to college, he'll value it more if he comes up with a way to do it himself." Billy's father looked me straight in the eye. "And he does better when his mother and I don't coddle him."

I was saddened but not surprised by what had happened to Billy when he attempted college. Like so many of the young people in our study, Billy's parents were both college educated and both had been given a higher education by their families. I had no doubt at all that if these two had stayed together, they would have sent Billy to college no questions asked. Moreover, their lack of concern for Billy's future was striking. I was certainly aware that a vulnerable young man like Billy needed a high level of specialized knowledge in order to enter the workplace because his poor health precluded so many jobs. But when I talked to Billy's mother she seemed politely regretful that her son hadn't continued in college. Billy's father told me flatly that he didn't care one way or another. Neither parent seemed to expect that Billy would achieve to at least their own educational and occupational levels. In fact, neither seemed to have many expectations for Billy at all.

When they reach their eighteenth birthday, many young adults in divorced families suddenly feel like second-class citizens. That's when the last child support check arrives and that's when they realize how disadvantaged they are compared with their friends in intact families. In California and the great majority of the states, a parent has no obligation to help a child after the age of eighteen or the end of high school. The child's continued education, including tuition, books, supplies, and living expenses, is all up to him. Many young people consider the cutoff at age eighteen the worst hit of their parents' divorce. They tell me bitterly, "I paid for my folks' divorce."

Among middle-class children, a college education is an expected rite of passage. Americans believe that the university is a necessary step for success in our technologically advanced, competitive society. Many parents in intact families make enormous sacrifices to send their children to college. As men and women of the world who benefited from their own professional training and contacts, they know that without a college education young people are handicapped all through their lives. Thus they save their money for many years ahead. In turn, they expect their kids to work hard as students and in part-time jobs. But they do not expect the children to do it all by themselves.

Billy's experience with higher education is typical of what happened to many of the young people in this study who had college-educated parents. In his case, support was cut off in the middle of his freshman year. For others the cut came later or was aborted from the start. These children worked hard to gain admittance to a public university with high standards and often found part-time jobs to help pay tuition. Their parents promised to foot all or part of the remaining expenses but then broke their promise, with no warning. Checks suddenly failed to arrive. Embarrassed, discouraged, and angry, they opted for a solution that fit their earlier experiences: they dropped out and gave up or they faced years of hard work that they viewed as simply another legacy of their parents' divorce. Their parents, meanwhile, offered no explanation or apology for their failure to help.

Numbers sometimes tell a very dramatic story. The people in our divorce and comparison groups grew up side by side on the same streets, attended the same public high schools, and most of their fathers earned the same good incomes. When I compared everyone's financial support for college, I was astounded. A little less than 30 percent of the youngsters from divorced families received full or consistently partial support for college compared with almost 90 percent of youngsters in intact families.[6] That's a whopping difference that speaks volumes about how children of divorce lead an entirely different life compared to their next-door peers in intact families. Their entry into adulthood begins painfully and precipitously—and very differently from their closest friends. The bottom line is that millions of young people, who might have expected and received financial help and encouragement from their families, now hear after divorce: You want a college education? You pay for it.

The economic plight of young people from divorced families who reach age eighteen and are faced with supporting themselves and their college educations is hardly ever discussed publicly or within the professional community. Among organizations of men and women who promote changes in divorce laws, the issue of financial support for college does not have priority. Women's groups concentrate on child support for young children. Men's groups lobby for presumptive joint custody. I've found no national statistics on the question of college support and no lobbying groups fighting for reform. But among children of divorce, it ranks near the top of the wish list. Legislators who speak on college campuses around the country get an earful from students on the ways in which their divorced parents are letting them down. I've had telephone calls from registrars at exclusive women's colleges asking me for insights into alumna families—the daughters have applied and are academically prepared but their parents won't pay and they do not qualify for financial aid. Most universities calculate need based on the income of both parents, but if one, often the father who has more money, is unwilling to contribute, the young person is denied scholarships. Ironically, if the father were deceased, the same young person would be eligible for scholarship aid.

Blunting of Father-Child Relationships

I CAN THINK OF several reasons for the sad state of affairs of college-bound children of divorce. First is the fact that in the vast majority of divorce settlements, college is not discussed and rarely is it covered. Like the whoosh of a falling guillotine, the law states that child support terminates at age eighteen. Except in a small number of states (Massachusetts, Hawaii, Washington, Oregon, and New Jersey), a judge cannot order support to continue even if a young person can show in court that her parents have the financial resources to send her to college, that higher education is a core family value, and that the student is serious and diligent. In other states like New Jersey, New York, and New Hampshire, support can be ordered up to age twenty-one if the family meets the criteria just mentioned and can show that, had the parents remained married, the child almost certainly would have had title to an "educational birthright" with full or partial funding of higher education. Pennsylvania used to have a similar law, but it was challenged successfully on constitutional grounds by a wealthy father who argued that he fully planned to pay for his daughter's college education but objected to being ordered to do so because parents in intact families have no such obligation. The court upheld his plea.

Despite court orders, collection of child support long relied heavily on voluntary cooperation and was rarely enforced. It took many years of seeing women and children intolerably impoverished before people realized that a system of child support would not work without serious enforcement measures. Thankfully, community attitudes have changed. Recent legislation has made it possible for states to go after "deadbeat" dads more vigorously and more efficiently, although a great many women and children are still in serious financial straits after divorce. Child support for college, however, remains in the voluntary realm of yesteryear.[7]

Family law attorneys tell me that they avoid negotiating college support at the time of divorce because it's likely to backfire. Introducing the subject into already delicate and difficult settlement talks, they say, is like pouring gasoline on a fire. It may further inflame the parties, resulting in a reduction of child support when the child is young. In a kind of twisted logic, a promise of support for a child's college education is regarded as a benefit for the mother, for which she will have to give up something in return. Attorneys tell their clients that if a father values education, has financial means, and regularly visits his child, he will assume responsibility for paying college tuition, just as if no divorce had occurred. Oh that it were so.

The sad truth is that many fathers feel differently about their voluntary responsibilities to their children after divorce. In the intact family, even among troubled intact families, a successful father is eager for his child to follow in his footsteps. Both parents are proud when their son or daughter attends their alma mater and many are pleased when their children join the same fraternities or sororities or live in the same dormitories. Other parents expect to attend alumnae events, both to enjoy with their children and to nostalgically recall their youth. As these passionate connections are revived, both generations feel part of a historic chain. But in divorced families, the line of succession between father and child is somehow weakened. The connection is strangely blunted by the marital rupture, by remaining anger between the couple, and by the many years of partial separation and the possible presence of a new wife and new children. An in-house parent is very different psychologically from a parent who lives far away. The child you see daily evokes different feelings of love and allegiance than the child you see at scheduled intervals, no matter how frequent they are. Despite their blood relationship some divorced fathers do not see their children as their moral or social heirs. They acknowledge their legal responsibility to help take care of the children, but this obligation ends at age eighteen. Although many fathers stay in close touch with their children and visit regularly, they nevertheless fail to contribute to their children's college support.

What is it with these dads? For clues, we can look to our study. Contrary to what many believe, the amount of past or present acrimony between parents was irrelevant to a father's willingness to help pay for college. I was very surprised to discover that the fathers who insisted on court-ordered visiting and held the children to a rigid schedule despite the youngsters' protests contributed partially or not at all to college expenses. When I asked these fathers about their failure to support their children at this juncture, none pleaded poverty or even temporary financial reverses. A few cited their greater obligations to their new family. Some felt a greater obligation to send their stepchildren to college over their biological children. None denied the value of a college education. Most said that they had paid child support over many years in accord with court orders and that they were finished with their legal obligations. "I did all that was required" was the recurrent theme.

As I talked to these fathers, I confess that I was shocked by the fact that no one seemed aware of or expressed concern over the hardships being endured by their children regarding the divorce, not being supported in higher education, and the serious consequences for their future economic well-being. Mothers for the most part were worried about the future and tried to contribute money for college. But only a few made the kind of incomes where they could really help, especially when they had more than one child. Others took second or third mortgages on their homes to pay tuition.

In none of these families did one or both parents gather around the kitchen table to discuss college and other future plans with their high school–aged children. Those kinds of conversations—what are you planning to do in a career, where do you want to go to school, what do you want to study—were commonplace in comparison group families. Even among the very troubled intact families, young people were provided with funds for college. It was simply a given. I also saw the same kind of commitment in families of very modest means. One father who drove a cab for a living sat down with his sixteen-year-old son and said, "Mike, you are going to college and we will help you." The boy was moved beyond words. But many children of divorce were not told by their dads, even wealthy ones, that there would be money to help them attend college. And the children were afraid to ask.

I remember a lecture that I gave on this subject to law students at Berkeley. When I finished, a young woman in her mid-twenties approached me.

"Professor," she said, "you have just given what to me is the most important lecture of my life."

I was taken aback. "How so?"

"I never thought I had the right to even ask my dad for support."

I couldn't believe my ears. A student at one of the most prestigious law schools in the country felt so removed from her father that she could not ask his help? The story has a sequel. Later she told me that after class that very day she called him and discussed her needs. He was grumpy and argued with her, maintaining that he was no longer legally obligated to support her, but he finally agreed to provide her with the financial help that she needed.

One of the interesting trends in American culture over the last ten years has been the growth of the men's movement in which men acknowledge their important roles as fathers and protectors of their families. However, in none of the many publications by the fathers' groups are fathers urged to support their children in college. Rather, they are encouraged in these publications to spend time with young children. The needs of older children are unacknowledged. At the same time, the cost of a university education has risen steeply. It's become much harder for young people to work their way through college. It may soon be impossible. A recent study shows that fewer children of divorce even apply to the nation's top colleges.[8] At the present time and in the foreseeable future, children from divorced families end up less well educated than their peers coming from intact homes. This is a dramatic example of the children's lament that they are the ones paying for their parents' divorce.

NINETEEN

Picking Up the Pieces, One by One

As I prepared to meet Billy for our twenty-five-year follow-up interview, I wondered if life had gotten any easier for him. I thought about the isolated life that he had led after his mother remarried and how at age sixteen he had moved out to live alone in his father's house. Were the wounds of feeling unwanted still open? Had he found any relationships to sustain and heal him? These questions swirled in my head as we sat down in the bakery shop, but nothing prepared me for the suffering he had experienced since our last meeting.

Two years earlier, the local newspaper reported that Billy's father had died in the crash of a small airplane that he was piloting. I wrote Billy a brief condolence note and he called me immediately to thank me for my interest. He cried bitterly, almost clinging to the connection with me over the phone. Between sobs he said that he knew his father had not been there for him as a child or as an adult. "But I never gave up hoping that someday he would take an interest in me, even if I wasn't the son he wanted. Now there's nothing more to hope for. I lost the father I had and I lost the father I never had." In rising distress he added, "My mother refused to come with me to the funeral. I hardly knew anyone there and no one knew me."

I had a poignant image in my head of a tearful young man sitting alone in the back of a dark church, leaving hurriedly after the funeral service—the dead man's only son, unrecognized. The longing and sadness that underlie a son's attachment to an absent father never ceases to move me. When several of the fathers in the divorce study died unexpectedly of heart attacks or strokes, the grieving of the fatherless children was passionate. They wept bitterly and clung to siblings, all crying for a man they had had little contact with over the years. I had the sense in hearing them talk and watching their tears that they were crying not for the father they knew but for the father they never had—the father they had hoped for and dreamt about as children.

Billy soon joined me at the table, placing a platter of freshly baked pastries between us. According to my records, he was now thirty-five; he still had the same slight build but his face looked older. As he smiled and extended his hand, I saw deeply etched worry lines between his eyebrows and down both sides of his mouth.

"I've been through hell," he announced as he sat down. "I think that I'm finally climbing out, but I'm not sure. I think there may be trouble ahead."

My heart sank. "What trouble do you mean?"

"My girlfriend Kristi has a son who is moving in with us. We're going to get married as soon as my divorce comes through and Kristi's divorce is final."

"And this worries you to be a stepfather?"

"It sure does. Basically I'm scared and unhappy. I hope that my attitude will change. I never saw myself with kids. I never liked little kids or babies."

"You'd prefer not to have kids?"

"I'm worried about money. But it's more than money. Being a dad has very little appeal. Look at my experience. Up until the time that he died I was still hoping for a dramatic change in my dad, that somehow he would become a guy who wasn't ashamed of me because I couldn't run or swing a bat, who would say, 'Go for it. Do what you can. I'm behind you.' As a kid I had this great image of him as a powerful man who would win the Olympics and build business empires. I used to wait for him to visit me like you wait for rain. After he died, I began to think a lot about him and I realized that never once did he encourage me to make something of myself. He weaseled out of paying my college after he promised. When I was really sick and so depressed I tried to commit suicide, he told me that my problems were all in my head. So you might say being a father is not something that comes naturally to me. How can you give somebody something you never had or saw?"

"So you don't think you can be a good stepfather to Kristi's son?"

"You may think that I'm being selfish but I'm afraid that the kid will come between Kristi and me and I'm not sure I can take that. My heart is not in any great shape. I've had some really rough years. So did she. But bottom line is that I really need for her to be there for me. I can't do with a handout now and then."

"And you think that you'll get less from Kristi after her son moves in."

"Yes, I do. Maybe I'm wrong. I hope that I am. But my whole life I've had to divide what I got into neat parcels. After my folks divorced, I always got what was left. I don't want that to happen to me in my marriage."

Spoken very clearly, I said to myself, and alas utterly realistic. There's no question that a child has first dibs on the mother, and unless the father can join in the giving there's serious trouble ahead. As Billy recognizes, he's not in the giving line. His own long-postponed needs are too great and too pressing. I was finding more and more confirmation for his prophecy of trouble ahead.

I wondered if he had other worries and asked, "How stable is your relationship with Kristi?"

"Stable relationship?" He snorted his reply. "I've never had a stable relationship with a woman, not ever. Even when I think it's stable, it blows up from under me."

"Billy," I sighed, settling back in my chair. "You've had a hard time with the women in your life. Can you bring me up to date from the start?"

"It's not a happy story and it's not a short one. But here goes. The truth is that when other guys in high school or later were dating or partying or screwing, I wasn't. I know you're going to ask me why so let me tell you short and sweet. I had no confidence that I would find a woman who would like me. Love I never even dreamed about. I figured anyone who went out with me was scraping the bottom of the barrel. Like she was desperate. I figured I was just not in the human race, sort of a mule supposed to pull his load and shut up. And if I ever found someone, she'd end up betraying me anyway, so why try?"

I was appalled at his terrible self-image and very distressed by his loneliness.

"How did you spend all those years in your early twenties?"

"You know, it's too painful to remember. I worked like a dog. I was exhausted most of the time. I came home and fell asleep. I sure drank more than was good for me. I taught myself to go without dinner because I was too upset and lonely when I had to eat alone. So I had breakfast and lunch at work and no supper. I had to get up at four so I had a good excuse to go to bed real early."

Passivity

ALTHOUGH BILLY SUFFERED with special physical difficulties, his story is familiar. Many young men from divorced families enter adulthood feeling lonely and utterly unlovable.[1] They are not angry like Paula or Larry, or unable to separate like Karen, but instead they are depressed and defeated. Billy was a poster child for this group.

"You said that you were worried about being betrayed? Has anyone ever cheated on you?"

"When I was twenty-three, I met this woman who sort of asked whether she could stay with me. She wasn't bad-looking so I said okay. We lived together for four months and I was getting to like her. Then one day I came home unexpectedly from a business trip. She had told me that she was going to be out with her girlfriends, but when I arrived, she was driving by, cute as a button, riding on the back of a guy's motorbike."

"What did you do?"

"Do?" Again that startled look. "Nothing. I didn't even mention it. I just moved out three weeks later without saying a word. I left all my belongings. It took me two years to write to her but I didn't mail the letter."

I was amazed at his reluctance to confront or even ask her. "Billy, why didn't you mention it?"

He looked sheepish and I decided to let it drop. But then with a passionate outburst, he let fly, "If I had mentioned it, what good would it have done? She would have said, 'Get lost! I'm with him now.' You're probably going to ask me why I'm so cautious. It's real simple. Name one thing I could have changed. Tell me one person who asked me. Did I want them to divorce? Did I like taking orders about all my chores from my stepfather? Did my dad want me around? Did my mother ask me before she got a whole new family? Did they ask me whether I wanted tuition money for college like the other guys? Who ever asked me anything? Who listened to me? Who helped me grow up? Life is the way it is. You know that Spanish expression? *Qué será será*, what will be, will be. Let me tell you something else while I'm spilling my guts. Say you came to see me or asked me like on a questionnaire or the phone (his voice rose to a quavering falsetto), 'How are you doing, Billy?' I would swear that I was fine. I would tell you that life's a breeze, great job, nice girl, parents' divorce super, no sweat. I would hide my feelings like I have learned all my life with smiles and lies, even when I feel like I'm dead or wish I was. But you would know that I was bullshitting you because you knew me when. So what I'm trying to say is, I'm not lying to you."

I thanked Billy for his trust in me but was shaken by his outburst. I have struggled for years to understand the powerlessness that so many of these men feel in their relationships with women. Why was it so rare for any of them to fight for someone they loved and wanted—or even to challenge her leaving? One man who suspected his wife of infidelity tapped her telephone for weeks and found his suspicions justified. Instead of confronting her, he filed for divorce. The fact that she was the mother of his two-year-old child didn't lead him to a moment's hesitation.

"Why didn't you talk with her?" I asked.

"What for?" he asked.

This kind of passivity was not as apparent in other parts of the men's lives. They were able to be reasonably competitive although not aggressive in the workplace. However, at home, when the partner's behavior coincided with what they feared, it's as if they lay down and played dead. The nightmare came alive.

I've seen this sort of passivity in both men and women who grew up in divorced families, although it seems to affect more men. In my earliest writing about the responses of children at the time of the breakup, I described how helpless children feel. As we've seen, they don't protest largely because no one is willing to take them seriously and listen to their complaints. They learn to keep their heads down, to lower their expectations, and to keep their feelings to themselves.

The passivity of young men like Billy makes sense if you think of it as a masked form of helpless rage. How else to explain their extraordinary willingness to put the worst face on incidents that might or might not have meaning? Does riding on a motorbike with a guy really establish infidelity and warrant the man's leaving? Perhaps she hurt her ankle. Perhaps the man was an old friend. Perhaps the meeting with her girlfriends was canceled. Of the many possibilities, Billy chooses infidelity. His suspicions are so powerfully convincing—and his fear of being hurt is so overriding—that he cannot summon the courage to ask the woman. His anger happens so fast that he loses his capacity to consider other alternatives rationally. If you suspect infidelity, then it must be true. This suspecting the worst and acting on it without thought and without delay is surely the most dangerous recipe for a stable relationship that anyone could devise.

Nothing Lasts

BILLY SIGHED RESIGNEDLY and shrugged. "To go on with the scenario, I was married for five years. We met when I was twenty-seven and she was twenty-five. I was managing one of the plants. She was a waitress in the bakery restaurant. I was also going to junior college in the morning to get a management degree. It wasn't a very good course but it was all I could afford. I think by then I'd gotten over being so scared of women and had decided to do something about being so alone. She was nice to be around. She smiled a lot. She was no beauty but neither was I. We soon found out that we had a lot in common. Her folks divorced when she was eight and she had a pretty miserable childhood, lots of moving around, money worries, and a hard time making friends because of all the moves. She was a lonely kid just like me. We agreed that it was the unhappiest time of our lives. We both understood how to put on a cheery face for the world and feel different inside. So we decided it was better to be together and that we would be less lonely."

"Were you pretty optimistic at that time?"

He looked forlorn. "I don't know whether I ever loved her or whether she loved me. How in hell would anyone love me anyway? What did I know about finding a wife? I thought at the time that it probably wouldn't last."

"Why did you think that it wouldn't last?"

"Because nothing in my life lasts," he said grimly. Then he broke into a grin. "You haven't noticed this little black cloud that follows me around?" He waved his arm at an imaginary cloud over his head. "It's like the weather. If things look fair, just wait a minute. That's how I live."

"What were you looking for in a wife?"

Billy looked startled. "Come again?"

"I just wondered what kind of person you thought would make you happy."

"I never thought much about that. I figured I didn't know any movie stars that week," he chuckled, "but a nice decent woman who wouldn't cheat and who could make a place look like a home would do fine."

When a Child of Divorce Marries Another Child of Divorce

I'VE TALKED ABOUT how children of divorce have trouble handling conflict in marriage. They are terrified of arguments that might start them down the same path as their parents. When a child of divorce marries another child of divorce, these problems and anxieties are doubled.[2] Children of divorce are often drawn to one another via their common histories. In high school and as young adults they are kindred souls who can share complaints about their past, specifics about custody or visiting arrangements, and how they put up with parents' problems. During adolescence especially, they hang out in packs, providing each other with the support and comfort they don't get at home. They take care of each other with money, sympathy, and a place to crash. I have seen several ersatz families, some in elegant neighborhoods, where the young people have left home or been ejected or the parent has walked away. As these children mature, they are drawn together by common worries about the future, concern for and resentment of parents, and their pervasive loneliness. They desperately need to tell their story, but agemates who have not lived through divorce are not all that sympathetic. So they look for and find someone who can listen and understand.

It's natural that Billy and Debbie would find each other. Unfortunately, their union was in peril from the start. Each brings a heavy load of distrust and fear to marriage. Each brings a great need for sympathy and comforting, which they hope the other person will provide in full measure. But if both people need to be nurtured who will provide what they both crave? Both have many past hurts that need to heal. They want and need the partner to be patient, loving, and forgiving. They are both vulnerable, easily hurt, and afraid of being unheard and unloved. And they are, as we have seen, quick to put the worst face on the other's behavior.

But I don't want to give the impression that these marriages cannot work or are doomed to end in divorce. In our society, with its growing number of children from divorce, these marriages will inevitably multiply. That said, some good marriages I have seen are between children from divorced families. Many of these marriages work for the very reason that each spouse is aware of the difficulties they face and resolve to help each other grow and change. They understand each other's history and are profoundly sympathetic to the other's fears of conflict and expectation that the marriage might fail. Such marriages provide a healing experience and restore each person's faith that they can find love and constancy in a troubled world. Karen's ability to hope and trust is restored by her marriage to a loving man who wants to undo her childhood deprivations by teaching her to lighten up. Larry learns to forgive himself for his earlier behavior by marrying a woman who, in his words, "brought love and laughter into my life." Their union rescues him from lifelong brooding and anger. Promiscuous women who meet and marry men who say "Stop it. I'm here and I'm planning to stay" are rescued from continuing infidelity. All of these marriages require enormous patience, a shared understanding of how easily children of divorce become discouraged, and knowing how important it is to stick it out despite the impulse to run. In my own research on good marriages, I became convinced that a good marriage more than any other adult relationship has a healing potential and the capacity to turn one or two tragic lives around.[3]

Unfortunately, such was not the case with Billy and Debbie. Certainly they set out to help one another in every possible way. "I thought the marriage with Debbie was okay," Billy continued. "She bought furniture and made curtains and fixed up our place. I was earning pretty good money so we bought a little house to make her feel better. But she kept saying that she wanted to do more stuff than we were doing. She wanted to go out once in a while when I came home from work, and I guess I didn't hear diddly. I worked long shifts at the plant. It was all my responsibility to make sure nothing burned. When I came home I was a couch potato. My heart wasn't good, I was short of breath, and I didn't have time to go to the doctor. She continued to cry and then to holler, but I was too tired and beat to listen. Anyway, to make it short I came home one day and the house was empty. She had moved out, taking the couch, the TV, the washer and dryer, her clothes, the whole frigging house. Fortunately she left my dog. I'll never forget it as long as I live. It was night. I walked in and out of the house four or five times. I couldn't believe it. I was sobbing like a baby. How could she? I nearly went mad. I mean it, Judy, mad, insane, bonkers. I couldn't eat. I went to work but I did nothing. I couldn't sleep. I couldn't go into the empty house. I stayed out on the porch for eight months, rain or shine. Depression set in like an anvil-shaped cloud. I was so overwhelmed with sadness, I said to myself, 'This is it. No one's ever wanted you—your wife, your dad, your mom.' I tried to kill myself with carbon monoxide four or five times. Actually the only way I slept at all was by wrapping my arms around my dog and dozing off at dawn."

I've seen many marriages come apart with the kind of severe reactions Billy described. (Often this kind of terrible trauma is what sparks a custody fight that never ends.) Still hurting from the unexpected and long-remembered loss of their intact family during childhood, they go on to lose the central relationship of their own adulthood *without any warning.* This confirms their view that they're doomed, that everything they need dies. The suffering is exactly as Billy described. They can't stand it. To come home to an empty house and be greeted by a note tacked to the door is a dreadful humiliation. The reaction—depression or explosive rage—can last for years. People blame the partner, the real or imaginary lover, the partner's family, the world. The trauma of the breakup can dominate their lives and lead to savage fighting over children or property.

But why didn't Billy have a clue about what was coming? For a woman to empty the household takes not only careful planning but a towering rage that builds over time until it explodes in an extraordinary act of hatred and revenge. Yet Billy was taken by surprise.

He was looking miserable. I touched his arm and said, "Billy, I can't think of anything worse that could happen. What she did was awful.

Thank God you didn't kill yourself. What led to her anger? Do you understand that?"

"If you mean did I hit her, I never laid a hand on her."

"Perhaps she felt trapped."

"I never thought of that."

"Do you think she was frustrated by having nothing to do except wait for an exhausted man to return home in time for sleep?"

"I never thought of that, either. She complained, but look, I'm used to women complaining."

The men in this study who divorced had experiences much like Billy's, although not as savage in their impact. In every case except one, the woman left in anger and the man was stunned. These young men genuinely liked their wives and wanted the marriage to continue. They later tried to explain what happened with platitudes—"she was too young," "she wanted somebody else"—but basically they had no idea why their wives had deserted them. Billy was one of the very few who honestly said, "I didn't hear her." None of these men had been violent in their marriages nor was infidelity a big issue, although it happened occasionally. They knew their wives had complaints but did nothing to deal with the problems. One man told me that he didn't notice that his wife had left a week earlier because he was working on a big computer assignment. When he realized she was gone, he went into an acute depression. Most recovered slowly. Several did not have any contact with another woman for years after. One man whose wife left when he was twenty-four was still not dating ten years later. He'd decided to remain alone rather than take another chance. "Once is enough," he stated.

Why don't these young men hear their wives' complaints? The men are intelligent and competent at work. They are decent people. But they are blind and deaf to their women and taken entirely by surprise when they leave.

I think they don't hear their wives because in large measure they don't hear themselves. They've told me many times that their own feelings are muted or shut down in situations that evoke strong feelings. They learned long ago in childhood that feelings are painful and that it's better and safer to shut down feelings and not respond to their own or to others. But sadly, people who are inhibited in acknowledging their own feelings also have trouble in recognizing the feelings of others. They're especially clueless about how to gauge the quality of a woman's feelings, needs, and wishes or how to assess the importance of her complaints.[4] It's as if everything is experienced in the same monotone key. Such men are hardly able to read a woman's facial expressions or her body language or to distinguish a minor upset from a serious grievance. They have no good models in their head for a good relationship between a man and a woman, and the subtleties of the interaction is a foreign language to them. Billy and the other young men in this group understood concrete requests. When Debbie wanted a house, he bought her a little house. Had she asked for shoes or a dress, he would have happily purchased these items for her. But she wanted her husband to talk to her in the evenings. She was lonely and wanted companionship. She was bored and wanted to go out dancing. These requests he found baffling and disconcerting. He failed utterly to observe the mounting distress or the rising anger that prompted these requests. Like others, he ignored all the signs of the coming storm. The woman became increasingly agitated and left in a towering rage. The men were shattered.

Vulnerability and Resilience

BY THE END of the interview I was keenly aware of how much Billy had suffered and how hard it had been for him to grow up with hardly any help from his family after the divorce. I was also impressed with his courage and perseverance. Despite his poor physical health, lack of education, and continuing sadness, he held a responsible, well-paying job that required skill, attention to detail, and an ability to make quick decisions. He had taken full responsibility for himself in recovering from a serious depression. And he had been able to live a life of extraordinary isolation and sadness without succumbing to alcoholism and drug abuse. He had survived each day while hoping that it would be his last. Last seen, Billy was starting a new relationship with a seemingly nice woman who had her own problems but was willing to work on the relationship. They at least had a fighting chance. I was also aware of how, with the help of his wry humor and courage, Billy had been able to hold on to his integrity and honesty. In all he was very likable, friendly, and generous. But he had been unhappy for most of his life.

What happened to Billy and how could his life have been different? This child suffered a great deal because his vulnerability was matched by a bleak, unsupportive environment that set in after the divorce. During the predivorce years when his mother took care of him, he was at the head of his class, had friends, and was a happy kid despite his handicap. His father never gave much personal support but he did pay for Billy's medical needs, games, books, and special tutors that were part of his everyday life. But after the divorce and his mother's remarriage, Billy lost all that had kept him afloat. With her new priorities, Billy's mother went from chief protector to chief critic of her young son. He was hurt, bewildered, and angry. As a vulnerable child who needed his mother's help, he had nowhere else to turn. Had she continued to support him in ways that he needed, Billy's life would unquestionably have been happier and more successful.

Other youngsters in this study showed impressive resiliency in similarly unsupportive environments. Larry rallied his resources to become his own father—as he said—to set his own goals in marriage, parenthood, and career choice. He had some help from his mother's ideals and courage but not really enough to ease his way. Had he been as vulnerable as Billy, I doubt that he could have made it. Karen also relied on herself and her own strength to overcome difficulties in her childhood. She had some help from her grandmother who loved her and helped pay for college, and later she found much help from her husband who supported her in breaking away from her demanding family. But if Karen had been a vulnerable child, she, too, would have had a different life in that she was raised by parents who had lost the ability to protect their children.

These examples reveal the important match between a child's temperament—their vulnerability, strength, or resiliency—and what the family environment is able to provide. Children with different levels of resilience need different kinds of support from their parents after the breakup. Highly competent children may be able to get along with little help. Those who are sensitive and more volatile in their temperament need more sustained parenting plus a range of supports at school and in their social lives. Vulnerable children need the most help because change is hardest for them.

In recent years the psychological concepts of resiliency and vulnerability[5] have become increasingly popular for explaining why some children succeed and others falter after divorce.[6] These concepts are important because, as we've seen throughout this book, children of divorce bear an unprecedented responsibility for raising themselves. It matters whether they can make friends easily or are frightened by strangers. It matters if they are bold or shy, agile or clumsy, quick-witted or slow to learn. The heroes of children's literature from Oliver Twist to Harry Potter are all held up as heroes who, surrounded by cruel or foolish adults, deal successfully with adversity. But real children have a much harder time, some more than others.

Most parents and children understand that every child, no matter how intrepid, has to rely on the family for help. More than this, each child needs a different kind of help from her family. One child can handle joint custody with aplomb. Others accept a mother's going back to full-time work with little stress. And others fall apart. One little boy can occupy himself alone after school with books, art, or calling a friend. Another sits alone in misery. Some children have loving, attentive grandparents, family friends, or neighbors who are happy to spend time with them because they are so appealing. Others sit alone and brood because they are not as outgoing or pleasant.

Although we can't wave a magic wand that will make all families sensitive and protective of children after divorce, we can promote a culture that helps people understand how and why their children are vulnerable after divorce. There's no question that Paula would have had a much easier time if she hadn't lost her stable home and her mother to a full-time job in one fell swoop. Billy would have benefited enormously from a careful transition between his life before and after divorce. For every Little Engine That Could there is a Little Engine That Couldn't. Many children need special care accepting the powerful changes that divorce brings. We have an obligation to help parents to provide it. As we have also seen, many adults cannot do it by themselves, either.

PART FIVE

My Best Case: Lisa

TWENTY

Is Not Fighting Enough?

For many years when I spoke about divorce and children at conferences around the world, I would begin my talk with excerpts from interviews with Lisa. She was an articulate child who immediately charmed people as she spoke about her parents with great love and compassion. As an adolescent, Lisa was doing remarkably well and I often referred to her as "my best case." Audiences liked to hear about her because it allayed their fears about the effects of divorce on children. If Lisa could make it, so could others. But when Lisa moved into adulthood, I began to see changes in her that hinted everything was not okay. Like other children I have described, Lisa took on a role in her family and played it well from the day her parents divorced. She was the model child who never rocked the boat. And although she was aware of the passions, jealousy, and hate that lay beneath the surface of her post-divorce family, she and everyone else pretended all was tranquil. In her core, Lisa was eager to protect her parents from feeling unhappy or guilty about the breakup. But her virtuous resolve no longer helped her when she came face-to-face with adult relationships. Lisa's story shows us that whatever we do to protect our children after divorce, residues appear in the realm of adult love and sexual intimacy.

Through the years, many people have asked me, "What if we don't fight after the divorce? What if we get along and put our child's best interest before our own? Surely we can protect our children from the harm that divorce can do. Can't we?"

Let's look at the evidence. It's true that fighting between parents, whether it takes place in the courtroom or bedroom, is harmful to children. As we've seen throughout this book, it offers a frightening model of adult behavior and it seriously erodes the quality of any parent-child relationship. Parents who engage in a conjugal jihad often lose sight of a child's needs. They easily confuse their own rage and anguished agenda with what they think the child wants. As a result, the child feels unloved and unsafe.

But there are millions of parents who, from day one of the divorce, are determined *not* to make their children suffer. They have the maturity and self-control to say, "We no longer can stay married but we can still put our children first. We will find ways to assure them that we both love them and we'll do everything we can to protect them." Amen. Post-divorce families that carry out this credo can and do protect their children from many of the adversities we have already discussed.

Yet here we need to face an uncomfortable truth. As Lisa's story shows, parents who cooperate fully with each other are not necessarily in touch with the feelings and needs of their child. Efforts to settle differences amicably do not automatically bring parents closer to understanding a child's concerns or make them more responsive to a child's distress. There's a good deal more to helping children than declaring a cease-fire. The prevailing divorce nostrum in this country—don't fight—does not, as so many lawyers, judges, and mental health professionals hope it will, protect children from experiencing the same sorts of difficulties in adulthood as we've seen in those raised in less cooperative families. Lisa represents a very large number of children in America's divorce culture. Her experience is instructive for us all.

Conflict and Suffering in the Midst of Cooperation

I FIRST MET Lisa when she was in nursery school—a charming four year old girl decked out in a raspberry red pantsuit with bright yellow ribbons in her hair. Her parents were successful professionals—

her mom a lawyer at the National Resources Defense Counsel office in Los Angeles and her dad a journalist who later went into public relations for several Silicon Valley corporations in Menlo Park. I asked Lisa what was going on in her family. She explained soberly, in a very grown-up way, "Daddy does not like Mommy so he's living in the city and Mommy likes Daddy and wants him back."

"That's an awful lot of changes," I said, with soberness to match hers. "What do you think is going to happen?"

Lisa shook her head silently and refused to say any more. But her play revealed all that she couldn't express in words. It had two acts. Each vividly portrayed her inner world. In the first episode, she placed the father, the mother, and the children dolls in the dollhouse living room where they all sat in a row watching television. Then they all lay in one big bed, hugging one another like puppies in a basket. Next they were all squashed together in the bathtub. Finally, they were perched precariously on the steep roof, holding on to each other to keep from falling. The togetherness wrought by little Lisa was overpowering. In the second act, the tiger, crocodile, giraffe, and bear all went mad with aggression, wildly biting each other. They snarled and leapt at one another's throats. Finally, carried away by her powerful feelings, Lisa bit the giraffe savagely and pummeled the tiger with her tiny fists. The message was clear. Lisa wanted desperately for her family to stay together but knew that it was coming apart. Underneath her composed, ladylike manner, fierce angers threatened to explode.

My records show that this was one of the few occasions—if not the only time—when Lisa allowed herself to express rage at the breakup of her family. She carefully hid her feelings for years. Mostly she was a very well-behaved, well-dressed, quiet child at home and at school. Her nursery school teacher told me that she often wished Lisa would do something naughty. A year later, her kindergarten teacher, in reply to an inquiry, dropped me a note saying she worried that this bright child showed so little fantasy or creativity in her play. "She's always on guard, looking around," the teacher reported.

At home, Lisa's upset, which she did not show in her parents' homes or in school, seeped through as fears—of the dark, of scary dreams, of fire, of sleeping alone. Lisa was frightened when her mother left town, even if she could stay at her dad's house. She was embarrassed to tell her father and stepmother how frightened she was at night. "I'm scared to tell Daddy that

I'm scared. I'd like them to leave a light on in the bathroom like my mom does but I'm too scared to ask them," she told me at our second meeting. Gradually her fears became more acute and she began to grind her teeth at night. Nevertheless, Lisa's mom, in trying to put her own life back together, went to visit her sister in Santa Fe for several weeks shortly after the breakup. She needed "space to think." Neither parent was aware of the extent of Lisa's grief and pain over the divorce. She seemed so self-controlled, so calm. Surely, they told themselves, her fears will disappear in time. Actually, they lasted for several years and worsened again when her mother took on a heavier work schedule. That's when Lisa began to worry daily that her mother would die.

In many divorces, one of the partners does not see the breakup coming and in fact has only a minor inkling that the other person is dissatisfied with the marriage. And tragically, the abandoned partner may be deeply in love with the spouse who wants out. When this happens, a sense of shock, betrayal, and rage can last for many years, if not forever.

Lisa's mother was stunned when her husband asked her for a divorce. She knew that he had minor complaints about the marriage but divorce had never crossed her mind. The fact that he remarried the day after their divorce was final compounded the blow. She was badly hurt, bewildered, and humiliated. She was, and still is, a very attractive professional woman who had no trouble finding dates, but casual liaisons depressed her. Tragically, she did not, despite many efforts, find a suitable partner. As Lisa told me, "She's an independent, strong woman, but I feel a lot of guilt, a lot of pity, and a lot of worry when I think of her."

Lisa's father was not happy being married to Lisa's mother. He complained that she was demanding, edgy, and uncaring. He wanted love and tenderness and, indeed, he quickly found a woman similar to his wife in age and education. By all accounts, this second marriage to Machiko, an accomplished Japanese American who was a senior executive at the Bank of America, was happy, lasting, and good for both partners. As a young adult, Lisa said, "I never want him to feel guilty about leaving my mom. He's been a good father and a good husband to my stepmother."

But this happy second marriage does not mean everything was hunky-dory right from the start. In this family, like the others we've met, parent and child relationships changed after divorce. Lisa's dad had always spent large amounts of time with her, reading her stories in the evenings, going places on weekends, making her breakfast in the morning. But as in other families, when the new stepparent objected to the amount of time he lavished on his child, he took her side. Lisa's mother was in no position to help her. She was herself in desperate need of love and comforting. And she had almost nothing left to give her little daughter. She was frantically engaged in keeping her own feelings under control, in strengthening her position at the government agency where she was employed, and in rebuilding her social life.

The message to Lisa from both parents at this time was to keep her distance and do the best she could. She was given no chance to cry by parents who truly loved her.

All the adults in this saga tried their level best to protect the child by not quarreling openly. But the passions evoked by the divorce, especially jealousy between the two women, did not lessen. As everyone cooperated for the sake of Lisa, close contact between Lisa's mother, father, and stepmother provided endless opportunity for misunderstanding, hurt, and envy. Lisa's mother knew when and where the stepmother and father went on vacation together, when they gave a party for the former mutual friends of the couple, what gifts the stepmother received from her former husband.

Lisa's mother continued to feel that her husband's happy remarriage was built upon her own unhappiness. This triangle remained central to Lisa's life as she grew up. Although little was said because Lisa's mother was a proud woman and did not dwell on her troubles, she continued to be hurt by what she considered her husband's betrayal. Lisa was acutely aware of her mother's loneliness and longing.

The Stepmother

LISA'S STORY ILLUSTRATES the many dilemmas that can arise between children and stepmothers. When Lisa's father met Machiko, he was immediately smitten by her sense of humor, her gentleness, and her good looks. She made him feel wonderful, sexy, alive, and wanted. In yet another example of how an adult unconsciously believes in the trickle-down theory of family happiness, he never questioned that his child would share his judgment. With the best intentions in the world, he expected Lisa to feel immediate affection for Machiko and after a brief period to accept her as a parent in situ.

In reality, neither the child nor the woman had an easy time developing their relationship. Machiko asserted her claim to be a bride, to come first as she and her husband built their life together. At the same time, Lisa was in crisis. Her family had evaporated. Her mother was depressed. Her beloved father had moved out and gotten involved with a stranger who took all his attention. Moreover, this new rival for her father's love was usurping her mother's place. This is the stuff of fairy tales and it is the stuff of modern life in America—with one difference. In fairy tales, the little girl is taken out into the deep dangerous forest where she is saved by a compassionate woodsman. In modern America, all the people stay together in the two households and life is ripe for conflict. In its early stages, the strife is not related to how nice or evil the stepmother is or to how well behaved or naughty the child is. The conflict is in the nature of the drama itself. There is one exalted king (the man), one princess (the child), one long and dark shadow (the ex-wife), and one usurper (the stepmother), who quite rightly wants the opportunity to enjoy her marriage. Such dramas play out differently in different families but they are never without travail. In Lisa's case, the stepmother shooed the little girl away and forbade her to sit in her father's lap. This was clearly a mistake that Machiko soon realized but Lisa never forgot or forgave. Nevertheless, in time the stepmother and stepdaughter did get to know each other, to like each other, and eventually to love and respect each other very much.

Other scenarios do not have happy endings. The stepmother, as many do, says: "I want the man, not the child." If the stepmother does not take the time and effort to cultivate a separate relationship with the child, the antagonism persists. Indeed, such rivalries tend to worsen as children move into adolescence and become angrier about the divorce or maintain covert plans to bring the biological parents back together. It's not unusual for a stepmother to say, "I cannot control this child. He hates me. You have to choose." The father's decision can go either way. Many second marriages (or live-in relationships) break up because of the jealousy between a stepparent and stepchild.

A father's commitment to his offspring is profoundly influenced by what his second or third wife says and does. Here's how it works: The man enters a second marriage with a strong desire to make it work. The last thing he wants is a second divorce, and so he is most likely to bow to the new woman's wants. In most instances I have seen, when push comes to shove he will side with his new mate over his own child. In this sense, stepmothers do have the power of fairy tales, which they can use for good or evil. The battle is the fight for the man. It can be kept under wraps and played out with good manners, as in Lisa's family, or it can rage in high C and end in more tragedy. It's also a battle over money, and this can become bitter indeed, with children mostly as losers.

The fairy tale continues with the rivalry between the stepmother and the ghost or actual presence of the first wife (whose influence can also be benevolent or evil). Who controls the roost—the new deal mom or the real mom? Whose convenience in setting schedules is more important? How important is the private school or the summer camp? Do we pay for the child's orthodontia or for our Paris vacation? Should the stepmom's salary be used at all for the support of children from the previous marriage? Should it be used for special but nonessential needs that enhance a child's life like the piano teacher or the school ski trips? Should it be used to help send the child to college? Is the child's visit an invasion that crosses the boundary of the stepmother's family or a pleasure? These questions and choices are never easy, but the attitudes of both women will influence and sometimes determine how the story plays out.

Finally, the plot thickens if the stepmother brings children from a previous marriage into the household. Endless triangles are formed as stepsiblings take up friendships or rivalries or, as sometimes happens with adolescents, become lovers themselves. All children watch each parent to see who is treated more or less favorably, who gets what at Christmas or Chanukah, who inherits grandma's locket or grandpa's binoculars. Although the addition of stepsiblings produces more fighting in some families, other children benefit greatly from having the protection of loving, older stepsiblings. Again, the fairy tale can have a happy or tragic ending depending on how the characters play their roles.

Lisa was fortunate because her stepmother was a decent, kind woman who built a loving, lasting marriage with Lisa's father. It's also lucky that in this case Lisa was very young at the time of the divorce. It's easier for an adult to play with a young child who in turn expects adults to take on authority roles. Adolescents, in contrast, have separate interests and resent being told what to do. This said, it's a mistake to think that little children have little feelings. Little children have powerful feelings and, despite their limited skills, can disrupt a second marriage as effectively as any adolescent on the warpath. Children of all ages have strong mixed feelings about stepparents. As I noted in discussing stepfathers, the stepmother also has to realize that it takes as long to cultivate the friendship and affection of a child as it does to cultivate the friendship and affection of an adult.

Two Worlds

IN LOOKING AT Lisa and others who were raised within the protection of good second marriages, I must admit my surprise that the good remarriage of one or both parents was not as influential as I had expected it would be in ameliorating the child's fear that her own adult relationships would fail. (All too often just one parent finds a happy, lasting remarriage and not both.) Although Lisa loved her father and stepmother, she never felt that their marriage was one that she would like for herself. She knew they were happy, but when she talked about them her tone was always bland. She never volunteered observations about them in the amused, pleased, or critical ways that the adults in intact families talked about their parents.

For reasons that we can only speculate about, children raised in remarried families often have a greater psychological distance between themselves and their parents compared with peers raised in an intact family. It was easier for Lisa to spend time with her father and stepmother separately than to feel truly at home with both together, although she loved and admired them. She could never quite visualize them as a couple. Perhaps loyalty to the excluded parent holds the key to these feelings.

As a young adolescent, Lisa took on the responsibility and role for keeping her two worlds separate. She tried with all her might to conform to the standards of each household and to say as little as possible, but she was an observant child and it was hard for her to keep everything to herself. Nevertheless, as I learned from talking with both of her parents, she was the soul of discretion. When she was fourteen, she explained to me, "I have two different lives. Everybody is happier this way. They have different expectations. Mom lets me do more of what I want. She has few rules. She understands me more. Dad expects a lot more, especially in schoolwork. He and my stepmother are into table manners and formal dinners. My parents still don't get along. My dad and stepmother really hate my mom. They would tell her how much they hate her except for me. I keep them apart. You see, my mom is pretty isolated. She would like a relationship with my dad and stepmother but there is nothing there for her. I don't want her to find out what they really think. So I keep it cool and I always, always watch what I say. And we manage."

This was the first inkling I had that the "don't fight" rule had limitations. In their behavior, Lisa's parents had had the most civilized divorce of all the couples in the study. If parents got grades for how they handled divorce and the postdivorce years, these people would have earned an A plus. There was no open fighting during the marriage and there was almost none after it ended. An only child, Lisa continued to see both parents in ways that felt fair and equitable to everyone. Sometimes her father and stepmother babysat her in her mother's home, which remained her primary residence. Both parents were devoted to their daughter. Money was adequate in both homes and included college support and vacation trips. Although her mother and stepmother experienced the kinds of ongoing tensions I just described, there was never any open conflict. Neither woman expected Lisa to take sides and both went out of their way not to criticize any family member.

But there are things that adults cannot hide from children. Continuing tensions between ex-partners and stepparents are conveyed directly to children via countless nonverbal signals. A roll of the eyes, a shrug of the shoulders, an edge in the voice are enough to tell any child the truth—these adults are getting along on my behalf but they're pretending. Lisa grew up aware of their intense enduring anger and her mother's hurt. Good intentions can always become undermined by the frailties of human nature and its passions.

Except for her continued worry about her mother and an occasional mother's "boyfriend who drives me up the wall," Lisa enjoyed her adolescence. Unlike children living under strict court-ordered visiting schedules, she had lots of choices about what she could do and when. Her father called her every week to arrange what they would do, according to her preferences—which included not seeing him if other activities were more desirable. She had many girlfriends at high school and prided herself on her skill in making friends. She grew up slowly. In fact, she seemed to be holding back from involvement with boyfriends. Unlike many in her generation, she was in no hurry to have a sexual relationship. The one boy she fell in love with from afar, she said sadly, "didn't like me back." School was enjoyable for Lisa; she got good grades and did well in sports and dance. She avoided drugs and alcohol. "They just don't interest me," she announced.

I asked Lisa, as I did all the youngsters, to draw on her own experience for any advice she might offer to parents and children in other divorced families. Lisa thought for several long minutes. Then she responded with a vehemence that took me by surprise: "Children should not hate their parents for the divorce. They should give their parents a chance." She stopped suddenly, as if she had let the cat out of the bag. More gently, she added, "As for parents, they should not get mad at the kids. They should try to understand that it's hard for the kids as well as for them." I was surprised by her strong use of the word "hate" and with her recurring theme of anger. Obviously this sweet, shy fifteen-year-old had struggled with powerful feelings of resentment toward her parents. Her advice to parents also implied that her own suffering had not been appreciated. Instead it was kept under wraps, for fear they might disapprove.

I remember the end of this interview when she talked happily about her future plans: "Marriage is a good thing if you love someone, but if you want a divorce you should get that also. I'd like to think that I won't, but you never can tell." Clearly these issues were hardly real at this point. But Lisa's final statement was hopeful and very reassuring: "I want to go to college, get a good job, get married, and have kids. Also maybe do something in math, maybe computer engineering or science." I was very taken with her spunkiness and self-confidence.

When I met with Lisa's mother and father and stepmother I congratulated them all. Lisa seemed to be developmentally on target and surging happily ahead toward adulthood. My notes were full of encouraging words. This youngster, who had experienced divorce under the best of circumstances, showed the care, love, and good financial support that had been given her. She was one of the few young people in the study who had maintained good relationships with both of her parents and her stepparent. Her mother and father had not made unreasonable demands on her for time or emotional support. She felt loved and respected by both. At the same time, she had been able to work out a balance that left her free to pursue her own interests with her girlfriends. She was doing well at school and in a range of extracurricular activities. She was one of the very few who was enjoying her adolescence.

I knew that compared to her peers, Lisa was a young fifteen-year-old who seemed to be delayed in her development, especially in her relationship with boys. I had no reading on how that would go once her full adolescent agenda came into play. Would she allow herself independence or even a little rebellion? I felt some disquiet about her inordinately close tie to her mother and wondered if leaving home would be a problem for her. Would she hold back on that, too? And I was concerned about her taking responsibility for the delicate equilibrium between her parents and for having to walk on eggs to maintain the precarious balance. But in all she showed me reserves of strength and good sense that left me enormously optimistic.

Feelings Are Painful

LISA AND I next met each other when she was twenty years old—a pretty, shy, and very appealing young woman who was finishing her second year at a small college in Oregon. Her hair was long and pulled up into a neat bun held with a chopstick, and she wore the usual college costume—faded jeans, Doc Martins, and a long sweater with a boat neck. She had added a bright red silk scarf that looked stunning in its simplicity. Lisa still liked school, continued to do well academically, and enjoyed a wide circle of women friends. But she was newly troubled by many questions about herself. Her major problem, as she described it, was feeling numb when she had sex.

"Have you had many boyfriends?" I asked.

"Not that many," she replied. "We have co-ed dorms and so lots of kids end up sleeping with each other. I'm not nearly as wild as some of my friends, but it'd be hard to stay a virgin around here. So sex is easy. But," she said, frowning, "sex with a guy I care about is hard for me. It's much easier to be with someone I don't feel close to. If I care about him, then when it's over I'm left with a sad feeling. When sex is just play and has nothing to do with love, I have no problem and I feel fine. Sometimes I feel that I was brought up on a desert island." She thought for a moment and summed up her feelings. "Love combined with sex is a strange idea to me." She paused again. "Sometimes I just get numb."

"Tell me about feeling numb."

"What you have to understand about me is that I'm able to cut off feelings instantly when they hurt. My feelings are there but it's hard for me to reach them. As a child I hardly knew what it was like to cry. Basically I still feel out of touch with my feelings. If you were to tell me right now that my lover died, I would not have feeling until tomorrow."

"This protected you?"

"One thing you learn very quickly as a child of divorce is that feelings are painful. It's a lot easier if you can learn to turn them off. It's not simple, but otherwise you spend a lot of time worrying about your family. You see, just because my parents didn't fight doesn't mean that I didn't know the truth about how they felt about each other. I knew every waking hour. My father and stepmother hated my mom and wished that she would disappear. My mom was jealous of my stepmom and felt that their happiness was built on the ruins of her life. All of these feelings went on my whole life. We all pretended they weren't there, but we all knew different. The divorce was like a skeleton that everyone pretended wasn't there."

Faced with high expectations for conformist behavior, with no shelter from the storm, four-year-old Lisa quickly learned not to show her feelings and to expect less from her parents. She became the unsmiling, courteous, supervigilant little girl described by her teachers. Her spontaneity ceased like an extinguished flame. And the nightmares erupted. Feelings that Lisa could not express during the day surfaced as terrors at night, as bad dreams that lasted for years.

I thought again how the child of divorce is shaped by what goes on in the postdivorce family. Paula and Larry were angry. Karen took care of everyone but herself. Billy turned passive. Lisa, however, is numb. I sat back and thought of Lisa as I had known her for so many years—the charming child with ribbons in her hair who realized in sheer terror that her home was breaking apart. She tried with all her might to keep her anger and fear from erupting. At sixteen, she was cloistered with schoolwork and surrounded by wholesome activities and girlfriends. Her main problem was in maintaining the precarious balance between her two homes. And now I see a very distressed young woman who is facing serious problems in achieving intimacy and fulfilling sexual relationships.

I realized then one of the hidden dynamics in Lisa's family. In their struggle to suppress their own angry feelings at the time of the breakup, Lisa's parents made the mistake of conveying to the child that she should not express her feelings, either. Again, it's all too easy to confuse the parents' agenda with that of the child. Of course parents should try to control their anger, but it's not advisable or beneficial to keep the child from giving vent to hers. Children naturally restrain themselves at the time of the breakup and don't express their full anger and terror at what is happening in their lives. They don't wish to burden their troubled parents and push them further over the brink. But parents need to comfort children, not silence them. If parents decide on divorce, they have to find the courage to accept the anger and sadness of their children and not deny it or slough it off or—worst of all—drive it underground.

How can a child's suffering be so invisible in a family where both parents are trying their best to ease the divorce for the child? We know how parents are preoccupied with the huge task of reorganizing their own lives and reshaping their relationships. But at the same time, both parents fully expect their children to accept the immense changes in their lives without protest and without serious distress. If the truth be told (and it's not a truth that people want to hear) parents *want* their children to conform and not give them any trouble. Many parents are worried about the rightness of their decision and don't want their children to make them feel even worse.

The problem of numb feelings among grown children of divorce is serious and more widespread than I initially realized. A thirty-two-year-old scientist put it very clearly in a letter: "It's taken me fifteen years to acknowledge that I felt anything during my parents' divorce. In fact, it's taken a chunk of my life to let myself feel anything at all—especially anger, pain, fear, and sexual pleasure." An architect in his late thirties said, "I frequently spend time not investing in relationships. I keep myself back from emotional involvement. When people first meet me, they think of me as open. Only the people who are close to me know this about me. I'm still the schoolboy I was when they broke up. I'm afraid to express myself and too vulnerable to feel. I've learned that lots of times it's better not to feel at all. Feelings can hurt. It's better not to have them."

The numbness reported by children of divorce who were raised in families that did not fight points to a troubling conclusion. The "don't fight" rule does not protect children from feeling anxious and worried when they grow up and go in search of love and intimacy. In this arena, they are no different from children raised in high-conflict families. Thus we are wrong to tell parents that not fighting will protect their children against the long-term effects of divorce that come into play in adulthood. The safety net that good postdivorce coparenting provides for children is irrelevant in adulthood. The sense that a faithful, lasting, and loving relationship remains out of reach is a residue of divorce that is unrelated to the conflict at the breakup. The impact of the parents' divorce echoes and crescendos in adulthood whether the parents were civil or not.

TWENTY-ONE

Children of Divorce

At the twenty-five-year follow-up, Lisa looked smashing. With her dark-rimmed glasses and curly auburn hair cut no-nonsense short and her elegantly tailored suit, she was a model of a poised young businesswoman. After college she went on to earn an M.B.A at Georgetown University and now held a middle management job at a Fortune 500 firm in Columbus, Ohio. At age thirty-one, Lisa owned her own home, had a new car, and was swiftly climbing the corporate ladder. She had been sent west by her company on a business trip and took time out for our meeting. She spoke directly, just like her attorney mother. It wasn't long before we were talking about her mom and Lisa's expression turned serious.

"I'd have to admit that my main worry right now is my mother."

"Why? Is she having health problems?"

"Oh no, nothing like that," Lisa said. "It's just, well, I know this sounds strange, but I'd rather she got married than me. She's going to retire in five years from her law firm and then what'll she do? She's sad and very lonely. I'm probably the only person who realizes it because she's so attractive and she looks so capable. To take care of her, I'd need to live in Los Angeles, but I want to lead my own life in Columbus where I have a great job." Lisa's tone then changed from sadness to anguish. "You see, I *have* to protect her. Ultimately she has no one else in the world to take care of her but me. Ever since I was four years old, when my dad asked for the divorce, I've felt it was my job to make her happy."

Mother and Daughter Traps

MOTHERS AND DAUGHTERS can become stuck in the relationships they have at the breakup. We see this most often when the mother cannot absorb the shock of the divorce and go on to rebuild her life in a different direction. Fully identified with their mothers' pain, the daughters cannot break away emotionally to establish truly separate lives even if they live three thousand miles away.

Problems begin when the adolescent girl, who for years may have been her mother's most stalwart supporter, begins to move away from her mother's orbit. She needs to try her own wings, to be proud of her femininity, to be independent and strong. For all children, the adolescent years involve moving out and away. Here the daughter's dilemma becomes increasingly acute as she approaches young adulthood. Her problem is this: How can I leave my mother who has no one but me? Who will take care of her in her loneliness? Who will comfort her? The Old Testament tells the story of Ruth, a young woman who loses her spouse and devotes herself to her mother-in-law. The mother, Naomi, is grief-stricken. Ruth captures the passionate relationship between the two women when she says, "Whither thou goest I will go." This ancient story translates easily into the love and compassion that daughters of divorce feel for their mothers who are grieving and alone. They are bound by the golden strands of love and compassion. Negotiating the separation is a heroic task for the daughter when the mother is lonely. Lisa sobs as she contemplates her mother's plight and wonders what she should do. Another young woman told me that when she closes her eyes, she sees the figure of her mother "for the sad, repressed woman that she is and I cry and cry and feel that I'll never stop crying." Another said, "It used to be that I wasn't sure where she left off and where I began. I feel more separate now but I pity her and I worry about her." Another said, "My mother is a fettered person. She has the right tools but she can't make the shift since the divorce. She's wandered around in chains." Most said that they don't want to be like their mothers because that would be courting failure. They think of their mothers as women who have not been able to keep their dad's love or to capture the love of another man. And they are terrified of growing up to be like them. The mother evokes an extraordinary mix of love, compassion, and frightened rejection.

Moreover, the girl is deeply afraid that she will succeed where her mother failed. Everywhere she walks, the ice is thin. If she follows in her mother's footsteps, she fears that she'll end up alone and miserable. If she leaves her mother to pursue her own career, she repeats her father's rejection and leaves her mother alone and grieving. If she stays at her mother's side, she'll give up a life of independence, her career, and the man she wants. If she's happy in a relationship with a desirable man, then she commits the ultimate betrayal. She has taken what her mother never had and never will have. This dilemma is widespread. In one form or another, it's the central drama of many sensitive, devoted daughters who grow up in the loving care of an unhappy, lonely mother who has been left by her husband or who may have sought the divorce but failed to fill the void that was left. For example, from age twenty to thirty-two, Denise lived with a man who criticized and humiliated her. "I believed him when he said that I was bad person," she told me. When I saw her in her early thirties she had finally left him and was dating an eligible, attractive man. "I've been on a long detour," she explained. "It's long overdue but I'm finally finding my way. I've been preoccupied with what happened to my mom when I was ten years old. I think I'm free of her now. My mind and her mind are not enmeshed anymore. I feel separate now, though I still feel guilty." Denise married her boyfriend of three years when she was thirty-seven. No one in her family, including her mom, was invited to the ceremony, which took place at dawn overlooking Zion National Park in Utah. But others like her have stayed single.

Ghosts of the Past

I ASKED LISA if she still felt numb while having sex.

"That hasn't changed," she confessed. "But on top of that, I've gotten myself entangled with some real losers since I saw you last."

"What do you mean, losers?" She sounded like Karen, who lived with a man she didn't love simply because she knew he'd never leave her.

"There have been several men in my life over the last ten years. My longest relationship was with Jim. We met during our senior year in college and then lived together for five years. I kept trying to break up with him but every time I tried, I went back the next day."

"What was wrong?"

"For starters, he was a party guy, I'm not. He drank heavily. I hardly drink. He did sports that don't interest me. We were really opposites. I had a hard time asking him for what I wanted. Like I really wanted him to show that he cared about me and get me a gift at Christmas, be sympathetic and nice and kind, but he didn't do any of those things. He was a pretty self-centered guy."

I thought to myself, "What a strange relationship. What did she find appealing in him?"

"I couldn't let go," Lisa said softly. "Every time I tried to leave, to tell him it was quits, I chickened out. I wanted to break it off but I couldn't."

"Why not?" I asked as gently as I could.

The reply came in a barely audible whisper. "Whenever I decided to quit, I panicked. I thought of my dad leaving my mom. And I said to myself, 'I can't do this to another human being.' "

"What did your mom and dad's experience have to do with you and Jim?"

Lisa looked at me, startled. "Everything!"

It took me a minute to absorb what she was saying. On the surface, Lisa's attachment to a man who didn't meet her needs looked very much like Karen's first relationship. But then I realized that the source of their entrapment was different. Karen couldn't leave because she had installed her caretaking role into her love life. She had to stay with her boyfriend to take care of him. But Lisa's boyfriend didn't need to be taken care of. Lisa couldn't leave because she didn't want to do to him what was done to her mother. She couldn't bear to repeat the hurt that she always understood was at the root of her mother's lifelong distress. In effect, she was blocked from defending her own interests out of her intense fear of hurting the other person. As she confessed, it made her feel like a bad person to tell a man that their relationship was over. It was too close a parallel to her mother's experience with her father, and in this, Lisa's identification with her mother blocked her ability to reject an unsuitable lover. As a result, she stayed with him unhappily for five very important years.

But it went deeper. Lisa's father also stood in her way.

"What do you mean that you couldn't do to your mom what your dad did?" I wondered if Lisa knew something about her parents' divorce that I didn't.

"I love my dad," Lisa said, "but we don't talk openly to each other. We both avoid conflict. We communicate a lot through our shared love of music, especially chamber music. He plays in a quartet with his friends and sends me the music reviews from the *San Francisco Chronicle.* We're on e-mail every couple of days, mostly talking about music. It's a bonding thing for us. I know he loves me more than anything and that he's proud of me. He wants to protect me. And I want to protect him. So we tiptoe around each other and try and take care of each other and we never really talk."

"What do you need to protect him from?"

Her response startled me. "I never want him to feel guilty about leaving his first marriage."

"And this puts you on guard in your dealings with him?"

"Yes. Always."

"What would you like to say to him if you could be totally honest?"

This question unleashed a torrent in Lisa. Tears streamed down her face as she said, "There's always been a deep dark secret in our family. Even though everyone walks around it, it keeps getting bigger and bigger. Did my dad have an affair while he was still married to my mom? Did something happen that I should know about? I know that my parents met in college and fell in love. They're both decent, hardworking people. So why did a good man like my dad break his marriage vows and walk away from his wife? I suppose it's silly, but I want to think of my dad as a good person. But is he?" She wiped away the tears. "You see it's not enough that he loves me. I need to respect him. My relationship with him is not separate from my relationship with my mom just because they divorced when I was four. Why doesn't he say that a long time ago he hurt my mom a lot and that he's sorry? I know my mom was hurt whether she says so or not. I know that she loved him and probably still does. Why did he walk out?" Lisa, in her elegant business suit, was sobbing.

At some point in her growing up, probably in adolescence, Lisa decided that her father had violated a fundamental moral code in leaving his wife and daughter to marry another woman. Because she dearly loves her father, she never discussed her conclusions with him. Undoubtedly he would have suffered greatly had his beloved daughter directly accused him of infidelity. Doubtless Lisa, a sensitive and loving daughter, understood this. As a result it was a dreaded secret, a ghost that stood between them that Lisa, during their many hours together, took great pains never to mention. Like many young people from divorced families, Lisa is preoccupied with the morality of her parents' behavior. I was startled the first time a teenager walked into my office and demanded to know if her mother was a good woman. But as I have since learned, this is a common concern among children of divorce. Siblings spend years speculating over the probability that there were affairs during or after the marriage. As adults, children of divorce are influenced by their moral judgment of who was wronged by the divorce.

No-fault divorce is a legal concept. It was never intended to mean no moral responsibility. Children never subscribe to the idea that no one is to blame for the divorce, although they are too protective of themselves and their parents to say so. As young children they blame themselves, and when they dare, they blame one or both parents. But as adolescents in search of moral values, suspicion of infidelity, other mistreatment, or exploitation can be a serious obstacle to developing a close or honest relationship with the parent they think behaved immorally. For thousands of children and parents the undiscussed past hangs heavily over both generations, keeping them emotionally distant from each other.

These moral issues are also kept alive by what happens to each parent in the postdivorce years. The discrepancy between her mother's loneliness and her father's happiness broke Lisa's heart. Thus, despite the lack of overt fighting in this family, Lisa has placed herself years later exactly in the middle. Ironically, this is what both parents sought to avoid by "not fighting." The ways of a child's heart are unpredictable and cannot be orchestrated from the outside. Children make moral judgments about their parents. They want and need virtuous parents. They are willing to forgive if asked, but when this fails to happen, they find the silence deafening.

After finally breaking up with Jim, Lisa told me that she had several boyfriends but no relationships that lasted more than a year or two at the most. "Look at my life," she said heatedly. "I have a great career and plenty of money. I've always had close women friends. I get along with all my parents. But for some reason I don't understand, my relationships with men are still bad news. I'm getting pretty discouraged. I have nothing at all against marriage, but it's not for me."

Although Lisa's message was troubling, her directness was utterly appealing. I felt on safe enough ground to ask, "You don't think you would enjoy marriage?"

Lisa snapped back, "That's not it!" These young people almost always correct me when I don't get their meaning straight. "I'd like to get married but I don't think that I ever will, not ever." She shook her head vigorously. "When I was just out of college and my friends started to get married I'd think, Oh my God, there is no way I could ever be in something that would work like this. For a few years I was envious. And now I just don't care anymore."

"Are you dating anyone?"

"Well, maybe you could call it that. A few months ago, John moved into my house. We'd been seeing each other for about six months and decided that we didn't like sleeping in two places. He's a nice guy, Judy. He likes me a lot. He's going to be forty-two next month. We've decided to live together but we're never going to get married or anything. He's gone through two divorces and he's had enough. We're not planning on having any children together, unless you count our golden retrievers as ersatz kids." She laughed at the very thought. "So to anticipate your next question, yes, I've pretty much decided to remain single for the rest of my life. John treats me well, but to be totally honest with you, I'm not in love with him. He keeps me from being lonely." Lisa looked away, as if embarrassed by this confession. "Sometimes I think it would be the most wonderful thing in the world to love somebody one hundred percent with my whole heart and soul. But that's never going to happen to me. It's a far-fetched dream. Living with John is a lot easier and pleasanter than any alternatives that I know. Love a man and expect to cry has become my mantra. Last Valentine's Day he gave me a diamond ring in a weak moment but I had the good sense to turn him down. 'Thanks but no thanks,' I told him. 'It's better for both of us not to go down that road. But it's a neat ritual. You can propose to me once a year. It's a no-risk proposition.' "

"What does that mean?" I was mystified by her comment.

"Simple. If you don't marry, you don't get betrayed. You don't divorce. You're safe from a whole lot of things. That's reality. I'm in my thirties and I've never been in love where I felt like somebody was the right person and that I'm going to spend the rest of my life with him. People say you just know it if you're in love. I've never known it and I doubt I ever will. I've pretty much been convinced my whole life that I'm not going to have a romantic relationship that works. I'm sure I'm not the first to tell you that."

A Generation Stays Single

LISA WAS RIGHT. She has lots of company. Forty percent of the men and women in this divorce study have never married, a figure that exceeds the national average for adults in this age group raised in intact families.[1] This never-married group is a mix, including people like Lisa who are cohabiting, those who have serial lovers, and those who lead solitary lives. The increase in unmarried adults nationwide is a trend that shows no signs of abating and is probably an inevitable consequence of our divorce culture.[2] Children of divorce know the script when it comes to marriage. So do adults from intact marriages. Why take that risk?

One young woman said scornfully, "You spend a fortune on the wedding and then when you're broke, you divorce." But most who choose not to marry frankly say they are scared by what they know from their own history and from the number of broken marriages they have seen. Like Lisa they hope for a loving commitment and have been disappointed or hurt in relationships. While they don't like living alone or in a cohabitation that is going nowhere, they say that they reluctantly but firmly change their expectations.

A few of the still single young women said that they hoped to marry and to have children some day. Several were living with men and had these plans in mind. But most had firmly decided against marriage and motherhood. They gave many reasons that mostly boiled down to a distrust of men. They felt safer without legal marriage to keep them tied. A few talked about the great advantages of lifelong freedom. They said cohabitation was safer than marriage because escape was easier if they needed to get out or if the man left.

I thought to myself that everything Lisa had said was logical, but it just wasn't very convincing. I couldn't help thinking how distressed I would feel if Lisa were my daughter and had decided to forgo ever finding a man she could love. Having been in a happy marriage for fifty-three years, I knew how much she would be missing. Of course, men and women can live rich and interesting lives without ever getting married, but Lisa's decision was coming not so much from disinterest in an intimate relationship as from her fear that trust and love were beyond her reach.

Compared to Lisa, young people raised within the protection of good intact marriages hold very different expectations about the future. Lisa's best friend, Bettina, grew up down the street in a home with parents who were among the happiest in our study. These were people content with their lives who didn't hesitate to show mutual affection and love for their two children. They went out of their way to make their children's friends feel welcome in their home. Lisa loved spending time with this family and accompanied them on several camping trips in the Sierras. The two girls were inseparable from first grade through high school graduation, and Lisa was maid-of-honor at Bettina's wedding. In fact, Lisa gave us Bettina's name as someone to include in our comparison group.

The thing I remember most about my interview with Bettina was her statement, "I always thought of myself as a good person, and I never doubted that I would find a good man to love me and to love in return." She referred to her home as being "rock solid."

Of course, being raised by parents who are happily married does not innoculate children against divorce or other serious troubles. Life is not so simple. In an earlier book, *The Good Marriage*, I interviewed several young adults who had been raised by parents who were very happy in sexually close, romantic marriages. Such parents were often so devoted to each other that their children, watching the ongoing love affair, sometimes felt excluded from the parents' orbit. When these youngsters grew up, they rejected their parents as role models and opted for more reserved behavior in their own marriages.

In other close-knit families, children grow so close to their parents that separation in adolescence and early adulthood is an issue. I was relieved when Bettina told me how she had decided to go to Cornell instead of her father's alma mater, Stanford University. When the acceptance letters came, Bettina yelped, "Cornell, here I come!" Her father said to her with thinly veiled irritation, "No one turns Stanford down."

"Well then," Bettina answered tartly, "here goes the first." And she tootled off.

As if turned out, Bettina married another Cornell graduate and settled in upstate New York, far away from her parents. She still visits them a couple of times a year and now that her dad is retired, her parents travel more widely and often stop off to see her when they're back east. "They're great role models for my husband and me," Bettina said. "They're really savvy about how to do each life stage. I hope that we can do as well." After talking to Bettina, I remember feeling struck by the fact that both girls started from almost the same place; they had outstanding parents, solid middle-class backgrounds, and happy memories from when they were very young. But after Lisa's parents divorced, their paths diverged in ways no one could have predicted.

"You know, I have a lot in common with my friends from divorced families," Lisa said. "We define ourselves as children of divorce."

I'd been hearing this from others and asked Lisa to explain what she meant.

"It's sort of a permanent identity, like being adopted or something like that. I guess you might say that our parents' divorce was the formative event in our lives. It explains why I feel the way I do. The divorce is a permanent part of me and in some ways I'll never get over it. But it's good and bad news. The bad part is that as far as men are concerned, I always seem to be settling. Like even now I ask myself what am I doing living with a man who is twelve years older than me who has had two divorces? He's nice but I'll never fall in love with him. And he doesn't love me. I worry about that." Lisa shook her head slowly. "Look at it this way. I grew up unprepared for adult relationships, especially for being a woman with a man. No one taught me what I could expect or ask for. My mother never taught me about men. She didn't know much herself. She never even taught me not to nag. And my father failed to keep his marriage vows. So it was hard for me to learn much from his marriage, although he's been a great father and second husband. I have no idea how to be with a man. I have no idea what to expect. When my boyfriends have not been loving or kind or caring and I felt disappointed, I blamed me for being greedy and selfish. I told myself I was wrong for wanting more than I was getting, like I was supposed to be content. Kent told me I was trying to control him when I asked him to call if he was coming home late. I was dumb enough to believe him. I was incredibly naïve.

"But look at the good news. I've had to become independent and strong. I can work well with change. When things get chaotic, I don't lose my cool. I'm a good diplomat. I really had to be with my parents. I'm a good mediator in business and I can work with difficult people. I'm a great negotiator. Look at the lifetime of experience I have had keeping peace in my family. Also I learned at an early age to think for myself and to rely on myself. This may surprise you because I know that compared to a lot of others I've led a protected life. But I consider myself a survivor."

All that Lisa said was true of her own life and her generation. Others spoke proudly and triumphantly about their achievements and the strength they acquired in having to do things on their own. "Because my parents were so different I learned to navigate my own way in the world," said Jerry, a thirty-one-year-old stockbroker. "I've learned to use my head and my heart. I'm not afraid of what comes along." Because they learn at an early age that their parents' values could differ sharply, children of divorce learn to think for themselves. Their independent thinking extends into learning not to take sides in any continued warfare between their parents. Barbs and criticisms often drone on for years between their divorced parents, but none of the children as older adolescents or adults in this study bought into the accusations. Quite the reverse. They were careful to form their own opinions based on their own perceptions. This, too, was a source of their pride. Given the continuing accusations of infidelity and selfishness in their families, they realized that they had to develop their own morality. Whatever their own family histories, they valued honesty, equality, faithfulness, and kindness in relationships. If they failed to meet their own standards—and many did—they were no different in their values from their peers within good intact families. They just knew a lot less how to live up to them.

This generation did not engage in self-pity. Having learned to trust their own judgment they were pragmatists to the core, showing grit and courage against the ups and downs of life. Most held on to the capacity to hope and with it their capacity to change. As Evan said, "The divorce was hard but we can move on and build riches out of it. There is a lot of mix in my family with my dad's three marriages and my mom's two

TWENTY-TWO

Conclusions

"What's done to children, they will do to society."
Karl A. Menninger

Around the time I was finishing this book, a very important judge on the family law bench in a large state I shall not name invited me to come see him. I was eager to meet with him because I wanted to discuss some ideas I have for educating parents under court auspices that go beyond the simple advice "don't fight." After we had talked for a half an hour or so, the judge leaned back in his chair and said he'd like my opinion about something important. He had just attended several scientific lectures in which researchers argued that children are shaped more by genes than by family environment. Case in point, studies of identical twins reared separately show that in adulthood such twins often like the same foods and clothing styles, belong to the same political parties, and even bestow identical names on their dogs. The judge looked perplexed. "Do you think that marriages and all their children. Mine is the generation to put things together after our parents' divorce."

I asked Lisa how firm her decision was about never marrying. Was she really sure at age thirty-one she would never fall in love or find a man who would love her?

She answered very soberly. "Look, I don't know a lot about love between a man and a woman, but I know a lot about love and faithfulness. I've been blessed with two parents and a stepmother who did their level best for me. So the truth is that I know a lot about love, and yes, I'd want that more than anything in the whole world. With all my big talk, that would be my first choice." She smiled impishly as she left. "If my luck changes you'll be among the first to know."

could mean divorce is in the genes?" he asked in all seriousness. "And if that's so, does it matter what a court decides when parents divorce?"

I was taken aback. Here was a key figure in the lives of thousands of children asking me whether what he and his colleagues do or say on the bench makes any difference. He seemed relieved by the notion that maybe his actions are insignificant.

I told him that I personally doubt the existence of a "divorce gene." If such a biological trait had arisen in evolution, it would be of very recent vintage. But, I added, "What the court does matters enormously. You have the power to protect children from being hurt or to increase their suffering."

Now it was his turn to be taken aback. "You think we've increased children's suffering?"

"Yes, Your Honor, I do. With all respect, I have to say that the court along with the rest of society has increased the suffering of children."

"How so?" he asked.

We spent another half hour talking about how the courts, parents, attorneys, mental health workers—indeed most adults—have been reluctant to pay genuine attention to children during and after divorce. He listened respectfully to me but I must say I left the judge's chambers that day in a state of shock that soon turned to gloom. How can we be so utterly lost and confused that a leading judge would accept the notion of a "divorce gene" to explain our predicament? If he's confused about his role, what about the rest of us? What is it about the impact of divorce on our society and our children that's so hard to understand and accept?

Having spent the last thirty years of my life traveling here and abroad talking to professional, legal, and mental health groups plus working with thousands of parents and children in divorced families, it's clear that we've created a new kind of society never before seen in human culture. Silently and unconsciously, we have created a culture of divorce. It's hard to grasp what it means when we say that first marriages stand a 45 percent chance of breaking up and that second marriages have a 60 percent chance of ending in divorce. What are the consequences for all of us when 25 percent of people today between the ages of eighteen and forty-four have parents who divorced? What does it mean to a society when people wonder aloud if the family is about to disappear? What can we do when we learn that married couples with children represent a mere

26 percent of households in the 1990s and that the most common living arrangement nowadays is a household of unmarried people with no children?[1] These numbers are terrifying. But like all massive social change, what's happening is affecting us in ways that we have yet to understand.

For people like me who work with divorcing families all the time, these abstract numbers have real faces. When I think about people I know so well, including the "children" you've met in this book, I can relate to the millions of children and adults who suffer with loneliness and to all the teenagers who say, "I don't want a life like either of my parents." I can empathize with the countless young men and women who despair of ever finding a lasting relationship and who, with a brave toss of the head, say, "Hey, if you don't get married then you can't get divorced." It's only later, or sometimes when they think I'm not listening, that they add softly, "but I don't want to grow old alone." I am especially worried about how our divorce culture has changed childhood itself. A million new children a year are added to our march of marital failure. As they explain so eloquently, they lose the carefree play of childhood as well as the comforting arms and lap of a loving parent who is always rushing off because life in the postdivorce family is so incredibly difficult to manage. We must take very seriously the complaint of children like Karen who declare, "The day my parents divorced is the day my childhood ended."

Many years ago the psychoanalyst Erik Erikson taught us that childhood and society are vitally connected. But we have not yet come to terms with the changes ushered in by our divorce culture. Childhood is different, adolescence is different, and adulthood is different. Without our noticing, we have created a new class of young children who take care of themselves, along with a whole generation of overburdened parents who have no time to enjoy the pleasures of parenting. So much has happened so fast, we cannot hold it all in our minds. It's simply overwhelming.

But we must not forget a very important other side to all these changes. Because of our divorce culture, adults today have a greater sense of freedom. The importance of sex and play in adult life is widely accepted. We are not locked into our early mistakes and forced to stay in wretched, lifelong relationships. The change in women—their very identity and freer role in society—is part of our divorce culture. Indeed, two-thirds of divorces are initiated by women despite the high price they pay in economic and parenting burdens afterward. People want and expect a lot more out of marriage than did earlier generations. Although the divorce rate in second and third marriages is sky-high, many second marriages are much happier than the ones left behind. Children and adults are able to escape violence, abuse, and misery to create a better life. Clearly there is no road back.

The sobering truth is that we have created a new kind of society that offers greater freedom and more opportunities for many adults, but this welcome change carries a serious hidden cost. Many people, adults and children alike, are in fact not better off. We have created new kinds of families in which relationships are fragile and often unreliable. Children today receive far less nurturance, protection, and parenting than was their lot a few decades ago. Long-term marriages come apart at still surprising rates. And many in the older generation who started the divorce revolution find themselves estranged from their adult children. Is this the price we must pay for needed change? Can't we do better?

I'd like to say that we're at a crossroads but I'm afraid I can't be that optimistic. We can choose a new route only if we agree on where we are and where we want to be in the future. The outlook is cloudy. For every person who wants to sound an alarm, there's another who says don't worry. For everyone concerned about the economic and emotional deprivations inherited by children of divorce there are those who argue that those kids were "in trouble before" and that divorce is irrelevant, no big deal. People want to feel good about their choices. Doubtless many do. In actual fact, after most divorces, one member of the former couple feels much better while the other feels no better or even worse. Yet at any dinner party you will still hear the same myths: Divorce is a temporary crisis. So many children have experienced their parents' divorce that kids nowadays don't worry so much. It's easier. They almost expect it. It's a rite of passage. If I feel better, so will my children. And so on. As always, children are voiceless or unheard.

But family scholars who have not always seen eye to eye are converging on a number of findings that fly in the face of our cherished myths. We agree that the effects of divorce are long-term. We know that the family is in trouble. We have a consensus that children raised in divorced or remarried families are less well adjusted as adults than those raised in intact families.

The life histories of this first generation to grow up in a divorce culture tell us truths we dare not ignore. Their message is poignant, clear, and contrary to what so many want to believe. They have taught me the following:

From the viewpoint of the children, and counter to what happens to their parents, divorce is a cumulative experience. Its impact increases over time and rises to a crescendo in adulthood. At each developmental stage divorce is experienced anew in different ways. In adulthood it affects personality, the ability to trust, expectations about relationships, and ability to cope with change.

The first upheaval occurs at the breakup. Children are frightened and angry, terrified of being abandoned by both parents, and they feel responsible for the divorce. Most children are taken by surprise; few are relieved. As adults, they remember with sorrow and anger how little support they got from their parents when it happened. They recall how they were expected to adjust overnight to a terrifying number of changes that confounded them. Even children who had seen or heard violence at home made no connection between that violence and the decision to divorce. The children concluded early on, silently and sadly, that family relationships are fragile and that the tie between a man and woman can break capriciously, without warning. They worried ever after that parent-child relationships are also unreliable and can break at any time. These early experiences colored their later expectations.

As the postdivorce family took shape, their world increasingly resembled what they feared most. Home was a lonely place. The household was in disarray for years. Many children were forced to move, leaving behind familiar schools, close friends, and other supports. What they remember vividly as adults is the loss of the intact family and the safety net it provided, the difficulty of having two parents in two homes, and how going back and forth cut badly into playtime and friendships. Parents were busy with work, preoccupied with rebuilding their social lives. Both moms and dads had a lot less time to spend with their children and were less responsive to their children's needs or wishes. Little children especially felt that they had lost both parents and were unable to care for themselves. Children soon learned that the divorced family has porous walls that include new lovers, live-in partners, and stepparents. Not one of these relationships was easy for anyone. The mother's parenting was often cut into by the very heavy burdens of single parenthood and then by the demands of remarriage and stepchildren.

Relationships with fathers were heavily influenced by live-in lovers or stepmothers in second and third marriages. Some second wives were interested in the children while others wanted no part of them. Some fathers were able to maintain their love and interest in their children but few had time for two or sometimes three families. In some families both parents gradually stabilized their lives within happy remarriages or well-functioning, emotionally gratifying single parenthood. But these people were never a majority in any of my work.

Meanwhile, children who were able to draw support from school, sports teams, parents, stepparents, grandparents, teachers, or their own inner strengths, interests, and talents did better than those who could not muster such resources. By necessity, many of these so-called resilient children forfeited their own childhoods as they took responsibility for themselves; their troubled, overworked parents; and their siblings. Children who needed more than minimal parenting because they were little or had special vulnerabilities and problems with change were soon overwhelmed with sorrow and anger at their parents. Years later, when contemplating having their own children, most children in this study said hotly, "I never want a child of mine to experience a childhood like I had."

As the children told us, adolescence begins early in divorced homes and, compared with that of youngsters raised in intact families, is more likely to include more early sexual experiences for girls and higher alcohol and drug use for girls and boys. Adolescence is more prolonged in divorced families and extends well into the years of early adulthood. Throughout these years children of divorce worry about following in their parents' footsteps and struggle with a sinking sense that they, too, will fail in their relationships.

But it's in adulthood that children of divorce suffer the most. The impact of divorce hits them most cruelly as they go in search of love, sexual intimacy, and commitment. Their lack of inner images of a man and a woman in a stable relationship and their memories of their parents' failure to sustain the marriage badly hobbles their search, leading them to heartbreak and even despair. They cried, "No one taught me." They complain bitterly that they feel unprepared for adult relationships and that they have never seen a "man and woman on the same beam," that they have no good models on which to build their hopes. And indeed they have a very hard time formulating even simple ideas about the kind of person they're looking for. Many end up with unsuitable or very troubled partners in relationships that were doomed from the start.

The contrast between them and children from good intact homes, as both go in search of love and commitment, is striking. (As I explain in this book, children raised in extremely unhappy or violent intact homes face misery in childhood and tragic challenges in adulthood. But because their parents generally aren't interested in getting a divorce, divorce does not become part of their legacy.) Adults in their twenties from reasonably good or even moderately unhappy intact families had a fine understanding of the demands and sacrifices required in a close relationship. They had memories of how their parents struggled and overcame differences, how they cooperated in a crisis. They developed a general idea about the kind of person they wanted to marry. Most important, they did not expect to fail. The two groups differed after marriage as well. Those from intact families found the example of their parents' enduring marriage very reassuring when they inevitably ran into marital problems. But in coping with the normal stresses in a marriage, adults from divorced families were at a grave disadvantage. Anxiety about relationships was at the bedrock of their personalities and endured even in very happy marriages. Their fears of disaster and sudden loss rose when they felt content. And their fear of abandonment, betrayal, and rejection mounted when they found themselves having to disagree with someone they loved. After all, marriage is a slippery slope and their parents fell off it. All had trouble dealing with differences or even moderate conflict in their close relationships. Typically their first response was panic, often followed by flight. They had a lot to undo and a lot to learn in a very short time.

Those who had two parents who rebuilt happy lives after divorce and included children in their orbits had a much easier time as adults. Those who had committed single parents also benefited from that parent's attention and responsiveness. But the more frequent response in adulthood was continuing anger at parents, more often at fathers, whom the children regarded as having been selfish and faithless.

Others felt deep compassion and pity toward mothers or fathers who failed to rebuild their lives after divorce. The ties between daughters and their mothers were especially close but at a cost. Some young women found it very difficult to separate from their moms and to lead their own lives. With some notable exceptions, fathers in divorced families were less likely to enjoy close bonds with their adult children, especially their sons. This stood in marked contrast to fathers and sons from intact families, who tended to grow closer as the years went by.

Fortunately for many children of divorce, their fears of loss and betrayal can be conquered by the time they reach their late twenties and thirties. But what a struggle that takes, what courage and persistence. Those who succeed overcome their difficulties the hard way—by learning from their own failed relationships and gradually rejecting the models they were raised with to create what they want from a love relationship. Those lucky enough to have found a loving partner are able to interrupt their self-destructive course with a lasting love affair or marriage.

In other realms of adult life—financial and security, for instance—some children were able to overcome difficulties through unexpected help from fathers who had vanished long before. Still others benefit from the constancy of parents or grandparents. Many men and women raised in divorced families establish successful careers. Their workplace performance is largely unaffected by the divorce. But no matter what their success in the world, they retain some serious residues—fear of loss, fear of change, and fear that disaster will strike, especially when things are going well. They're still terrified by the mundane differences and inevitable conflicts found in every close relationship.

I'm heartened by the hard-won success of these adults. But at the same time, I can't forget those who've failed to straighten out their lives. I'm especially troubled by how many divorced or remained in wretched marriages. Of those who have children and who are now divorced, many, to my dismay, are not protecting their children in ways we might expect. They go on to repeat the same mistakes their own parents made, perpetuating problems that have plagued them all their lives. I'm also concerned about many who, by their mid- and late thirties, are neither married nor cohabiting and who are leading lonely lives. They're afraid of getting involved in a relationship that they think is doomed to fail. After a divorce or breakup, they're afraid to try again. And I'm struck by continuing anger at parents and flat-out statements by many of these young adults that they have no intention of helping their moms and especially their dads or stepparents in old age. This may change. But if it doesn't, we'll be facing another unanticipated consequence of our divorce culture. Who will take care of an older generation estranged from its children?

What We Can and Cannot Do

Our efforts to improve our divorce culture have been spotty and the resources committed to the task are pitifully small. The courts have given the lion's share of attention to the 10 to 15 percent of families that continue to fight bitterly. Caught between upholding the rights of parents and protecting the interests of children, they have tilted heavily toward parents. Such parents allegedly speak in the name of the child just as those who fight bloody holy wars allegedly speak in the name of religion. Thus, as I explained to the judge with whom I began this chapter, our court system has unintentionally contributed to the suffering of children. At the same time, most parents receive little guidance. Some courts offer educational lectures to families at the time of the breakup, but the emphasis is on preventing further litigation. Such courses are typically evaluated according to how much they reduce subsequent litigation and not on how they might improve parenting. Curricula to educate teachers, school personnel, pediatricians, and other professionals about child and parenting issues in divorce are rare. Few university or medical school programs in psychiatry, psychology, social work, or law include courses on how to understand or help children and parents after separation, divorce, and remarriage. This lack of training persists despite the fact that a disproportionate number of children and adolescents from divorced homes are admitted as patients for psychological treatment at clinics and family agencies. In many social agencies, close to three-quarters of the children in treatment are from divorced families. Some school districts have organized groups for children whose parents are divorcing. And some communities have established groups to help divorcing parents talk about their children's problems. A few centers such as ours have developed programs to help families cope with high conflict and domestic violence. But such efforts are not widespread. As a society, we have not set up services to help people relieve the stresses of divorce. We continue to foster the myth that divorce is a transient crisis and that as soon as adults restabilize their lives, the children will recover fully. When will the truth sink in?

Let's suppose for a moment that we had a consensus in our society. Suppose we could agree that we want to maintain the advantages of divorce but that we need to protect our children and help parents mute the long-term effects of divorce on future generations. Imagine we were willing to roll up our sleeves and really commit the enormous resources of our society toward supplementing the knowledge we have. Suppose we gave as much time, energy, and resources to protecting children as we give to protecting the environment. What might we try?

I would begin with an effort to strengthen marriage. Obviously, restoring confidence in marriage won't work if we naively call for a return to marriage as it used to be. To improve marriage, we need to fully understand the nature of contemporary man-woman relationships. We need to appreciate the difficulties modern couples confront in balancing work and family, separateness and togetherness, conflict and cooperation. It's no accident that 80 percent of divorces occur in the first nine years of marriage. These new families should be our target.

What threats to marriage can we change? First, there's a serious imbalance between the demands of the workplace and the needs of family life. The corporate world rarely considers the impact of its policies on parents and children. Some companies recognize that parents need time to spend with their children but they don't understand that the workplace exerts a major influence on the quality and stability of marriage. Heavy work schedules and job insecurity erode married life. Families with young children especially postpone intimate talk, sex, and friendship. These are the ties that replenish a marriage. When the boss calls, we go to the office. When the baby cries, we pick up the child. But when a marriage is starving, we expect it to bumble along. Most Western European countries provide paid family leave. What about us? Why do we persist in offering unpaid leave and pretend that it addresses the young family's problem? One additional solution might be social security and tax benefits for a parent who wants to stay home and care for young children. That alone would lighten the burden on many marriages. Other suggestions for reducing the stresses on young families include more flex time, greater opportunities for part-time work, assurances that people who take family leave will not lose their place on the corporate ladder, tax advantages for families, and many other ideas that have been on the table for years. Public policy cannot create good marriages. But it can buffer some of the stresses people face, especially in those early, vulnerable years when couples need time to establish intimacy, a satisfying sex life, and a friendship that will hold them together through the inevitable challenges that lie ahead. Ultimately, if we're really interested in improving marriage so that people have time for each other and their children, we need to realign our priorities away from the business world and toward family life.

We might also try to help the legions of young adults who complain bitterly that they're unprepared for marriage. Having been raised in divorced or very troubled homes, they have no idea how to choose a partner or what to do to build the relationship. They regard their parents' divorce as a terrible failure and worry that they're doomed to follow in the same footsteps. Many adults stay in unhappy marriages just to avoid divorce. We don't know if we can help them with educational methods because we haven't tried. Our experience is too limited and our experimental models nonexistent. But when so many young people have never seen a good marriage, we have a moral obligation to try to intervene preventively. Most programs that give marital advice are aimed at engaged couples who belong to churches and synagogues. These are very good beginnings that should be expanded. But many offer too little and arrive too late to bring about changes in any individual's values or knowledge. Nor is the excitement that precedes a wedding the best time for reflection on how to choose a lifetime partner or what makes a marriage work. Academic courses on marriage mostly look at families from the lofty perch of the family scholar and not from the perspective of children of divorce who feel "no one ever taught me."

In my opinion, a better time to begin helping these youngsters is during mid-adolescence, when attitudes toward oneself and relationships with the opposite sex are beginning to gel. Adolescence is the time when worries about sex, love, betrayal, and morality take center stage. Education for and about relationships should begin at that time, since if we do it right, we'll have their full attention. It could be based in the health centers that have been established in many schools throughout the country. Churches and synagogues and social agencies might provide another launching place. Ideally, adolescents in a well-functioning society should have the opportunity to think and talk about a wide range of relationships, issues, and conflicts confronting them. As an opening gambit, think about asking the deceptively simple question: "How do you choose a friend?" A group of teenagers considering this problem could be drawn to the important question of how to choose a lover and life partner—and even more important, how not to choose one. Specific topics such as differences between boys and girls, cultural subgroups, and how people resolve tensions would follow based on the teenagers' interests and their willingness to discuss real issues. Colleges could also offer continuing and advanced courses on an expanded range of subjects, including many problems that young men and women now struggle with alone.

We are on the threshold of learning what we can and cannot do for these young people. Still one wonders, can an educational intervention replace the learning that occurs naturally over many years within the family? How do we create a corps of teachers who are qualified to lead meaningful courses on relationships? By this I mean courses that are true to life, honest, and respectful of students. I worry about the adult tendency to lecture or sermonize. In a society where the family has become a political issue, I'm concerned about attacks from the left and the right, about the many people who would attack such interventions the way they've attacked the Harry Potter books. Mostly I'm concerned about finding a constituency of adults who would rally behind an idea that has so many pitfalls. But I'm also convinced that doing nothing—leaving young people alone in their struggles—is more dangerous. We should not give up without a try.

For the Children

EXCEPT FOR THOSE raised in divorced families, few people realize the many ways that divorce shapes not only the child's life but also the child. As we have seen in many homes, parenting erodes almost inevitably at the breakup and does not get restored for years, if ever. The changes in parenting and in the structure of the family place greater responsibilities on the child to take care of herself. And she, in turn, becomes a different person as she adjusts to the new needs and wishes of her parents and stepparents. All of the children I have described in this book took on new roles in direct response to changes that occurred during the postdivorce years. Many were acutely aware of their parents' distress and tried to rescue them. Others remained angry at their parents' diminished attention and judged them harshly. Others longed for the family they had lost and tried to reverse the divorce decision. And still others took responsibility for keeping the peace and walked on eggs throughout their childhoods. These children took many paths, but all changed significantly in the wake of divorce. And because the children's character and conscience were still being formed during the postdivorce years, the new roles they assumed in the family had profound effects on who they became and on the relationships they established when they reached adulthood.

As an adult child of divorce reading this book, I hope you have gained a better understanding of who you are today and how you got here. I hope you realize that you have millions of peers who share your worries about relationships and who understand the seriousness of your predicament. Your fears and feelings were forged in the crucible of your parents' divorce years ago and strengthened over the years that followed. These emotions, which are often hidden from consciousness, have the power to affect your marriage, your parenting, indeed the quality of your entire life.

An important task for your generation is to achieve better relationships. But how to go about it? You still wonder what motivated your parents' decision to divorce. Some people find that it helps to sit down and talk candidly with their parents. You may not believe or like the answers, but the exercise can provide new and useful perspectives. Not everyone can do this, nor should they, since it may cause both parent and child unnecessary suffering. But for many, it's worth trying to lift the curtain of silence that has troubled the parent and child relationship for years.

My next advice is to delay marriage or commitment until you have learned more about yourself and what you want in a partner. A good relationship cannot be created if you're expecting to fail. You can learn about people by observing them and by observing yourself together with them. Look around and try to see relationships that are working. You might learn something. You should consider individual or group therapy as a bridge to understanding yourself. You need to learn how to resolve conflict without becoming terrified. In mastering this skill, you'll gain confidence that you can influence your relationships instead of passively settling for whatever comes your way. Before you settle for disappointment, try to learn about the parts of life that you missed. In the end, each person finds his or her own way. Ultimately, your goal is to close the door on your parents' divorce, to separate the now from the then. By giving up wanting what you didn't have, you can set yourself free.

For the Parents

IN TALKING TO young adults who were raised in unhappy intact families, it became clear to me that their parents could have gone either way—stay together or get a divorce. This older generation of parents certainly had enough legitimate complaints about their spouses to consider divorce. But their marriages were not so explosive or chaotic or unsafe that husband and wife felt living together was intolerable.

What can we learn from them? Is their example useful to people today who share similar problems? If this describes you, I think you should seriously consider staying together for the sake of your children. The couples who stayed unhappily married in this study struggled with all the problems that beset modern marriage—infidelity, depression, sexual boredom, loneliness, rejection. Few problems went away as time wore on, but that's not what mattered most to these adults. Given their shared affcction and concern for their children, they made parenting their number onc priority. As one woman explained, "There are two relationships in this marriage. He admires me as a wonderful mother. As a wife, I bore him in every way possible. But our children are wonderful and that's what counts." If a couple can maintain their loving, shared parenting without feeling martyred, this is a choice to consider seriously. Many people make it. The notion that open conflict is always the hallmark of unhappy marriages is simply not true. That children are aware of their parents' unhappiness and are themselves unhappy because of it is also not true. It depends on whether the parents are able with grace and without anger to make the sacrifice required to maintain the benefits of the marriage for their children.

For those parents who decide to divorce, I have other advice. First, don't act impulsively. A visit to an attorney will give you very important information about finances, your legal rights and other aspects of the law, and court or mediation practice. This is vital information but only a small part of what you will need. Think realistically about what your life will be like after divorce. If you need to go back to school, think about doing it before you divorce. Add up the pros and cons carefully. Keep in mind that you will need to spend far more time with your children, giving them extra support and encouragement after the divorce, and that your presence may be even more needed during their adolescence. This means you won't have time to look for the new lover you may have dreamed about or to begin a new marriage right away, especially if your new partner has children. Your children may well be more demanding, more symptomatic, angrier, and harder to handle than ever before. No matter what custody arrangement you work out, you will *still be a single parent* in decision making, in responsibility, and in guiding your child. So be prepared for a lonely, hectic time. Yes, it can be done. Yes, it's much harder than you think. At least one parent, you or your ex-spouse, must be willing to give the children priority. The time that you invest in comforting your children, in being available to them in the evenings, is the most important investment you can make in your future relationship with them. Try your best not to delegate parenting tasks to your eldest or most competent child. If you do, then be sure to make the job temporary. As I said in earlier chapters, you need to maintain household structure and routines in childhood as well as during adolescence. And what has emerged clearly from this work is that your children will continue to need your help in entering young adulthood and during their early twenties.

If a very young child has enjoyed having one parent at home part- or full-time, you should consider finding ways to maintain this arrangement for at least a year after the breakup. Little children who lose both parents because daddy moves out and mommy goes to work full-time suffer terribly. These children pathetically search for their lost parents everywhere. The youngsters in our study, who had so little capacity to understand the changes in their lives or to provide for their own care, remained vulnerable throughout their growing up years and had more trouble in adulthood than children who were older at the breakup. Just as postponing the sale of the home can be built into the divorce agreement, I recommend that parents delay the mother's reentry into full-time work until the youngest child has had time to adjust. This investment in our youngest children of divorce is something we would celebrate in future years. These little ones are the most vulnerable. Their feelings of pain, anger, and abandonment endure into adulthood. They need special protection.

I also want to amplify another finding of this study having to do with support for higher education. Children who would have received financial help for their college educations should not, at age eighteen, feel they're paying for their parents' divorce with the forfeiture of their future careers. This is an intolerable injustice. The children will never forgive their parents for this betrayal, nor should they. If parents cannot afford to pay for college, children understand that just fine. But if a parent has the means to help pay tuition but says he or she is not "obligated," then the child has every right to be furious—at the parent and even more at a society that has sanctioned the child's heavy loss with its divorce laws. When a stingy parent gives priority to a new family—new spouse, new children, new life—the child of divorce is doubly wounded.

Professors in several law schools have suggested that money for college along with other funds for the children be set aside at the time of the breakup—before the community property is divided.[2] For families with the means to do so, trust funds would assure that children are able to get the educations they deserve. Although a few states have enacted legislation that enables the court to order support for college under certain circumstances, most states have no laws that extend child support beyond age eighteen. Surely all children deserve the same legal protection and the financial and emotional support and encouragement that is critical to their future. The children who would benefit from such legislation, as usual, have no voice, no constituency, no power to influence their futures. But the rest of us can and should speak up for them.

For Society

IF WE WANT to improve our divorce culture, we can begin with better services for families that are breaking up. Our focus should not be on parental rights but on what needs to be done to protect each individual child in each household. Such services could be offered under court auspices, clinics, or independently by a new agency. Basically this new agency would be a place for divorcing parents to come and make long-term plans for their children—not just for this year or next but for many years into the future. Parents can be helped to anticipate the changes that lie ahead and to learn critical skills for protecting their children. This new agency would represent a significant expansion of mediation and parent education services that already exist in several states. It would provide education, counseling, and mediation to divorced and remarried families. It would be staffed by people with a knowledge of children and parents and a range of psychological and mediation skills. Divorcing couples would be required to participate in a comprehensive course on the many aspects of coparenting. In small groups and at lectures, they would learn about the particular problems associated with visiting and joint custody families, moving, and the burdens on a child who travels long distances between two homes. The staff would teach parents how to help children with difficult transitions at both ends and how to make sure that going back and forth, whether for visiting or for custody, does not break up the child's playtime and activities. Parents would discuss how to plan visits with their child at different ages. The goal would be to help parents prepare for the challenges of bringing up children in the postdivorce and remarried family, recognizing that everything will be different. And children in this new system could be given a real voice in what happens to them.

Parents and children in violent or high-conflict families will need another set of services provided by people with specialized training.[3] Current arrangements in most courts are insufficient for the needs of these troubled and often tormented families. As we've seen, they use an inordinate amount of court time and attention. Without specialized programs there is little evidence that the children from such families can be protected. Moreover, they often require help over many years. Obviously, all of these services require training or personnel that is not currently available at universities although knowledge to design appropriate graduate courses surely exists.

These new centers could establish special playgroups for young children providing an oasis of pleasant contact with peers to help offset their sense of isolation. In my experience, it's not necessarily helpful to tell a child that she needs to "express her feelings" or that she's not the cause of her parents' divorce. But it does reduce a child's anxiety to understand the changes happening in her life and to help her think of ways to actively deal with those changes. In these circumstances, a playgroup leader can be especially helpful in imparting information calmly and slowly. An intervention like this lasting several weeks will not prevent children from running into difficulties in the postdivorce family (and it will certainly not affect their anxieties when they reach adulthood), but it can give them a larger framework for understanding their situation—and it could go far in lessening their loneliness and suffering. Moreover, teachers working with children at this time can be trained to spot problems such as uncontrolled aggression, speech disturbances, or depression and to refer the family for expert help before the problems become chronic.

Groups for adolescents are not easy to set up at the time of the breakup despite the fact that they would be very useful. It takes considerable skill to get teenagers into group settings at the time of the breakup. Once they get going, however, groups can provide an excellent vehicle for clarifying divorce, ventilating anger at parents, dealing with issues of morality, and discussing the adolescents' fears that their own future relationships might fail. Groups are also a good way to diminish or even abort the early acting out and sexual behavior that is rampant in this age group. Group leaders who gain the respect and empathy of young people have an opportunity to help them understand the impact of seeing parents with new lovers or their anxiety at becoming the too close confidant of one parent—and how to deal with these issues.

For the Courts

THE COURTS, BY virtue of their centrality to the divorce process, have been leaders in setting our national policies and priorities. Many judges are sensitive people who have great compassion and sympathy for children. But with all due respect, our rigid court structure may be the wrong forum for making decisions about parents and children at the time of divorce. Judges have no special training to help them deal with families in crisis. They are charged with safeguarding the best interests of children without knowledge about the needs of children at different developmental stages. Few have been exposed to studies on the impacts of divorce on children and what helps or hinders their adjustment. Moreover, the courts are hard pressed for time and staff. This frustration with our current system is widely shared among judges.

Findings from this twenty-five-year study challenge the central assumption of our court policy: namely, that if parents refrain from conflict, issues around custody, contact, and economic support will be settled expeditiously, both parents will resume their parenting roles, and the child will resume her normal developmental progress. But it is manifestly misguided to expect that muting conflict between divorced parents by itself will reinstate the course of parenting observed in intact families. It is in fact misguided to expect that arrangements made at the time of the breakup will effectively shape the child's future. What influences the child are the long-term circumstances of life during the postdivorce years. As couples exit the courthouse steps, profound changes in parent-child relationships lie ahead. Parenting in the postdivorce family is far less stable than parenting in the functioning intact family. Visiting or custody arrangements that work immediately after the divorce when both parents are single often collapse when a new wife or husband has priorities that may not include time or sacrifices on behalf of children from the former marriage. Everything changes when a second marriages fails, or when the individual circumstances of each parent zig and zag, or when the child gets older and has different needs plus a mind of her own. Only a very small handful of children in this study continued to have close relationships with both parents during the postdivorce years. The course of parent-child relationships is far less predictable than either parents or courts acknowledge.

To help parents and children in divorcing families, our courts and mental health professionals associated with the legal system need a more realistic view of the postdivorce family. Parent educators should address the long-term needs of children and help parents anticipate the changes and stresses that lie ahead as they try to meet those challenges. Although discouraging conflict is important, parent education courses should prepare mothers and fathers for the long haul. They will be coparents for many years, meeting the challenges of sole or joint custody, visiting, and myriad financial and emotional crises that inevitably arise until the child becomes an adult.

Courts could ease children's lives many ways. After examining dozens of court-issued guidelines for visiting and attending many court sessions, I'm astonished at the silence surrounding the child. Lawyers speak up for what parents want but no one speaks for the child. As we saw in many stories in this book, her wishes, her preferences, how she feels about the proposed plans, and how she wishes to spend her time separate from each parent are considerations that are hardly ever raised. In our current system, a child is treated like a rag doll that quietly sits wherever it is placed. The children of divorce that I know would be startled to learn that the courts were ever seriously concerned with their interests. Despite our bright assurances that children are central in divorce proceedings, they remain voiceless. No provisions are made for changing visiting arrangements as the child matures and wishes to make her own vacation and weekend plans. School-age children in intact families spend most of their time with friends and playmates, in school and on the playground—and not in the company of their parents. Adolescents in intact families are encouraged to participate in planning their own activities. But children from divorced families whose schedules are dictated by rigid court or mediated orders complain bitterly that they feel like second-class citizens. Compared to their peers from intact homes, they have fewer rights and privileges and fewer opportunities for social relationships and activities that could enrich their lives. When they are able to speak honestly, they express intense anger at the courts and the parent or parents who insist on maintaining orders that the children feel no longer suit their needs. Most of all, they want a say in their own lives and feel aggrieved at being excluded from the planning process. They want respect for choosing their own friends and interests. These youngsters are right on every count. Peer relationships are not only important to a child, they are critical to her development as a good citizen and cooperative member of a group. Visiting orders for children should be flexible and subject to review and change at regular intervals as each child matures.

Children exposed to violence are especially vulnerable, but they are not being protected by the courts. Court orders and mediated agreements about visiting generally ignore the violence of one parent toward the other. Many judges believe that if a violent man hits his wife but not his children, such brutality is not an issue in making a court order in reference to the children. From the silence, children receive the message that violence is acceptable to society. Thus divorce can rescue the parent who is a victim of violence but it does not rescue the child who has witnessed that violence. Many studies show that children who have witnessed violence suffer severe, long-term effects in their ability to form relationships, to develop a conscience, and to control their own aggressive impulses. The court's failure to address this issue has grave consequences because domestic violence typically occurs behind closed doors and only surfaces at the breakup. Thus courts have a onetime opportunity to intervene on behalf of the child by providing counseling and education for parents and children—before orders for visiting or custody are written. This does not mean that the violent parent will be prevented from seeing the children. But it does mean that the parents and children will get help before visiting arrangements are set.

Courts are guilty of one other unforeseen consequence stemming from their rigid policies. Children locked into inflexible, court-ordered visiting arrangements until age eighteen grow up rejecting the parent who insisted on the plan. As young adults, they refuse further contact with the parent who held them to the rigid visiting plan. Parents and attorneys forget that growing youngsters hold the trumps. So if the purpose of court-ordered visiting is to enable a child and parent to get to know each other better and enjoy a friendly or even loving relationship, the strategy boomerangs badly. Children's resentment grows during adolescence. The lesson is clear. Parents cannot rely on the courts to enforce their rights with a child the way they can with property. Unfortunately, the current system encourages parents to think exactly in this way. Sooner than expected, the child will grow up and express her resentment at the tyranny of the courts and the parent. The parent who desires the love and respect of his or her child cannot rely on the power of the courts to create a relationship. Court orders can create the opportunity for a relationship, but the responsibility for cultivating a loving, concerned friendship with the child only begins there. It would be helpful to many parents if the courts and attorneys directly conveyed this understanding.

I have already reviewed issues around joint custody and will not repeat them here except to note again that joint custody is helpful to some children and detrimental to others. It can help some at one age and be harmful at a later age. Despite the courts' wish for a policy that can be applied across the board, one size will never fit all or most children. Perhaps it would be wise to teach judges to be suspicious of policies for children that apply across the board.

Finally, judges, attorneys, mediators, and the mental health professionals who work in the courts should consider building in means to follow up their actions. For example, when young children are required to fly unaccompanied to maintain visiting, both child and parents should be expected back in court one year later to review the impact of the traveling on the child's feelings and general adjustment. Unlike the fields of medicine and psychology, courts have no built-in review processes at their disposal. Flawed court orders or mediated agreements remain hidden because their results are not regularly held to the light and examined. Rulings in family law—with their long-term consequences for children—have a complexity that requires an assessment that goes beyond questions of following laws appropriately. It would be very helpful and reassuring to parents, to the courts themselves, and to society as a whole if court policies and related practice had a built-in, regular review process. Such assessments might lead to important changes that would greatly improve the quality of the children's lives.

• • •

THESE SUGGESTIONS ARE just some of the things we might do to reduce the suffering of children and adults in our divorce culture. I'm sure that gifted minds will come up with many others as we learn more about the long-term consequences of divorce on the American family. In fact, it's likely that many new ideas will come from those who have lived firsthand the experience of growing up in divorced families—the generation of young adults that we met in this book. They are now of an age when they're entering responsible positions in politics, law, entertainment, science, medicine, education, and other professions. They are our future, and thank God, they are dubious but not entirely cynical. Quite the opposite. They have demonstrated a startling capacity to change, to put aside their fears, and to learn how to trust the people they love.

We now come to a final, critical question. What values does this generation hold regarding marriage and divorce? Have they given up on marriage or committed cohabitation? Is it fated to disappear as a human institution? The vote of this generation is clear. Despite their firsthand experience of seeing how marriages can fail, they sincerely want lasting, faithful relationships whether in marriage or a lasting cohabitation. No single adult in this study accepts the notion that marriage is going to wither away. They want stability and a different life for their children. They fully accept divorce as an option but they believe that divorce in a family with children should be an absolute last resort. Those who are happily married feel blessed. They never expected to have a happy family of their own and they're grateful for their great good fortune. As children of divorce they are all eager to rewrite history, not to repeat it. They want to do things better than their parents.

Over the years, many of the children in this study have kept in touch with me. I've been invited to their weddings and attended several of them. Others send color photographs, including images of romantic weddings with all the trimmings. In one, a crateful of white doves was released after the vows were spoken. One garlanded bride got married on top of a mountain to the sound of a shepherd's flute. Some did not invite their parents. Others invited everyone, including former and present wives and husbands of their parents. For all young people, a wedding still symbolizes lifetime commitment. But among children of divorce, the wedding represents a triumph over fear. For those whose weddings I attended, I think my presence may have provided a sense of closure on their past and strengthened their sense of having made it against the odds. I am the tribal elder who was there at the major battles of their lives, who carries their history, including their dreams, hopes, and fears, in my keeping.

I end this book with a passionate wedding toast offered at the marriage of a young man named Michael who just turned thirty-two. Like so many others in this study it had taken Michael years to overcome his intense fear of commitment. He said: "Every time I decided to go through with it, I would be overcome by an awful feeling of sadness, just like I felt when I was a little boy." Finally he managed to conquer his fear and marry Elizabeth, the woman he had lived with and loved for over five years. These words were spoken by his best man, who is also a child of divorce. His toast conveys the yearning, uncertainty, and youthful self-confidence of his generation:

> To many here today it feels strange to find that one of us is getting married. It's strange because we are a generation of cynical children when it comes to marriage. We came of age during a time when divorce became an acceptable alternative. Ultimately this is good. But the effect on us is one of caution, of skepticism. Who needs marriage? It's an outdated institution. Why be burdened? But while we were uttering these cynicisms, we were privately nurturing the hope that we could rediscover and experience the romantic and very profound magic that we had heard existed in a far-off time—to see marriage through innocent eyes. But we didn't realize it's not about innocence. It's about realism, about seeing what's really there and not deluding ourselves with false expectations. Ironically, the wonderful thing about growing up in the Age of Divorce is that we have learned so much. It's been very painful but we learned. So we look for signals. When one of our friends tells us he's getting married, we look for signals to assess his chances. Well, I got a signal this morning. As the bride stepped out of the door, I caught my breath. I felt a lump in my throat and I leaned against the car for support. I was stunned. She was so beautiful. But it wasn't just physical beauty. As Elizabeth walked behind Michael, he turned slowly and took her hand. I felt that calm electricity that happens when it's right—the thing, whatever it is, that doesn't happen unless it's basically right. And I paused to appreciate the knowledge that our cynical generation has gained. And I choked back a tear. We're okay, Michael and Elizabeth. Speak the truth to each other and be happy.

Appendix: Research Sample

Divorced Sample

ORIGINAL SAMPLE AND DEMOGRAPHICS

The study began in 1971 with 131 children and adolescents from 60 families in which the parents had recently separated and filed for divorce in Marin County, California. These families were selected out of a much larger group of people who were referred to us by their family law attorneys on the basis of the parents' willingness to participate and using the criteria that all of the children had to be developmentally on track, never having been referred for emotional or developmental problems. Each child, 59 of the mothers, and 47 of the fathers were studied intensively for a six-week period near the time of the marital separation, which was defined as the time when the parents physically separated and remained permanently apart. Parents and children were recontacted and reexamined at eighteen months postseparation, at five years, and at ten years. A subset of the parents and children were contacted and interviewed at the fifteen-year mark, although this was not a formal follow-up. At the twenty-five-year follow-up the children, now adults, were located and studied intensively.

The 131 children consisted of 52 percent girls and 48 percent boys. Fifty-three percent were 8 years old or younger and 47 percent ranged in age from 9 to 18 when they were first studied. Number of children per family averaged 2.2. Eighty-eight percent of the families were white; 3 percent were African American, and 9 percent were interracial, with one Asian and one white spouse. The mothers' average age was 34.1; the fathers' age averaged 36.9. This was the first marriage for 90 percent of the men and 93 percent of the women. At the decisive separation they had been married an average of 11.1 years with length of marriages ranging from 4 to 23 years. For the early 1970s they were a relatively well-educated group. Twenty-five percent of the fathers held graduate degrees in medicine, law, or business administration (and close to one-half had bachelor's degrees). One-third of the mothers had completed college; 5 percent held graduate degrees. Eighteen percent of the men and 24 percent of the women had ended their formal education with a high school degree. (Ten percent of the men and one-third of the women had completed a year or more of college coursework.) Prior to their divorce the families fell largely in the middle-class socioeconomic range as measured by the Hollingshead Two-Factor Index of Social Position. Forty-three percent fell into the two highest levels, 29 percent were in the middle level, and 28 percent ranked at the two lowest levels.

EIGHTEEN-MONTH FOLLOW-UP SAMPLE

Fifty-six of the 60 families participated in the eighteen-month follow-up. Two families had reconciled, one could not be located, and one declined to participate. Full data were obtained on 108 children, 41 fathers, and 53 mothers. Fifty-five percent of the participating children were girls and 45 percent were boys.

FIVE-YEAR FOLLOW-UP SAMPLE AND DEMOGRAPHICS

At five years, 58 of the 60 families were recontacted and members of 56 families participated in the extensive interview process. These families consisted of 96 children, 54 mothers, and 41 fathers. Sixty percent of the women and children had suffered a precipitous decline in income and standard of living with their socioeconomic level being two or more ranks below what it was before the divorce.

TEN-YEAR FOLLOW-UP SAMPLE AND DEMOGRAPHICS

Fifty-four (90%) of the original 60 families were located and members of 52 (87%) of the families were interviewed. Full data were obtained for 113 children, which consisted of 56 percent females and 44 percent males, 47 mothers, and 36 fathers. At the ten-year mark the average time since separation was 10.9 years. Fifty percent of the fathers ranked in the two highest socioeconomic status (SES) categories and 17 percent fell into the two lowest categories. Mothers had regained some economic advantage with 40 percent now ranking in the two highest socioeconomic categories, but 30 percent still fell into the bottom two levels.

One-fourth of the women were experiencing serious financial difficulties as compared to 18 percent of the men.

TWENTY-FIVE-YEAR FOLLOW-UP SAMPLE AND DEMOGRAPHICS

Forty-eight (80%) of the original 60 families were located twenty-five years later. In two families the fathers were unwilling to provide information as to the whereabouts of the children. In another family the adult child was out of contact and his mother was unable to locate him. Forty-five families (75% of the original group) participated. At this follow-up only the children, now adults, were formally studied, although we spoke to many of the parents in the process of locating their children. Ninety-three (71%) of the original 131 were interviewed, consisting of 38 (41%) males and 55 (59%) females. Their mean age was 33; ages ranged from 28 to 43 years. In the 45 families, 2 mothers and 4 fathers were deceased and 1 father had disappeared. Twenty-five years after their divorce, one-third of the fathers ended up in the upper socioeconomic level as compared to only 5 percent of their former wives. Almost half of the fathers (48%) and a little over half of the mothers (53%) ended up in above adequate economic circumstances. A third of the mothers were at a socioeconomic level that was only adequate as compared to 20 percent of the fathers. Ten percent of mothers and 5 percent of fathers lived in below adequate to poverty conditions.

Comparison Sample

Our main objective in including a comparison group was to compare the nature and quality of their experience growing up and in their adult relationships to that of our divorced group. Although we provide numerical comparisons between the two groups, the purpose is not to compare them statistically but to illustrate the differences in their life course. Forty-four adults from 27 families comprised the comparison group. Twenty-eight (64%) were women and 16 (36%) were men. Their ages ranged from 28 to 43 years; the mean age was 34.9. Forty-two of the comparison group participants were Caucasian. Two were African Americans.

We use the term "comparison group" rather than the better-known "control group" as we feel it more accurately describes both its structure and function in this study. A formal control group is matched to the study group for every possible source of variation except the one in question. As we did not expect to find people who matched our divorced group in every way except that their parents had not divorced, we settled on controlling for only those areas we felt were most relevant: age, socioeconomic status of the parents, growing up in the same neighborhoods, and attending the same elementary and high schools. Our goal was to interview people who had grown up alongside our divorced kids—but whose parents had stayed married. Putting ads in local newspapers, on the Internet, and in the community schools yielded only a few appropriate participants. More personalized methods worked much better and provided the bulk of our comparison group. Several of the people in our divorced group referred friends and acquaintances. The method that provided the most participants was through high school alumni networks—locating the organizers of alumni reunions at the high schools that our divorced kids attended and for the relevant years. These alumni "queens" and "kings" not only had lists of classmates but had kept in personal contact with many over the years and were able to guide us to those whose parents were still married.

Participants provided information as to their parents' education level, which we compared to the parents in the divorced group.

Education Level of Parents

	Comparison Group		***Divorced Group***	
	Mothers	*Fathers*	*Mothers*	*Fathers*
Graduate degree	4%	41%	5%	25%
Bachelor's degree	37%	33%	33%	47%
Some college	19%	0	30%	10%
H.S. degree	40%	22%	24%	18%
No H.S. degree	0	4%	8%	0

It was not possible to get an accurate estimate of the parents' socioeconomic level twenty-five years ago to compare to the SES of the divorced sample at that time.

We were able to estimate the current SES level of both the comparison group parents and the divorced parents from what their adult children reported. These statistics are as follows:

Current SES Level

	Comparison Group Parents	*Divorced Fathers*	*Divorced Mothers*
Very comfortable	30%	33%	5%
Above adequate	44%	47%	53%
Adequate	15%	20%	32%
Below adequate	11%	0	5%
Poverty level	0	0	5%

Methodology

This investigation was originally started as a hypothesis-generating study in which the goal was to explore and track the perceptions and experiences of family members, particularly the children, following divorce. It is a qualitative study primarily, using the structured interview method in which each participant is seen individually and intensively in an open-ended interaction with a trained clinician who guides the interview to cover a predetermined set of questions. Participants are encouraged, within the privacy and safety of the interview, to explain in detail their feelings, perceptions, behaviors, decisions, opinions, hopes, and anxieties about targeted aspects of their lives. This method of data gathering results in a rich record of the participant's story and the clinician's professional impressions from the interview. The way the data have been treated—the development of coding categories, the creation of variables, the choice of data analytic techniques—derives from the primary goal of maintaining and reflecting the richness and complexity of each person's full experience as he or she negotiated the years following divorce.

INITIAL ASSESSMENT

Each parent was interviewed for at least an hour, sometimes much longer, weekly for six weeks. Children were seen for fifty minutes for three to four sessions. Families were not excluded if a member refused to participate. The same clinician generally saw all family members, although this practice varied according to availability and scheduling. The average number of interviews per family was fifteen. Independent reports on each child's functioning were obtained from interviews with school personnel, usually teachers and occasionally principals. The content areas of the interviews are presented here in a chart that outlines interview content at each time period.

Extensive summaries of the interviews were prepared by the clinicians and the summaries were transcribed. Each transcription was coded according to a series of rating scales and categorical items.[1] Interrater reliability in coding was established using the consensus method. Each discrepancy was discussed and resolved. After consensus was reached the same coder finished coding the transcript.

EIGHTEEN-MONTH, FIVE-YEAR, AND TEN-YEAR ASSESSMENTS

The method of assessment remained essentially the same for these follow-up periods. The same semistructured interview outline was used with portions modified and added that addressed demographic, life history, and psychological issues relevant to each time period. Interview content having to do with premarital and marital history as well as circumstances of the divorce were not repeated. Whenever possible the clinician who had seen the participant at previous follow-ups did the interviewing. By the ten-year follow-up four of the original six interviewers were still with the study.

As before, interviews were summarized, transcribed, and coded. Coding followed categories used at earlier time periods and new categories reflecting added questions. As much more information was added than was deleted, the number of coding items increased at each time period. At the ten-year follow-up a total of 710 items were coded for each child and 398 for the parents combined. Coding items requiring clinical judgment were discussed extensively by trained raters. Operational criteria anchoring rating points were included. Interrater reliability was developed using randomly selected transcripts from 10 percent of the sample. Level of reliability was computed using Kendall's tau *b* statistic for ordinal-level items and the kappa statistic for nominal-type coding items. Sixty-two percent of the ordinal codes and 54 percent of the nominal codes had acceptable levels of agreement ($p < .05$). The discrepant coding items were reviewed and operational anchor points further defined. When acceptable reliability could not be attained, those codes were eliminated from the formal analyses.[2]

TWENTY-FIVE-YEAR ASSESSMENT

The same structured interview method was used at twenty-five years for both the divorced group and for the comparison group, which was added at this time period. In addition, a structured questionnaire covering routine demographic questions and self-report ratings of key areas was administered. Eighty percent of the divorced participants and 100 percent of the comparison group completed the questionnaire. The structured interview outline was further modified to include relevant life changes and circumstances for the divorced group. A parallel interview outline was developed for the comparison group. Where appropriate the same questions were used. A set of new questions relevant to the ever-married status of the parents and to capture the experience of growing up in the family was developed. Excepting the senior author, this round of interviews was conducted by a new group of trained clinicians.

Transcription, coding, and obtaining interrater reliability were conducted using the same methods and procedures reported for the ten-year follow-up. The self-reporting from the questionnaire was included in the coding as another source of information, in addition to what participants said face-to-face and the clinician's professional impressions. Because only the children (now adults) were interviewed at this time period, the total number of items coded was less: 308 for each participant in the divorced group and 293 for those in the comparison group.

Summary of Content Areas in Structured Interview[a]

Regarding Parents:[b]

Premarital history (0, C)
Marital history (0, C)
Divorce Circumstances (0)
Marital Status (1, 2, 3, 4)
Employment (0, 1, 2, 3, 4, C)
Schooling/Training (0, 1, 2, 3, C)
Economic Circumstances (0, 1, 2, 3, 4, C)
Living Situation (0, 1, 2, 3, 4, C)
Social Relationships (0, 1, 2, 3, C)
Supports/Needs (0, 1, 2, 3, C)
Parenting (0, 1, 2, 3, 4, C)
Health Status (0, 1, 2, 3, 4, C)
Psychological Functioning (0, 1, 2, 3, 4, C)
Treatment History (0, 1, 2, 3)
Attitude toward the Divorce (0, 1, 2, 3)
Coparental Relationship (0, 1, 2, 3, C)
Interparental Relationship (0, 1, 2, 3, 4, C)
Grandparental Relationship (3, 4, C)

Regarding Children (Adult Children):

Living Situation (0, 1, 2, 3, 4, C)
Visitation and Custody (0, 1, 2, 3)
Memories of Parental Divorce (3, 4)
Memories of Childhood (4, C)
Pattern of Contact with Father (0, 1, 2, 3, 4, C)
Pattern of Contact with Mother (0, 1, 2, 3, 4, C)
Attitudes toward Parent Contact (0, 1, 2, 3, 4, C)
Schooling/Training (0, 1, 2, 3, 4, C)
Employment (3, 4, C)
Economic Situation (3, 4, C)
Adolescent Achievements (3, 4, C)
Early/Middle Adolescent History (3, 4, C)
Later Adolescent History (3, 4, C)
Adult Achievements (4, C)
Supports (0, 1, 2, 3, 4, C)
Peer Relationships (0, 1, 2, 3, 4, C)
Sexual/Love Relationships (1, 2, 3, 4, C)
Marital Status/History (3, 4, C)
Children/History (3, 4, C)
Divorce Circumstances/History (3, 4, C)
Psychological Functioning (0, 1, 2, 3, 4, C)
Psychotherapy and Health History (0, 1, 2, 3 4, C)
Relationship with Father (0, 1, 2, 3, 4, C)
Relationship with Mother (0, 1, 2, 3, 4, C)
Relationship with Siblings (0, 1, 2, 3, 4, C)
Relationship with Spouse (3, 4, C)

[a] Time period indicated: 0 = original contact; 1 = 18-month follow-up; 2 = 5-year follow-up; 3 = 10-year follow-up; 4 = 25-year follow-up; C = Comparison group interview

[b] Asked of parents when parents participated in interviews. Asked of children when parent did not participate.

Regarding Children (Adult Children):
Relationship with Children (3, 4, C)
Relationship with Stepchildren (4, C)
Children's Relationship with Grandparents (4, C)
Management of Conflict (4, C)
Perceptions of Parents' Marriage (C)
Parenting (4, C)
Attitude/Mother's Remarriage (0, 1, 2, 3, 4)
Attitude/Father's Remarriage (0, 1, 2, 3, 4)
Attitude/Parents' Divorce (0, 1, 2, 3, 4)
Attitudes/Marriage and Divorce (0, 1, 2, 3, 4, C)
Expectations for Future (0, 1, 2, 3, 4, C)

Data Analysis

Before the ten-year mark the data were analyzed by hand using mainly correlational techniques. At ten years all of the data, including data from the earlier time periods, were put on the computer. Cross-sectional and longitudinal analyses of the divorced sample at ten years and at twenty-five years followed essentially the same procedures. Data from the comparison group were reduced and described in a comparable manner. Additional analyses comparing the two groups were performed at the twenty-five-year mark.

Data were reduced by obtaining frequencies of all coding items. Items whose frequencies did not discriminate between categories were eliminated if not clinically meaningful. Appropriate measures of association were run between remaining items; those associated above the 80 percent level were either combined or collapsed. The surviving items provided the data base.

The primary test used in the cross-sectional analyses of the data at ten and at twenty-five years was the chi-square statistic, which best fit the categorical nature of the data. Primary independent variables were sex, age group, remarriage history of parents, relationship with each parent, quality of parental marriage (for the comparison group).

Grouping by age changed over the course of the study, the choice of age group at each point determined by developmental relevance and statistical considerations. At twenty-five years we used three age groups based on age at the time of the parents' decisive separation: ages 2–6 (n = 29), ages 7–10 (n = 41), and ages 11–15 (n = 23).

Relationship with each parent was a code that took into consideration the self-report on the questionnaire, the participant's report and attitude about the parent during the interview, the impression of the interviewer, and the clinical judgment of the coder.

Based on how the comparison group described their parents' marriage, we categorized them into one of three groups: "A" parental marriages (n = 12), which their child thought were perfect or nearly so, "B" parental marriages (n = 23), where the child was aware of problems but felt there was "good enough" parenting, and "C" parental marriages (n = 9), where the marital relationship seriously disrupted parenting.

Dependent measures were organized into dimensions reflecting psychological, social, and economic functioning; attitudes toward relationships, divorce, and the future; and clinical judgments on the long-term residual impact of growing up in the divorced or intact family.

Outcome was assessed using a global measure and then three more specific measures. The global measure, EgoCope, was the overall measure of outcome taking into consideration the individual's internal functioning, including psychological integration, affective stability, and strength of defensive structure and level of functioning in the environment. We also assessed dimensions of functioning separately using three measures reflecting emotional capacity, quality of social relationships, and occupational competence and satisfaction.

Longitudinal analyses were organized using two methods. Changes in the postdivorce family over time were captured by creating profile variables[3] that reflected patterns across the years in targeted areas: psychological change in the parents, quality of life, socioeconomic variation, degree of conflict and anger between the parents, parental cooperation over visiting, attitudes toward the ex-spouse as parent, and degree of felt responsibility for the children. These profile variables are an attempt to combine individual information into family-level variables that more accurately represent the experience of the postdivorce environment for the child. Measures of child outcome and functioning associated with these family profiles provided a way of conceptualizing triadic or system-level functioning over time.

The course of individual stability and change was tracked by constructing pathway variables that reflect patterns of variation over time.[4] Key dimensions of outcome, relationship with parents, contact with parents, and degree of divorce resolution were transformed into pathway variables and then compared with outcome at each time period. In this manner both longitudinal patterns were ascertained and predictive power from one time period to the next was tested.

Notes

Introduction

1. J. Guidubaldi, H. K. Cleminshaw, J. D. Perry, and C. S. McLoughlin, "The Impact of Parental Divorce on Children: Report of the Nationwide NASP Study," *School Psychology Review* 12 (1983): 300–23; N. Zill and C. Schoenborn, *Developmental, Learning and Emotional Problems: Health of Our Nation's Children, United States, 1988. Advance Data*, Vital and Health Statistics of the National Center for Health Statistics (Washington, D.C.: National Center for Health Statistics, no. 190, November 16, 1990); S. McLanahan, *Growing Up with a Single Parent: What Hurts, What Helps* (Cambridge, Mass.: Harvard University Press, 1994).

2. A. J. Cherlin, P. L. Chase-Lansdale, and C. McRae, "Effects of Parental Divorce on Mental Health Throughout the Life Course," *American Sociological Review*, 63 (April 1988): 239–49; J. S. Wallerstein and J. B. Kelly, *Surviving the Breakup: How Children and Parents Cope with Divorce* (New York: Basic Books, 1980); N. Zill, D. R. Morrison, and M. J. Coiro, "Long-Term Effects of Parental Divorce on Parent-Child Relationships, Adjustment and Achievement in Young Adulthood," *Journal of Family Psychology* 7, no. 1 (1993): 91–103.

3. National Center for Health Statistics, *Births, Marriages and Deaths for 1996. Monthly Vital Statistics Report*, vol. 45, no. 12 (Hyattsville, Md.: National Center for Health Statistics, 1997).

4. According to figures estimated from the 1995 National Survey of Families and Households and the 1997 Statistical Abstract of the U.S. Bureau of the Census.

5. General Social Survey, 1996 (National Sample).

6. Wallerstein and Kelly, *Surviving the Breakup*; J. S. Wallerstein and S. Blakeslee, *Second Chances: Men, Women, and Children a Decade after Divorce* (Boston: Houghton Mifflin, 1989).

7. The Judith Wallerstein Center for the Family in Transition was established in Marin County in 1980 in response to findings reported in *Surviving the Breakup* and rising community concern. The initial grant from the San Francisco Foundation was for $3.5 million over a five-year period. Known nationally and internationally for its research and its training programs for mental health professionals, educators, pediatricians, ministers, and attorneys, the center has served as a model for research, intervention, and social policy addressing the changes in the American family.

One

1. J. Johnston, "High-Conflict Divorce," *The Future of Children* 4 (1994): 165–82.

Two

1. For a review including references, see J. S. Wallerstein, "Children of Divorce," in *All Our Families: New Policies for a New Century. A Report of the Berkeley Family Forum*, ed. M. A. Mason, A. Skolnick, and S. D. Sugarman (New York: Oxford University Press, 1998).

2. Arundhati Roy, *The God of Small Things* (New York: Random House, 1997), p. 1.

3. J. R. Harris, *The Nurture Assumption* (New York: The Free Press, 1998).

Three

1. F. F. Furstenberg and J. A. Seltzer, "Divorce and Child Development," in *Sociological Studies of Child Development*, vol. 1, ed. P. A. Adler and P. Adler (Greenwich, Conn.: JAI Press Inc., 1986), pp. 127–160; P. R. Amato and A. Booth, "Consequences of Parental Divorce and Marital Unhappiness for Adult Well-Being," *Social Forces* 69 (1991): 905-14.

2. D. M. Capaldi and G. R. Patterson, "Relation of Parental Transition to Boys' Adjustment Problems: I. A Linear Hypothesis. II. Mothers at Risk for Transitions and Unskilled Parenting," *Developmental Psychology* 27 (1991) 489–504. According to the U.S. National Center for Health Statistics, one-half of those marrying in the 1990s were getting married for the second time. In one in seven weddings one or both were getting married for the third time.

3. This question is discussed in N. G. Glenn and K. Kramer, "The Marriages and Divorces of the Children of Divorce," *Journal of Marriage and the Family* 49 (1987): 811–25.

Figures from the 1990–96 General Social Surveys (National Samples) for persons ages 28–43 show significantly higher divorce rates in people from divorced families compared to those from nondivorced families. The figures for rate of marriage, age at marriage, and rate of divorce for our adult children of divorce as compared to their cohorts in our comparison group and to available national figures are as follows:

Adult Children of Divorce		Adult Children from Intact Families	
Our Sample	*National Figures*[a]	*Our Sample*	*National Figures*
60% married	76% married	80% married	84% married
40% of marriages ended in divorce	43% of marriages ended in divorce	9% of marriages ended in divorce	35% of marriages ended in divorce

Adult Children of Divorce *(Our Sample)*	Adult Children from Intact Families *(Our Sample)*	National Figures[b]
50% married before age 25	11% married before age 25	34% married before age 25[c]
57% of those married before age 25 divorced	25% of those married before age 25 divorced	not available

FIVE

1. The figures for success of later marriages (married at age 25 or later) for men and women in our adult children of divorce group, and our comparison group, along with the available national figures, are as follows:

Adult Children of Divorce *(Our Sample)*	Adult Children from Intact Families *(Our Sample)*	National Figures[d]
Of those who married, 50% married later	Of those who married, 89% married later	Of those who married, 65.5% married later[e]
Of men who married, 59% married later	Of men who married, 80% married later	Of men who married, 71% married later
Of women who married, 44% married later	Of women who married, 95% married later	Of women who married, 60.1% married later
21% of later marriages ended in divorce	6% of later marriages ended in divorce	not available

2. The numbers of those who had children in our adult children of divorce group and in our comparison group are as follows:

Adult Children of Divorce	Adult Children from Intact Families
38% have children	61% have children
32% of men have children	75% of men have children
42% of women have children	54% of women have children

[a]Tabulations from the 1990–96 General Social Surveys (National Samples): Persons Ages 28–43. (Figures averaged over men and women.)

[b]From N. Glenn, "Courtship and Marital Choice: Why They Are Important and What We Need to Learn about Them," working paper no. 70, Council on Families, Institute for American Values, 1999.

[c]Figure averaged over men and women. (Figures broken down between people from divorced versus intact families not available.)

[d]From Glenn, "Courtship and Marital Choice."

[e]Figure averaged over men and women.

Of those who have children, 17% had children out of wedlock	None had children out of wedlock

The average (mean) number of children per adult in our children of divorce group, and our comparison group as compared to national figures:

Adult Children of Divorce		**Adult Children from Intact Families**	
Our Sample	*National Figures*[a]	*Our Sample*	*National Figures*
Overall: .57	Overall: 1.6	Overall: 1.2	Overall: 1.6
Men: .42	Men: 1.4	Men: 1.4	Men: 1.5
Women: .67	Women: 1.8	Women: 1.0	Women: 1.7

3. Rates of divorce with and without children for the adult children of divorce and for the comparison group, along with national figures:

Adult Children of Divorce	**Adult Children from Intact Families**	**National Figures**[b]
Of those who divorced, 36% had children	Of those who divorced, 33% had children	Of divorcing couples, 53% had children
14% of men who divorced had children	Numbers too small	not available
47% of women who divorced had children	Numbers too small	not available

4. See this chapter, note 2, for exact figures.

SIX

1. See Glenn and Kramer, "The Marriages and Divorces of the Children of Divorce."

SEVEN

1. O. W. Barnett, C. L. Miller-Penn, and R. D. Penin, *Family Violence Across the Lifespan* (Thousand Oaks, Calif.: Sage, 1997); *The Impact of Domestic Violence on Children.* A report to the president of the American Bar Association, August 1994. Prepared by the American Bar Association Center on Children and the Law, a Program of the Young Lawyer's Division.

2. Y. Ito et al., "Increased Prevalence of Electrophysiological Abnormalities in Children with Psychological, Physical, and Sexual Abuse," *Journal of Neuropsychiatry and Clinical Neuroscience* 5, no. 4 (1993): 401–8; F. Schiffer, M. H. Teicher, and A. C. Papanicolaou, "Evoked Potential Evidence for Right Brain Activity during the

[a]Tabulations from the 1990–96 General Social Surveys (National Samples): Persons Ages 28–43. (Overall figures averaged over men and women.)

[b]From Centers for Disease Control and Prevention, *Monthly Vital Statistics Report*, vol. 43, no. 9, Supplement, March 22, 1995. (Figure is for the years 1989–90, the years in which the modal number of divorces occurred in our samples.)

Recall of Traumatic Memories," *Journal of Neuropsychiatry and Clinical Neuroscience* 7, no. 2 (1995): 169–75.

EIGHT

1. M. A. Strauss, R. J. Gelles, and S. K. Steinmetz, *Behind Closed Doors: Violence in the American Family* (Garden City, N.Y.: Anchor Press/Doubleday, 1980).

2. L. Pagani, et al., "Verbal and Physical Abuse toward Mothers: The Role of Family Configuration, Environment and Coping Strategies," *American Journal of Psychiatry*, in press.

3. M. A. Strauss, "Children as Witnesses to Marital Violence: A Risk Factor for Lifelong Problems among a Nationally Representative Sample of American Men and Women" (paper presented at the Ross Roundtable on Children and Violence, Washington, D.C., 1991).

4. There is emerging concern among judges and mental health professionals about these issues and some seminal programs. A recent report recommended that a legal advocate be provided for every victim seeking a protection order. For a summary of these issues and programs see *Family Violence: Emerging Programs for Battered Mothers and Their Children.* A report from the Family Violence Department of the National Council of Juvenile and Family Court Judges, Reno, Nevada, 1998.

5. For a more detailed description of the dynamics of these alliances see Wallerstein and Blakeslee, *Second Chances.*

TEN

1. Two excellent reviews of this literature appear in M. E. Lamb, ed., *The Role of the Father in Child Development*, 3rd ed. (New York: Wiley, 1997), and in K. Pruett, *Fatherneed: Why Father Care Is as Essential as Mother Care for Your Child* (New York: The Free Press, 2000).

2. C. Leland and M. Lozoff, "College Influences in the Role Development of Female Undergraduates" (paper prepared for the Institute for the Study of Human Problems, Stanford University, 1969).

3. J. S. Wallerstein and S. Blakeslee, *The Good Marriage: How and Why Love Lasts* (New York: Houghton Mifflin, 1995).

4. See B. S. Shone and L. E. Pezzin, "Parental Marital Disruption and Intergenerational Transfers: An Analysis of Lone Elderly Parents and Their Children," *Demography* 26, no. 3 (August 1999): 287–97, for an illustration of the falling away of caregiving for elderly divorced and remarried parents.

5. This clinical finding from our twenty-five-year study receives mixed support from the existing literature. A 1990 national study found that the propensity to become a victim of physical violence is stronger than the likelihood to become an aggressor in both men and women who come from violent families. See C. Cappell and R. B. Heiner, "The Intergenerational Transmission of Family Aggression," *Journal of Family Violence* 5 (1990): 135–52. An extensive critical review concludes there is general support for the intergenerational transmission of violence but points out the issue has been too narrowly focused on whether children from violent families become violent themselves and not on the more likely but far more complex outcome of damage or distortion in the capacity to form and sustain satisfying and ethical intimate relationships. See J. Johnston, "The Intergenerational Legacy of Family Violence: A Critical Review and Reformulation," in *Violence and Hate in the Family*, eds.

J. Johnston (Champaign, Ill.: ERIC Clearinghouse on Elementary and Early Childhood Education, University of Illinois at Urbana, 1992).

ELEVEN

1. Our figures and comparable national figures on those who remained single are as follows:

Adult Children of Divorce		Adult Children from Intact Families	
Our Sample	*National Figures*[a]	*Our Sample*	*National Figures*
40% never married	24% never married[b]	29% never married	16% never married[b]
42% of men never married	29% of men never married	6% of men never married	19% of men never married
38% of women never married	18% of women never married	28% of women never married	13% of women never married

The history of intimate relationships for our adult children of divorce and our comparison group is as follows:

Adult Children of Divorce	Adult Children from Intact Families
Of Men Who Never Married	
45% have had relationships 56% had no relationships	The one man who was not married was in a relationship
Of Women Who Never Married	
95% have had relationships One had no relationships	All have had relationships

TWELVE

1. Personal communication from Norval Glenn, November 1999.

2. J. Teachman and K. Paasch, "Financial Impact of Divorce on Children and Their Families," *The Future of Children* 4 (1994): 63–83.

3. J. Seltzer, "Legal Custody Arrangements and Children's Economic Welfare," *American Journal of Sociology* 94 (1991): 895–929.

4. A. Gopnik, A. Meltzoff, and P. Kuhl, *The Scientist in the Crib: Minds, Brains and How Children Learn* (New York: William Morrow, 1999).

5. Our overall measure of outcome was one that we had used at the earlier follow-up points. It is a measure of functioning considering both internal organization and stability and competence in life tasks. See J. L. Lewis and J. S. Wallerstein, "Methodological Issues in Longitudinal Research on Divorced Families," in *Advances in Family Intervention, Assessment and Theory*, vol. 4, ed. J. P. Vincent (Greenwich, Conn.: JAI Press, 1987) for details on this outcome measure.

At the twenty-five-year follow-up we found that 30 percent of the participants

[a]Tabulations from the 1990-96 General Social Surveys (National Samples): Persons Ages 28–43.

[b]Figures averaged over men and women.

in our study were doing poorly, with functioning significantly impaired and below average. Thirty-four percent were in the average range, and 36 percent were doing very well to outstanding in all areas of their life tasks.

We knew from our extensive contact with them that one measure of overall outcome didn't tell the whole story of how our adult children of divorce were doing in their adult lives. We were repeatedly struck with their struggles in the relationship arenas of their lives and their relative success and competence in other areas, particularly in work. We had another outcome measure that broke down the different dimensions of functioning and rated them separately. Sixty-seven percent were rated as being above average in their work competence. Only 40 percent were seen as above average in their functioning in social relationships, with 60 percent falling below average.

Men and women were similar in these patterns as were people in different age groups. The few notable differences were that overall, men were doing more poorly, with more men in the lower level of functioning and more women in the highest levels of functioning. People who were younger when their parents divorced looked less competent overall twenty-five years later. This was most notable in girls who had been preschoolers and in boys who had been early school age when their parents divorced.

Thirteen

1. This study is included in *Evaluation of the Child Access Demonstration Projects.* Report to Congress prepared by the Center for Policy Research and Policy Studies, Inc. Submitted to the Federal Office of Child Support Enforcement, U.S. Department of Health and Human Services, Washington, D.C., July 1996.

2. There are no formal studies on children who fly alone. In a *New York Times* article appearing November 15, 1998, it was estimated that on average one child flew alone on 22,000 domestic flights per day. Airlines generally accept children as lone passengers as young as age five.

Most U.S. courts don't count up the orders that they issue for children. There are no national or pooled state records that could tell us how many children are in sole or joint custody. We have no idea how many children are flying unaccompanied to visit their parents or what ages they are when such long-distance visiting begins. We have no count on how many infants are ordered to spend overnights in their fathers' homes. Some states keep no records at all on these issues while others have some record keeping but no uniform standards. We have no way to follow up on the condition of children after court orders have been in place for some time. Custody issues tend to get discussed in legislatures when organized constituences representing mothers or fathers groups start arguing. These issues are also discussed at professional conferences involving attorneys, mediators, and mental health professionals—all without the help of knowing the scope of the problem.

Fourteen

1. Our figures on age of first use and the extent of use of drugs and alcohol for both our adult children of divorce group and the comparison group as compared to national statistics are as follows:

Adult Children of Divorce	Adult Children from Intact Families	National Statistics[a]
	Use of Alcohol/Drugs before Age 14	
25%	9%	7%
	Use of Alcohol/Drugs by Age 17	
30%	47%	30%
	Heavy Use (Significant Interference) among Users during High School	
85%	24%	18%

2. McLanahan, *Growing Up with a Single Parent.*

3. See Chapter 3, note 3.

FIFTEEN

1. Figures for heavy use of drug/alcohol during late teens and twenties as compared to rates of heavy use in the age range of late twenties to early forties in the men and women of our adult children of divorce sample are as follows:

Adult Children of Divorce: Males	Adult Children of Divorce: Females
29% used drugs/alcohol heavily during late teens/twenties	38% used drugs/alcohol heavily during late teens/twenties
21% used drugs/alcohol heavily during late twenties to early forties	6% used drugs/alcohol heavily during late twenties to early forties

SIXTEEN

1. R. Emory and P. Dillon, "Divorce Mediation and Resolution of Child-Custody Disputes: Long-Term Effects," *American Journal of Orthopsychiatry* 66 (1996): 131–40.

2. As reported in E. Maccoby and R. Mnookin, *Dividing the Child: Social and Legal Dilemmas of Custody* (Cambridge, Mass.: Harvard University Press, 1992).

3. See C. Albiston, E. Maccoby, and R. Mnookin, "Does Joint Legal Custody Matter?" *Stanford Law and Policy Review* 2 (1990): 167–79.

4. J. Johnston, M. Kline, and J. Tschann, "Ongoing Postdivorce Conflict in Families Contesting Custody: Effects on Children of Joint Custody and Frequent Access," *American Journal of Orthopsychiatry* 59 (1989): 576–92.

5. M. Kline, J. Tschann, J. Johnston, and J. Wallerstein, "Children's Adjustment in Joint and Sole Physical Custody Families," *Developmental Psychology* 25 (1989): 430–38.

6. J. Johnston, "Research Update: Children's Adjustment in Sole Custody Compared to Joint Custody Families and Principles for Custody Decision Making," *Family Conciliation Courts Review* 33 (1995): 415–25; P. R. Amato, "Children's Adjustment to

[a]As reported in M. D. Resnick et al., "Protecting Adolescents from Harm: Findings from the National Longitudinal Study on Adolescent Health," *Journal of the American Medical Association* 278, no. 10 (1997): 823–32.

Divorce: Theories, Hypotheses and Empirical Support," *Journal of Marriage and the Family* 55 (1992): 23–38.

7. C. M. Heinke and I. Westheimer, *Brief Separations* (New York: International University Press, 1965).

8. J. Soloman and C. George, "The Development of Attachment in Separated and Divorced Families: Effects of Overnight Visitation, Parent and Couple Variables," *Attachment and Human Development* 1, no. 1 (April 1999): 2–33.

Seventeen

1. There do not appear to be any formal comparisons of rates of divorce in families with exceptional children. However, professional opinion generally supports the clinical impression that divorce is higher. See B. Tew, H. Payne, and K. Lawerence, "Must a Family with a Handicapped Child Be a Handicapped Family?" *Developmental Medicine and Child Neurology* 16 (1974): 95; and C. Telford and J. Sawrey, *The Exceptional Individual*, 4th ed. (Englewood Cliffs, N.J.: Prentice Hall, 1981). Professor Marci Hansen, an expert in special education at San Francisco State University, uses the concept of multiple stressors to explain why families containing members with exceptional needs may be at greater risk for divorce.

Eighteen

1. E. M. Hetherington and K. M. Jodl, "Stepfamilies as Settings for Child Development," in *Stepfamilies: Who Benefits? Who Does Not?* ed. A. Booth and J. Dunn (Hillsdale, N.J.: Lawrence Erlbaum Associates, 1994).

2. Glenn, *Courtship and Marital Choice.*

3. For a review and discussion see E. M. Hetherington et al., "Coping with Marital Transitions: A Family Systems Perspective," *Monographs of the Society for Research in Child Development* 57, no. 227 (1992).

4. Zill and Schoenborn, *Developmental, Learning and Emotional Problems.*

5. Hetherington et al., "Coping with Marital Transitions."

6. The level of higher education achieved and the extent of financial support for higher education in our adult children of divorce group compared to our comparison group is as follows:

Adult Children of Divorce	**Adult Children from Intact Families**	**Relevant Comparison Figures**
77% attempted college	100% attempted college	85–92% attempted college from the same high schools[a]
24% attempting college dropped out	11% attempting college dropped out	
4% did not complete high school	All finished high school	

[a]These figures were garnered from a telephone survey in which we contacted each of the four public high schools that our adults from divorced and intact families attended. Two high schools had records extending back to the time period (1973–88) in which our samples graduated from high school. Administrators at the other two schools provided an estimate.

29% ended with a high school diploma	7% ended with a high school diploma	
10% achieved a 2-year degree or certification	4% achieved a 2-year degree or certification	
39% achieved a bachelor's degree	52% achieved a bachelor's degree	
18% earned a postgraduate degree	37% earned a postgraduate degree	
29% received full or consistent partial support from parents	88% received full or consistent partial support from parents	49–83% of California college students received some parental support[b]
44% received erratic, inconsistent partial support from parents	2% received erratic, inconsistent partial support from parents	
26% received no parental support	10% received no parental support	

7. N. M. Astone and S. S. McClanahan, "Family Structure, Parental Practices and High School Completion," *American Sociological Review* 56 (1991): 309–20; M. A. Powell and D. L. Parcel, "Effects of Family Structure on the Earnings Attainment Process: Differences by Gender," *Journal of Marriage and the Family* 59, no. 2, (1997): 419–33.

8. D. Lillard and J. Gerner, "Getting to the Ivy League: How Family Composition Affects College Choice" (paper presented at the Annual Meetings of the Population Association of America, New Orleans, 1996).

Nineteen

1. See Chapter 11, note 1. Also see R. Simons et al., "Explaining the Higher Incidence of Adjustment Problems of Children of Divorce," *Journal of Marriage and the Family*, in press.

2. In P. Amato, "Explaining the Intergenerational Transmission of Divorce, *Journal of Marriage and the Family* 58 (1996): 628–40; Dr. Amato notes the high divorce rate when two children of divorce marry and discusses the nature of their difficulties in terms of "lack of social skills."

3. This type of healing marriage is discussed in some detail as a "rescue marriage" in Wallerstein and Blakeslee, *The Good Marriage.*

4. Barbara Dafoe Whitehead also uses the term "clueless" to describe the difficulty that children of divorce have in understanding intimate relationships. See B. D. Whitehead, *The Divorce Culture* (New York: Alfred A. Knopf, 1997).

[b]Taken from *A Report on the Expenses and Resources of Undergraduate Students Enrolled in California Post-Secondary Institutions during the 1982–83 Academic Year.* California Student Aid Commission, February 1985. (The years 1982–83 were the modal years in which the people in our samples were attending college; there were ranges in mean levels of parental support across the different California college systems.)

5. The concepts of stress, risk, buffering, and resiliency were developed in the 1970s and 1980s to explain the wide range of individual differences in how children react to traumatic experiences in their environment. For an overview of this literature see N. Garmezy and M. Rutter, *Stress, Coping and Development in Children* (New York: McGraw Hill, 1983).

6. These concepts were then applied to how children cope with divorce and remarriage. The ways that authors use these concepts in this area can be seen in E. M. Hetherington, ed., *Coping with Divorce, Single Parenting, and Remarriage: A Risk and Resiliency Perspective* (Mahwah, N.J.: Lawrence Erlbaum Associates, 1999).

Twenty-one

1. According to tabulations from the 1990–96 General Social Survey (National Sample): Persons Ages 28–43, 80.6% of males and 87.4% of females from intact families marry. See Chapter 3, note 3, for rates of marriage for our comparison group and for our adult children of divorce group.

2. Pamela J. Smock, "Cohabitation in the United States: An Appraisal of Research, Themes, Findings and Implications," *Annual Review of Sociology* 26 (2000).

Twenty-two

1. According to figures published in T. Smith, *The Emerging Twenty-First-Century American Family* (National Opinion Research Center, University of Chicago, November 24, 1999).

2. For a discussion of this "children first" policy, see M. A. Glendon, *Abortion and Divorce in Western Law* (Cambridge, Mass.: Harvard University Press, 1987), and M. A. Mason, *The Custody Wars* (New York: Basic Books, 1999).

3. The development of some of these services is described in J. Johnston and V. Roseby, *In the Name of the Child* (New York: The Free Press, 1997).

Appendix

1. For details see Wallerstein and Kelly, *Surviving the Breakup*.

2. For a more thorough review of this assessment process see J. S. Wallerstein, S. B. Corbin, and J. L. Lewis, "Children of Divorce: A Ten-Year Study," in *Impact of Divorce, Single Parenting, and Stepparenting on Children*, ed. E. M. Hetherington and J. D. Arasteh (Hillsdale, N.J.: Lawrence Erlbaum, 1988).

3. For a discussion of the "profile" methodology see Lewis and Wallerstein, "Methodological Issues in Longitudinal Research on Divorced Families."

4. This method of longitudinal data analysis is thoroughly discussed in S. B. Corbin, "Factors Affecting Long-Term Similarities and Differences Among Siblings Following Parental Divorce" (Ph.D. diss., Pacific Graduate School of Psychology, Calif., 1988).

Index